# DEMOCRATIC STATEHOOD IN INTERNATIONAL LAW

This book analyses the emerging practice in the post-Cold War era of the creation of a democratic political system along with the creation of new states. The existing literature either tends to conflate self-determination and democracy or dismisses the legal relevance of the emerging practice on the basis that democracy is not a statehood criterion. Such arguments are simplistic. The statehood criteria in contemporary international law are largely irrelevant and do not automatically or self-evidently determine whether or not an entity has emerged as a new state. The question to be asked, therefore, is not whether democracy has become a statehood criterion. Rather, the emergence of new states is a law-governed political process in which certain requirements regarding the type of government may be imposed internationally. And in this process the introduction of a democratic political system is equally as relevant or irrelevant as the statehood criteria. The book demonstrates that via the right of self-determination, the law of statehood requires for state creation to be a democratic process, but that this requirement should not be interpreted too broadly. The democratic process in this context governs independence referenda and does not interfere with the choice of a political system.

**Volume 46 in the series Studies in International Law**

# Studies in International Law

## Recent titles in this series

**For the complete list of titles in this series, see 'Studies in International Law' link at www.hartpub.co.uk/books/series.asp**

# Democratic Statehood in International Law

## The Emergence of New States in Post-Cold War Practice

Jure Vidmar

·HART·
PUBLISHING
OXFORD AND PORTLAND, OREGON
2013

Published in the United Kingdom by Hart Publishing Ltd
16C Worcester Place, Oxford, OX1 2JW
Telephone: +44 (0)1865 517530
Fax: +44 (0)1865 510710
E-mail: mail@hartpub.co.uk
Website: http://www.hartpub.co.uk

Published in North America (US and Canada) by
Hart Publishing
c/o International Specialized Book Services
920 NE 58th Avenue, Suite 300
Portland, OR 97213-3786
USA
Tel: +1 503 287 3093 or toll-free: (1) 800 944 6190
Fax: +1 503 280 8832
E-mail: orders@isbs.com
Website: http://www.isbs.com

British Library Cataloguing in Publication Data
Data Available

ISBN: 978-1-84946-469-7

Typeset by Hope Services, Abingdon
Printed and bound in Great Britain by
CPI Group (UK) Ltd, Croydon, CR0 4YY

# *Acknowledgements*

This book was initially written as a PhD thesis, defended at the University of Nottingham. I had the good fortune to be supervised by Robert McCorquodale, to whom I will always remain indebted for three years of inspiring supervision and challenging discussions as well as constant support and invaluable advice during my PhD years and afterwards. Whenever I was lost in research and ideas, I would talk to Robert, who always had the magic formula to get me focused again, while encouraging my own thinking. Robert managed to motivate me and keep me realistic at the same time.

I owe a big thank you to the University of Nottingham's International Office and the School of Law for awarding me the two grants without which my research would not have been (financially) feasible. Nottingham also provided me with excellent facilities and expertise in international law that made my research a really pleasurable experience.

The examiners, James Crawford and Dino Kritsiotis, gave me excellent comments and detailed feedback on my thesis. Their suggestions and constructive criticism were most helpful when preparing the manuscript for publication.

The book was finalised at the University of Oxford, at the time when I was an Anglo-German 'State of the State' Fellow, kindly supported by the Volkswagen Foundation. I am thankful to Stefan Vogenauer for accommodating me at the Institute of European and Comparative Law at Oxford, to Dan Sarooshi for reading the manuscript and giving me helpful suggestions, and to Dapo Akande for inspiring conversations about statehood and other topics in international law.

After leaving Nottingham and prior to moving to Oxford, I worked as a post-doc at the Amsterdam Center for International Law, University of Amsterdam. My mentor, Erika de Wet, showed a great measure of understanding whenever statehood was on my mind, even when it was not supposed to be. I am also thankful to Erika for her energetic support, friendly advice, constant encouragement on my career path, and, most importantly, for teaching me that international law is not only about statehood!

While at Amsterdam, I also benefited greatly from discussions with a number of distinguished academics as well as younger colleagues, in particular: Jean d'Aspremont, Kiki Brölmann, Lisa Clarke, Yvonne Donders, Christina Eckes, Stephan Hollenberg, Louwrens Kiestra and André Nollkaemper. Thank you for a wonderful time at the *Universiteit van Amsterdam*, for all your help and comments, for being good friends and for putting up with me. I know this was not always easy.

I am grateful to my colleagues and friends Michal Bobek, Thomas Dietz, Jolyon Ford and Amrei Müller for their advice, humour, enlightening discussions on history, and for being very, very understanding.

My interest in international law and global developments started in my childhood. Growing up in Slovenia, I experienced the emergence of a new (democratic) state when I counted toward the body of its 'permanent population' under the Montevideo Convention. It was, however, my parents and my late grandfather who inspired my curiosity for developments around the world, enabled me to travel and encouraged me to consider different views and perspectives. They always supported me and trusted I knew what I was doing. And it was always good to know I had this support. *Hvala za vse!*

But most of all, I will never be able to thank enough my wife Carly for her love, support and sacrifices. We were married in the first year of my PhD and I even conducted some research for this book on our honeymoon. I am fully aware that this was not entirely normal. Carly not only accepted that I was a somewhat 'absent' husband, as my thesis needed lots of my attention, she also helped me with brainstorming, proofreading and editing. Carly has also followed me when moving between a number of institutions and countries (or shall I say states) and has always been supportive of my pursuits, or at least the sensible ones. Thank you so much! This book is thus dedicated to my wonderful wife!

It is my intention that the research is current as of 31 October 2012.

Jure Vidmar

St John's College, Oxford
1 March 2013

# Table of Contents

# Table of Cases

## The Arbitration Commission of the Conference on Yugoslavia
## (Badinter Commission)

# Table of Materials

**International instruments**

## Domestic legislation

# 1

# *Democracy and Statehood in International Law*

## 1 INTRODUCTION

### 1.1 Background

AT THE END of the Cold War, two multiethnic socialist federations were dissolved: the Union of Soviet Socialist Republics (the Soviet Union) and the Socialist Federal Republic of Yugoslavia (SFRY).[1] This period thus marked not only the end of the communist/socialist social, political and economic order but also the emergence of a number of new states.[2] The entanglement of post-Cold War political developments and the emergence of new states led to the idea that democracy should be brought into international law as a normative framework in relation to both existing and emerging states. This was at a time when some international legal scholars argued that democracy had become a

---

[1] Legal analyses of the two dissolutions include the following works: C Warbrick, 'Recognition of States' (1992) 41 *ICLQ* 473; A Pellet, 'The Opinions of the Badinter Arbitration Committee: A Second Breath for the Self-Determination of Peoples' (1992) 3 *EJIL* 178; D Türk, 'Recognition of States: A Comment' (1993) 4 *EJIL* 66; R Rich, 'Recognition of States: The Collapse of Yugoslavia and the Soviet Union' (1993) 4 *EJIL* 36; S Trifunovska, *Yugoslavia through Documents: From its Creation to its Dissolution* (Dordrecht, Martinus Nijhoff, 1994); M Craven, 'What's in a Name?: The Former Yugoslav Republic of Macedonia and Issues of Statehood' (1995) 16 *Australian Yearbook of International Law* 199; M Craven, 'The European Community Arbitration Commission on Yugoslavia' (1996) 66 *British Yearbook of International Law* 333; D Bethlehem and M Weller, *The 'Yugoslav' Crisis in International Law* (Cambridge, Cambridge University Press, 1997); T Grant, *The Recognition of States: Law and Practice in Debate and Evolution* (Westport, Praeger, 1999); S Terrett, *The Dissolution of Yugoslavia and the Badinter Arbitration Commission: A Contextual Study of Peace-Making Efforts in the Post-Cold War World* (Aldershot, Ashgate, 2000); P Radan, *The Break-up of Yugoslavia and International Law* (London, Routledge, 2002); I Ziemele, *State Continuity and Nationality: The Baltic States and Russia: Past Present and Future as Defined by International Law* (Leiden, Martinus Nijhoff, 2005); J Crawford, *The Creation of States in International Law* (Oxford, Oxford University Press, 2006).

[2] New states emerging in the territory of the SFRY were: Bosnia-Herzegovina, Croatia, the Federal Republic of Yugoslavia (FRY), Macedonia and Slovenia. See ch 2, 3.1. The new states emerging in the territory of the Soviet Union were: Armenia, Azerbaijan, Belarus, Georgia, Kazakhstan, Kyrgyzstan, Moldova, Russia, Tajikistan, Turkmenistan, Ukraine and Uzbekistan. Estonia, Latvia and Lithuania became independent states prior to the dissolution of the Soviet Union. See ch 2, 2.1.

normative entitlement of all individuals[3] and when the European Community (EC) Member States adopted documents which explicitly expressed the willingness to (collectively) grant recognition only to those new states which had *constituted themselves on a democratic basis.*[4]

The dissolutions of the Soviet Union and of the SFRY were followed by the dissolution of a third (then already formerly) socialist federation – Czechoslovakia.[5] Shortly afterwards, Eritrea successfully seceded from Ethiopia.[6] In due course, East Timor[7] and Montenegro also became independent states.[8] In 2008, Kosovo declared independence.[9] Kosovo has attracted a significant number of recognitions, but its legal status remains ambiguous. Most recently, South Sudan emerged as an independent state.[10]

In the language of international law, these new states emerged as a result of consensual and non-consensual dissolutions of federations; as a result of consensual secessions from their parent states, and in one case perhaps even as a result of a successful unilateral secession (Kosovo). Some of these states satisfied the statehood criteria upon their emergence and others had problems in this respect. Most new states were recognised promptly, but some were not and were nevertheless considered to be states. The new states may have emerged upon the exercise of the right of self-determination and some of them possibly even under the doctrine of remedial secession. With regard to self-determination, most states emerged with the overwhelming support of the will of the people, expressed at independence referenda. And many of the post-Cold War

[3] See especially T Franck, 'The Emerging Right to Democratic Governance' (1992) 86 *American Journal of International Law* 46; T Franck, 'Democracy as a Human Right' in L Henkin and J Hargrove (eds), *Human Rights: An Agenda for the Next Century* (Washington DC, ASIL, 1994); T Franck, 'Legitimacy and the Democratic Entitlement' in G Fox and B Roth (eds), *Democratic Governance and International Law* (Cambridge, Cambridge University Press, 2001); F Teson, 'The Kantian Theory of International Law' (1992) 92 *Columbia Law Review* 53; F Teson, *A Philosophy of International Law* (Boulder, Westview, 1998); AM Slaughter, 'International Law in a World of Liberal States' (1995) 6 *EJIL* 503; AM Slaughter, 'The Real New World Order' (1997) 76 *Foreign Affairs* 183.

[4] See the *EC Guidelines on Recognition* of New *States* in Eastern Europe and in the Soviet Union (16 December 1991), para 3 (emphasis added).

[5] See E Stein, *Czechoslovakia: Ethnic Conflict, Constitutional Fissure, Negotiated Breakup* (Ann Arbor, University of Michigan Press, 1997); Crawford (n 1) 402.

[6] See M Haile, 'Legality of Secessions: The Case of Eritrea' (1994) 8 *Emory International Law Review* 479; Crawford (n 1) 402.

[7] See I Martin, *Self-Determination in East Timor: The United Nations, the Ballot, and International Intervention* (Boulder, Lynne Rienner Publishers, 2001); Crawford (n 1) 560–62; R Wilde, *International Territorial Administration: How Trusteeship and the Civilizing Mission Never Went Away* (Oxford, Oxford University Press, 2008) 178–88. See also UN Doc S/RES/1338 (31 January 2001) and UN Doc A/RES/57/3 (27 September 2002).

[8] See UN Doc A/RES/60/264 (28 June 2006). With this resolution, Montenegro was admitted to the United Nations (UN).

[9] See the Kosovo Declaration of Independence (2008).

[10] See UN Doc GA/11114 (14 July 2011).

state creations were marked by international involvement, which included the creation of democratic institutions.[11]

The question now arises whether the language being used in the discourse of state creation is still that of international law. Concepts such as statehood criteria, recognition, secession and dissolution are traditional concepts in the law of statehood. As we move through self-determination towards democracy, it becomes unclear whether one is still on the terrain of the law of statehood or is rather dealing with issues of policy. Yet even policy, if followed universally, could be reflective of state practice and *opinio juris*.

In essence, the post-1990 developments were marked by an entanglement of the processes of democratisation and state creation; however, what is the legal significance of such an entanglement?

The place of democracy in the international law of statehood remains unclear. It is commonly argued that if democracy were accepted as a statehood criterion, 'a territorial entity which did not come about in a democratic procedure and which does not seek to establish democratic government structures would not qualify as a state'.[12] This argument carefully avoids pronouncing democracy a statehood criterion and holds that democracy in the law of statehood is concerned with two basic concepts: (i) a 'democratic procedure' required by international law in the process of state creation (altering the legal status of a territory in accordance with the will of the people); and (ii) a requirement for 'democratic government structures' in a new state (creating new states that adhere to a particular political system).

Doctrinal writings have not established a proper distinction between these two concepts subsumed under democracy in the international law of statehood. Scholarship in this area of international law has also remained too narrowly focused on the statehood criteria and has not analysed state creation as an internationalised *process*, to some extent influenced by the statehood criteria but also by other factors – democracy being a prominent example of one.

## 1.2  Context and Existing Literature

In 1992, Thomas Franck authored 'The Emerging Right to Democratic Governance', an article which adopts an election-centric definition of

---

[11]  J d'Aspremont, 'The Rise and Fall of Democratic Governance in International Law' in J Crawford and S Nouwen (eds), *Select Proceedings of the European Society of International Law* (Oxford, Hart Publishing, 2012) 61.

[12]  A Peters, 'Statehood after 1989: "Effectivités" between Legality and Virtuality' in J Crawford and S Nouwen (eds), *Select Proceedings of the European Society of International Law* (Oxford, Hart Publishing, 2012) 171.

democracy, deriving the putative new right from a selection of civil and political rights.[13] A related idea stems from the writings of Fernando Teson[14] and Anne-Marie Slaughter,[15] who suggest the reconceptualisation of international law as law among democratic states.

The ideas of both normative democratic entitlement and international law as law among democratic states have attracted strong criticism. Susan Marks argues that these endeavours are overtly ideological and points out the inadequacy of an election-centric definition of democracy.[16] José Alvarez questions the idea of legal prescriptions being based on the election-centric democratic self-image of some states and argues that the democratic enterprise in international law proposes to disrupt the United Nations (UN) Charter system.[17] Brad Roth cautions that even from the perspective of the election-centric definition of democracy, a democratic bias in reading universal human rights standards cannot be assumed.[18] Steven Wheatley notes that although there is 'a commitment of the international community to democracy as the only legitimate form of government . . . [t]here is . . . no "hard" international law norm that all governments should be democratic'.[19]

These discussions on the idea that international law supports only one particular type of government relate predominantly to the governments of *existing* states and deal with the origins of their legitimacy. In contrast, this book explores the legal significance of democratic procedures, institutions and even postulates of substantive democracy for *new* state creations.

The concept of the state and its emergence has been subject to notable controversy in international legal scholarship. In one view, states emerge as 'a matter of fact', upon meeting the Montevideo statehood criteria.[20] However, as Hersch Lauterpacht argued, in order to accept this explanation, one needs to accept the rather awkward idea that 'a State exists in international law as soon as it exists'.[21] The emergence of a new state may thus rather depend on *international acceptance* of the existence of a new state rather than on a presumption that its existence is a self-evident fact.[22] Lauterpacht explained international acceptance in the context of constitu-

---

[13] Franck (n 3, 1992); Franck (n 3, 1994); Franck, (n 3, 2001).

[14] Teson (n 3, 1992); Teson (n 3, 1998).

[15] Slaughter (n 3, 1995); Slaughter (n 3, 1997).

[16] S Marks, *The Riddle of All Constitutions* (Oxford, Oxford University Press, 2000).

[17] J Alvarez, 'Do Liberal States Behave Better? A Critique of Slaughter's Liberal Theory' (2001) 12 *EJIL* 183.

[18] B Roth, *Governmental Illegitimacy in International Law* (Oxford, Oxford University Press, 1999), especially 324–38.

[19] S Wheatley, *The Democratic Legitimacy of International Law* (Oxford, Hart Publishing, 2010) 228.

[20] S Talmon, *Kollektive Nichtanerkennung illegaler Staaten* (Tübingen, Mohr Siebeck, 2004) 218–24.

[21] H Lauterpacht, *Recognition of States in International Law* (Cambridge, Cambridge University Press, 1948) 66.

[22] ibid.

tive recognition,[23] but this view is problematic in light of the general perception in contemporary international law of recognition being a declaratory act. However, existing practice on new state creations in contemporary international law may well suggest that Lauterpacht was right in arguing that states do not emerge automatically upon meeting the Montevideo statehood criteria. As Marc Weller argues, the emergence of a new state may instead depend on 'a grant of legal authority'.[24]

The existing literature has not adequately explored the legal nature of international acceptance of the existence of a new state in the absence of a presumption that recognition is constitutive. If the emergence of a new state is not a matter of meeting the statehood criteria, and the practice shows that this is the case, it is questionable on which other requirements a state creation depends and how these requirements are grounded in contemporary international law.

Based on the practice of states and UN organs, James Crawford argues that the traditional statehood criteria have been supplemented by additional ones, and an entity which does not meet them is not a state.[25] John Dugard bases his arguments on the general principle of law *ex injuria jus non oritur* and in the concept of *jus cogens*, and argues that the creation of an entity in breach of *jus cogens* is illegal and cannot produce legal rights to the wrongdoer; in other words, such an entity cannot become a state.[26]

While the concept of the additional statehood criteria can explain why certain illegally created effective entities did not become states (eg, Southern Rhodesia),[27] it cannot explain why some other effective entities cannot become states even in the absence of territorial illegality (eg Somaliland).[28] Statehood criteria (traditional and additional) are not the only parameters in the equation that explains whether and why an entity is a state. This book thus considers the emergence of new states in the broader context of an internationalised process which also prescribes certain democratic procedures.

Prior to 1990, it was generally not maintained that judging the type of government based on electoral practices could be determinative of a successful state creation.[29] After the end of the Cold War, this perception changed to some degree. Part of the EC's response to the events in the territories of the SFRY and the Soviet Union was to issue a set of guidelines

---

[23] ibid.

[24] M Weller, 'Modesty Can Be a Virtue: Judicial Economy in the ICJ *Kosovo* Opinion' (2011) 24 *Leiden Journal of International Law* 127, 129–30.

[25] Crawford (n 1) 96–173.

[26] J Dugard, *Recognition and the United Nations* (Cambridge, Grotius Publications, 1987).

[27] See ch 1, 3.5.3.

[28] See Crawford (n 1) 404, who argues that that Somalia remains the only internationally recognised state in that territory.

[29] See JES Fawcett, 'Security Council Resolution on Rhodesia' (1965–66) 41 *British Yearbook of International Law* 104, 112; DJ Devine, 'The Requirements of Statehood Re-examined' (1971) 34 *Modern Law Review* 410, 410–17 and Fawcett's response at 417.

for recognition of new states emerging in these two territories. In the case of the SFRY, the EC also established a mechanism for recognition.[30]

The legal significance of international involvement – most notably of the EC – in the dissolution of the SFRY has been examined by writers in international law and international relations. David Raič argues that the requirement for states to constitute themselves on a democratic basis, expressed in the EC Guidelines on recognition, should, as suggested by the title of this document, be regarded as a recognition requirement and not a statehood criterion.[31] However, as Richard Caplan argues, although the EC termed its involvement as that of recognition of new states, this was rather an exercise in collective state creation.[32]

This book demonstrates that the act of recognition was not crucial for the emergence of new states in the territory of the federation. It was rather that the international involvement led to an internationalised extinguishing of the SFRY's personality, which made its claim to territorial integrity inapplicable . . . Considerations for democracy by the international community were thus not necessarily applied only in the process of granting recognition, but rather in the process of international acceptance of the dissolution of the SFRY. What implications does this practice have for the contemporary law of statehood?

Existing analyses of the dissolution of the SFRY do not thoroughly deal with the substance of the EC's requirement for new states to adhere to democratic practices. It has been insufficiently explored how these requirements were implemented and what their significance was under international law. Although it is acknowledged that international involvement in the process of dissolution of the SFRY may well have had constitutive effects, little attention has been paid to the phenomenon of international (attempts at) imposition of democratic institutions in a new state being dependent on the *mode of a certain state creation*. As Jean d'Aspremont notes, there exists significant practice of an entanglement of the processes of internationalised transitions to both statehood and democracy.[33]

To date, this entanglement has not been analysed from the perspective of international law. In other words, scholarship has not explained the legal nature of the interplay between the mode of state creation and the international imposition of democratic institutions; neither has it divorced the issue of imposition of democratic institutions in the new state from the

---

[30] See the EC Declaration on Yugoslavia (16 December 1991).

[31] D Raič, *Statehood and the Law of Self-Determination* (The Hague, Kluwer Law International, 2002), especially 436.

[32] R Caplan, *Europe and Recognition of New States in Yugoslavia* (Cambridge, Cambridge University Press, 2005); see also S Terrett, *The Dissolution of Yugoslavia and the Badinter Arbitration Commission: A Contextual Study of Peace-Making Efforts in the Post-Cold War World* (Aldershot, Ashgate, 2000); Grant (n 1) especially 168.

[33] D'Aspremont (n 11) 12

democratic principles operating in the law of statehood via the right of self-determination.[34]

The principle of self-determination and democratic political theory have been expressly wedded in the ideas of the American and French Revolutions and in the writings and speeches of the US President Woodrow Wilson.[35] Yet self-determination also featured prominently in Lenin's writings and thus in the socialist interpretation of law and society.[36] It is thus questionable whether self-determination can be linked exclusively to democratic political theory.

Robert McCorquodale argues that self-determination as a human right,[37] like most rights, is not an absolute entitlement but is limited by other rights.[38] The right of self-determination is also limited by and weighed against the principle of territorial integrity of states[39] and would normally be consummated in its internal mode, ie its exercise will normally not result in a new state creation.[40] However, the internal mode of self-determination gave rise to some speculation that this is, in fact, a manifestation of the 'right to democracy'.[41] The right of self-determination is also one of the cornerstones of Franck's normative democratic entitlement thesis.

The association of democracy as a political system with the right of self-determination has been criticised by some writers.[42] However, it remains unexplored how the requirement for a representative government for the purpose of the right of self-determination – as a matter of law – differs from the requirement for a representative government in democratic political

[34] See Wheatley (n 19) 217, who argues that: 'Increasingly, it is accepted that the right of peoples to self-determination should be understood in terms of democratic government in accordance with the will of the people.'

[35] See W Wilson, *President Wilson's Foreign Policy: Messages, Addresses, Papers* (collected by J Brown Scott) (New York, Oxford University Press, 1918); R Baker and W Dodd (eds), *War and Peace: Presidential Messages, Addresses, and Public Papers* (New York, Harper, 1927).

[36] See VI Lenin, *Questions of National Policy and Proletarian Internationalism* (Moscow, Foreign Languages Publishing House, year of publication unknown).

[37] The right of self-determination is codified in the common Article 1 of the International Covenant on Civil and Political Rights (ICCPR) (1966) and International Covenant on Economic, Social and Cultural Rights (ICESCR) (1966).

[38] R McCorquodale, 'Self-Determination: A Human Rights Approach' (1994) 43 *International & Comparative Law Quarterly* 857, 875–76.

[39] See the Declaration on Principles of International Law Concerning Cooperation and Friendly Relations among States in Accordance with the Charter of the United Nations (hereinafter the Declaration on Principles of International Law), UN Doc A/RES/2625 (24 October 1970), annex, principle 5, para 7.

[40] See *Reference re Secession of Québec* [1998] 2 SCR 217 (Supreme Court of Canada) (hereinafter the *Québec* case), para 126.

[41] P Thornberry, 'Self-Determination, Minorities, Human Rights: A Review of International Instruments' (1989) 38 *International & Comparative Law Quarterly* 341. See also Wheatley (n 19) 217.

[42] A Cassese, *Self-Determination of Peoples: A Legal Reappraisal* (Cambridge, Cambridge University Press, 1995).

theory.[43] In other words, via the right of self-determination, international law requires a *representative* government, but representative is not necessarily a synonym for democratic. This issue not only needs to be considered in the context of the internal mode of the right of self-determination but also in the context of the so-called doctrine of remedial secession.[44]

Authors discussing the link between democracy and the right of self-determination have also insufficiently stressed the difference between democracy as a political system and the operation of democratic principles within the right of self-determination. Jean Salmon cautions that there are many governments in the world that do not adhere to democratic practices but are nevertheless representative of their peoples.[45] However, the General Assembly has clearly called for one-man-one-vote principles in the context of the exercise of the right of self-determination.[46] The International Court of Justice (ICJ) has pronounced that, in principle, a popular consultation needs to be held before a change of the legal status of a territory can occur[47] and the Badinter Commission reaffirmed this standard.[48] These can be described as calls for the adoption of (some) democratic principles in the process of collective decision-making for the purpose of the exercise of the right of self-determination. However, it remains to be clarified why such calls should not be interpreted too broadly to mean a requirement for democracy as a political system.

In this vein, Peters argues that secession is a regulated process which prescribes 'peaceful and democratic procedures'.[49] For Peters: 'Any extraordinary allowance to secede has to be realized in the appropriate procedures, notably under recourse to a free and fair referendum on independence or after democratic elections, ideally under international supervision.'[50] While this position rightly maintains that secession, and state creation in general, requires a democratic process, it blurs the differ-

---

[43] Malcolm Shaw notes that '[t]he traditional exposition of the [statehood] criterion of government concentrated upon stability and effectiveness needed for this factor to be satisfied, while [as a consequence of operation of the right of self-determination] the representative and democratic nature of the government has also been forward[ed] as a requirement'. M Shaw, *International Law* (Cambridge, Cambridge University Press, 2008) 205.

[44] See Wheatley (n 19) 230, who argues that 'the relationship between territorial integrity and the right of peoples to self-determination can only be understood by reference to the principle of democracy'. For an overview of remedial secession, see Crawford (n 1) 188–222; A Tancredi, 'A Normative "Due Process" in the Creation of States Through Secession' in M Kohen (ed.), *Secession: International Law Perspectives* (Cambridge, Cambridge University Press, 2006).

[45] J Salmon, 'Aspects of the Right to Self-Determination: Towards a Democratic Legitimacy Principle?' in C Tomuschat (ed.), *Modern Law of Self-Determination* (Dordrecht, Martinus Nijhoff, 1993) 280.

[46] UN Doc A/RES/2022 (5 November 1965), para 8 (on Southern Rhodesia).

[47] *Western Sahara Advisory Opinion*, ICJ Rep 1975, para 55.

[48] The Badinter Commission, Opinion 4 (11 January 1992), para 4.

[49] A Peters, 'Does Kosovo Lie in the Lotus-Land of Freedom?' (2011) 24 *Leiden Journal of International Law* 95, 117.

[50] ibid.

ence between independence referenda and general elections in the context of the law of statehood. This book argues against such an approach and demonstrates that these are two separate issues in the law of statehood as well as in international law in general.

This book also considers the limitations that international law imposes on the will of the people in the context of the right of self-determination. One source of such a limitation is the principle of territorial integrity of states, which prevents the popular support in favour of independence from automatically resulting in statehood. Another, arguably even more controversial, limitation on the will of the people may become evident once the claim to territorial integrity is no longer applicable, when new states are created and new international borders need to be confined. As Crawford argues, the rules of international law pertaining to the confinement of borders of new states are one of the non-democratic features of international law, but 'may well serve other values'.[51]

In the territory of the SFRY, the Badinter Commission applied the *uti possidetis* principle in order to confine the new international borders along previously existing internal boundaries.[52] This application created new minorities and numerically inferior peoples. The application of what is a colonial principle in a non-colonial situation has been criticised by several scholars, including Robert McCorquodale and Raul Pangalangan,[53] Michla Pomerance,[54] Peter Radan[55] and Steven Ratner.[56] On the other hand, Alain Pellet[57] and Malcolm Shaw[58] advocate the use of *uti possidetis* and argue that respect of the will of the people cannot result in all border arrangements being in flux when new states are created. In their view, this would be an invitation to territorial conquest.

The common patterns of determination of new international borders in the territory of the former SFRY and the determination of new international borders in subsequent state creations remain insufficiently considered in the relevant literature. This book argues that the *uti possidetis* principle is

---

[51] Crawford (n 1) 153.

[52] The Badinter Commission, Opinion 3 (11 January 1992), especially para 2.

[53] R McCorquodale and R Pangalangan, 'Pushing Back the Limitation of Territorial Boundaries' (2001) 12 *EJIL* 867, especially 875.

[54] M Pomerance, 'The Badinter Commission: The Use and Misuse of the International Court of Justice's Jurisprudence' (1998–99) 20 *Michigan Journal of International Law* 31.

[55] P Radan, 'Post-Secession International Borders: A Critical Analysis of the Opinions of the Badinter Arbitration Commission' (2000) 24 *Melbourne University Law Review* 50.

[56] S Ratner, 'Drawing a Better Line: *Uti Possidetis* and the Borders of New States' (1996) 90 *American Journal of International Law* 590.

[57] A Pellet, 'Avis juridique sommaire sur le projet de loi donnant effet à l'exigence de clarté formulae par la Cour suprême du Canada dans son avis sur le Renvoi sur la sécession du Québec' quoted in English translation in S Lalonde, 'Québec's Boundaries in the Event of Secession' (2003) 7 *Macquarie Law Journal* 129, 137.

[58] M Shaw, 'The Heritage of States: The Principle of *Uti Possidetis* Today' (1996) 67 *British Yearbook of International Law* 75; M Shaw, 'Peoples, Territorialism and Boundaries' (1997) 8 *EJIL* 478.

not applicable outside of the process of decolonisation; however, this does not mean that outside of colonialism all borders are in flux when new states emerge. The latest internal boundary arrangement, even if it enjoys little support among the people, will nevertheless form a strong base for new international delimitation. In this context, scholarship thus far has insufficiently considered what kind of internal boundaries are capable of becoming international borders. This book analyses the practice which reveals that these are only those boundaries which delimit historically realised self-determination units.

In sum, this book takes a different focus than the existing literature on the international law of statehood. In particular, it does not focus on the statehood criteria or consider whether democracy has become one of them. Rather, it analyses the post-Cold War practice of the emergence and delimitation of new states and develops an argument that state creation is an internationalised law-governed process of overcoming an applicable counterclaim to territorial integrity. This process is influenced by the statehood criteria, among other factors. The process prescribes certain democratic procedures and may even result in the international imposition of democratic institutions. But how has this practice shaped contemporary international law and what is the legal framework governing the creation of states that stretches beyond the statehood criteria?

## 1.3 The Main Objectives of the Book

There are two main reasons why the law of statehood needs to be updated with post-Cold War practice. First, new states in this period have emerged outside the colonial context and in the absence of an entitlement to independence. Therefore, new states in contemporary practice emerge in different legal circumstances than was the case in the past; independence-seeking entities are faced with the applicable claim to territorial integrity of their parent states. Second, in the new legal circumstances, the emergence of new states has become increasingly dependent on international acceptance rather than meeting the statehood criteria. In recent practice, this dependence has been used for an internationalised imposition of certain democratic standards on the newly created states.

In contemporary international law, the statehood criteria seem to be largely disregarded in practice. But how do new states come into existence if meeting the statehood criteria is neither sufficient nor necessary? This book demonstrates that the emergence of a new state is not a factual occurrence but a law-governed political process which leads to a change in the legal status of a certain territory. Under international law, this process requires some democratic procedures to be followed. However, several difficult issues arise in this context.

How does a territory become an independent state?; who decides on the change of the legal status and what is the procedure leading to this effect?; how and by whom are the boundaries of the new state confined and why is the emergence of a new state very unlikely, even where it is favoured by the democratically expressed will of the people? Which democratic principles are to be followed and what are the limits on these principles in the process of state creation? How do the will of the people and the principles of democratic decision-making interact with the principles of international law, such as the territorial integrity of states, *uti possidetis* and the free choice of the political system?[59] How does the process of acquiring statehood accommodate the practice of the international imposition of a democratic political system and what is the legal significance of this practice? And how do the legal rules governing the democratic process of state creation differ from the post-Cold War law and practice of internationalised creations of democratic states?

In answering these questions, this book: (i) comprehensively analyses the practice of the post-Cold War emergence of new states and considers the legal significance of international involvement in the process of new state creations; (ii) takes the international law of statehood further than the prevailing doctrinal debates on statehood criteria and recognition theories, and determines the legal implications of the principle of territorial integrity; (iii) considers the international legal relevance of the emerging post-Cold War practice of internationalised parallel creations of democratic political systems along with the creation of new states; (iv) thoroughly analyses the practice of democratic expression of the will of the people at independence referenda in terms of legal effects as well as procedural standards and determines the international legal limitations imposed on the democratic process; (v) explains why even in the absence of the *uti possidetis* presumption outside of the process of decolonisation, new international borders tend to be confined along the lines of the previously existing internal boundaries and argues why delimitation is not subject to popular decision-making; (vi) provides for an indepth analysis of legal sources which demonstrate how principles of general international law limit the democratic expression of the will of the people in the context of the law of statehood; and (vii) systematically demonstrates that democracy as a political system and the exercise of the right of self-determination are two separate issues in the international law of statehood.

In sum, analysing the law and practice of post-Cold War state creations, the book seeks to update the inadequate theory of statehood. In practical terms, it will provide answers to questions which the law of statehood in its present state cannot answer exhaustively. These questions include:

---

[59] *cf* Wheatley (n 19) 245–46, who argues that: 'Democracy does not define its own borders; the borders of democracy are defined by international law.'

why do certain entities meet the statehood criteria but are not considered states and vice versa?; what is the role of recognition in contemporary international law; does a new state need to adopt a certain institutional design or have a government of a particular type?; under what circumstances can an independence referendum actually lead to independence?; who is entitled to vote at independence referenda and what kind of majority is internationally accepted as an expression of the will of the people?; and how is the international border of the new state determined?

## 1.4 Structure of the Book

*Chapter one* locates the concepts of democracy and statehood within international legal scholarship. It initially outlines the ideas of bringing democracy into international law through the provisions of international human rights law and the ideas about reconceptualising international law as law among democratic states. Such arguments have prompted sceptical voices from both international law and political science scholarship. It is argued that when one brings democracy into international law, one also brings along the quarrels about the meaning and definition of democracy. This chapter thus deals with different understandings of democracy and cautions that the one adopted by the 'democratic endeavour' within international law attracts notable criticism in political science scholarship.

Subsequently, the chapter considers the concept of the state in international law; the statehood criteria; recognition requirements; the relationship between statehood and recognition in contemporary international law; and the legal effects of non-recognition (as well as the development of the doctrine of non-recognition in the pre-1990 practice). An argument is made that in contemporary international law, meeting the statehood criteria and the existence of an effective entity do not necessarily imply the existence of a state, not even a non-recognised one. Certain human rights may well be important for the legality of a new state creation. Yet in the pre-1990 practice, democracy as a political system did not play any role in the emergence of new states. This may be different when democratic principles operating within the right of self-determination are concerned.

However, even if an entity meets the Montevideo statehood criteria and certain legality requirements, it does not automatically and self-evidently become a state. The hurdle which the entity also needs to overcome is its parent state's counterclaim for territorial integrity. The chapter argues that this hurdle may be overcome, inter alia, through internationalised action. However, the international involvement into the process of state creation brings a possibility of internationalised interference into the choice of a political system in the new state.

*Chapter two* turns to the post-Cold War practice of state creations. The main concern is the role of the requirements other than those identified in chapter one for the emergence of new states. It is demonstrated that in a number of post-Cold War developments, new states were created as a result of international action and such action was coupled with international attempts to create a democratic political system along with the new state. It is, however, questionable whether considerations for democracy in this context can only be seen as a matter of recognition requirements. It may well be that international involvement can produce rather than merely acknowledge the emergence of a new state.

Presenting state creation as an internationalised process, this chapter considers case studies of all successful post-1990 state creations, including the controversial case of Kosovo and the recent emergence of South Sudan as an independent state. Drawing on the analysis in chapter one, chapter two considers the legal significance of the post-1990 attempts of the international community to contribute towards the creation of new states which are organised along democratic lines.

In *chapter three*, the discussion turns to the relationship between democracy and the right of self-determination. The chapter defines the difference between internal and external aspects of self-determination and considers the link between self-determination and democratic political theory. It argues that the right of self-determination requires a representative government, yet governmental representativeness in this context is defined differently than in the context of democratic political theory. The right of self-determination is not exclusively compatible with only one particular political system.

The chapter further identifies the democratic principles operating in the context of the external aspect of the right of self-determination and analyses the procedural standards of independence referenda. It is considered whether the practice of such referenda gives a suggestion as to the generally applicable standards of popular consultation in the framework of the right of self-determination. For this purpose, the post-1990 independence referenda practice is analysed from the perspectives of procedural referenda rules and the legal effects of the expressed will of the people on the international law of statehood.

This chapter draws on democratic political theory, initially to consider the link between democracy and the principle of self-determination and, subsequently, to analyse how the will of the people operates within the right of self-determination and how it is limited by general international law, in particular by the principle of the territorial integrity of states.

*Chapter four* is the final substantive chapter and is concerned with the limitations on the will of the people in the context of new state creations. Such limitations may also stem from the previous internal boundary arrangement. This chapter begins with the controversy over the applicability of the *uti possidetis* principle outside of colonial situations and questions whether all 'upgrades' of internal boundaries to international borders may be ascribed to the operation of *uti possidetis*. It further seeks to clarify the circumstances in which the will of the people pertaining to a new international delimitation may be rightfully limited by a pre-existing internal boundary arrangement.

The main argument of this chapter is that in the post-Cold War practice, new international borders are not colonial-like arbitrarily drawn boundaries, but rather are historically realised lines delimiting self-determination units. The criticism that such borders create new minorities ignores the fact that mono-ethnic 'nation states' do not exist in reality and for this reason it cannot be expected that such a state could be newly created. The latest internal boundary arrangement thus forms a strong base for the new international delimitation; nevertheless, international law does not exclude the possibility of territorial rearrangements.

*Chapter five*, the final chapter, provides for conclusions and summaries on the role and legal relevance of democracy and democratic principles in successful post-1990 state creations. It brings together the analysed law and practice on the emergence and delimitation of new states in the post-Cold War period, synthesises the theory of state creation as an internationalised *process*, and presents the legal nature and significance of democracy and democratic principles in this process.

## 2  INTERNATIONAL LAW AND (NON-)DEMOCRATIC STATES

### 2.1  Democracy, Elections and Human Rights

Free and fair elections are an integral part of the right to political participation and also a concept in democratic political theory, yet the relationship between democracy, elections and human rights remains somewhat controversial. In democratic political theory, there is an ongoing dispute as to whether elections should be considered a necessary or a sufficient condition for democracy. At the same time, it is ambiguous what the international legal threshold is of free and fair elections and whether such elections necessarily need to take place in a multiparty setting. This section outlines the procedural (ie, election-centric) and substantive definitions of democracy and argues that while the procedural definition may be inadequate, it is difficult to conceive democracy as an international legal principle on the postulates of its substantive definition. The concept of democracy in international human rights law is therefore often reduced to the procedural understanding and to the question of whether human rights standards require multiparty elections. However, multiparty elections should not be seen as an equivalent to democracy.

*2.1.1 Elections and the Procedural Understanding of Democracy*

The term 'democracy' is a synthesis of the Greek words *demos*, meaning 'people', and *kratos*, meaning 'rule'.[60] Semantically, the term 'democracy' stands for 'rule by the people'; however, in democratic political theory, there has been much ambiguity surrounding both components of the word 'democracy'. While a consensus has been reached that the term 'people' means all adult women and men,[61] a consensus over the meaning of the term 'rule' is more elusive. The controversial question now is no longer who rules, but rather how people exercise their rule.

The classical modern theory of democracy, adopted at the end of the eighteenth century, was government-centric and defined democracy 'in terms of sources of authority for government, purposes served by government, and procedures for constituting government'.[62] In the early years of modern democracy, when the category of 'people' was severely restricted, predominantly to wealthy men of a specific societal status determined by birth and education, the democratic method was confined to a small elite, which ruled on behalf of the majority, itself excluded from the power to rule.[63] The democratic method of this kind still resembled non-democratic methods.[64] This was rather a situation of '[a] society divided between a large impoverished mass and a small favoured elite [which] would result either in oligarchy (dictatorial rule of the small upper stratum) or in tyranny (popularly-based dictatorship)'.[65]

With the extension of the category 'people', the inadequacy of the government-centric definition of the rule became evident. The most tangible and quantitatively provable switch to the real rule of people happened by the adoption of electoral laws that enacted universal suffrage.[66] This enabled everyone to participate in the democratic process. Thus, the classical, ie, government-centric, understanding of democracy was challenged within the electoral process and the latter became the most visible component of the democratic rule.

[60] See G Sorensen, *Democracy and Democratization: Processes and Prospects in a Changing World* (Boulder, Westview, 1993) 3.

[61] Relatively recently, women in many states deemed democratic did not constitute the category of 'people who rule'. Many male citizens had long been excluded from this category based on reasons such as ethnic and racial background, class background, level of education and wealth. See Sorensen (ibid) 9–16.

[62] S Huntington, *The Third Wave* (Norman, University of Oklahoma Press, 1990) 6.

[63] See D Held, *Democracy and the Global Order: From the Modern State to Cosmopolitan Governance* (Cambridge, Polity Press, 1995) 9–12.

[64] In some sense, such rule was similar to that later established in apartheid South Africa, where democratic rule was in the hands of a minority determined by race, while the majority could not participate in the exercise of rule. See Sorensen (n 60) 14–17.

[65] SM Lipset, *The Encyclopedia of Democracy* (Washington DC, Congressional Quarterly, 1994) 75.

[66] It is argued that elections are the most tangible part of the democratic process and therefore are often considered a synonym for democracy. T Carothers, 'Empirical Perspectives on the Emerging Norm of Democracy in International Law' (1992) *ASIL Proceedings* 261, 264.

On this basis, a new understanding of democracy was developed, which is well-captured in the writings of Joseph Schumpeter: 'The democratic method is that of institutional arrangement for arriving at political decisions in which individuals acquire the power to decide by means of a competitive struggle for the people's vote.'[67] His ideas have remained both influential and criticised up to the present day.[68]

If one literally follows Schumpeter's definition, democracy would only be a matter of electoral process. In such an understanding, people periodically have a chance to elect their political leaders, while in the period between the elections, their participation within the society is limited to the status of observers who assess the actions of their leaders in order to decide whether to re-elect or replace them.[69] In this understanding, one could argue that the only action that political leaders are precluded from is the suspension of the following elections.

It may well be that the 'institutional arrangement'[70] necessary for the election of leaders presumes an arrangement wider than merely that of electoral law which is not to be suspended. Indeed, the Schumpeterian definition of democracy already looks beyond the electoral process as the sole criterion of democracy and 'elucidates the link between democracy, rights and the rule of law'.[71] If everyone is allowed to compete for political leadership, 'this will in most cases though not in all mean a considerable amount of freedom of discussion for all. In particular it will normally mean a considerable amount of freedom of the press',[72] which enables an individual to obtain more information on the candidates and their programmes, and thus optimise the electoral choice. In essence, even the Schumpeterian understanding of the electoral process is not only about standing for an election and casting a vote, but rather means that 'the institution of periodic elections must go hand in hand with the necessary institutions for securing respect for the rule of law and constitutional guarantees of civil and political rights'.[73]

The Schumpeterian understanding of democracy does not literally refuse to look beyond elections, but rather puts elections at the centre of

---

[67] J Schumpeter, *Capitalism, Socialism, and Democracy* (New York, Harper, 1942) 269.

[68] See ch 1, 2.1.1.

[69] Such an understanding of democracy may be challenged by the question of whether a democratic political system would not be 'more democratic if ordinary citizens (as they typically do) lobbied their representatives between elections, organized campaigning groups, engaged in consultative processes, took part in demonstrations . . . if they actively regarded public matters as their affair, and if representatives were systematically required to listen to them'. D Beetham, *Democracy and Human Rights* (Cambridge, Polity Press, 1999) 3. In other words, the democratic process operates even between elections and not only at elections.

[70] Schumpeter (n 67) 269.

[71] Marks (n 16) 51.

[72] Schumpeter (n 67) 271–72.

[73] Marks (n 16) 51.

the democratic method.[74] In this perception, free and fair elections are seen not as a necessary condition of democracy, but as a sufficient one. While such a narrow (ie, procedural) understanding of democracy acknowledges the necessity for other rights to be respected – expressly the freedoms of speech and assembly – it defines these rights vis-a-vis the right to political participation rather than vis-a-vis the entire human rights framework. In other words, the freedoms of speech and assembly in this model are the *sine qua non* of democracy because they are the *sine qua non* of the right to political participation.[75] Such a definition of democracy is thus based on a hierarchical order of a selection of civil and political rights.

### 2.1.2 *The Substantive Definition of Democracy in Relation to Human Rights*

In contrast to the procedural definition, the substantive definition of democracy is based on democracy's underlying principles rather than merely the electoral process. In this view:

> The core idea of democracy is that of popular vote or popular control over collective decision-making. Its starting point is with the citizen rather than with the institutions of government. Its defining principles are that all citizens are entitled to a say in public affairs, both through participation in government, and that this entitlement should be available on terms of equality to all. Control *by* citizens over their collective affairs and equality *between* citizens in the exercise of that control are the basic democratic principles.[76]

Democracy is defined in a much broader sense of popular control and equality for all. Such a definition makes it possible to address the issue of 'why particular institutions or procedures have a claim to be democratic, and what needs to be changed to be more so'.[77] Democracy is thus not defined as something absolute or as a promised destination, but rather as a continuous journey.[78]

In the substantive definition, civil and political as well as social, economic and cultural rights are an integral part of democracy.[79] Indeed, 'if

---

[74] The Schumpeterian definition of democracy expressly echoes within the normative democratic entitlement theory: 'The existence of a democratic form of government – evidenced by fair and free periodic elections, three branches of government, an independent judiciary, freedom of political expression, equality before the law, and due process – is *sine qua non* to the enjoyment of human rights.' C Cerna, 'Universal Democracy: An International Legal Right or the Pipe Dream of the West?' (1995) 27 *New York University Journal of International Law & Politics* 289, 295.

[75] *cf* the UN Human Rights Committee (HRC), General Comment 25, UN Doc CCPR/C/21/Rev.1/Add.7 (1996), para 12.

[76] Beetham (n 69) 90–91 (emphasis in original).

[77] S Marks and A Clapham, *International Human Rights Lexicon* (Oxford, Oxford University Press, 2005) 3.

[78] Marks (n 16) 73.

[79] Beetham (n 69) 114.

public decision-making is the business of all citizens equally, then all must be not just entitled, but also enabled, to undertake it, and that calls for access to the requisite social, economic and cultural resources. Political equality depends on overcoming material deprivation'.[80] This relationship is one of mutual dependency between economic, social and cultural rights on one side and democracy on the other.[81] As argued by Beetham, the absence of social, economic and cultural rights 'compromises civil and political equality, the quality of public life and the long-term viability of democratic institutions themselves; democracy, on the other hand, constitutes a necessary if not sufficient condition for the protection of economic and social rights'.[82]

Two main challenges to the argument of mutual dependency between social, economic and cultural rights and democracy have been invoked. First, proponents of the procedural understanding argue that social, economic and cultural rights lack normative precision and, consequently, democracy cannot be normatively defined. Such a view is well-captured in the following observation:

> To some people democracy has or should have much more sweeping and idealistic connotations. To them, 'true democracy' means *liberté, egalité, fraternité*, effective citizen control over policy, responsible government, honesty and openness in politics, informed and rational deliberation, equal participation and power, and various other civic virtues. These are, for the most part, good things and people can, if they wish, define democracy in these terms. Doing so, however, raises the problems that come up with the definitions of democracy by source or by purpose. Fuzzy norms do not yield useful analysis.[83]

Second, the mutual dependence between social, economic and cultural rights on the one hand and democracy on the other has been challenged by the neoliberal[84] view that social, economic and cultural rights contradict some of the rights from the civil and political cluster. Fukuyama defines 'fundamental rights' as civil and political rights and rejects social, economic and cultural rights, arguing that 'the achievement of these

---

[80] Marks and Clapham (n 77) 64–65.
[81] Beetham (n 69) 114.
[82] ibid.
[83] Huntington (n 62) 9.
[84] Consider the following definition of neoliberalism: 'Neoliberalism is in the first instance a theory of political economic practices that proposes that human well-being can best be advanced by liberating individual entrepreneurial freedoms and skills within an institutional framework characterized by strong private property rights, free markets, and free trade. The role of the state is to create and preserve an institutional framework appropriate to such practices . . . [I]f markets do not exist . . . then they must be created, by state action if necessary. State interventions in markets (once created) must be kept to a bare minimum because, according to the theory, the state cannot possibly possess enough information to second-guess market signals (process) and because powerful interest groups will inevitably distort and bias state interventions (particularly in democracies) for their own benefit.' D Harvey, *A Brief History of Neoliberalism* (Oxford, Oxford University Press, 2005) 2.

rights is not clearly compatible with other rights like those of property or free economic exchange'.[85] Such an argument has been described as 'the extreme neo-liberal view that private property and the freedom of exchange constitute absolute and untouchable "natural rights"'.[86] This is, however, to overlook that both private property and freedom of exchange are 'socially constructed and validated institutions, whose primary justification lies in their effectiveness in securing people's means of livelihood'.[87] Ultimately, '[a] democratic society . . . requires both the institutions of private property and free exchange and the guarantee of basic economic rights, if it is to be founded upon a general consent'.[88]

In sum, democratic political theory does not have a unitary definition of democracy. The procedural definition understands democracy in terms of the electoral process. In this understanding, democracy can be expressed with a selection of civil and political rights, most commonly with the right to political participation and freedoms of speech and assembly. It is highly controversial as to whether democracy is only a matter of electoral process. Therefore, the substantive definition of democracy looks beyond the electoral process. However, as the critique of such a definition suggests, substantive democracy can be a philosophical ideal, while it is not possible to define it by a set of legal prescriptions. Thus, in international legal parlance, references to democracy are most commonly made with tenets of procedural democracy in mind. Even if the procedural understanding is adopted and democracy is primarily associated with free and fair elections, it still remains questionable whether international human rights law requires that such elections be held in a multiparty setting.

## 2.2 Democracy and International Human Rights Law

### 2.2.1 Linking International Law and Democracy

The interdependence between human rights and democracy makes international human rights law the most suitable framework for invoking democracy as a principle of international law, but the word 'democracy' does not appear in either the UN Charter or universal human rights instruments, nor has the International Court of Justice (ICJ) 'based any of its decisions on the legal application of democratic principles'.[89] Some international human rights instruments, however, make references to 'democratic society'.

[85] F Fukuyama, *The End of History and the Last Man* (New York, Free Press, 1992) 42–43.
[86] Beetham (n 69) 101.
[87] ibid.
[88] ibid, 100–01.
[89] R Rich, 'Bringing Democracy into International Law' (2001) 12 *Journal of Democracy* 20, 20.

Such a reference initially appeared in the Universal Declaration of Human Rights (UDHR),[90] where the expression 'democratic society' is employed in the context of the limitation clause: human rights may be limited if the interest of 'democratic society' so requires. But how broadly does international law understand the adjective 'democratic'? Its inclusion at the time of the adoption of the UDHR in 1948 could hardly reflect a customary rule of international law requiring a particular political system or electoral method. 'Democratic' at the time was hardly more than a synonym for 'non-fascist'.[91] Subsequently, the expression 'democratic society' found its place into a number of international human rights treaties, where it was also employed within the limitation clauses.[92]

The meaning of 'democratic society' within the universal treaties was not seen as a requirement for a particular political system or electoral method. Moreover, it is not the limitation clauses where the links between democracy and human rights are normally established. Arguments are instead advanced that democratic principles operate within certain human rights provisions. In one such view, 'by becoming a party to an international human rights instrument, a state agrees to organize itself along democratic lines by establishing independent tribunals, allowing freedom of expression, and conducting free elections'.[93]

This understanding is a reflection of the procedural understanding of democracy, which places free and fair elections at the centre of the democratic process, while it acknowledges that some other rights are also important for the conducting of such elections. Human rights which are most notably associated with the electoral process are sometimes referred

[90] Article 29(2) of the UDHR provides: 'In the exercise of his rights and freedoms, everyone shall be subject only to such limitations as are determined by law solely for the purpose of securing due recognition and respect for the rights and freedoms of others and of meeting the just requirements of morality, public order and the general welfare in a democratic society.'

[91] Roth (n 18) 326.

[92] The International Covenant on Economic, Social and Cultural Rights (ICESCR) comprehends a general limitation clause in Article 4: 'The States Parties to the present Covenant recognize that, in the enjoyment of those rights provided by the State in conformity with the present Covenant, the State may subject such rights only to such limitations as are determined by law only in so far as this may be compatible with the nature of these rights and solely for the purpose of promoting the general welfare in a democratic society.' The ICESCR also refers to 'democratic society' as part of the limitation clause in the elaboration subparas (a) and (c) of Article 8 (the right to form trade unions). The International Covenant on Civil and Political Rights (ICCPR) attaches the interest of 'democratic society' as one of the limitation clauses to Articles 14 (the right to a fair trial), 21 (the right to freedom of assembly) and 22 (the right to freedom of association). The Convention on the Rights of the Child (CRC) invokes, inter alia, restrictions 'which are necessary in a democratic society' as a limitation clause to Article 15 (the rights of a child to freedom of association and assembly). The International Convention on the Protection of the Rights of All Migrant Workers and Members of Their Families attaches the interest of 'democratic society' within the limitation clause to Articles 26 (the right of migrant workers to take part in trade unions) and 40 (the freedom of assembly of migrant workers).

[93] Cerna (n 74) 295.

to as 'democratic rights'.[94] However, even if one accepts the electoral-centric (procedural) definition of democracy, it is questionable whether the universal understanding of the right to political participation can *only* be fulfilled in a multiparty political system.

### 2.2.2 *The Right to Political Participation and Democracy*

The right to political participation is elaborated in Article 21 of the UDHR and in Article 25 of the International Covenant on Civil and Political Rights (ICCPR). In the Cold War environment, the scope of the formulations the 'will of the people'[95] and the 'will of the electors'[96] were not to be interpreted too broadly.[97] This was due to there being two competing interpretations of democracy and democratic principles. The Western[98] world adopted the model of 'liberal democracy', which presupposes elections in a multiparty setting,[99] while the interpretation of the Soviet Bloc was 'people's democracy'.[100]

Neither Article 21 of the UDHR nor Article 25 of the ICCPR specifically requires multiparty elections or establishes a specific link between elections and government formation.[101] In other words, nothing in these provisions defines the extent to which a government needs to reflect the electorate's will.[102] If in a liberal-democratic understanding the composition of government needs to reflect electoral results[103] and elections need

---

[94] The term 'democratic rights' in this book will describe those civil and political rights which are most relevant for the procedural definition of democracy. The right to political participation, freedom of assembly and freedom of expression can be most notably identified as such.

[95] UDHR, art 21(3).

[96] ICCPR, art 25(b).

[97] A possible interpretation could also be that, for example, multiparty elections are not required if the will of the people is against them. See Rich (n 89) 23.

[98] The term 'Western states' at that time implied states belonging to the regional group 'Western European and Others', which was unofficially used within the UN system. Yet, after the end of the Cold War, such a definition of 'Western states' is no longer adequate. References to 'Western states' in the post-Cold War era should then be understood as states of Europe, broadly understood, and non-European states in which societies are of European historical, cultural, religious and linguistic origin. In this context, Carothers (n 66) 263 argues that: 'Latin America and Eastern Europe are essentially parts of the Western world.'

[99] See Roth (n 18) 325–32.

[100] Consider especially the following argument given by Roth (ibid) 331: 'In the Marxist-Leninist view, multi-party competition [otherwise a crucial postulate of the Western concept of liberal democracy] masks the inalterable structure of power rooted in the concentrated ownership and control of the major means of production, distribution and exchange.'

[101] The amendment to Article 21 of the UDHR, which would call for multiparty elections, was withdrawn after a protest by the Soviet government. See Roth (n 18) 326–27.

[102] ibid, 330.

[103] This postulate of liberal democracies is subject to caution. Since the liberal-democratic model does not prescribe a single model of government formation or a single constitutional system (presidential, semi-presidential or parliamentary), the 'representative government' may significantly differ from electoral results. What is more, the question of what is a 'representative government' to a great degree becomes subject to subjective analyses. See also ch. 3, 3.

to take place in a true multiparty setting,[104] such an interpretation is not acceptable for the Leninist concept of democracy.[105] Indeed, the drafting history shows that many, if not actually most, signatory states would have refused to ratify the ICCPR were it to bind them to democratic institutions, most notably to multiparty elections.[106] Thus, the language of the UDHR and the ICCPR is to be understood as an attempt 'to avoid controversy over institutional requisites, while still asserting a universal human interest in political participation that states are bound to satisfy in some manner',[107] but one cannot proclaim the liberal interpretation of democracy as being the only authoritative one.

The position that human rights treaty provisions and customary international law do not require a state to adopt any particular electoral method or, in general, any political, social, economic and cultural system was confirmed by the ICJ in the *Nicaragua* case: '[T]he Court cannot find an instrument with legal force, whether unilateral or synallagmatic, whereby Nicaragua has committed itself in respect of the principle or methods of holding elections.'[108] The Court took this position despite the fact that Nicaragua was a party to the ICCPR and continued:

> [A]dherence by a State to any particular doctrine does not constitute a violation of customary international law; to hold otherwise would make nonsense of the fundamental principle of State sovereignty, on which the whole of international law rests, and the freedom of choice of the political, social, economic and cultural system of a State . . . The Court cannot contemplate the creation of a new rule opening up a right of intervention by one State against another on the ground that the latter has opted for some particular ideology or political system.[109]

If such an interpretation of the ICCPR and of customary international law was accurate in 1986, this may have changed since the end of the Cold War.

---

[104] Even this postulate is subject to caution as the liberal-democratic model does not prescribe a single model of the party system, which is also a consequence of different electoral systems. The model of two-party democracy may lead to significant considerations regarding its democratic quality and so can a fragmented, so-called hundred-party system. A detailed analysis of these deficiencies would, however, be beyond the scope of this book. For more on this, see K von Beyme, 'Institutional Engineering and Transitions to Democracy' in R Elgie and J Zielonka (eds), *Democratic Consolidation in Eastern Europe* (Oxford, Oxford University Press, 2001) 3–24; R Elgie and J Zielonka, 'Constitutions and Constitution Building: A Comparative Perspective' in R Elgie and J Zielonka (eds), *Democratic Consolidation in Eastern Europe* (Oxford, Oxford University Press, 2001) 25–47.

[105] See ch 3, 2.

[106] Roth (n 18) 332.

[107] ibid.

[108] *Military and Paramilitary Activities in and Against Nicaragua (Nicaragua v United States)*, Merits, Judgment of 27 June 1986, [1986] ICJ Rep 14, at 132, para 261 (hereinafter the *Nicaragua* case).

[109] ibid, para 263.

## 2.3  A Democratic Bias in Post-Cold War International Law?

### 2.3.1  *The Theories of Normative Democratic Entitlement and Democratic Peace*

At the end of the Cold War, in the triumphal age of democracy and ideological proclamation of the 'end of history',[110] an attempt was made to proclaim democracy itself a human right. In his groundbreaking article entitled 'The Emerging Right to Democratic Governance',[111] Thomas Franck derived the right to democratic governance from the right of self-determination, freedom of expression and the right to political participation.[112] He remained aware that this was a rather narrow concept of democracy; however, he was prepared to accept it in order to find the lowest common denominator in the politically and culturally diverse world.[113] Further, he saw that a right to democratic governance, so underpinned, benefits from a relatively clear normative framework and thus appears to be much more persuasive as a legal norm.[114]

Although the three cornerstones of the right to democratic governance (the right of self-determination, freedom of expression and the right to political participation) have been codified as international human rights, the proponents of the theory of normative democratic entitlement argue that it was the international circumstances at the end of the Cold War which led to the reinterpretation of the norms of international human rights law with a pro-democratic bias.[115] According to Franck, especially relevant in this regard were the international responses to the coups in the Soviet Union and Haiti in 1991.[116] In this perception, a global switch to democracy after the Cold War has occurred and democracy has become the only form of government deemed legitimate by the world's population.

However, when pronouncing Western-style democracy as the universally accepted, sole legitimate system of government, Franck gave little evidence for such a claim. Relevant evidence may exist within newly democratised Western societies.[117] Yet Western-style democracy cannot be assumed to be the preference of all of humanity.[118] The right to democratic

---

[110] For more on the critique of 'democratic ideology', see Marks (n 16) 8–49.
[111] Franck (n 3, 1992).
[112] ibid, 52
[113] ibid, 90.
[114] ibid. *cf* Huntington (n 62) 9–10. *cf* also ch 1, 2.1. For a critique of an attempt to fit democracy into the legal prescription, see also Carothers (n 66) 265, who argues that: 'International law, like most law, tends to look for bright lines, but it is very hard to find one when dealing with democracy.'
[115] On the other hand, it was argued that '[d]emocracy, or the right to live under a democratic form of government, became an international legal right in 1948 [by the UDHR], although for decades it was honored more in breach than in observance'. Cerna (n 74) 290.
[116] Franck (n 3, 1992) 47.
[117] See Carothers (n 66) 262–63.
[118] ibid, 263.

governance also provokes a question associated with the definition of democracy, ie, to what one is entitled by the proposed normative entitlement.

The decisive criterion for the exercise of the right to democratic governance appears to be formation of a government based on free and fair elections. In Franck's words:

> The right to democracy is the right of people to be consulted and to participate in the process by which political values are reconciled and choices made.[119]
>
> The term 'democracy', as used in international rights parlance, is intended to connote the kind of governance that is legitimated by the consent of the governed. Essential to the legitimacy of governance is evidence of consent to the process by which a populace is consulted by its government.[120]

In this understanding, elections are seen as a sufficient rather than a necessary criterion for democracy.[121] The right is thereby premised on the procedural understanding of democracy, the shortcomings of which have been discussed above.[122] As elections are the most tangible part of the democratic process,[123] it is relatively easy to monitor them and determine whether or not they were (sufficiently) free. According to Franck, the legitimacy of government would ultimately depend on this determination.[124] Indeed, the idea of the right to democratic governance proposes that electoral monitoring become an institutionalised instrument.[125] Merely refusing electoral monitoring – not necessarily the failure to hold free and fair elections, let alone democracy as it is broadly understood – might then constitute a breach of international legal obligations.[126] This further narrows the focus of the right to democratic governance from the electoral process to electoral monitoring. The right to democratic governance thus effectively becomes a right to monitored elections. Yet, as one author has put it, 'electoral monitoring has not been the democratic panacea',[127] as it is much easier to implement democratic institutions and observe this part of the democratisation process than to consolidate democracy and assess the progress in this phase.[128]

A related idea to normative democratic entitlement is that of bringing the democratic peace theory into international law.[129] In 1795, Immanuel

---

[119] Franck (n 3, 2001) 25.

[120] Franck (n 3, 1994) 75.

[121] *cf* ch 1, 2.1.

[122] See ch 1, 2.1.

[123] Carothers (n 66) 264.

[124] See Franck (n 3, 1992) 90–91.

[125] Franck (n 3, 2001) 41–47.

[126] ibid, 47, arguing: 'If monitoring evolves into a universal obligation, perhaps consequences will attach even to a refusal to be monitored.'

[127] Rich (n 89) 26.

[128] ibid. *cf* also ch 1, 2.2.

[129] The democratic peace theory has both philosophical and empirical foundations. Philosophically, it is founded on the Kantian assumption that people are rational and prefer

Kant wrote a work entitled 'Perpetual Peace: A Philosophical Sketch'[130] in which he laid out an idea of perpetual peace among states with a republican form of government which form a federation of *free* states. Kant saw democracy in the domestic setting as the decisive factor for peaceful behaviour internationally.[131]

The neo-Kantian understanding of international law rejects the Kelsenian concept of a presupposed validity of the *Grundnorm*[132] and instead anchors the validity of the legal norm in the people's consent, which is presumed to be a consequence of rational choice.[133] The first premise is that people are rational and peace-loving, and therefore their democratic choice is peace rather than war. If the second premise is that people exercise final control over decision-making, the conclusion should follow that democracies pursue peaceful behaviour in international affairs.

In part of the post-Cold War international law scholarship, an attempt was made to accommodate the neo-Kantian ideas of democratic peace within contemporary international law. In this theory, the domestic consent of people has direct implications for the law of statehood, as '[i]ndividuals must give consent to governments in order that they can possess the formal credentials of statehood'.[134] Consent of the people is

peace to war: Kant (1795), Section II, First Definitive Article for Perpetual Peace. Consequently, if the people have control over decision-making and access to information, which are qualities of democratic states, their governments will conduct peaceful policies. The empirical foundation of the theory is based on studies proving the absence of war between any two democracies. Perhaps the most influential study of this kind is that of Michael Doyle, who traces peace between democracies from 1817: M Doyle, 'Kant, Liberal Legacies, and Foreign Affairs' (1983) 12 *Philosophy and Public Affairs* 205. However, the democratic peace theory is controversial for its questionable methodological manoeuvres in order to prove the absence of a war between two democracies and for not addressing the problem of wars waged by states which perceive themselves to be democratic against those states which they perceive to be non-democratic. Moreover, it is questionable to what extent the 'rational citizenry' in modern democracies really exercises the control over war-making. A thorough scrutiny of the democratic peace theory would fall beyond the scope of this book. For more, see, for example, G Simpson, 'Two Liberalisms' (2001) 12 *EJIL* 537, especially 122–23; and Alvarez (n 17), especially 234–38.

[130] I Kant, 'Perpetual Peace' (1795) in T Humphrey (ed), *Perpetual Peace and Other Essays on Politics, History, and Morals* (Indianapolis, Hackett, 1983).

[131] Kant held: (1) 'The civil constitution of every country shall be republican.' (2) International law shall be based on a federation of free states. In the neo-Kantian scholarship, the notion of a republican constitution is understood as a constitution of a democratic state. Teson (n 3, 1998) 61, for example, argues: 'By "republican", Kant means what we would call today a liberal democracy, a form of political organization that provides full respect for human rights.'

[132] For Kelsen, 'the affirmation of the foundational norm is "presupposed" by any express or implied affirmation of individual legal rules. This affirmation of the foundational norm of a legal system ("one ought to do whatever is authorized by the historically first constitution"), is what Kelsen calls the *"Grundnorm"* or "Basic Norm".' B Bix, *Jurisprudence: Theory and Context* (London, Sweet & Maxwell, 2006) 59.

[133] Teson (n 3, 1998) 5.

[134] Simpson (n 129) 115.

premised on the existence of a democratic political system, which is typically deemed to require the following qualities:

> [1] formal legal equality for all citizens and constitutional guarantees of civil and political rights such as freedom of religion and the press; [2] broadly representative legislatures exercising supreme sovereign authority based on the consent of the electorate and constrained only by a guarantee of basic civil rights; [3] legal protection of private property rights justified either by individual acquisition, common agreement or social utility; [4] market economies controlled primarily by the forces of supply and demand.[135]

The proponents of the democratic peace theory in international law argue that international law should be conceived as law among democratic states, while states with a different form of government would not be part of this arrangement.[136] The relationship between democratic states vis-a-vis those with other forms of government would be governed by different legal rules and democracies would have a duty to take action for the implementation of the will of the people (ie, democratic institutions) in states where the will of people is disregarded (ie, democratic institutions are absent).[137]

In the context of international action, Teson differentiates between illegitimate governments and illegitimate states.[138] Illegitimate governments are those that are not representative of their people, ie, they do not come to power by means of democratic electoral process.[139] Illegitimate states, on the other hand, are those in which human rights are systematically breached and their peoples no longer consent to the existence of such a state.[140] In both circumstances, it is suggested, such states would no longer be deemed sovereign in their territories.[141] The concept of illegitimate states, to some degree, falls close to arguments in favour of the 'remedial secession doctrine' and might also underpin an argument in favour of dissolution of non-representative multiethnic states,[142] both of which will be thoroughly discussed below. Yet Teson, at this point, does not make an argument in favour of 'remedial secession', but one in favour of military intervention which he terms 'humanitarian', although instead it appears to be pro-democratic:[143]

> [F]orce will sometimes have to be used against nonliberal regimes as a last resort in self-defence or in defence of human rights. Liberal democracies must

---

[135]   Doyle (n 129) 207–08.
[136]   Slaughter (n 3, 1995) 528–34.
[137]   Teson (n 3, 1998) 64–65.
[138]   ibid, 57–58. There is also a possibility that a government was initially legitimate, ie elected, but later lost its legitimacy (eg, by grave breaches of human rights). ibid, 57.
[139]   ibid, 57.
[140]   ibid, 58.
[141]   ibid.
[142]   *cf* ch 3, 6.
[143]   Teson (n 3, 1998) 59–64.

seek peace and use all possible alternatives to preserve it. In extreme circumstances, however, violence may be the only means to uphold the law and defend
the liberal alliance against outlaw dictators that remain nonmembers. Such . . .
is the proper place of war in the Kantian theory.[144]

Such an argument has been described by sceptics as consistent with democratic peace but inconsistent with Article 2(4) of the UN Charter.[145] The
right to self-defence is not debatable and applies to all states under Article
51 of the UN Charter and customary international law. As such, it does
not need to be specifically invoked as a postulate of a new international
law, only applicable among democratic states. The perspective, however,
changes if a non-democratic government is per se seen as a threat to international peace and security. This is what the interventionist argument
within the so-called Kantian theory of international law implies: '[A] war
of self-defence by a democratic government and its allies against a despotic aggressor is a just war.'[146] From the context of this statement, it is
clear that the reference to self-defence against a despotic aggressor is not
meant as against an aggressor from outside but against an aggressor who
is deemed to lack domestic (democratic) legitimacy. In this understanding, states would enjoy attributes of statehood, including the protection of
Article 2(4) of the UN Charter, based on the democratic legitimacy of their
governments.

A less radical proposal comes from Slaughter, who concentrates on the
expansion of the zone of democracy – and consequently of democratic
peace – by peaceful means. Slaughter's theory looks under the layer of
state sovereignty and focuses on cooperation and networking between
professionals from different states working in the same or similar
branches, which impact governance both globally and within individual
states.[147] The foundation for such transnational networking is a common
democratic identity in which societies arguably pursue similar goals.[148] In

---

[144] ibid, 90.
[145] Alvarez (n 17) 236.
[146] Teson (n 3, 1998) 91.
[147] See generally AM Slaughter, *A New World Order* (Princeton, Princeton University Press, 2004).
[148] Pursuing common goals in liberal democracies is a rather risky statement. Slaughter argues that regarding the death penalty, the Constitutional Court of South Africa resorted to the reasoning of the courts of Hungary, India, Tanzania, Germany and of the European Court of Human Rights (ECtHR): ibid, 186–87. However, Slaughter does not mention that in the same judgment in which foreign jurisprudence was considered in order to establish that the death penalty was unconstitutional in South Africa, the Constitutional Court of South Africa also considered the jurisprudence of the Supreme Court of the United States on this matter. The South African Constitutional Court identified several breaches of human rights stand-ards stemming from the death penalty and decided not to follow the US's example. See *State v T Makwanyane and M Mchunu* (1995) CCT 3-94 (South Africa) (the *Makwanyane case*), paras 40–62. Notably, had the South African Constitutional Court followed the US doctrine, it could have reached a diametrically opposite conclusion than it did. However, such a conclusion would still be underpinned by a cross-jurisdictional citing from a fellow liberal democracy.

Slaughter's view, such networking should not be an exclusive club for professionals from democratic states. Indeed, the cooperation with professionals from non-democratic states is of crucial importance for Slaughter and serves as a means for non-democratic states to get accustomed to democratic practices.[149] Slaughter ultimately sees a possibility for an expansion of the democratic zone in this 'tutorial approach' of professionals from democratic states towards their 'non-democratic' counterparts.[150] Such tutelage and networking between professionals from democratic and non-democratic states should lead to the adoption of democratic practices in non-democratic states, which would, according to the neo-Kantian postulates, lead to peaceful behaviour in international affairs.[151]

However, such a conceptualisation draws parallels with the system of international law developed in the nineteenth century, where a 'standard of civilisation' was applied in order to decide on whether a state was to be admitted into the system of international law.[152] The idea thus gets a neo-colonial spin, where the old colonial 'civilising missions' would be renamed 'democratisation and pacification missions'.

Slaughter further proposes a development of an adequate normative framework which would allow us to distinguish between democratic and non-democratic states as well as provide us with a set of rules which would govern relations between them.[153] Such a normative framework is, however, conceived on the platform of the procedural understanding of democracy, the association of democracy with certain democratic institutions and postulates of the free market economy, and with the established hierarchy of civil and political rights.[154] In short, the normative system to distinguish between democratic and non-democratic states adopts Fukuyama's pattern, which pronounces democracy wherever a capitalist economy is in existence.[155]

Conceptualising international law as law among democratic states rejects the principle of the sovereign equality of states and replaces the concept of state sovereignty with the concept of popular sovereignty, which originates in democratic political theory.[156] It attempts to create a

[149]  Slaughter (n 3, 1997) 194.
[150]  ibid, 185–86.
[151]  See n 129, above.
[152]  Consider especially the following argument posited by Simpson (n 129) 546: 'Civilisation was a usefully illusive term'; however, even at that time it was perceived that 'a civilised state was one that accorded basic rights to its citizens'.
[153]  Slaughter (n 3, 1995) 506.
[154]  Slaughter adopts the definition of a liberal state developed by Doyle (n 129). See AM Burley, 'Toward an Age of Liberal Nations' (1992) 33 *Harvard International Law Journal* 393, 1915. At a later point, Slaughter (n 3, 1997, 196) defines a non-liberal state as one that 'has neither a representative government nor a market economy'.
[155]  See Fukuyama (n 85) 42.
[156]  *cf* ch 3, 2 and 3, 3.

system of international law based on the exclusive-club approach and an expansion of this club would be sought. The proposed means for the expansion of this club differentiate and range from informal networking among professionals from different states to pro-democratic interventions. Such views are difficult to reconcile with the UN Charter system, which is based on the sovereign equality of states. Yet proponents of such a new international law do not seem to seek reconciliation with the UN Charter. Indeed, they seem to seek the invention of a new international legal system[157] which would take different types of governments into account. Democratic governments would be at least strongly favoured by the new international system, if not actually pronounced the only legitimate ones. As Koskenniemi argues, international law has been there before – when 'civilisation' was applied as a qualifying criterion.[158]

The related ideas of normative democratic entitlement and democratic peace in international law are reflective of democratic triumphalism at the end of the Cold War, yet they are questionable from the aspect of positive law. The following subsection is concerned with the practice of post-Cold War practice of states and UN organs regarding the democratic interpretation of international (human rights) law.

### 2.3.2  Interpretations of 'Democratic Rights' in the UN Framework

After the end of the Cold War, a number of references to democracy were made in the documents adopted in the UN framework. Democracy and its connection to human rights features very prominently in Commission of Human Rights Resolutions, entitled 'Promotion of the Right to Democracy',[159] 'Promoting and Consolidating Democracy'[160] and 'Further Measures to Promote and Consolidate Democracy'.[161]

The first two resolutions refer to elections within the limits of Article 25 of the ICCPR, which, inter alia, provides that elections shall be based on 'universal and equal suffrage and shall be held by secret ballot, guaranteeing the free expression of the will of the electors.'[162] Resolution 2002/46, however, goes further and links democracy and multiparty elections: '[T]he essential elements of democracy include . . . the holding of periodic free and fair elections by universal suffrage and by secret ballot as the expression of the will of the people, a pluralistic system of political parties

---

[157] Slaughter (n 3, 1997) 183.
[158] See M Koskenniemi, 'Carl Schmitt, Hans Morgenthau and the Image of Law in International Relations' in M Byers (ed), *The Role of Law in International Politics* (Oxford, Oxford University Press, 2000) 17.
[159] Commission on Human Rights Resolution 1999/57 (27 April 1999).
[160] Commission on Human Rights Resolution 2000/47 (25 April 2000).
[161] Commission on Human Rights Resolution 2002/46 (23 April 2002).
[162] ICCPR, art 25(2).

and organizations.'[163] However, the legal relevance of this resolution is very weak. First, by its very nature, it is a 'soft law' document. Second, it was adopted by 43 votes to none, with nine abstentions.[164] Such a support does not prove the existence of general practice and *opinio juris*, and the provisions of this resolution cannot be said to reflect customary international law in the same way that the provisions of unanimously or nearly unanimously adopted General Assembly resolutions are capable of expressing customary norms.[165]

The issues of democracy and free and fair elections were also invoked in a number of General Assembly resolutions, but in all of them the understanding of democracy was expressed very cautiously, without a reference to elections in a multiparty setting. Between 1988 and 1993, a set of General Assembly resolutions, entitled 'Enhancing the Effectiveness of the Principle of Periodic and Genuine Elections', was adopted.[166] The most instructive in this context are Resolutions 45/150 and 45/151. Resolution 45/150, inter alia, provides: '[T]he efforts of the international community to enhance the effectiveness of the principle of periodic and genuine elections should not call into question each State's sovereign right freely to choose and develop its political, social, economic, and cultural systems, whether or not they conform to the preferences of other States.'[167] And Resolution 45/151:

> Recognizing that the principles of national sovereignty and non-interference in the internal affairs of any State should be respected in the holding of elections;
>
> Also recognizing that there is no single political system or single model for electoral process equally suited to all nations and their peoples, and that political systems and electoral processes are subject to historical, political, cultural and religious factors;
>
> Urges all states to respect the principle of non-interference in the internal affairs of States and the sovereign right of peoples to determine their political, economic and social system.[168]

---

[163] Commission on Human Rights Resolution 2002/46 (23 April 2002), para 1.
[164] ibid.
[165] In the *Nicaragua* case (n 108), at 99, para 188, the ICJ held that *opinio juris* may be, inter alia, deduced from the attitude of states towards relevant General Assembly resolutions and concluded that consent to the text of a resolution 'may be understood as an acceptance of the rule or set of rules declared by the resolution'. See also D Harris, *Cases and Materials on International Law* (London, Sweet & Maxwell, 2010) 54, who argues that: 'The process by which they [General Assembly resolutions] are adopted (adopted unanimously, or nearly unanimously, or by consensus or otherwise) establishes whether the practice is a "general" one.'
[166] See UN Doc A/RES/43/157 (8 December 1988); UN Doc A/RES/44/146 (15 December 1989); UN Doc A/RES/46/137 (17 December 1991); UN Doc A/RES/47/138 (18 December 1992); UN Doc A/RES/48/131 (20 December 1993). The latter two resolutions mainly deal with electoral assistance.
[167] UN Doc A/RES/45/150 (18 December 1990). The resolution was adopted with a vote of 129 in favour and eight against, with nine abstentions.
[168] UN Doc A/RES/45/151 (18 December 1990). The resolution was adopted with a vote of 111 in favour and 29 against, with 11 abstentions.

These resolutions not only fail to specify that elections need to take place in a multiparty setting but also affirm that the choice of a political system is a domestic matter for each state.

References to democracy and to the will of the people also appear in the set of General Assembly resolutions, entitled 'Support of the United Nations System of the Efforts of Governments to Promote and Consolidate New or Restored Democracies'. However, when referring to elections, these resolutions use the language of the UDHR and do not mention that elections need to take place in a multiparty setting.[169] Furthermore, it is specifically affirmed that 'while democracies share common features, there is no single model of democracy and that [democracy] does not belong to any country or region'.[170] In the context of these resolutions, similar observations were expressed by the UN Secretary-General: '[T]he United Nations system does not promote any specific form of Government. Democracy is not a strict model to be copied, but a goal to be attained. It may take many forms, depending on the characteristics and circumstances of cultures and societies.'[171] In his letter to the General Assembly, the Secretary-General further stated: '[T]here is no one model of democratization or democracy suitable to all societies . . . individual societies decide if and when to begin democratization.'[172]

References to democracy are also made in some other documents adopted in the UN framework, such as the Vienna Declaration and Programme of Action[173] and the Millennium Declaration,[174] but these documents do not go beyond general references to democracy, no definition is attempted and no link between democracy and multiparty elections is established.

Arguably, these General Assembly resolutions may be considered to reflect customary international law regarding the relationship between obligations imposed by the right to political participation and the principle of non-interference into matters essentially in domestic jurisdiction,

---

[169] UN Doc A/RES/50/133 (20 December 1995), UN Doc A/RES/51/31 (13 December 1996), UN Doc A/RES/52/18 (21 November 1997), UN Doc A/RES/53/31 (23 November 1998), UN Doc A/RES/54/36 (29 November 1999), UN Doc A/RES/55/43 (27 November 2000), UN Doc A/RES/58/13 (17 November 2003), UN Doc A/RES/58/281 (9 February 2004), UN Doc A/RES/60/253 (2 May 2006), UN Doc A/RES/61/226 (22 December 2006) and UN Doc A/RES/55/2 (8 September 2000) – the Millennium Declaration.

[170] UN Doc A/RES/60/253, preamble, para 11; UN Doc A/RES/61/226, preamble, para 7 and UN Doc A/RES/62/7, preamble, para 7.

[171] UN Doc A/51/512 (18 October 1996), para 4 – Support of the United Nations System of the Efforts of Governments to Promote and Consolidate New or Restored Democracies, Report of the Secretary-General.

[172] UN Doc A/51/761 (20 December 1996), para 4 – Support of the United Nations System of the Efforts of Governments to Promote and Consolidate New or Restored Democracies, letter dated 17 December 1996 from the Secretary-General addressed to the President of the General Assembly.

[173] UN Doc A/CONF.157/23 (12 July 1993) – Vienna Declaration and Programme of Action.

[174] UN Doc A/RES/55/2 (8 September 2000), paras 24 and 25.

such as adoption of a particular political system and/or electoral method. While several references to democracy have been made, there is no indication of how international human rights law understands democracy.[175] References to multiparty elections are carefully omitted and the resolutions commonly affirm that international human rights standards do not prescribe any specific political system or electoral method. This was clearly stated even by the UN Secretary-General.

The link between democracy and human rights has been developed by the Human Rights Committee (HRC). In General Comment 25, the HRC held that the right to political participation 'lies at the core of democratic government based on the consent of the people and in conformity with the principles of the Covenant'.[176] Further, it established that the right to political participation depends on some other rights: 'Freedom of expression, assembly and association are essential conditions for the right to vote and must be fully protected.'[177]

In one view, General Comment 25 'gives teeth to the Covenant's obligation to hold "genuine periodic elections"'.[178] What is evidently absent in General Comment 25 is a specific reference to elections in a multiparty setting. Consequently, not even General Comment 25 allows us to adopt a democratic bias when reading the elaboration of the right to political participation in the ICCPR, as '[t]here is a great difference . . . between obliging States to address seriously their citizens' interest in participation in governance and imposing on a state a specific political solution in a given circumstance'.[179]

Despite numerous references to democracy in the documents adopted in the UN framework, an analysis of these documents confirms the *Nicaragua* case standard: obligations imposed on states by the right to political participation and other human rights provisions do not demand a specific political system or electoral method.

### 2.3.3 Democracy and Internationalised Regime Change in the Practice of States and UN Organs

Although electoral democracy is not a universal entitlement, some collective practice has developed which denies the legitimacy of coup-

---

[175] The UN Secretary-General has affirmed that due to different understandings of democracy in various societies, the UN system does not attempt to define democracy. See UN Doc A/51/512 (18 October 1996), para 4 – Support of the United Nations System of the Efforts of Governments to Promote and Consolidate New or Restored Democracies, Report of the Secretary-General.

[176] HRC, General Comment 25, UN Doc CCPR/C/21/Rev.1/Add.7 (1996), para 1.

[177] ibid, para 12.

[178] Rich (n 89) 23.

[179] Roth (n 18) 343.

governments overthrowing democratically elected ones.[180] In 2009, the General Assembly condemned the coup in Honduras and demanded the restoration of the *elected* government.[181] The Security Council has developed even more significant practice in this regard. In the case of Sierra Leone, the Security Council, acting under Chapter VII of the UN Charter, demanded that 'the military junta take immediate steps to relinquish power in Sierra Leone and make way for the restoration of the democratically-elected Government and a return to constitutional order'.[182]

The collective response to the situation of Haiti was even more determined as the Security Council authorised an intervention for the return of an ousted democratically elected government. In 1994, the Security Council, acting under Chapter VII, adopted Resolution 940 on Haiti. Based on this resolution, the US led a multinational effort to bring the overthrown elected President Jean-Bertrande Aristide back to power. The legally binding resolution, inter alia, spelled out:

> Reaffirming that the goal of the international community remains the restoration of democracy in Haiti and the prompt return of the legitimately elected President, Jean-Bertrande Aristide, within the framework of the Governors Island Agreement . . .
>
>   . . .
>
>   Acting under Chapter VII of the Charter of the United Nations, authorizes Member States to form a multinational force under unified command and control and, in this framework, to use all necessary means to facilitate the departure from Haiti of the military leadership, consistent with the Governors Island Agreement, the prompt return of the legitimately elected President and the restoration of the legitimate authorities of the Government of Haiti.[183]

Importantly, Resolution 940 thereby authorised an intervention for the purpose of restoration of an elected government and not for the imposition of democracy.

The entire role of the UN in the Haiti events, which ultimately led to intervention under Chapter VII, is to some degree in line with the pro-democratic advocacy within international law. The internationalisation of the internal matters of Haiti was the key to intervention. Namely, the UN observed the Haitian election in 1990 and, after it had verified the electoral results, was unwilling to accept the nullification of these results by a coup.[184] As noted in Resolution 940, the Governors Island

---

[180] See generally J d'Aspremont, 'Responsibility for Coups in International Law' (2010) 18 *Tulane Journal of International & Comparative Law* 451.
[181] UN Doc A/RES/63/301 (1 July 2009).
[182] UN Doc S/RES/1132 (8 October 1997), para. 1
[183] UN Doc S/RES/940 (31 July 1994).
[184] Roth (n 18) 385.

Agreement[185] further internationalised the internal conflict. In the process of the negotiation of this agreement between the de facto government of Haiti and the government-in-exile, the UN also became a party and thus became responsible for the implementation of the solutions foreseen by the agreement. It follows from Resolution 940 that the failure of the de facto government of Haiti to comply with this agreement was also a reason for intervention.

It should be noted that the Security Council acted under Chapter VII of the UN Charter, although it is questionable whether a threat to international peace and security existed in the traditional sense.[186] Indeed, Haiti was a domestic matter, but in contemporary international law even domestic behaviour of governments can be of international interest and seen as a threat to international peace and security.[187]

Nevertheless, Resolution 940 should not be understood too broadly, as the previous engagement of the UN in the electoral process in Haiti makes the situation somewhat specific. It is further debatable to what degree other Chapter VII resolutions addressing the governance problem in a certain territory have been founded on express pro-democratic rather than general human rights arguments. There exists practice established in regard to the legitimacy of those governments that are in effective control but are 'unwilling to carry out essential international law duties and obligations'.[188] Grave breaches of international human rights and threats to international peace fall under this category, but the absence of a democratic government does not. This seems to have been affirmed in subsequent Security Council Resolutions.

Kosovo[189] and East Timor[190] were put under international territorial administration by Security Council Resolutions adopted under Chapter VII of the UN Charter. However, the reason for this was not the absence of democratic practices, but rather the abuses of sovereign powers of their parent states, which resulted in gross breaches of human rights and in grave humanitarian situations.[191] The Security Council, acting under Chapter VII of the UN Charter, denied legitimacy to the Taliban government of Afghanistan and called for a government representative of the

---

[185] The Governors Island Agreement, concluded on 3 July 1993, was a UN-sponsored agreement between the elected overthrown President Aristide and the de facto government of Haiti which foresaw a retreat of the non-elected de facto government from power in exchange for an amnesty. For more on this, see UN Doc S/26063 (12 July 1993).
[186] See R Falk, 'The Haiti Intervention: A Dangerous World Order Precedent for the United Nations' (1995) 36 *Harvard International Law Journal* 341, 342.
[187] See nn 183–84, above.
[188] Roth (n 18) 149.
[189] UN Doc S/RES/1244 (10 June 1999).
[190] UN Doc S/RES/1272 (25 October 1999).
[191] R Wilde, 'From Danzig to East Timor and Beyond: The Role of International Territorial Administration' (2001) 95 *American Journal of International Law* 503, 503.

Afghan people.[192] However, despite some references to democratic principles, such as a 'broad-based' government, which is 'multi-ethnic and fully
representative of all the Afghan people',[193] one cannot argue that the
Security Council expressed support for a particular political system. The
term 'democracy' was avoided and there is no indication in any of
the Security Council Resolutions dealing with the Taliban regime in
Afghanistan that a representative government should be understood as
one which comes to power upon multiparty elections.[194] Instead, governmental representativeness was defined in terms of gender, ethnicity and
religion.[195]

From the perspective of democracy, the significance of the international
legal responses to the 'Arab Spring' should not be exaggerated either. In
the binding Security Council Resolutions 1970 and 1973 on Libya, the
Security Council identified the existence of a threat to international peace
and security and drew a number of legal consequences, such as a travel
ban,[196] asset freezing,[197] referral to the International Criminal Tribunal[198]
and an arms embargo.[199] In order to protect civilians, the Security Council
authorised the use of *all necessary means*, which can be seen as a deliberate
ambiguity that authorises the use of force.[200] However, in so doing, the
Security Council specifically excluded 'a foreign occupation force of any
form on any part of Libyan territory'.[201]

The resolutions are not concerned with the choice of a political system.
Resolution 1970, for example, urged the Libyan authorities to: 'Act with the
utmost restraint, respect human rights and international humanitarian law,

---

[192]  UN Doc S/RES/1363 (30 July 2001).

[193]  ibid.

[194]  It needs to be noted that no reference to democracy or elections was made in order to
establish the non-representativeness of the Taliban government. However, references to
democracy and elections appeared in subsequent resolutions, after the Taliban government
had already been removed from power. See UN Doc S/RES/1453 (14 December 2002), preamble, para 3; UN Doc S/RES/1471 (28 March 2003), preamble, para 3; UN Doc S/RES/1536
(26 March 2004), preamble, paras 3, 5 and 7; UN Doc S/RES/1589 (24 March 2005), preamble
at para 5, main text at para 5; UN Doc S/RES/1623 (13 September 2005), preamble at para 6;
UN Doc S/RES/1746 (23 March 2007), preamble, para 3; UN Doc S/RES/1806 (20 March
2008), preamble, para 3; UN Doc S/RES/1817 (11 June 2008), preamble, para 4; UN Doc
S/RES/1868 (23 March 2009) preamble, para 4 and 10, main text, para 7. References to
democracy and elections in these resolutions may point out a collective belief that governmental representativeness in the post-Taliban era should be achieved by a democratic (electoral) process. But it is nonetheless significant that the representativeness of the Taliban
regime itself was not challenged on the tenets of electoral democracy.

[195]  UN Doc S/RES/1378 (14 November 2001), para 1.

[196]  UN Doc S/RES/1970 (26 February 2011), para 15.

[197]  ibid, paras 17–21.

[198]  ibid, paras 4–8.

[199]  ibid, paras 9–14.

[200]  See C Henderson, 'International Measures for the Protection of Civilians in Libya and
Cote D'Ivoire' (2011) 60 *ICLQ* 767, 770-71.

[201]  UN Doc S/RES/1973 (17 March 2011), para 4.

and allow immediate access for international human rights monitors.'[202] Resolution 1973 condemned 'the gross and systematic violation of human rights, including arbitrary detentions, enforced disappearances, torture and summary executions'.[203]

Unlike the relevant resolutions on Afghanistan, the resolutions on Libya did not explicitly deny the legitimacy of the sitting government or call for a regime change, not even when, at that time, the Benghazi–based government of the National Transitional Council was already in control of large parts of the Libyan territory. Indeed, the language used in the resolutions on Afghanistan clearly denied the legitimacy of the Taliban government,[204] while the resolutions on Libya referred to the Gaddafi government as 'the Libyan authorities'. The authorisation of the use of force was limited to the protection of the civilian population.[205]

Nevertheless, the change of government in Libya was not only a domestic but also an internationalised issue.[206] It is debatable whether the international support for the National Transitional Council overstepped the Security Council's mandate and at which point international involvement should have ceased.[207] As argued above, an internationalised government change was not authorised by the applicable Security Council Resolutions and nor was a requirement expressed for enactment of a particular political system.

The human rights violations and grave humanitarian situation in Syria also triggered an international response and a draft Security Council Resolution.[208] The draft went much further than the resolution on Libya and explicitly called for a regime change. The draft thus called for a transition 'to a democratic, plural political system'[209] and for the formation of a national unity government.[210] It did not specify or operationalise the meaning of a democratic, plural political system and nor did it challenge the legitimacy of the government of Syria on the basis of democracy. For this purpose, it instead invoked human rights and humanitarian grounds, but nevertheless reflected the view that respect for human rights can only be achieved upon a change of government and in a democratic setting.

---

[202] UN Doc S/RES/1970, para 2(a).
[203] UN Doc S/RES/1973, preamble, para 4.
[204] ibid.
[205] See Henderson (n 200) 772.
[206] See generally M Payandeh, 'The United Nations, Military Intervention, and Regime Change in Libya' (2012) 55 *Virginia Journal of International Law* 355.
[207] ibid.
[208] See 'Draft of Security Council Resolution on Syria', *New York Times* (31 January 2012), at http://www.nytimes.com/2012/02/01/world/middleeast/draft-of-security-council-resolution-on-syria.html?pagewanted=all
[209] ibid, para 7.
[210] ibid.

If it were adopted, the resolution would have been rather far-reaching. Yet it was subject to a double veto (China and Russia).[211] This indicates that the universal perception of governmental legitimacy has not entirely shifted away from the requirement of effective control over a territory. As Stefan Talmon argued in the context of the Gaddafi regime in Libya: 'Even gross and systematic violations of human rights by a government . . . do not *automatically* lead to its loss of status as a government in international law or make it any less a government than it would otherwise be.'[212] With regard to Syria, this means that in the absence of the Security Council's action or collective de-recognition of the Syrian government, the latter remains the government of Syria, despite the gross and systematic human rights violations.

Subsequently, the Security Council adopted a set of legally non-binding resolutions on the situation in the Middle East, in which Syria featured prominently.[213] The resolutions called on the parties to reach and implement a political solution to the conflict.[214] Specific references are made to the Syrian government and the opposition,[215] thus leaving no doubt that, despite the grave humanitarian situation and gross violations of human rights, the incumbent government still has international legitimacy to speak on behalf of Syria. In the preamble, Resolution 2042 also reaffirms 'its strong commitment to the sovereignty, independence, unity and territorial integrity of Syria, and to the purposes and principles of the Charter'.[216] This is a clear indication that the outcome of the internal struggle in Syria needs to be determined in a domestic process.

These otherwise non-legally-binding resolutions do not make any provisions for a regime change and continue to regard the Assad government as the legitimate government of Syria. However, nothing in the resolutions implies that overthrowing a government by extra-constitutional means would not be allowed; they only determine that such an outcome would need to result from domestic processes. This is different from the above-discussed resolution on Haiti, in which the extra-constitutional changes of the government were internationally condemned.

It seems that a terminological difference in doctrine is emerging between 'coup' and 'regime change'. Strictly speaking, a coup is a regime change, but in some circumstances it will be condemned and in others at least tolerated, if not endorsed. Indeed, no one speaks about a coup against Colonel

---

[211] See 'Russia and China Veto Resolution on Syria at UN', *BBC News* (4 February 2012), http://www.bbc.co.uk/news/world-16890107.

[212] S Talmon, 'De-Recognition of Colonel Qaddafi as Head of State of Libya?' (2011) 60 *ICLQ* 759, 765 (emphasis added).

[213] UN Doc S/RES/2042 (14 April 2012); UN Doc S/RES/2043 (21 April 2012); UN Doc S/RES/2051 (12 June 2012).

[214] SC Res 2042, para 1; SC Res 2043, para 1; SC Res 2051, para 1.

[215] SC Res 2042, para 1; SC Res 2043, para 1; SC Res 2052, para 1.

[216] SC Res 2042, paras 2 and 4; SC Res 2043, paras 2, 3 and 4.

Gaddafi or President Assad. Of crucial importance for the label 'coup' or 'regime change' appears to be the nature of the government.[217] Overthrowing democratic governments has brought universal condemnation, while overthrowing abusive governments is a practice that is internationally at least tolerated and sometimes even specifically endorsed. But this practice should not be generalised to imply a general entitlement to democracy.

Despite some support for the restoration of democratically elected governments and action taken against governments that have been grossly abusive of their people, the practice of the Security Council does not deny legitimacy to non-democratic governments in general, nor does it establish a link between human rights and multiparty democracy.

The analysis in this section thus leads to the conclusion that, even in the post-Cold War era, international law prescribes no particular political system or electoral method.

## 2.4 The Place of Democracy in Post-1990 International Law

Democracy has come into international legal parlance through human rights law. In the building period of the UN system, the noun 'democracy' was omitted from the relevant documents, while the provisions of human rights law left some space for the interpretation that international human rights standards can only be met in a setting of a democratic political system.[218] However, in the Cold War period, the *Nicaragua* case confirmed that neither the ICCPR nor customary international law binds states into adopting a particular political system or electoral method. The ICJ thereby confirmed that universal human rights instruments and customary international law are not to be read with the idea of multiparty electoral democracy in mind.

The age of democratic triumphalism in the post-Cold War period inspired some legal scholars to proclaim democracy to be a human right and to redesign international law as an exclusive club of democratic states. In this view, states deemed non-democratic could even lose some attributes of statehood. However, such interpretations do not find much support in positive law. Indeed, in the post-Cold War era, references to democracy have been made in several documents adopted in the framework of the UN. The scope of these references should not be overstretched. The relevant General Assembly resolutions, which are capable of reflecting customary international law, make no mention of elections in a multiparty setting. Furthermore, these resolutions commonly affirm that the

---

[217]  *cf* D'Aspremont (n 180) 563, who argues that the debate on democracy promotion in the immediate years after the end of the Cold War has now shifted to the debate on 'regime change'.

[218]  See ch 1, 2.2.1.

choice of a political system remains in the exclusive domestic jurisdiction of states. Despite the proliferation of references to democracy in post-Cold War documents adopted in the framework of the UN, no attempt has been made to carve a universally accepted legal definition of this concept.

Despite the developing practice of denying legitimacy to coup governments and of taking measures against governments that are grossly abusive of their peoples, collective practice has failed to deny legitimacy to a firmly established non-democratic government exclusively on the basis of the absence of democratic elections. From the aspect of the procedural understanding of democracy, there exists no universally applicable authority holding that international (human rights) law requires a particular political system or elections in a multiparty setting.

Even in the post-Cold War period, international law remains neutral with regard to the choice of a political system and/or electoral method. The theories of normative democratic entitlement and international law as law among democratic states do not have support in international law *de lega lata*. Indeed, even in the post-Cold War period, democracy cannot be regarded as a continuous requirement for states in order to possess the attributes of statehood. However, it will be discussed below that the type of government and some democratic standards may well be applied in international practice when new states are created; it remains questionable whether democratic standards operate within the concept of statehood criteria, recognition requirements or influence the law of statehood in some other way. The discussion thus turns to the analysis of international law governing the creation and recognition of states and the exercise of the right of self-determination.

## 3  THE EMERGENCE OF STATES IN INTERNATIONAL LAW

### 3.1  The Statehood Criteria

The Montevideo Convention on Rights and Duties of States, in its Article 1, provides: 'The State as a person of international law should possess the following qualifications: (a) a permanent population; (b) a defined territory, (c) government; and (d) capacity to enter into relations with other states.'[219] These provisions have acquired the status of statehood criteria under customary international law.[220] While the Montevideo criteria usually serve as the starting point for any research in the law of statehood, they also lead to many difficult questions regarding their interpretation, legal effects and (in)adequacy. These issues will now be considered.

---

[219]  The Montevideo Convention on Rights and Duties of States 165 LNTS 19 (1933), art 1.
[220]  See Harris (n 165) 92.

The criteria of a permanent population and a defined territory do not prescribe any minimum population figure or a minimum requirement of the surface area.[221] As to the criterion of defined territory, international law does not require that all borders of a state need to be undisputed, but rather demands 'sufficient consistency' of the territory.[222] Further, 'a group of people without a territory cannot establish a State'[223] and nor can a territory alone become a state without a group of people intending to inhabit it permanently. A qualifying group of people may, however, consist of different peoples,[224] and of people of different nationalities;[225] as such, a permanent population has been defined as '[a]n aggregate of individuals of both sexes who live together as a community in spite of the fact that they may belong to different races or creeds, or be different in colour'.[226]

The criterion of government has been described as 'the most important single criterion of statehood, since all the others depend upon it'.[227] This is so because 'governmental authority is the basis for normal inter-State relations; what is an act of a State is defined primarily by reference to its organs of government, legislative, executive or judicial'.[228] A government of a state needs not only to exist as an authority but also to exercise effective control in the territory of a state, as well as to operate independently from the authority of governments of other states.[229] In this regard, the International Commission of Jurists held that the Finnish Republic in the period from 1917 to 1918 did not become a sovereign state 'until the public authorities had become strong enough to assert themselves throughout the territories of that State without the assistance of foreign troops'.[230] It is

---

[221] See Crawford (n 1) 46–47 and 52–53.

[222] See the German-Polish Mixed Arbitral Tribunal: 'It is enough that this territory [of a state] has sufficient consistency, even though its boundaries have not yet been accurately delimited, and that the State actually exercises independent public authority over that territory.' *Deutsche Continental Gas-Gesellschaft v Polish State* (1929) 5 ILR 11 (German Polish Mixed Arbitral Tribunal) 11–15. This position was later confirmed by the ICJ: 'There is . . . no rule that the land frontiers of a State must be fully delimited and defined, and often in various places and for long periods they are not.' *North Sea Continental Shelf* cases, ICJ Rep 1969, para 46.

[223] Raič (n 31) 60.

[224] ibid, 58.

[225] See Crawford (n 1) 52–53.

[226] L Oppenheim, *International Law: A Treatise* (H Lauterpacht (ed.)) (London, Longmans, 1955) 118.

[227] Crawford (n 1) 56.

[228] ibid.

[229] See A Aust, *Handbook of International Law* (Cambridge, Cambridge University Press, 2005) 136–37, who argues that: 'There must be a central government operation as a political body within the law of the land and in effective control over the territory . . . The government must be sovereign and independent, so that within its territory it is not subject to [the] authority of another state.' See also Raič (n 31) 75, defining independence of a state as possessing 'the *legal capacity* to act as it wishes, within the limits given by international law' (emphasis in original).

[230] Report of the International Committee of Jurists Entrusted by the Council of the League of Nations with the Task of Giving an Advisory Opinion upon the Legal Aspects of the Aaland Islands Question. LNOJ Spec Supp 3 (1920) (hereinafter the *Aaland Islands* case (1920)), 8–9.

important to note that the type of government was traditionally not important.[231] It will be considered at a later point how and to what extent this has changed.

The capacity to enter into relations with other states is said to be a corollary of a sovereign and independent government, which exercises jurisdiction on the territory of the state.[232] As such, it is 'a consequence of statehood, not a criterion for it'.[233] Indeed, the criterion is self-fulfilling as non-state entities cannot enter into relations with foreign states on the same level as do states. They have this capacity once they become states. Nevertheless, non-state actors have some limited capacity to enter into relations with states, as the '[c]apacity to enter into relations with States at the international level is no longer, if it ever was, an exclusive State prerogative'.[234] This capacity is also a prerogative of international organisations and even subunits of states.[235] However, such a limited capacity cannot imply statehood of the subunit in question.

The capacity to enter into relations with other states needs to be distinguished from the actual existence of relations, which is a matter of policy for states.[236] In other words, the international law of statehood does not impose an obligation upon states to enter into relations with other states if they do not wish to do so.

Once states have acquired statehood, the latter is difficult to lose, even when the Montevideo criteria are no longer met. Indeed, statehood criteria only apply to newly created states and not to existing ones.[237] A good example is Somalia, which continues to be a state even though its government does not exercise effective control over its territory.[238] This proves that a state can exist as virtually no more than a legal fiction.

The Montevideo statehood criteria are criticised for being 'essentially based on the principle of effectiveness',[239] as nineteenth-century international law was ready to acknowledge statehood to any entity fulfilling

---

[231] See H Charlesworth and C Chinkin, *The Boundaries of International Law* (Manchester, Manchester University Press, 2005) 132.

[232] ibid, 132: 'Sovereignty means both full competence to act in the external arena, for example by entering into treaties or by acting to preserve state security, and exclusive jurisdiction over internal matters.'

[233] Crawford (n 1) 61.

[234] ibid.

[235] See Raič (n 31) 73. See also Harris (n 220) 98, who argues that: 'Units within a *federal state* may or may not be allowed by the federal constitution some freedom to conduct their own foreign affairs. If, and to the extent that, they are allowed to do so, such units are regarded by international law as having international personality . . . Such units are not thereby states but international persons *sui generis*' (emphasis in original).

[236] See Raič (n 31) 73.

[237] R McCorquodale, 'The Creation and Recognition of States' in S Blay, R Piotrowicz and BM Tsamenyi (eds), *Public International Law: An Australian Perspective* (Melbourne, Oxford University Press, 2005) 192.

[238] T Lyons and A Samatar, *Somalia: State Collapse, Multilateral Intervention, and Strategies for Political Reconstruction* (Washington DC, Brookings Institution Press, 1995).

[239] Crawford (n 1) 97.

the traditional statehood criteria and 'showing sufficient durability of its existence'.[240] However, in contemporary international law, effectiveness is no longer the only principle governing the law of statehood and 'the question remains whether [the Montevideo] criteria are sufficient for Statehood, as well as being necessary'.[241]

It has been suggested in international legal scholarship that contemporary international law also knows of a set of additional statehood criteria, which are not found in the Montevideo Convention, but can be derived from a more recent practice of states and UN organs.[242] The criteria described as 'additional' do not originate specifically in the law of statehood, but rather are concepts developed in other fields of international law which impact the law of statehood. The underlying idea behind the concept is that an illegally created entity, even if it becomes effective, cannot become a state.[243]

It is most commonly identified that the legality-based additional statehood criteria require that a state is not created as a result of the illegal use of force, in violation of the right of self-determination or in pursuance of racist policies.[244] The legal norms underlying the concept of additional statehood criteria are often considered to be of a *jus cogens* character[245] and therefore it may be said that a state creation in violation of norms of this particular character would be illegal.[246] The association of illegality of state creation with the concept of *jus cogens* was given some cautious support even in the *Kosovo Advisory Opinion*, where the ICJ held that illegality of a declaration of independence may stem from 'the unlawful use of force or other egregious violations of norms of general international law, in particular those of a peremptory character (*jus cogens*)'.[247]

However, this pronouncement of the ICJ remains somewhat ambiguous and does not link the illegality of a state creation exclusively to *jus cogens*. Moreover, it remains controversial whether the illegality is really a matter of additional statehood criteria or should better be seen as a matter of recognition requirements.[248]

---

[240] Raič (n 31) 57.

[241] M Dixon, R McCorquodale and S Williams, *Cases and Materials in International Law* (Oxford, Oxford University Press, 2011) 158.

[242] See McCorquodale (n 237) 191.

[243] ibid. See also Crawford (n 1) 107.

[244] See McCorquodale (n 237) 191.

[245] See Crawford (n 1) 105

[246] See Crawford (n 1) 105; Dugard (n 26) 135–37 and 152–61.

[247] *Accordance with International Law of the Unilateral Declaration of Independence in Respect of Kosovo (Request for Advisory Opinion)*, ICJ Rep 2010 (hereinafter the *Kosovo Advisory Opinion*), para 122.

[248] See n 268, below.

## 3.2 Recognition and Non-recognition of States

Traditionally, any discussion on recognition considers two theories: constitutive theory and declaratory theory. The constitutive theory perceives recognition as 'a necessary act before the recognized entity can enjoy an international personality',[249] while the declaratory theory perceives it as 'merely a political act recognizing a pre-existing state of affairs'.[250]

In the constitutive perception, the question of 'whether or not an entity has become a state depends on the actions [ie, recognitions] of existing states'.[251] However, the situation in which one state may be recognised by some states but not by others is an evident problem and is thus a great deficiency of the constitutive theory.[252] In the absence of a central international authority for granting recognition, this would mean that such an entity at the same time has and does not have an international personality.[253]

Most writers have adopted a view that recognition is declaratory.[254] This means that a 'state may exist without being recognized, and if it does exist, in fact, then whether or not it has been formally recognized by other states, it has a right to be treated by them as a state'.[255] According to this explanation, when recognition is granted, other states merely recognise a pre-existing situation. However, not even this explanation seems to be entirely satisfactory. As Shaw argues, recognition is 'a method of accepting factual situations and endowing them with legal significance, but this relationship is a complicated one'.[256] It is not only the relationship that is complicated; it is also questionable what defines a 'factual situation' which needs to be recognised and how does recognition endow a new factual situation with legal significance, especially if recognition is considered to be a declaratory act. The answers to these questions depend on how one understands the legal nature of emergence of a new state. These issues will be now discussed, first in relation to the obligation to withhold recognition and subsequently by considering the concept of the state in international law.

McCorquodale argues that recognition is an act which has legal consequences while it is 'primarily based on political or other non-legal considerations'.[257] Because of the political nature of this act, states are never under an obligation to grant recognition.[258] As a consequence, there may

[249] Dixon, McCorquodale and Williams (n 241) 158.
[250] ibid.
[251] Grant (n 1) 2.
[252] J Brierly, *The Law of Nations* (Oxford, Clarendon Press, 1963) 138.
[253] ibid.
[254] See Harris (n 220) 131.
[255] Brierly (n 252) 138.
[256] Shaw (n 43) 207.
[257] McCorquodale (n 237) 193.
[258] See n 299, below.

be states which remain non-recognised, sometimes virtually universally, on political grounds.[259] However, the withholding of recognition is not always a matter of policy, but may be required by international law. This obligation thus makes the political act of recognition an act which is at least partly governed by law – in the sense that states are not always free to grant recognition.

The obligation to withhold recognition is reflected in the practice of states and UN organs[260] and has been adopted in the International Law Commission (ILC) Articles on State Responsibility.[261] Article 41(2) provides that 'no State shall recognize as lawful a situation created by a serious breach [of *jus cogens*] nor render aid or assistance in maintaining that situation'.[262] It further specifies that states owe an obligation *erga omnes* to withhold formal or implied recognition of an effective territorial situation created in breach of *jus cogens*.[263] In this context, it needs to be noted that according to the Commentary to the ILC Articles on State Responsibility, norms of a *jus cogens* character include the prohibition of the illegal use of force, the right of self-determination and the prohibition of racial discrimination.[264]

Advocates of the declaratory theory who adopt the concept of the additional set of legality-based statehood criteria argue that the purpose of collectively withholding the recognition of illegally created entities is not that recognition could constitute statehood of such an entity but that it would merely affirm a legally non-existent situation. One such argument is well-captured in the following paragraph:

> [T]he obligation of non-recognition has a declaratory character in the sense that States are considered to be under a legal obligation not to recognize a specific situation which is *already* legally non-existent. Thus, the obligation of withholding recognition is not the cause of the fact that an illegal act does not produce the intended results, that is, legal rights for the wrongdoer. Non-recognition merely declares or confirms that fact and the obligation not to grant recognition prevents the validation or 'curing' of the illegal act or the situation resulting from that act.[265]

Such an argument is not entirely persuasive. As Talmon argues, the call for collective non-recognition of an illegally created effective entity implies only that such an entity could become a state through recognition and proponents of the declaratory theory do not adequately prove that this is not

[259] See ch 3, 3.5 and 3, 3.6.
[260] See ch 1, 3.5.
[261] ILC Articles on Responsibility of States for Internationally Wrongful Acts, arts 40 and 41. UN Doc A/RES/56/83 (hereinafter the ILC Articles on State Responsibility).
[262] ibid, art 41(2).
[263] Commentary to Article 40, Report of the ILC. UN Doc A/56/10 (2001) 283.
[264] Commentary to Article 41, Report of the ILC. UN Doc A/56/10 (2001) 286–90.
[265] Raič (n 31) 105 (emphasis in original).

so.[266] Indeed, illegality being 'cured' through recognition is just a way of saying that recognition could create a state without actually saying this directly. The problem here is that the creation of an illegal state triggers an obligation to withhold recognition; at the same time, it is proposed that the underlying illegality results in an entity's non-meeting of the (additional) statehood criteria. Consequently, the territorial illegality triggers an obligation to withhold recognition of an entity which is not considered to be a state in the first place. Why would that be necessary if recognition could not constitute a state? One then needs to accept either that recognition may constitute a state or that the illegally created effective entities are, in fact, states and non-recognition does not interfere with an entity's legal status.

The view of treating illegally created effective entities as states and preserving the declaratory nature of recognition is very prominently advocated by Talmon, who argues that '[t]he collectively non-recognized States may be "illegal States" [but] they are nevertheless still "States"'[267] and that 'the additional criteria of legality proposed are not criteria for statehood but merely conditions for recognition, *viz* reasons for not recognizing *existing* States'.[268] This explanation thus introduces the concept of 'illegal states', which employs the word 'states' and thereby accepts that collectively non-recognised 'illegal states' are prima facie states. Since they are already states, no constitutive effects are ascribed to the act of recognition. In other words, non-recognition only interferes with the adjective 'illegal' and not with the noun 'state'.

However, the qualification with the adjective 'illegal' makes these states somewhat different from those states which are not illegal. This is problematic because the concept suggests that a (non-recognised) 'illegal state' does not have all the rights stemming from statehood, ie, it does not have all the attributes of statehood.[269] Yet it is somewhat difficult to accept that there exist two types of states in international law: those with all and those with only some attributes of statehood. In order to accept this argument, one would also need to accept the notion of some states being more equal than others.[270] This seems to be unacceptable from the perspective of the sovereign equality of states.[271]

---

[266] S Talmon, 'The Constitutive versus the Declaratory Doctrine of Recognition: *Tertium Non Datur?*' (2004) 75 *British Yearbook of International Law* 101, 138.

[267] ibid, 125.

[268] ibid, 126 (emphasis in original).

[269] Having entities called states without the full attributes of statehood is problematic in light of Lauterpacht's observation that 'it seems irrelevant to predicate that a community exists as a State unless such existence is treated as implying legal consequences': Lauterpacht (n 21) 39. In other words, a state must have the full attributes of statehood or it cannot be considered a state.

[270] This does not mean that non-recognised states cannot exist. An argument will be made below that states not recognised on political (not legal) grounds have indeed been treated as states.

[271] UN Charter, art 2(1).

Moreover, the concept of 'illegal states' does not solve the problem of ascribing recognition with constitutive effects. Indeed, unlike 'states', 'illegal states' in this perception do not have the full attributes of statehood. By holding that non-recognition 'only' withholds 'the rights inherent in statehood', it is actually implied that recognition could endow an 'illegal state' with the full attributes of statehood. This is how the constitutive effects of recognition are, then, admitted through the back door and the problem is merely pushed to another level: it is not a state itself that could be constituted by recognition; 'only' the attributes of statehood could be constituted if recognition were not withheld.[272]

A more plausible explanation of the purpose of the obligation to withhold recognition is thus that under some circumstances, recognition could have constitutive effects. Certainly, recognition cannot be seen as a constitutive act if this were to mean that a state cannot exist without being recognised. States which were universally non-recognised on political grounds have existed without a doubt of their being states.[273] Non-recognition of such states does not interfere with their legal status. The situation is different where recognition is withheld not on political but on legal grounds.

The declaratory nature of recognition should not be taken as a dogma and defended in all circumstances. The arguments that a state may exist without being recognised and that recognition may create a state are not mutually exclusive. These are two separate issues.[274] As will be set out in detail below, where unilateral secession is concerned, the effects of recognition may be constitutive.[275] Similarly, if virtually universal (collective) recognition were granted to an illegally emerged entity, it would be difficult to claim that this entity is not a state. Now it needs to be clarified how a state comes into existence. It will be argued that the answer is determined by the understanding of the concept of the state in international law.

## 3.3 Defining the State in International Law

Discussing the *Kosovo Advisory Opinion*, Marc Weller exposes the question of whether 'new states [are] created as a matter of fact, or does their existence depend on a grant of legal authority?'.[276] This dilemma recalls the two fundamentally different concepts of the state. In one perception, a state comes into existence as an objective fact upon meeting the statehood

---

[272] This view falls close to the idea of 'natural statehood', developed by Jellinek and Oppenheim, whereby states become states 'by birth', yet their membership of the international community may depend on recognition. *cf* n 277, below.
[273] See ch 2, 3.5 and ch 2, 3.6.
[274] *cf* ch 2, 3.5, ch 2, 3.6 and ch 2, 6.
[275] See ch 2, 6.
[276] Weller (n 24) 129.

criteria and its emergence is merely acknowledged by international law.[277] Hence, the existence of a state is understood as virtually a physical fact or, at least, the concept of the state in international law is explained by an analogy to physical facts.

In another view, however, a state cannot be seen as an objective (physical) fact. As Crawford argues: 'A State is not a fact in the sense that a chair is a fact; it is a fact in the sense in which it may be said a treaty is a fact: that is, a legal status attaching to a certain state of affairs by virtue of certain rules or practices.'[278] The emergence of a new state is not a simple matter of a self-evident fact, but rather a matter of an (international) legal acceptance of a certain territory having a specific legal status.

The concept of 'international acceptance' may be seen as a synonym for what Weller refers to as 'a grant of legal authority' for the emergence of a new state. Indeed, in Weller's words, 'such a grant might be made either by the predecessor states through their consent to secession or, perhaps, exceptionally, by collective international action of the UN Security Council or widespread recognition triggered by the opposed, but effective, unilateral creation of statehood'.[279] In other words, the success of an (attempt at) state creation depends on either acceptance by the parent state or acceptance by the international community, either acting through the UN organs or (collectively) through the act of recognition.

The concept of the state and the related question of how a new state emerges have been the subject of notable discussion by (international) legal scholars.[280] This debate is marked by the controversy of how one understands the traditional statehood criteria. Is an entity which meets these criteria automatically considered a state?[281] If so, how can we objectively know that these criteria have been met, especially within the decentralised legal system of international law? It is argued that in the absence of a central authority which could determine whether or not a certain

---

[277] See Talmon (n 20) 218–20. The view of a state being a matter fact, not law, was very prominently advanced by Oppenheim. For him, however, a new state does not acquire an international personality by 'natural birth', but rather by recognition. See L Oppenheim, *International Law* (London, Longmans, 1905) 264. However, as Lauterpacht (n 21) 38, noted, such a distinction adopts Jellinek's 'confusing distinction between (natural) statehood, which is independent of recognition, and membership of the international community (or full international personality), which alone is a source of rights and which is dependent on recognition.' As Lauterpacht (n 21) 38–39, continues: 'The distinction seems to be of little value. There is, in law, no substance in the assertion that a community is a State unless we attach to the fact of statehood rights and competencies within the internal or international sphere, which international law is ready to recognize. It seems irrelevant to predicate that a community exists as a State unless such existence is treated as implying legal consequences.'

[278] Crawford (n 1) 5.

[279] Weller (n 24) 129–30.

[280] ibid. See also Crawford (n 1) 6–36; Lauterpacht (n 21) 38–66; Talmon (n 20) 83–213; H Kelsen, *General Theory of Law and State* (New York, Russell & Russell, 1961) 181–269.

[281] For such an argument, see Talmon (n 20) 222–23.

entity is a state, this duty needs to be performed by other states.[282] However, this explanation sparks the debate on the nature and legal effects of recognition in international law.[283] This section argues that the concept of international acceptance of the existence of a new state does not need to presuppose that recognition is primarily a constitutive act. In so doing, the section also develops an argument that a state is a legal concept, not a physical fact resulting from meeting the statehood criteria. Consequently, emergence of a new state can only be a question of law and not a matter of an objective fact.

### 3.3.1 *Problems with the 'State-as-a-Fact' Approach*

The Montevideo Convention, inter alia, invokes a defined territory.[284] This means that a state indeed needs to possess 'something physical' in order to be a state. But what does the requirement that a state needs to have 'a defined territory' actually mean? A territory itself is certainly an objective physical fact. However, its delimitation (which defines a territory) can only be a matter of law.[285] For example, if the territory of a new state is defined by the international legal principle of *uti possidetis*,[286] this does not mean that the territory of the newly emerged state is only a matter of physical fact; it is clearly also a matter of law. Indeed, the continents and the oceans are physical facts, while delimitation on these physical facts is a legal concept.[287] The surface of the Earth does not have any boundaries between states and, indeed, also defines no states. Boundaries are thus confined, territories defined and states created on the basis of legal principles. For this reason, 'a defined territory' cannot be a purely factual concept.

Even if one took the existence of 'a defined territory' as a physical fact, the concept of the state could still not be seen as such. No doubt, the (defined) territory of Kosovo exists physically.[288] It is ambiguous whether or not Kosovo is a state under international law.[289] Looking at a chair, for example, we objectively know this is a chair. We do not need to analyse the law to know this. The law may determine whether or not the chair was acquired or indeed manufactured legally, but regardless of what the law has to say on this, it is a matter of objective physical fact that the chair exists physically.

[282] See, for example, Kelsen (n 280) 223.

[283] This issue was more thoroughly discussed in ch 1, 3.2.

[284] See n 219, above.

[285] See Kelsen (n 280) 213, who argues that: 'Traditional theory distinguishes between "natural" and "artificial," ie, legal, boundaries; but the boundaries of a State always have a legal character, whether or not they coincide with such 'natural' frontiers as, for instance, a river or a mountain range.'

[286] For more on *uti possidetis* see ch 4, 2.

[287] *cf* Kelsen (n 280) 213.

[288] For history of Kosovo as an entity see ch 2, 6.1.

[289] For ambiguity with regard to Kosovo's legal status see ch 2, 6.5.

Looking at a territory is a different thing. Even if the territory is defined and populated by a permanent population which is represented by a government with the capacity to enter into relations with other states, we may still not know whether or not we are looking at a territory which forms a separate state or one which forms part of a larger state. If we want to know whether a certain territory is a separate state, we are interested in knowing its legal status. Merely knowing that the territory exists physically is not enough to determining its legal status.

Thus, a state cannot be understood as a physical fact. Statehood is an entirely legal construction; it is *legal status*. But legal status is not always as clear as are physical facts. This section thus turns to the problem of an objective definition of a state on the basis of the Montevideo criteria.

### 3.3.2 The Statehood Criteria and Problems with the Self-Evident-Fact Approach

Writing in 1900, Georg Jellinek argued that in order to find a state, one needs to look for three elements: a territory, a population and a sovereign.[290] It is notable that the Montevideo criteria fall very close to Jellinek's definition of a state. However, can we really objectively identify a state only by looking at Jellinek's elements? In normative language, do we have a state as soon as we can say that the Montevideo criteria are met? Are these criteria virtually a checklist that tells us whether or not an entity is a state?

Hersch Lauterpacht argued that such an explanation presupposes that 'fulfilment of the Montevideo criteria is self-evident.'[291] However, the 'self-evident-perception' leads to the conceptual problem of identifying an 'objective fact' in the decentralised legal system of international law. It is true that this is a problem of international law in general, not only in the context of statehood specifically.[292] However, it is also true what Lauterpacht observed, namely that if we accept that a state comes into existence objectively and automatically upon meeting the Montevideo criteria, we need to accept the rather awkward proposition that 'a State exists in international law as soon as it exists'.[293]

In response to such an illogical and circular explanation, Lauterpacht tried to prove that recognition was constitutive.[294] In the absence of a central authority for determining whether or not a certain entity is a state, this duty needs to be performed by (existing) states.[295] Once the statehood criteria are met, other states objectively confirm this fact by granting

---

[290] G Jellinek, *Allgemeine Staatslehre*, 2nd edn (Berlin, O Häring, 1905) 137.
[291] Lauterpacht (n 21) 41.
[292] Talmon (n 20) 218–19.
[293] Lauterpacht (n 21) 66.
[294] ibid, 58.
[295] See n 253, above.

recognition and then no doubt exists that a new state has emerged.[296] At least, this is the case if recognition is granted universally. If it is not, the old problem of the constitutive theory arises: how many and whose recognitions are necessary to create an objective legal fact of the existence of a new state?[297]

Lauterpacht tried to solve this problem by arguing that once the statehood criteria are met, foreign states have a *duty* to grant recognition.[298] This is precisely the Achilles' heel of Lauterpacht's proposition – the existence of such an obligation is not supported by state practice.[299] In the absence of an obligation to grant recognition, Lauterpacht's constitutive approach does not work. Indeed, if recognition is constitutive and no *duty* exists to grant recognition, we may have entities that are recognised as states by some states but not by others. As a consequence, we still do not objectively know whether or not they are states.

Nevertheless, what can be said of Lauterpacht's proposition is that it very accurately diagnoses the problem: the explanation that 'a state exists as soon as it exists' is inadequate. The fulfilment of the statehood criteria is not self-evident and states do not emerge as a matter of (virtually) physical fact by meeting 'Montevideo'. This chapter accepts the diagnosis but argues that the solution does not lie directly within the constitutive nature of recognition. The answer needs to be sought more broadly, in the context of (international) acceptance of an entity's new legal status.

## 3.4  Territorial Integrity and the Emergence of New States

In the process of decolonisation, 'the only territorial relationship to be altered was that with the metropolitan power. Achieving independence . . . did not come at the expense of another sovereign state's territory or that of an adjacent colony'.[300] The process of decolonisation is virtually over. The world nowadays is completely divided into states and for this reason all permanently populated territories have a parent state which is, in turn, protected by the principle of territorial integrity.[301] It is thus impossible to make a claim for independence in the contemporary world in the absence of a competing claim to territorial integrity by a parent state.

The principle of territorial integrity of states is one of the cornerstones of the UN Charter system and the post-Second World War international

---

[296] See, for example, Lauterpacht (n 21) 65–66.

[297] See n 252, above.

[298] See Lauterpacht (n 21) 65–66.

[299] Kelsen (n 280) 223; K Marek, *Identity and Continuity of States in Public International Law* (Geneva, Librairie Droz, 1968) 137; Talmon (n 266) 103.

[300] G Fox, 'Self-Determination in the Post-Cold War Era: A New Internal Focus' (1994–95) 16 *Michigan Journal of International Law* 733, 736.

[301] See, for example, Peters (n 12) 8.

legal order. In this era, it appears to be the most challenging hurdle an entity needs to overcome on its path to statehood.[302] However, in the UN Charter, a reference to territorial integrity only appears in Article 2(4). This reference is thus contextualised with the prohibition of the use of force. As has been argued above, this prohibition also has an impact on the law of statehood.[303] What is discussed at this point is the territorial integrity of states in the context of claims for independence not involving the use of force in international relations. The UN Charter is silent on this issue.

The Declaration on Principles of International Law,[304] which is reflective of customary international law,[305] makes a reference to the principle of territorial integrity in two instances. In one instance, the Declaration provides: 'Every State shall refrain from any action aimed at the partial or total disruption of the national unity and territorial integrity of any other State or country.'[306] This elaboration obviously understands territorial integrity of states more broadly than Article 2(4) of the UN Charter and liberates the principle from the context of the use of force. Nevertheless, it remains confined to relations between states.

In another elaboration, however, the principle is invoked as a limitation on the right of self-determination. As the right of self-determination applies to peoples, not states, it follows that the principle of territorial integrity is not applicable in relations between states exclusively.[307] The relevant provision reads:

> Nothing in the foregoing paragraphs [referring to the right of self-determination] shall be construed as authorizing or encouraging any action which would dismember or impair, totally or in part, the territorial integrity or political unity of sovereign and independent States conducting themselves in compliance with the principle of equal rights and self-determination of peoples as described above and thus possessed of a government representing the whole people belonging to the territory without distinction as to race, creed or colour.[308]

The principle of territorial integrity is thus not only liberated from the context of the use of force but also from its applicability in international relations. As it provides for limitations on the right of self-determination,

---

[302] For an overview of a number of unsuccessful attempts at secession, see Crawford (n 1) 403

[303] See n 244, above.

[304] The Declaration on Principles of International Law, GA Res 2625 (24 October 1970), annex, principle 5.

[305] *Kosovo Advisory Opinion*, para 80.

[306] ibid.

[307] This elaboration was ignored by the ICJ in the *Kosovo Advisory Opinion*, where the Court, by selective references to the Declaration on Principles of International Law, wrongly established that the principle of territorial integrity only applies in relations between states. *Kosovo Advisory Opinion*, para 80. For more on this, see J Vidmar, 'The *Kosovo* Advisory Opinion Scrutinized' (2011) 24 *Leiden Journal of International Law* 355, 368–69.

[308] See n 304, above.

the elaboration is reflective of the doctrine that outside of colonialism the right of peoples to self-determination will be normally consummated internally, ie, within the international borders of the parent state, and will not result in a new state creation.[309]

In one view, the operation of the principle of territorial integrity leads to an absolute prohibition of unilateral secession.[310] This argument has little support in positive international law. The first elaboration of the principle of territorial integrity provides that secession is not 'authorised' or 'encouraged', yet nowhere does it say that secession would be prohibited or even illegal. The elaboration is thus evidence of the neutrality of international law with respect of secession.[311] In this vein, the ICJ in the *Kosovo Advisory Opinion* recalled the extensive practice of state creations upon an initial issuing of a unilateral declaration of independence, and such state creations were not considered to be illegal only because independence was declared against the applicable claim to territorial integrity of the parent state.[312] The accurate position of international law is that the secession and emergence of a new state against the applicable claim to territorial integrity is not an entitlement under international law,[313] but neither is it prohibited.[314]

The consequence of the neutrality of international law in respect of unilateral secession is that an entity which issues a unilateral declaration of independence is at the same time not precluded from becoming a state, yet achieving independence, and thus the status of a state under international law, is not only a matter of declaring it. In other words, a declara-

---

[309] See ch 2, 2.2.

[310] Consider the following argument: 'As soon as the principle of territorial integrity applies, it necessarily outlaws secession without the consent of the parent state. Such understanding avoids systemic inconsistency under which international law would guarantee territorial integrity yet would not prohibit secession.' A Orakhelashvili, 'Statehood, Recognition and the United Nations System: A Unilateral Declaration of Independence in Kosovo' (2009) 12 *Max Planck Yearbook of United Nations Law* 1, 13.

[311] See Crawford (n 1) 390.

[312] See *Kosovo Advisory Opinion*, para 79. The Court argued: 'During the eighteenth, nineteenth and early twentieth centuries, there were numerous instances of declarations of independence, often strenuously opposed by the State from which independence was being declared. Sometimes a declaration resulted in the creation of a new State, at others it did not. In no case, however, does the practice of States as a whole suggest that the act of promulgating the declaration was regarded as contrary to international law. On the contrary, State practice during this period points clearly to the conclusion that international law contained no prohibition of declarations of independence. During the second half of the twentieth century, the international law of self-determination developed in such a way as to create a right to independence for the peoples of non-self-governing territories and peoples subject to alien subjugation, domination and exploitation . . . A great many new States have come into existence as a result of the exercise of this right. There were, however, also instances of declarations of independence outside this context. The practice of States in these latter cases does not point to the emergence in international law of a new rule prohibiting the making of a declaration of independence in such cases.'

[313] The *Québec* case (n 40), para 126.

[314] ibid, para 155.

tion of independence does not create the legal fact of the existence of a new state, even if the entity, in principle, exhibits the attributes of statehood. In the end, this entity may or may not become a state. But it is not a state if the claim to territorial integrity is not waived by the parent state or universally disregarded by the international community.

The principle of territorial integrity thus establishes a sphere of legal neutrality in which entities make claims for independence but do not necessarily also emerge as states; they are not simply entitled to independence, even where they are deemed to exhibit the attributes of statehood. The sphere of legal neutrality also means that the principle of territorial integrity does not generate a norm which would absolutely prohibit the emergence of a new state. It was argued above that such norms otherwise exist in international law;[315] however, these are the norms of peremptory character and a putative 'right of states to territorial integrity' is not one of them.[316] Rather, what can be said is that although unilateral secession is not illegal, its success is very unlikely in contemporary international law. This is because the burden of moving the territorial status quo lies on the independence-seeking entity.

By consent to secession, the parent state waives its claim to territorial integrity.[317] Such a waiver may also be produced by international involvement, especially if this is done collectively through the actions of the UN.[318] Moreover, the claim to territorial integrity may be removed by the dissolution of the parent state. The international legal effect of dissolution is that the parent state no longer exists and its claim for territorial integrity becomes inapplicable. As will be argued in the next chapter, dissolution can be either consensual or non-consensual.[319] The claim to territorial integrity by the parent state may also be disregarded and foreign states may decide to grant recognition to an entity which is unilaterally seeking secession.[320] This is the most controversial removal of the claim to territorial integrity because it: (i) implies that a new state may be constituted through recognition; and (ii) this, in turn, leads to the problem of how many and whose recognitions are necessary for an entity to become a state.[321]

However, it is not claimed here that recognition is primarily constitutive and that a non-recognised entity cannot exist as a state. The argument here is rather that where an entity declares independence unilaterally, international recognition could have constitutive effects. But recognition of such an entity needs to be virtually universal. If it is not, widespread

---

[315] See nn 244–46, above.
[316] See Peters (n 12) 8.
[317] *cf* ch 2, 2.3, ch 2, 2.4 and ch 2, 4.
[318] *cf* ch 2, 5.
[319] *cf* ch 2, 2.1 and ch 2, 3.
[320] *cf* ch 2, 6.
[321] *cf* n 252, above.

international recognition may create ambiguity rather than clarify the legal status of a territory.[322] At the same time, where recognition of a secession-seeking entity is universal, it may well be difficult to establish a doctrinal difference between collective recognition and collective state creation.[323]

State creation in contemporary international law is not an exercise in meeting the statehood criteria, either traditional or additional, but rather an internationalised process of overcoming the applicable claim to territorial integrity. The next chapter will argue that the international involvement in this process leads to the possibility of the imposition of certain democratic standards. It still remains for this chapter to consider the practice of non-recognition on legal grounds in the era pre-1990 . It will be demonstrated that the effective entities which were generally perceived as having satisfied the Montevideo statehood criteria were not considered to be states. However, in post-1990 practice, the question of statehood did not interfere with the question of a political system.

## 3.5  The Development of the Obligation to Withhold Recognition in Practice

This chapter has already discussed the additional statehood criteria as well as the obligation to withhold recognition. It has been established that a state creation in violation of certain norms of general international law, in particular those of a *jus cogens* character, is illegal.[324] The consequence of breaches of these norms is that the international community does not accept the illegally emerged effective entities as states.[325] Now it remains to be clarified how this doctrine has developed in the practice of the UN organs and why this practice cannot be seen as being a matter of adopting a particular political system.

### 3.5.1  *Manchukuo and European Annexations*

The development of the doctrine of collective non-recognition of illegally created effective entities arguably began in the era of the League of Nations and the collective response to the creation of Manchukuo and of European annexations and puppet states.

After Japan's occupation of Manchuria in 1931 and establishment of the state of Manchukuo,[326] the latter was not universally recognised as a state.

---

[322] See ch 2, 6.6.
[323] Crawford (n 1) 501.
[324] See n 245, above.
[325] See ch 1, 3.2.
[326] See Raič (n 31) 116.

On 11 March 1932, the Assembly of the League of Nations adopted a reso-lution in relation to Manchukuo in which it held that: 'It is incumbent upon the Members of the League of Nations not to recognize any situa-tion, treaty or agreement which may be brought about by means contrary to the Covenant of the League of Nations or to the Pact of Paris.'[327] Despite this proclamation, it remains questionable whether Manchukuo may really serve as an early example of the doctrine of obligatory non-recognition on legal grounds. Indeed, the Lytton Commission, established by the League to examine the case of Manchukuo, found that the entity lacked independence and was a puppet state of Japan.[328] Manchukuo did not satisfy the Montevideo criterion of an independent government.[329]

International responses to the annexations and establishing of puppet states in Europe and in Africa by Fascist Italy and Nazi Germany[330] as well as by the Soviet Union[331] do not give a unitary answer to whether the new effective situations were recognised. Indeed, '[t]he extinction of Austria, Albania and Czechoslovakia was recognized by most European Powers'[332] and the submergence of the Baltic States was 'widely if tacitly accepted',[333] while the Independent State of Croatia was recognised only by Germany, Italy, Slovakia, Bulgaria, Romania and Japan.[334]

Like Manchukuo, the situation in Europe also invoked questions relat-ing to the independence of the newly created states. Albania, Slovakia and Croatia, though each in a constitutionally different position, could be merely described as puppet states of Fascist Italy and Nazi Germany, respectively.[335] Thus, like Manchukuo, it was the traditional statehood criterion of independent government which was obviously not met. It therefore remains somewhat unclear whether the unlawful use of force in

---

[327] LNOJ (March 1932) 384. Notably, the Covenant of the League of Nations dealt with the prohibition of the use of force in Article 10. The resolution thus adopted the doctrine previously expressed by the US (also known as the Stimson Doctrine), according to which the US did not 'admit the legality of any situation de facto . . . and [did] not . . . recognize any situation, treaty or agreement . . . brought about by means contrary to the covenants and obligations of the Treaty of Paris of August 27, 1928'. Statement of Foreign Secretary of the United States Henry Stimson, reprinted in (1932) 26 *American Journal of International Law* 342. In the Treaty of Paris (1928), the contracting states condemned the recourse to war and subscribed themselves to the peaceful settlement of disputes. See http://www.yale.edu/lawweb/avalon/imt/kbpact.htm.

[328] Report of the Commission of Enquiry, League of Nations Publications, vol 7, no 12 (1932) 97 (hereinafter the Lytton Commission).

[329] Crawford (n 1) 133. It should be noted that Manchukuo was still recognised by a num-ber of states besides Japan: El Salvador, Italy, Spain, Germany, Poland, Hungary, Romania and Finland. Dugard (n 26) 34.

[330] Ethiopia (1935), Austria (1938), Slovakia (1939), Albania (1939) and Croatia (1941).

[331] For more on the Baltic States, see ch 2, 2.1.

[332] Dugard (n 26) 37–38. Significantly, only the US strictly adhered to the Stimson Doctrine, which was also adopted by the League in relation to Manchukuo (ibid).

[333] Crawford (n 1) 690.

[334] AP Sereni, 'The Status of Croatia under International Law' (1941) 35 *American Political Science Review* 1144, 1144.

[335] ibid, 1151.

the interwar period was considered a barrier which prevented Manchukuo and some European entities from being internationally accepted as states. One can say that there existed insufficient state practice, as well as insufficient *opinio juris*, to support such a claim.[336] Nevertheless: 'State and League practice, albeit inconsistent, demonstrated a clear trend in favour of the non-recognition of territorial conquests, if necessary, of the non-recognition of an aspirant State produced by conquest.'[337] This practice became more uniform and consistent in the UN Charter era.

### 3.5.2 *The Turkish Republic of Northern Cyprus*

In 1974, the officers of the Greek Cypriot National Guard, which was backed by Greece, overthrew the central government of Cyprus.[338] In response, Turkey militarily intervened and established an effective Turkish entity in Northern Cyprus.[339] Turkey maintained that the intervention aimed to protect Turkish Cypriots;[340] however, the Security Council adopted Resolution 353 in which the intervention was condemned.[341] The Turkish Republic of Northern Cyprus (TRNC) declared independence on 15 November 1983[342] after negotiations on a possible federal arrangement between the Turkish and Greek Cypriot entities failed.[343]

Upon the proclamation of independence of the TRNC, the Security Council adopted Resolution 541 in which it, inter alia, called 'upon all States to respect the sovereignty, independence, territorial integrity and non-alignment of the Republic of Cyprus',[344] and called 'upon all States not to recognise any Cypriot state other than the Republic of Cyprus'.[345] While Resolution 541 was not adopted under Chapter VII of the UN Charter, the TRNC was not recognised by any state other than Turkey.[346]

Illegal creation is not the only controversial issue under the law of statehood in relation to the TRNC. The continuous presence of the Turkish military and its political dependence on Turkey lead to the conclusion that the TRNC does not have a government independent of Turkey. This also follows from the reasoning of the ECtHR in *Cyprus v Turkey*:

> [T]he Court's reasoning is framed in terms of a broad statement of principle as regards Turkey's general responsibility under the Convention for the policies

---

[336] Dugard (n 26) 39.
[337] ibid, 39–40.
[338] See Raič (n 31) 123.
[339] ibid.
[340] ibid.
[341] UN Doc S/RES/353 (20 July 1974).
[342] See Raič (n 31) 123.
[343] ibid.
[344] UN Doc S/RES/541 (18 November 1983), para 6.
[345] ibid, para 7.
[346] See Crawford (n 1) 144.

and actions of the 'TRNC' authorities. Having effective overall control over northern Cyprus, its responsibility cannot be confined to the acts of its own soldiers or officials in northern Cyprus but must also be engaged by virtue of the acts of the local administration which survives by virtue of Turkish military and other support. It follows that, in terms of Article 1 of the Convention, Turkey's 'jurisdiction' must be considered to extend to securing the entire range of substantive rights set out in the Convention and those additional Protocols which she has ratified, and that violations of those rights are imputable to Turkey.[347]

One possible argument is therefore that Turkey is in effective control of the TRNC, which is a puppet state of Turkey. Nevertheless, if the TRNC attracted a significant number of recognitions, it would be difficult to argue that it is not a state.

### 3.5.3 Southern Rhodesia

On 11 November 1965, the government of Southern Rhodesia issued the Unilateral Declaration of Independence (UDI).[348] This was done despite the fact that both the General Assembly and the Security Council adopted a set of resolutions in which the white-minority government, due to the exclusion of the black population from political participation, was proclaimed as non-representative of the entire population of Southern Rhodesia and was thus held not to be the right authority to declare independence.[349] The Security Council called on the UK not to decolonise Southern Rhodesia and on other states to withhold recognition.[350]

Upon the issuing of the UDI, the UN organs continued the initiative for collective non-recognition. Resolution 2024 of the General Assembly condemned 'the unilateral declaration of independence made by the racialist minority in Southern Rhodesia'[351] and recommended the matter to the Security Council.[352] The Security Council adopted Resolution 216, in which it condemned 'the unilateral declaration of independence made by a racist minority in Southern Rhodesia'.[353] It further decided 'to call upon all States not to recognize this illegal racist minority regime in Southern Rhodesia and to refrain from rendering any assistance to this illegal regime'.[354] This Resolution was followed by Resolution 217, in which the

---

[347] *Cyprus v Turkey*, 35 EHRR 30 (2002), para 77.
[348] Dugard (n 26) 90. The UDI included a provision that the government of Southern Rhodesia would act as the representative of the Queen: UDI, s 2 (1)(b). However, in 1970, Southern Rhodesia proclaimed itself a republic: ibid, 90–91.
[349] See UN Doc A/RES/1747 (XVI) (27 June 1962), UN Doc S/RES/202 (6 May 1965), UN Doc A/RES/2022 (XX) (5 November 1965).
[350] See UN Doc S/RES/202, paras 3, 4 and 5.
[351] UN Doc A/RES/2024 (XX) (11 November 1965), para 1.
[352] ibid, para 3.
[353] UN Doc S/RES/216 (12 November 1965), para 1.
[354] ibid.

Security Council condemned 'the usurpation of power by a racist settler minority in Southern Rhodesia and [regarded] the declaration of independence by it as having no legal validity'[355] and called 'upon all States not to recognize this illegal authority and not to entertain any diplomatic or other relations with it'.[356]

All states, including apartheid South Africa,[357] complied with the resolutions and 'Rhodesia was at no stage recognized by any State'.[358] This was the legal situation despite the fact that there was no doubt that Southern Rhodesia met the traditional criteria for statehood.[359] None of the relevant resolutions directly invoked Chapter VII of the UN Charter, although references to international peace and security were made. The legal status of some of the resolutions may thus be questionable;[360] however, in the absence of a direct reference to Chapter VII, they were probably not legally binding.

Upon Southern Rhodesia's proclamation of a republic on 18 March 1970,[361] the Security Council, acting under Chapter VII of the UN Charter, adopted Resolution 277, in which it decided 'that Member States shall refrain from recognizing this illegal regime or from rendering assistance to it'.[362] The call for the non-recognition of Southern Rhodesia thus doubtlessly became legally binding, although full compliance had already been achieved after previous resolutions, even though they had probably not been legally binding.[363]

The Security Council and General Assembly Resolutions on Southern Rhodesia avoided the use of the term 'state', or even 'illegal' or 'illegally-created' state. The reason for this avoidance needs to be sought in the purpose of these resolutions, namely preventing Southern Rhodesia from acquiring statehood. The Security Council and the General Assembly obviously did not want to cause any ambiguity, which could have resulted if the term 'state' were used.[364]

In the context of Southern Rhodesia, Resolutions of UN organs mention democracy and democratic principles, even political parties.[365] However, references to democracy and democratic principles in the relevant resolutions were limited to the framework of the right of self-determination and

[355] UN Doc S/RES/217 (20 November 1965), para 3.
[356] ibid, para 6.
[357] Dugard (n 26) 91: 'South Africa, with which Rhodesia maintained diplomatic relations and close economic and political ties, refrained from according express recognition to Rhodesia.'
[358] ibid, 91.
[359] ibid.
[360] ibid, 95.
[361] ibid, 92–93.
[362] UN Doc S/RES/277 (18 March 1970), para 2.
[363] *cf* nn 353–56, above.
[364] Dugard (n 26) 94
[365] See UN Doc A/RES/2022 (XX) (5 November 1965), para 8.

to the question of how this right is to be exercised.[366] Indeed, democratic principles in the Resolutions on Southern Rhodesia were invoked because the government, which declared the UDI, was not representative of the people of the entity and as such did not have the competence to make such a proclamation.[367] In other words, the change of legal status of the territory would not occur 'in accordance with . . . freely expressed will and desire'[368] of all of the people of Southern Rhodesia, as demanded by the General Assembly Resolution 1514. In order for the 'freely expressed will and desire' to be ascertained, some democratic principles obviously need to be followed, but it is too ambitious to conclude that the operation of the right of self-determination necessarily requires democracy as a political system.[369]

### 3.5.4 The South African Homelands

The development of the 'Homeland policies' in South Africa began in the 1950s as a response to international pressure on the apartheid regime.[370] These policies attempted to attach indigenous Africans to separate territorial entities, based on their respective tribal origins.[371] With the quasi-independence of the Homelands, these people would lose South African citizenship.[372] Further, there was an extensive indigenous African population living outside of their Homelands, who would also become 'Homeland citizens' and would thus likewise be denationalised as citizens of South Africa.[373] Consequently, as one author noted:

> Should all the *Bantustans* become independent, then theoretically there would no longer be any black citizen of South Africa; instead, the urban blacks would all be tied by citizenship clauses . . . to one of the various homelands. The material wealth of the country would remain in the hands of the white minority.[374]

The creation of the Homelands as quasi-independent states was in obvious pursuance of racist policies of their parent state, South Africa.

---

[366] See J Nkala, *The United Nations, International Law, and the Rhodesian Independence Crisis* (Oxford, Clarendon Press, 1985) 57. See also Fawcett (n 29) 112; Devine (n 29) 410–17 and Fawcett's response to Devine's article at 417.

[367] *cf* n 349, above.

[368] UN Doc A/RES/1514 (XV) (14 December 1960), para 5.

[369] For a thorough analysis of the link between democracy and self-determination see ch 3, 3 and 3, 4.

[370] See Raič (n 31) 135.

[371] See Crawford (n 1) 339.

[372] ibid, 340–41.

[373] Transkei, for example, which was a Homeland of the Xhosa-speaking peoples, had resident population of 1.7 million. In addition, there were another 1.3 million people classified as citizens of Transkei who had no real links to its territory. See M Faye Witkin, 'Transkei: An Analysis of the Practice of Recognition – Political or Legal?' (1977) 18 *Harvard International Law Journal* 605, 610.

[374] ibid, 622.

With regard to the right of self-determination, this right was not applied to the entirety of peoples who would qualify for it and the 'initial organization of the black population of South Africa into *bantustans* was imposed without their participation'.[375] Thus, the creation of the Homelands as quasi-independent states was not an expression of the right of self-determination, as maintained by South Africa,[376] but its violation, which attempted to prevent self-determination of a larger unit.[377]

Between 1976 and 1981, Transkei,[378] Bophuthatswana,[379] Venda[380] and Ciskei[381] were granted quasi-independence by South Africa as a parent state. Even before the declaration of independence of the four 'Homelands', the General Assembly Resolutions 2671F[382] and 2775E[383] held that the Homeland policies were expressions of apartheid and were against the right of self-determination.

After the declaration of independence of Transkei, the General Assembly adopted Resolution 31/6A in which it called upon 'all Governments to deny any form of recognition to the so-called independent Transkei and to refrain from having any dealings with the so-called independent Transkei or other Bantustans'.[384] The General Assembly thus held that the creation of the Homelands was not a real expression of the right of self-determination, but rather meant a pursuance of racist policies and called for non-recognition. This view was subsequently confirmed by Security Council Resolutions 402[385] and 407,[386] and after the admission to quasi-independence of the three other Homelands also by General Assembly Resolutions 37/43[387] and 37/69A.[388]

None of these Security Council Resolutions was adopted under Chapter VII of the UN Charter. Nonetheless, the full compliance of third states was achieved. Further, the fact that the Security Council did not act under Chapter VII of the UN Charter 'does not necessarily mean that States [were] not under any legal obligation to withhold recognition of the

---

[375] ibid, 621. Notably, the Homelands were not entirely forced into (quasi-)independence. Indeed, 'it seems more likely that the Homeland leaders chose the course of separation as the only means open to them to further the interest of their tribes [in the absence of a popular consultation] . . . It is . . . unclear whether the goal of independence was shared equally by the populace of the *bantustan*': ibid, 614.

[376] See Raič (n 31) 135.

[377] Crawford (n 1) 128.

[378] Status of Transkei Act 100 (26 October 1976).

[379] Status of Bophuthatswana Act 89 (6 December 1977).

[380] Status of Venda Act 107 (13 September 1979).

[381] Status of Ciskei Act 110 (4 December 1981).

[382] UN Doc A/RES/2671 F (8 December 1970), especially para 3.

[383] UN Doc A/RES/2775 (29 November 1971).

[384] UN Doc A/RES/31/6 A (26 October 1976), para 3.

[385] UN Doc S/RES/402 (22 December 1976).

[386] UN Doc S/RES/407 (25 May 1977).

[387] UN Doc A/RES/37/43 (3 December 1982).

[388] UN Doc A/RES/37/69A (9 December 1982).

Homeland-States'.[389] The character of norms violated in the case of the South African Homelands may be argued to be that of *jus cogens* and, consequently, states may have been 'under a general legal obligation to withhold recognition of such an illegality'.[390]

While it can be generally concluded that the violation of the right of self-determination and the pursuance of racist policies were the source of the illegality of the state creations in the case of the South African Homelands, it also needs to be noted that these cases may serve as examples of limitations on state creations with the consent of a parent state. In other words, even if the parent state waives its claim for territorial integrity, the entity will nevertheless not become a state where it would emerge in breach of certain fundamental norms of international law, in particular those of a *jus cogens* character.

### 3.6  The Emergence of New States as an Internationalised Process: A Place for Democracy?

Knowing that a certain territory physically exists does not mean that the territory in question constitutes a separate state. A territory can only be defined according to the law and the question of whether or not a certain 'defined territory' is a state is a question of its legal status.

The interpretation that a state emerges 'as a matter of fact'[391] is thus problematic as it tries to interpret the creation of legal status as though this were a matter of the existence of an objective physical fact. In this interpretation, it is presumed that an entity which meets the (traditional) statehood criteria automatically and self-evidently becomes a state. Such an interpretation is difficult to accept. The traditional statehood criteria are not a simple checklist which could objectively determine whether or not an entity is a state.

Contemporary international law also knows of the concept of additional statehood criteria.[392] These criteria are defined in negative terms: a state must not emerge as a result of the (illegal) use of force, in violation of the right of self-determination and/or in pursuance of racist policies.[393] Does this mean that an entity becomes a state simply by not breaching these norms?

Discussing the episode of Southern Rhodesia,[394] Crawford explains that three interpretations are possible: (i) Southern Rhodesia was a state;

---

[389] Dugard (n 26) 102.
[390] Ibid.
[391] See ch 1, 3.3.2.
[392] See n 242, above.
[393] See n 243, above.
[394] *cf* ch 1, 3.5.3.

(ii) Southern Rhodesia was not a state because recognition was collectively withheld; and (iii) Southern Rhodesia was not a state because 'the principle of self-determination in this situation prevented an otherwise effective entity from being regarded as a State'.[395] Crawford then argues that in the light of international practice, the first possibility needs to be rejected.[396] The second possibility is also rejected with the explanation that recognition is declaratory and Crawford thus accepts the third option – although the effectiveness-based Montevideo criteria were met, Southern Rhodesia was not a state because it would have emerged in breach of the right of self-determination.[397]

This reasoning underlies the concept of the additional statehood criteria and is premised on the assumption that certain entities (eg, Southern Rhodesia) would have been states if the Montevideo criteria were the only applicable statehood criteria. If such entities are not states, this means that a set of additional statehood criteria must exist. This is, however, an equation with too few parameters.

The logic of this argument works *only* if it is accepted that states emerge *automatically* upon meeting the statehood criteria, except that here the statehood criteria are not only those elaborated in the Montevideo Convention but also a set of legality-based criteria. This is problematic as recent practice demonstrates that entities can meet both sets of statehood criteria (the Montevideo as well as additional criteria), but are nevertheless not states.

The concept of the additional statehood criteria is influenced by the zeitgeist of Southern Rhodesia, the South African Homelands and Northern Cyprus;[398] while it does not take into account the subsequent situations in which no territorial illegality was involved. Therefore, the reasoning behind the concept of the additional statehood criteria only works where territorial illegality *is* indeed attached to the creation of an effective entity. It can explain why Southern Rhodesia was not a state, but cannot explain what prevents Somaliland from becoming a state. A strong argument can be made that Somaliland meets the Montevideo criteria.[399] It did not become effective as a result of the use of force in the sense of Article 2(4) of the UN Charter, in denial of the right of self-determination or in pursuance of racist policies. It is thus safe to assume that Somaliland, in principle, meets both the traditional and the additional statehood criteria. Why, then, is it not a state?

[395] See Crawford (n 1) 129.
[396] ibid.
[397] ibid.
[398] *cf* Raič (n 31) 151–58, who builds the concept of the additional statehood criteria exclusively on the examples of Southern Rhodesia, the South African Homelands and Northern Cyprus.
[399] See n 28, above.

Recourse to the statehood criteria, traditional and additional, is not enough to answer whether or not an entity is a state. Even under the presumption that these criteria are met, the entity in question will not necessarily become a state. The hurdle which the entity needs to overcome is the territorial integrity of its parent state. All claims for independence outside of colonialism are prima facie faced with the principle of territorial integrity, which protects their parent states.[400]

It would be erroneous to interpret the principle of territorial integrity as being an absolute principle which could prohibit the emergence of a new state. The operation of the principle in the context of new state creations only means that independence is not a right or an entitlement under international law.[401] The emergence of a new state is thus not a matter of declaring independence, but rather a matter of acceptance of such a declaration.[402] The notion of the 'acceptance of a declaration of independence' falls within the sphere of what Weller refers to as 'a grant of legal authority'.[403]

Acceptance of a declaration of independence means that the claim to territorial integrity becomes either inapplicable or internationally disregarded. There generally appear to be four modes of such acceptance: (i) consent by the parent state; (ii) dissolution of the parent state; (iii) internationalised action, either institutionalised or informal; (iv) and 'constitutive recognition' of unilaterally declared independence (in spite of the parent state's continued claim for territorial integrity).

The boundaries between these four modes may be blurred; for example, the dissolution of the parent state may be consensual or, as will be seen in the next chapter, the result of an internationalised action. Furthermore, internationalised action may procure the consent of the parent state. State creation via recognition remains very controversial; however, this chapter shows that where an entity attempts to emerge as a state unilaterally, recognition may well have constitutive effects. This issue will be further discussed in the next chapter in relation to Kosovo.[404]

This chapter has showed that statehood is not a fact dependent on meeting the statehood criteria, but rather is a *legal status*. States are legal constructions, not physical facts. And the emergence of a new state is a law-governed political *process*, not an automatic occurrence. This process may be subject to significant international involvement. Such involvement,

---

[400] See n 301, above

[401] See nn 313 and 314, above.

[402] *cf* ICJ, Accordance with International Law of the Unilateral Declaration of Independence by the Provisional Institutions of Self-Government of Kosovo, public sitting held on Thursday 10 December 2009, CR 2009/32, 47, para 6 (argument of James Crawford on behalf of the UK); 'State practice confirms that the adoption of a declaration of independence, or similar legal acts, frequently occurs during the creation of a new State. As such, this very act – the act of declaring independence – is legally neutral.'

[403] Weller (n 24) 129–30.

[404] See ch 2, 6.

however, raises the possibility of entanglement of the process of internationalised state creation and internationalised transition to democracy in the new state. Post-1990 practice of state creations has evidenced such an entanglement and this is where the book turns next.

It needs to be recalled that even in pre-1990 practice, the influence of the right of self-determination and human rights in general on the international law of statehood has led to some controversy in interpreting the scope of the requirements that these criteria set for a lawful state creation. While early developments in the UN Charter era show that effectiveness is not enough for the international acceptance of a successful state creation, it would be an exaggeration to claim that this practice lends support to a conclusion that the emergence of a new state depends on the adoption of a certain political system or electoral method. The practice of state creations in the Cold War era was not only marked by the competing sociopolitical ideologies but also by the process of decolonisation, in which former colonies emerged as independent states in the absence of a presumption of the territorial integrity of the parent state.[405] In the post-Cold War era, however, claims to independence are faced with the prima facie applicable claim of territorial integrity, which, as shown in this chapter, can be removed by international involvement. As will be seen in the next chapter, international involvement in the (law-governed) process of new state creations to some extent adopted the idea of the post-Cold War global switch to democracy.

---

[405] See n 300, above.

# 2

# *The Practice of Post-Cold War State Creations: The Statehood Criteria, Democracy and Human Rights*

## 1 INTRODUCTION

IT WAS SHOWN in chapter one that states do not emerge auto-matically and self-evidently upon meeting the Montevideo state-hood criteria. Even under presumption that an entity has met the effectiveness-based Montevideo criteria and does not attempt to emerge as a state illegally, the legal status of such an entity remains, at best, ambiguous if the claim for territorial integrity of the parent state contin-ues to apply and is not internationally disregarded. The emergence of a state is thus not a mere matter of meeting the statehood criteria, but rather a result of a political *process* which is often internationalised.

In the pre-1990 UN Charter era, the process of state creation was shaped by certain human rights norms, violations of which were capable of ren-dering a state creation illegal under international law. However, in this period, the nature of an entity's political system did not play any role in the process of the emergence of new states.

This chapter considers how democracy as a political system has shaped the practice of post-Cold War state creations and what the consequences are of this practice for the international law of statehood. It will be argued that the role of democracy as a political system in the international law of statehood is not determined narrowly by the generally accepted legal position that democracy is *not* an ongoing statehood criterion.[1] Indeed, an exclusive focus on the statehood criteria does not pay sufficient attention to the legal nature of state creation as a *process*. This chapter shows that in the post-Cold War era, the creation of a democratic political system may well have become an integral part of this process. As d'Aspremont argues, '[e]ntities which have reached statehood in the last few years thanks to the support of the involvement of the international community have been induced to adopt democratic institutions. Likewise, each experience of

[1] See J Crawford, *The Creation of States in International Law* (Oxford, Oxford University Press, 2006) 150–55.

international administration of territory has led to creation of democratic states'.[2]

The chapter draws a distinction between internationalised and non-internationalised processes of state creations in post-Cold War practice and demonstrates that the practice of international imposition of a democratic political system on new states depends on the mode of state creation. Where states emerge as a result of domestic consensus and the parent state waives its claim to territorial integrity, no international inquiry is made into domestic institutions of government. This is different when state creation depends on international involvement.

The chapter initially considers the consensual dissolutions of the Soviet Union and Czechoslovakia as well as the consensual creations of Eritrea and South Sudan. It then moves on to an internationalised attempt at the creation of new (democratic) states resulting from the dissolution of the SFRY, the secession of Montenegro and the internationalised guidance of East Timor and Kosovo towards statehood and democracy.

The chapter demonstrates that little regard was paid to the statehood criteria in the practice of post-1990 state creations. This practice instead proves that state creation is a political *process* with legal implications. The international imposition of democracy has become a part of this process, but what are the legal consequences of this practice and how does it relate to the statehood criteria?

## 2  THE EMERGENCE OF STATES AS A RESULT OF DOMESTIC CONSENSUS

The dissolutions of the Soviet Union and Czechoslovakia as well as the emergences of Eritrea and South Sudan as independent states were the outcomes of rather complicated internal political processes. But these processes removed the applicable counterclaim to territorial integrity and led to a new legal situation: that of the emergence of new states. An argument will be made in this section that in instances of domestic consensus, the international community merely accepts the existence of a new state, without any inquiry into the methods of government.

### 2.1  The Dissolution of the Soviet Union

With regard to the dissolution of the Soviet Union, two separate occurrences need to be considered: first, the regaining of independence by

---

[2] J d'Aspremont, 'The Rise and Fall of Democratic Governance in International Law' in J Crawford and S Nouwen (eds), *Select Proceedings of the European Society of International Law* (Oxford, Hart Publishing, 2012) 61.

Estonia, Latvia and Lithuania; and, second, the establishment of the Commonwealth of Independent States (CIS).

In the interwar period, Estonia, Latvia and Lithuania were independent states and were members of the League of Nations.[3] On the basis of the Ribbentrop–Molotov Pact, signed in 1939, the three Baltic States were annexed by the Soviet Union in 1940.[4] While '[t]he international community almost uniformly refused to grant *de jure* recognition to the 1940 Soviet annexation of the Baltic States',[5] it was de facto accepted that they were constitutive republics of the Soviet Union.[6]

Lithuania declared independence on 11 March 1990.[7] At a subsequent referendum held in February 1991, 90.47 per cent of votes cast were in favour of independence.[8] Estonia declared independence on 20 August 1991, following a referendum at which 77.83 per cent of votes cast were in favour of independence.[9] Latvia declared independence on 21 August 1991, following a referendum at which 73.68 per cent of votes cast were in favour of independence.[10] Subsequently, '[o]n 6 September 1991, the State Council of the Soviet Union voted unanimously to recognize the independence of the Baltic States'[11] and thereby consented to independence of the three states.

Some states granted recognition to the Baltic States prior to recognition granted by the Soviet Union. Notably, the EC Member States recognised the Baltic States on 27 August 1991.[12] Due to different interpretations of their legal status during the time of Soviet annexation, there existed different views on the question of whether this was an act of recognition of new states or an acknowledgement of a revival of the states in existence prior to (illegal) annexation in 1940:

> A distinction was drawn in the [EC] Presidency statement between the position of the Netherlands and Spain which had recognised the annexation of the Baltic

---

[3] See Crawford (n 1) 393.

[4] Article 1 of the Secret Additional Protocol to the Ribbentrop-Molotov Pact reads: 'In the event of a territorial and political rearrangement in the areas belonging to the Baltic States (Finland, Estonia, Latvia, Lithuania), the northern boundary of Lithuania shall represent the boundary of the spheres of influence of Germany and [the] U.S.S.R. In this connection the interest of Lithuania in the Vilna area is recognized by each party.' The German-Soviet Non-Aggression Pact (the Ribbentrop-Molotov Pact) (23 August 1939), Secret Additional Protocol, art 1, http://www.fordham.edu/halsall/mod/1939pact.html

[5] S Himmer, 'The Achievement of Independence in the Baltic States and its Justification' in A Sprudzs (ed), *The Baltic Path to Independence* (Buffalo, WS Hein, 1994) 323.

[6] ibid, 324.

[7] Crawford (n 1) 394.

[8] ibid.

[9] ibid.

[10] ibid,

[11] ibid.

[12] C Warbrick, 'Recognition of States' (1992) 41 *ICLQ* 473, 474. Recognition was thus granted before adoption of the EC Guidelines (see ch 2, 3.2.1). The latter document was therefore not applicable in this situation.

States and which, accordingly, needed to recognise their revived status, and the remainder of the Community States, for which the act of 27 August [1991] was not an act of recognition.[13]

The dilemma is also captured in the position of the UK government, which held that the act of 27 August 1991 was an act of recognition; however, 'it has yet to take a position on whether the present Baltic States are simply revivals of the ones existing before 1940'.[14] Warbrick concludes that: 'From a purely legal point of view, the outcome will depend to an extent on what view is taken of the legality of the Ribbentrop–Molotov Pact and the subsequent incorporation of the territories into the USSR.'[15]

Estonia, Latvia and Lithuania were admitted to the UN on 17 September 1991.[16] Notably, '[t]he Security Council did not consider the applications for recognition made by the Baltic States until 12 September 1991, six days after the Soviet Union had agreed to recognize them'.[17] As Crawford notes, this implies that 'the position of the Soviet authorities was treated as highly significant even in a case of suppressed independence'.[18] It also needs to be noted that Lithuania declared independence more than 17 months before the EC extended recognition and held a referendum six months before receiving recognition. Lithuania may be an example of a state creation where a unilateral declaration of independence was subsequently acknowledged by the parent state. On the other hand, Estonia and Latvia declared independence after a period of negotiations with the Soviet authorities and in a more favourable political situation.[19] Estonia and Latvia, unlike Lithuania, were recognised as states and received approval of the parent state almost immediately after the declaration of independence.[20]

After the three Baltic States became independent, the Soviet Union continued in existence as a federation of 12 republics. On 8 December 1991, the Presidents of Belarus, Russia and Ukraine signed the Agreement on the Establishment of the Commonwealth of Independent States,[21] which, inter alia, comprehends the following formulation: 'We, the Republic of Belarus, the Russian Federation . . . and Ukraine, as founder states of the Union of Soviet Socialist Republics and signatories of the Union Agreement of 1922

---

[13] ibid.
[14] ibid.
[15] ibid.
[16] UN Doc A/RES/46/4 (17 September 1991) (Estonia); UN Doc A/RES/46/5 (17 September 1991) (Latvia); UN Doc A/RES/46/6 (17 September 1991) (Lithuania).
[17] Crawford (n 1) 394.
[18] ibid.
[19] For more on this, see I Ziemele, *State Continuity and Nationality: The Baltic States and Russia: Past Present and Future as Defined by International Law* (Leiden, Martinus Nijhoff, 2005) 43.
[20] *cf* nn 7–11, above.
[21] The Agreement on the Establishment of the Commonwealth of Independent States 1991 (hereinafter the Minsk Agreement), (1992) 31 *International Legal Materials* 138.

. . . hereby declare that the Union of Soviet Socialist Republics as a subject of international law and a geopolitical reality no longer exists.'[22]

On 21 December 1991, a protocol to the Minsk Agreement was adopted by the remaining Soviet Republics, with an exception of Georgia (The Alma Ata Protocol),[23] by way of which the CIS was extended to these former republics from the moment of ratification of the Minsk Agreement.[24] On the same day, 11 Soviet Republics (in the absence of Georgia) also adopted the Alma Ata Declaration, which, inter alia, declared: 'With the establishment of the Commonwealth of Independent States, the Union of Soviet Socialist Republics ceases to exist.'[25]

The Minsk Agreement further expressed the intention to set up 'lawfully constituted democratic States'[26] and:

> [T]o develop . . . relations on the basis of mutual recognition of and respect for State sovereignty, the inalienable right to self-determination, the principles of equality and non-intervention in internal affairs, of abstention from the use of force and from economic or other means of applying pressure and of settling of controversial issues through agreement, and other universally recognized principles and norms of international law [and confirmed] adherence to the purposes and principles of the Charter of the United Nations, the Helsinki Final Act and the other documents of the Conference on Security and Co-operation in Europe.[27]

Similar commitments were also expressed in the Alma Ata Protocol.[28]

The Agreement adopted the commitment to standards similar to those expressed in the EC Guidelines on Recognition of New States in Eastern

---

[22] ibid, preamble, para 1.

[23] The Protocol to the Agreement Establishing the Commonwealth of Independent States signed at Minsk on 8 December 1991 by the Republic of Belarus, the Russian Federation (RSFSR) and Ukraine 1991(hereinafter the Alma Ata Protocol), (1992) 31 *International Legal Materials* 147.

[24] Ratifications took place on the following dates: Belarus (10 December 1991), Ukraine (10 December 1991), Russia (10 December 1991), Kazakhstan (23 December 1991), Turkmenistan (26 December 1991), Uzbekistan (4 January 1992), Armenia (18 February 1992), Kyrgyzstan (6 March 1992), Tajikistan (26 June 1993), Azerbaijan (24 September 1993) and Moldova (8 April 1994). Eventually Georgia also ratified the Minsk Agreement on 3 December 1993. See the Minsk Agreement (1991).

[25] The Alma Ata Declaration 1991, (1992) 31 *International Legal Materials* 147.

[26] The Minsk Agreement (1991), para 3.

[27] ibid, paras 3 and 4.

[28] The Alma Ata Declaration, inter alia, invokes the following commitments: '[S]etting up lawfully constituted democratic States, the relations between which will be developed on the basis of mutual recognition and respect for State sovereignty and sovereign equality, the inalienable right to self-determination, the principles of equality and non-intervention in internal affairs, abstention from the use of force and the threat of force and from economic or any other methods of bringing pressure to bear, peaceful settlement of disputes, respect for human rights and freedoms including the rights of national minorities, conscientious discharge of obligations and the other universally acknowledged principles and norms of international law.' The Alma Ata Declaration (1991), para 2.

Europe and in the Soviet Union.[29] Yet the Minsk Agreement was concluded eight days before the EC Guidelines were adopted, so its commitments were obviously not expressed in order to comply with the EC Guidelines. The latter document, which made international recognition dependent on the implementation of some democratic standards, was ultimately applied only to the situation of the SFRY,[30] although it also contained the Soviet Union in the title.

Unlike in the case of the SFRY, where none of its former republics had an exclusive right to continue the SFRY's international personality,[31] in the process of dissolution of the Soviet Union it was mutually accepted by members of the CIS that Russia continued the membership of the Soviet Union in international organisations. Such a position was expressed in the Decision by the Council of Heads of State of the CIS, adopted on 21 December 1991: 'The States of the Commonwealth support Russia's continuance of the membership of the Union of Soviet Socialist Republics in the United Nations.'[32] Subsequently, on 24 December 1991, the President of the Russian Federation addressed a letter to the UN Secretary-General, stating:

> The membership of the Union of the Soviet Socialist Republics in the United Nations, including the Security Council and all other organs and organizations of the United Nations system, is being continued by the Russian Federation (RSFSR) with the support of the countries of the Commonwealth of Independent States.[33]

Crawford notes that '[n]o resolution confirming the continuity of membership was passed but Russia took up the seat of the Soviet Union without objections'.[34] Some have questioned whether Russia's continuity of the Soviet Union's UN membership is compatible with the legal effects of the dissolution of a parent state. The Minsk Agreement extinguished the international personality of the Soviet Union. In one view, 'its membership in the UN should have automatically lapsed and Russia should have been admitted to membership in the same way as the other newly-independent republic (except for Belarus and Ukraine [which were members of the UN already as Soviet republics])'.[35] If the former Soviet

---

[29] EC Guidelines on Recognition of New States in Eastern Europe and in the Soviet Union (16 December 1991), reprinted in S Trifunovska, *Yugoslavia through Documents: From its Creation to its Dissolution* (Dordrecht, Martinus Nijhoff, 1994) 472 (hereinafter the EC Guidelines). For a detailed analysis of the EC Guidelines, see ch 2, 3.2.1.

[30] *cf* ch 2, 3.2.1.

[31] See ch 2, 3.4.6.

[32] The Decision by the Council of Heads of State of the Commonwealth of Independent States (1991) 31 *International Legal Materials* 138 (1992), para 1.

[33] The Letter of the President of the Russian Federation to the UN Secretary-General, 31 *International Legal Materials* 138 (1992).

[34] Crawford (n 1) 395.

[35] Y Blum, 'Russia Takes Over the Soviet Union's Seat at the United Nations' (1992) 3 *EJIL* 354, 359.

Republics wanted to achieve independence yet secure Russia's continuity of the Soviet Union's international personality, '[t]he correct legal path to this end would have been for all the republics of the Soviet Union except Russia to secede from the union'.[36] It is questionable whether this path was feasible in the political situation which led to the dissolution of the Soviet Union.[37]

All newly emerged states in the territory of the former Soviet Union were rapidly admitted to the UN and no objections were raised with regard to their new legal status.[38] By the indirect references to democracy, invoking 'the Helsinki Final Act and the other documents of the Conference on Security and Co-operation in Europe',[39] the Minsk Agreement reflected the 'democratic rhetoric' at the end of the Cold War, while in the circumstances of consensual dissolution the democratic standards in the former Soviet Republics were not internationally scrutinised and had no implications for their statehood.

Since the dissolution of the Soviet Union was a consensual political process whereby the federation ceased to exist consensually, the emergence of new states in its territory was not subject to international involvement. As soon as the Soviet Union no longer existed, foreign states had no other choice but to acknowledge that its former republics had become independent states, regardless of how (non-)democratic they were.

## 2.2 The Dissolution of Czechoslovakia

The dissolution of Czechoslovakia was negotiated among, at that time already elected, political elites,[40] while it was unclear whether the people of either federal unit supported the creation of separate Czech and Slovak states:

---

[36]  ibid, 361.

[37]  For more on the political situation which lead to the legal arrangement for the dissolution of the Soviet Union see ch 3, 7.3.2.

[38]  Moldova, Kazakhstan, Kyrgyzstan, Uzbekistan, Armenia, Tajikistan, Turkmenistan and Azerbaijan all became members of the UN on 2 March 1992, and Georgia, who made its application belatedly, on 31 July 1992. UN Doc A/RES/46/223 (Moldova), UN Doc A/RES46/224 (Kazakhstan), UN Doc A/RES46/225 (Kyrgyzstan), UN Doc A/RES/46/226 (Uzbekistan), UN Doc A/RES/46/227 (Armenia), UN Doc A/RES/46/228 (Tajikistan), UN Doc A/RES/46/229 (Turkmenistan), UN Doc A/RES/46/230 (Azerbaijan), UN Doc A/RES/46/241 (Georgia). Ukraine and Belarus were original members of the UN and continued their membership. See A Aust, *Handbook of International Law* (Cambridge, Cambridge University Press, 2005) 18.

[39]  See n 27, above. For an analysis of these documents, see ch 2, 3.3.

[40]  The first post-communist multiparty parliamentary elections in Czechoslovakia took place on 8 and 9 June 1990. Elections were held to both the federal assembly and the assembly of the constitutive republics. For more on this, see 'Czechoslovakia: Parliamentary Elections', www.ipu.org/parline-e/reports/arc/2084_90.htm.

[The dissolution] was the result of almost three years of constitutional negotiations which ended in deadlock when the Slovak side demanded a confederation or a 'union' and the Czech side refused to accept anything but 'a functional federation'. In the face of the 'no exit' situation the two sides agreed, with the blessing of the Federal Parliament, on an orderly breakup and on a dense network of international agreements between the nascent republics defining their future relations.[41]

The dissolution of Czechoslovakia was thus not initiated by secessionist attempts in either republic, but rather was a result of different views on the internal organisation of the common state and an inability to reconcile these views. In this negotiated settlement, Czechoslovakia ceased to exist on 31 December 1992.[42] On 1 January 1993, the Czech Republic and Slovakia were proclaimed independent states.[43] Both were admitted to the UN on 19 January 1993[44] Czechoslovakia was thus a clear example of consensual dissolution and the existence of the two new states was not contested.

Notably, consent of the people for the alteration of the legal status of the territory was not unequivocally given. The fact that the political leaders who carried out the dissolution were democratically elected does not change this consideration.[45] The international community, however, accepted the dissolution and, consequently, the emergence of two separate states. The absence of the support of the will of the people for the changed legal status of the territory was not invoked before recognitions were granted. Further, the questionable quality of democracy in Slovakia during the tenure of Prime Minister Vladimír Mečiar did not play any role in the international recognition of Slovakia.[46]

After the political process in Czechoslovakia extinguished the federal state, there was no applicable counterclaim for territorial integrity. The international community could only accept the emergence of two separate states.

## 2.3 The Independence of Eritrea

Eritrea was a former Italian colony. After Italy's defeat in the Second World War, it was temporarily put under British administration.[47] In 1950,

[41] E Stein, *Czechoslovakia: Ethnic Conflict, Constitutional Fissure, Negotiated Breakup* (Ann Arbor, University of Michigan Press, 1997) 45.

[42] See Crawford (n 1) 402.

[43] ibid,

[44] UN Doc A/RES/47/221 (19 January 1993) (Czech Republic); UN Doc A/RES/47/222 (19 January 1993) (Slovakia).

[45] See ch 3, 4 for discussion on the shortcomings of the electoral process when the exercise of the right of self-determination is in question.

[46] See SP Ramet, *Whose Democracy?: Nationalism, Religion, and the Doctrine of Collective Rights in Post-1989 Eastern Europe* (Lanham, Rowman & Littlefield, 1997) 85–90.

[47] For more on this, see M Haile, 'Legality of Secessions: The Case of Eritrea' (1994) 8 *Emory International Law Review* 479, 482–87.

UN General Assembly Resolution 390 proposed a federal arrangement for Eritrea and Ethiopia, under the Ethiopian Crown.[48] The arrangement foresaw meaningful self-government for Eritrea.[49]

In 1952, a federal constitution 'was adopted unanimously by the Eritrean Assembly and the Government of Eritrea and its federation with Ethiopia came into being'.[50] Faced with growing Eritrean dissatisfaction over the federation with Ethiopia and calls for independence, the federal arrangement was unilaterally terminated by Ethiopia in 1962.[51] Subsequently, the Eritrean People's Liberation Front (EPLF) emerged, which sought Eritrean independence.[52] This became feasible after the change of government in Ethiopia in 1991, when the Ethiopian military regime was defeated by the Ethiopian People's Revolutionary Democratic Front, backed by the EPLF.[53] In Eritrea, a provisional government was established, which co-brokered the ceasefire agreement between the conflicting parties within Ethiopia[54] and scheduled a referendum on independence.[55]

The referendum was held in 1993, under the auspices of the UN, at which overwhelming (99.8 per cent) support was given for independence.[56] In this context, the General Assembly adopted Resolution 47/114 on 16 December 1992, in which it observed 'that the authorities directly concerned have requested the involvement of the United Nations to verify the referendum in Eritrea'[57] and supported 'the establishment of a United Nations observer mission to verify the referendum'.[58] Eritrean independence was accepted by the Transitional Government of Ethiopia, which previously came to power with the help of the EPLF.[59] Eritrea was admitted to the UN on 28 May 1993.[60]

Although one could advance an argument that Ethiopian suppression of the right of self-determination in Eritrea might have given support to remedial secession,[61] it is notable that Eritrea only became independent

---

[48]  UN Doc A/RES/390 (V) A (2 December 1950).

[49]  Resolution 390 (V), inter alia, provides: 'Eritrea shall constitute an autonomous unit federated with Ethiopia under the sovereignty of the Ethiopian Crown.' ibid, para 1.

[50]  Haile (n 47) 487. See also generally A Schiller, '*Eritrea*: Constitution and Federation with Ethiopia' (1953) 2 *American Journal of Comparative Law* 375, 375–82.

[51]  See Crawford (n 1) 402. Ethiopia was at that time still ruled by Emperor Haile Selassie, whose government was ousted in 1974 by the military regime, which stayed in power until 1991. See Haile (n 47) 487 and S Haile, 'The Origins and Demise of the Ethiopia-*Eritrea* Federation Issue' (1987) 15 *Journal of Opinion* 9, 9–17.

[52]  See Crawford (n 1) 402.

[53]  ibid.

[54]  Keesing's World News Archive (1992) 38855.

[55]  Keesing's World news Archive (1992) 39085.

[56]  Crawford (n 1) 402.

[57]  UN Doc A/RES/47/114 (5 April 1993), preamble, para 3.

[58]  ibid, para 1.

[59]  ibid.

[60]  UN Doc A/RES/47/230 (28 May 1993).

[61]  For more on the remedial secession doctrine, see ch 3, 6.

once the consent of its parent state was given. This consent was an out-come of a rather complex political process and civil war, but once it was given, the central government of Ethiopia waived its claim to territorial integrity. International involvement into the state creation of Eritrea was limited to observing the independence referendum and did not address governance issues.[62]

## 2.4 South Sudan: Independence Stemming from the Peace Agreement

Sudan became an independent state in 1956, comprising of northern and southern parts which were settled by diverse peoples in terms of ethnic-ity, religion and language.[63] A detailed account of the history of Sudan and the north–south divide, lengthy civil wars and atrocities has been given elsewhere.[64] For the purposes of this section, it needs to be recalled that South Sudan's path to independence followed on from the legal regime established under the Comprehensive Peace Agreement, signed on 9 January 2005, between the central government of Sudan and the Sudan People's Liberation Movement/Sudan People's Liberation Army.[65] The Comprehensive Peace Agreement resulted from the efforts of the regional peace initiative to end the civil war.[66]

The Comprehensive Peace Agreement is comprised of texts of previously signed agreements and protocols.[67] These are: the Machakos Protocol (20 July 2002); the Protocol on Power Sharing (26 May 2004); the Agreement on Wealth Sharing (7 January 2004); the Protocol on the Resolution of the Conflict in the Abyei Area (26 May 2004); the Protocol on the Resolution of the Conflict in Southern Kordofan and Blue Nile States (26 May 2004); the Agreement on Security Arrangements (25 September 2003); the Permanent Ceasefire and Security Arrangements Implementation Modalities and Appendices (30 October 2004); and the Implementation Modalities and Global Implementation Matrix and Appendices (31 December 2004).[68]

The Machakos Protocol specified that the people of South Sudan have the right of self-determination and shall determine their future legal

[62] *cf* ch 2, 5 and 2, 6 for different accounts on East Timor and Kosovo.

[63] MW Daly, 'Broken Bridge and Empty Basket: The Political and Economic Background of the Sudanese Civil War' in MW Daly and AA Sikainga (eds), *Civil War in the Sudan* (London, British Academic Press, 1993) 2–3.

[64] See, eg, D Johnson, *The Root Causes of Sudan's Civil Wars: Comprehensive Peace or Temporary Truce?* (Oxford, James Currey, 2011); E Grawert (ed), *After the Comprehensive Peace Agreement in Sudan* (Oxford, James Currey, 2010).

[65] See the Comprehensive Peace Agreement (2005), www.sd.undp.org/doc/CPA.pdf.

[66] For more on this, see United Nations Mission in Sudan, Background to Sudan's Comprehensive Peace Agreement, http://unmis.unmissions.org/Default.aspx?tabid=515.

[67] See the Comprehensive Peace Agreement, Chapeau of the Comprehensive Peace Agreement, xii, para 2.

[68] ibid, para 3.

status at a referendum.[69] The Protocol further established a six-year interim period in which the internationally monitored referendum was to take place.[70] The parties later also agreed on the implementation modalities of the permanent ceasefire and security arrangement.[71] This Agreement did not only make references to self-determination and independence referendum but also invoked some specific solutions to be implemented in the event of South Sudan's decision for independence.[72]

After the adoption of the Comprehensive Peace Agreement, Sudan promulgated a new interim constitution which granted substantive autonomy to Southern Sudan.[73] The Constitution further specified that a referendum on the future status of Southern Sudan would be held six months before the end of the six-year interim period.[74]

The interim Constitution of Sudan thus defined Southern Sudan as a self-determination unit and, in principle, created a 'constitutional right to secession'. The right was then operationalised in the Southern Sudan Referendum Act, promulgated on 31 December 2009. Article 41 of the Act specified the referendum rules and made specific provisions for the required quorum (60 per cent of all eligible to vote) as well as the winning majority (50 per cent plus one vote of the total number of votes cast).[75] Article 66 of the Act specified that the decision taken at the referendum would be binding,[76] and Article 67, inter alia, provided that in the event of Southern Sudan's vote for secession, the government would apply the constitutional provisions which foresaw Southern Sudan's withdrawal from the Sudanese institutional arrangement.[77]

The option for secession was given overwhelming support by 98.83 per cent of voters, at a turnout of 97.58 per cent. The central government of Sudan announced that it would respect the referendum results.[78] South Sudan declared independence on 9 July 2011 and the central government in

---

[69] The Comprehensive Peace Agreement, the Machakos Protocol (20 July 2002), pt A, s 1.3.

[70] ibid, pt B, s 2.5. The six-year interim period started at the time of the conclusion of the Comprehensive Peace Agreement.

[71] See the Comprehensive Peace Agreement, Agreement on Permanent Ceasefire and Security Arrangements Implementation Modalities between the Government of Sudan (GOS) and the Sudan People's Liberation Movement/Sudan People's Liberation Army (SPLM/SPLA) During the Pre-Interim and Interim Periods (31 December 2004).

[72] See ibid, ss 17.8, 20.1, 20.2 and 21.2.

[73] The Interim National Constitution of the Republic of Sudan (2005). It needs to be noted that legal instruments prior to independence refer to 'Southern Sudan', while the independent state chose the name 'South Sudan'.

[74] ibid, art 222(1).

[75] The Southern Sudan Referendum Act (31 December 2009), art 41, paras 2 and 3, at http://saycsd.org/doc/SouthernSudanReferendumActFeb10EnglishVersion.pdf.

[76] ibid, art 66

[77] ibid, art 67(2).

[78] See, eg, 'President Omar Al-Bashir Gives South Sudan His Blessing', *BBC News* (7 July 2011), www.bbc.co.uk/news/world-africa-14060475.

Khartoum announced its formal recognition a day before the declaration of independence was issued.[79]

South Sudan's path to independence was marked by a lengthy civil war, atrocities and a grave humanitarian situation.[80] However, these circumstances did not create a 'right to independence'. In terms of international law, it is significant that South Sudan did not become an independent state before the central government of Sudan formally agreed to hold a binding referendum on independence, at which secession was supported by an overwhelming majority. South Sudan emerged as a state in the political process which led to approval being given by its parent state. The mechanism for secession was rooted in the 2005 Peace Agreement and the constitutional arrangement which resulted from this. The international recognition of South Sudan followed promptly.[81] On 14 July 2011, South Sudan became a member of the UN.[82]

The peace process in Sudan was also marked by the implementation of democratic institutions. The Sudanese 2005 Interim Constitution made several references to democracy and made a commitment to a multiparty system of government. The preamble to the Constitution, inter alia, expresses a commitment to 'a decentralized multi-party democratic system of governance'.[83] In the operative articles, the Constitution provides for periodic elections[84] and further specifies that 'every person shall have the right to freedom of association with others, including the right to form or join political parties, associations and trade or professional unions for the protection of his/her interests'.[85]

Upon issuing the declaration of independence, the President of South Sudan promulgated the Transitional Constitution of the Republic of South Sudan.[86] The transitional constitution of the new state contains general references to, as well as specific provisions for, the political system of multiparty democracy. The preamble, inter alia, expresses a commitment 'to establishing a decentralized democratic multi-party system of governance in which power shall be peacefully transferred and to upholding values of human dignity and equal rights and duties of men and women'.[87] The operative articles of the Constitution provide that 'every person shall

---

[79] See 'South Sudan Counts Down to Independence', *BBC News* (8 July 2011), www.bbc.co.uk/news/world-africa-14077511.

[80] See n 64, above.

[81] See 'South Sudan: World Leaders Welcome New Nation', *BBC News* (9 July 2011), www.bbc.co.uk/news/world-africa-14095681.

[82] See UN Doc GA/11114 (14 July 2011).

[83] The Interim National Constitution of the Republic of Sudan (2005), preamble, para 6.

[84] ibid, ch 2, art 41(2).

[85] ibid, ch 2, art 40(1).

[86] The Transitional Constitution of the Republic of South Sudan (2011).

[87] ibid, preamble, para 6.

have the right to freedom of association with others, including the right to form or join political parties, associations and trade or professional unions for the protection of his or her interests'[88] and that '[e]very citizen shall have the right to take part in any level of government directly or through freely chosen representative, and shall have the right to nominate himself or herself or be nominated for a public post or office in accordance with this Constitution and the law'.[89]

The institutional arrangement for multiparty democracy was thus built into the legal foundations of the new state. The emergence of South Sudan as an independent state resulted from a peace process which also included the creation of democratic institutions and a popular consultation on the future legal status of the territory. Nevertheless, unlike in some other post-Cold War state creations,[90] the legal significance of the establishment of democratic institutions in South Sudan played little role in its path to independence. Even the recognition texts predominantly refer to the civil war and the years of struggle of South Sudan for independence, and avoid any reference to (procedural) democracy.[91] The international community did not link the question of statehood and the adoption of a particular political system.

The case of South Sudan is a good illustration of the nature of the emergence of new states in contemporary international law. This does not happen automatically on the basis of meeting the statehood criteria and/or the existence of a historic entitlement; rather, it is a political process which leads to a new legal situation. The more this process is internationalised, the more likely it is that democratic institutions will be built into the foundational instruments of the new state. This will now be further demonstrated on the examples of the emergence of new states in the absence of a domestic consensus.

---

[88] ibid, pt 2, art 25(1).
[89] ibid, pt 2 art 26(1).
[90] See ch 2, 3.4, 2, 5 and 2, 6.
[91] The President of the United States, for example, stated: 'As Southern Sudanese undertake the hard work of building their new country, the United States pledges our partnership as they seek the security, development and responsive governance that can fulfill their aspirations and respect their human rights.' A reference to democracy remained very general: 'Together, we can ensure that today marks another step forward in Africa's long journey toward opportunity, democracy and justice.' See the White House, 'Statement of President Barack Obama Recognition of the Republic of South Sudan' (9 July 2011), www.whitehouse. gov/the-press-office/2011/07/09/statement-president-barack-obama-recognition-republic-south-sudan.

## 3  THE EC GUIDELINES AND EC DECLARATION:
## BEYOND THE STATEHOOD CRITERIA

### 3.1  Background to the Yugoslav Crisis and the EC Involvement

After Slovenia and Croatia both declared independence on 25 June 1991,[92] an armed conflict between Slovenia and the Yugoslav National Army (YNA) broke out.[93] While there was no major outbreak of hostilities between Croatia and the YNA immediately after Croatia's proclamation of independence, there had been conflicts between Serb paramilitaries and Croatian police since early 1991.[94]

Upon the outbreak of hostilities, foreign ministers of the Netherlands, Luxembourg and Italy – the 'EC Troika' – were sent to Slovenia 'in order to negotiate the withdrawal of Slovenia's declaration of independence [and] a cease-fire between the warring factions'[95] along with the re-establishment of normal functioning of federal organs.[96] The efforts resulted in an agreement signed on 7 July 1991 at the Brioni Islands, Croatia.[97] The Brioni Agreement was concluded by the EC, represented by the EC Troika,[98] representatives of the Yugoslav federal organs,[99] and representatives of Slovenia[100] and Croatia.[101]

The Brioni Agreement regulated a three-month suspension period in which the situation of 25 June 1991 (prior to Slovenia's and Croatia's declarations of independence) was to be re-established.[102] In this period,

---

[92] Declaration of Independence of the Republic of Slovenia (1991), reprinted in Trifunovska (n 29) 286; and Declaration of Independence of the Republic of Croatia (1991), reprinted in Trifunovska (n 29) 301.

[93] See Crawford (n 1) 396.

[94] S Terrett, *The Dissolution of Yugoslavia and the Badinter Arbitration Commission: A Contextual Study of Peace-Making Efforts in the Post-Cold War World* (Aldershot, Ashgate, 2000) 31.

[95] ibid, 72.

[96] The Yugoslav political crisis culminated in Serbia's usurpation of federal organs such as the collective presidency, in which it controlled three out of eight seats, and the non-appointment of the Croatian member of the presidency to its constitutionally established rotating chairmanship. See ibid, 32.

[97] See the Brioni Agreement, http://www.uradni-list.si/dl/vip_akti/1991-02-0001.pdf

[98] ibid, The composition of the Troika of foreign ministers was changed due to the EC's policy of rotating the presidency. The foreign minister of Italy was followed by the foreign minister of Portugal.

[99] The federal organs were represented by the premier, the Minister of Internal Affairs, the Deputy Minister of Defence, and members of the Federal Presidency. ibid.

[100] The Slovenian representatives included the Chairman of the Slovene presidency, the Slovene Premier, the Slovene Foreign Minister, the Speaker of the Slovene Assembly and the Slovene Representative in the Federal Presidency. ibid.

[101] Croatia was represented by its president (ibid). The few-in-number Croatian representation can be understood in the context of the Agreement, which predominantly dealt with Slovenia.

[102] The Brioni Agreement, Annex 1, para 4.

further negotiations on the future of Yugoslavia were to take place.[103] The Agreement also foresaw the withdrawal of YNA units to their barracks as well as the demobilisation of the Slovene military units.[104] It further established a monitoring mission under the auspices of the Conference for Security and Co-operation in Europe (CSCE), for which it was specifically stated that it was not a peace-keeping mission and that the observers were unarmed.[105] In the latter context, Croatia was also mentioned, although the entire text predominantly referred to the situation in Slovenia and aimed at ending hostilities between Slovenia and the YNA.[106] Although the provisions of the Agreement effectively regulated the ceasefire in Slovenia, in general terms they also applied to Croatia and thus the three-month suspension of Croatia's declaration of independence was also enforced.[107]

On 27 August 1991, the EC and its Member States founded the Conference on Yugoslavia, under whose auspices the Arbitration Commission was established.[108] The Arbitration Commission was chaired by the President of the French Constitutional Court, Robert Badinter.[109] As noted by Grant, 'the authority of the Commission . . . derived from two related but distinct sources: from the European Community as a legal entity unto itself and from the constituents of the Community'.[110] The mandate of the Commission and the scope of its decisions were, however, not entirely defined.[111] Indeed, '[m]inority rights, use of force, border changes, the rule of law, state succession, and recognition all eventually fell within the Commission's brief'.[112] The opinions of the Badinter Commission were formally not legally binding.[113]

---

[103]  ibid.

[104]  ibid, Annex 1, para 5.

[105]  ibid, Annex 2.

[106]  It should be noted that the YNA was, at least formally, a military force of the federation. Although hostilities between Croatian police forces and Serb paramilitary units had already begun in early 1991, the latter, unlike the YNA, could not be perceived as agents of the federation. In Slovenia, however, police and military units were involved in an armed conflict with a federal agent. This situation would soon develop in Croatia, but had not openly occurred at the time that the Brioni Agreement was reached. See n 102, above.

[107]  See n 101, above.

[108]  See Crawford (n 1) 396.

[109]  Hereinafter the Badinter Commission. The other four members of the Commission were the Presidents of the Constitutional Courts of Germany and Italy, the President of the Court of Arbitration of Belgium and the President of the Constitutional Tribunal of Spain. See A Pellet, 'The Opinions of the Badinter Arbitration Committee: A Second Breath for the Self-Determination of Peoples' (1992) 3 *EJIL* 178, 178. The terms 'Badinter Commission' and 'Badinter Committee' are used interchangeably. References to the 'Badinter Committee' in secondary sources should therefore be understood as synonyms for the 'Badinter Commission'.

[110]  T Grant, *The Recognition of States: Law and Practice in Debate and Evolution* (Westport, Praeger, 1999) 154.

[111]  Pellet (n 109) 178.

[112]  Grant (n 110) 156.

[113]  See D Türk, 'Recognition of States: A Comment' (1993) 4 *EJIL* 66, 70.

At the Council of Ministers meeting on 16 December 1991, the EC adopted two documents in which it expressed its recognition policy in regard to the new states emerging in the territories of the SFRY and of the Soviet Union, respectively:[114] the EC Guidelines[115] and the EC Declaration on Yugoslavia.[116]

These documents were part of a broader political involvement of the EC in the processes of dealing with the disintegration of the two federations, which were in large part motivated by stopping ongoing and preventing future armed conflicts in their respective territories.[117]

## 3.2  Substance of the EC Guidelines and the EC Declaration

### 3.2.1  The EC Guidelines

The EC Guidelines invoked 'the normal standards of international practice and the political realities in each case'[118] when recognition was to be granted. This may be understood as a reference to the traditional statehood criteria.[119] Further, the EC Guidelines, inter alia, invoke 'the principle of self-determination,'[120] 'rights of ethnic and national groups and minorities',[121] 'respect for the inviolability of all frontiers which can only be changed by peaceful means and by common agreement'[122] and spell out the point that: 'The Community and its Member States will not recognize entities which are the result of aggression.'[123] The standards invoked in this context, which refer to the prohibition of the unlawful use of force, respect for the right of self-determination and even a limited

---

[114] See D Harris, *Cases and Materials on International Law* (London, Sweet & Maxwell, 2010) 132–36.

[115] See n 29, above. As the dissolution of the SFRY coincided with the dissolution of the Soviet Union, 'many of the same issues were raised in relation to both cases': Terrett (n 94) 80. Notably, the EC became much more involved in the dissolution of the SFRY, which was a source of instability in the geographical proximity of a number of the EC Member States. Hence, the EC Declaration only dealt with the SFRY.

[116] EC Declaration on Yugoslavia (16 December 1991), reprinted in Trifunovska (n 29) 474 (hereinafter the EC Declaration).

[117] See R Caplan, *Europe and Recognition of New States in Yugoslavia* (Cambridge, Cambridge University Press, 2005) 15–16. It should be noted that 1991 was the year of the final negotiations on the Treaty on European Union (TEU), which also foresaw the creation of the 'second pillar', ie, Common Foreign and Security Policy (CFSP). During the time when the EC became involved in the Yugoslav crisis, the TEU had not been ratified by all EC Member States, while 'Yugoslavia became an experimental test-case' for the EC Member States and their commitment to the CFSP. Terrett (n 94) 72.

[118] EC Guidelines (1991), para 2.

[119] See Harris (n 114) 133.

[120] EC Guidelines (1991), para 2.

[121] ibid, para 3.

[122] ibid.

[123] ibid, para 4.

reference to human rights, could arguably fall within the scope of the additional statehood criteria, developed in the era of the UN Charter.[124]

The document, however, also spells out that new states must 'have constituted themselves on a democratic basis, have accepted the appropriate international obligations and have committed themselves in good faith to a peaceful process and to negotiations'.[125] To these general requirements, stretching beyond the statehood criteria, a much more specific meaning is attached by the demand that new states need to have 'respect for the provisions of the Charter of the United Nations and the commitments subscribed to in the Final Act of Helsinki and in the Charter of Paris, especially with regard to the rule of law, democracy and human rights'.[126] As already discussed, the provisions of the UN Charter cannot be interpreted as favouring a particular type of political system, ie, they do not require the Western style of (liberal) democracy.[127] However, this might not be true in relation to the Charter of Paris and the Final Act of Helsinki. The image of democracy in these two documents determines the image of democracy in the EC Guidelines. This issue will be dealt with below.

### 3.2.2 *The EC Declaration*

The EC Declaration referred specifically to the SFRY. The Declaration, inter alia, provides:

> The Community and its Member States agree to recognize the independence of all the Yugoslav Republics fulfilling all the conditions set out below. The implementation of this decision will take place on 15 January 1992.
>
> They are therefore inviting all Yugoslav Republics to state by 23 December [1991] whether:
>
> – they wish to be recognized as independent States
> – they accept the commitments contained in the above-mentioned Guidelines
> – they accept the provisions laid down in the draft Convention – especially those in Chapter II on human rights and rights of national or ethnic groups – under consideration by the Conference on Yugoslavia
> – they continue to support the efforts of the Secretary General and the Security Council of the United Nations, and the continuation of the Conference on Yugoslavia.
>
> The applications of those Republics which reply positively will be submitted through the Chair of the Conference to the Arbitration Commission for advice before the implementation date.[128]

[124] See ch 1, 3.1.
[125] EC Guidelines (1991), para 2.
[126] ibid, para 3.
[127] See ch 2, 2.4.
[128] EC Declaration (1991), para 3. For explanation on 'the provisions laid down in the draft Convention', see ch 2, 3.4.3.

The EC Declaration recognition procedure leads to the question of whether it established a mechanism to create new states and if the practice in regard to the SFRY may be seen as being similar to the historically well-known practice of collective state creations.[129] In the absence of a universal body for the granting of recognition,[130] the Badinter Commission played this role to a certain degree. Its decisions were not legally binding, not even for EC Member States,[131] and '[v]esting an arbitration panel with authority to study and advise on recognition is not the same as vesting such an organ with authority to recognize'.[132] The Badinter Commission was thus not a body that granted recognition, but rather a body that 'to some extent . . . influenced state practice'.[133] Yet it was also a body composed of eminent legal experts with a sense of strong legal persuasiveness in its opinions.[134] The legal significance of its opinions will be further discussed below.

Conditions set for recognition make a general reference to the EC Guidelines[135] and more specifically define a required commitment to human rights protection (especially the rights of minorities),[136] a commitment to a peaceful resolution of the conflict in the territory of the SFRY[137] and an assurance that the new state would have no territorial claims towards neighbouring states.[138] From the point of view of the conditions set for recognition, the EC Declaration followed the EC Guidelines and partially supplemented them with requirements which specifically addressed the situation in the territory of the SFRY in December 1991. The EC Declaration is therefore a technical and SFRY-specific document, and its main relevance is that it established a mechanism for recognition in this particular situation. In order to determine the image of democracy in the EC's involvement in the new state creations in the territories of the SFRY and the Soviet Union, the relevant document to be analysed is the EC Guidelines.

---

[129] Caplan (n 117) 61–62.

[130] See ch 1, 3.2.

[131] See n 113, above.

[132] Grant (n 110) 168. The creation of such a body to deal with recognition, among other questions, was not unprecedented. Previous examples include the Commission of Jurists, established under the auspices of the League of Nations, which dealt with the territorial status of the Aaland Islands (see ch 1, 3.1) and the Lytton Commission, also established by the League of Nations, which dealt with the status of Manchukuo (see ch 1, 3.5.1).

[133] ibid.

[134] *cf* ch 2, 3.4.3.

[135] EC Guidelines (1991), para 3.

[136] ibid.

[137] ibid.

[138] ibid, para 5. This requirement specifically had in mind the dispute between Greece and Macedonia over the latter's name. See Grant (n 110) 158. *cf* ch 2, 3.4.5.

## 3.3  Democracy, Human Rights and a Commitment to Peace in the EC Guidelines

It has been established that the EC Guidelines spelt out some require-ments that arguably fall within either the traditional or additional statehood criteria.[139] These will not be discussed at this point. The focus will be on: first, requirements that do not belong to the statehood criteria; and, second, requirements that stem from the (additional) statehood crite-ria, but extend the scope of their operation. The requirement for new states 'to have constituted themselves on a democratic basis'[140] falls within the first group. The image of democracy within this requirement will be examined in this context. Into the second group may fall: (i) the require-ment for respect of human rights; and (ii) the requirement that states must refrain from the illegal use of force. As argued above, the respect for the right of self-determination and the prohibition of racial discrimination may well be relevant for the law of statehood.[141] However, the EC Guidelines invoke human rights in general; moreover, the commitment to peace required by the EC Guidelines may reach beyond the requirement that a state cannot be created as a result of an illegal use of force.

### 3.3.1 Democracy in the EC Guidelines

The EC Guidelines, inter alia, provide:

> [The EC and its Member States] affirm their readiness to recognize, subject to the normal standards of international practice and the political realities in each case, those new States which, following the historic changes in the region, have constituted themselves on a democratic basis, have accepted the appropriate international obligations and have committed themselves in good faith to a peaceful process and to negotiations.[142]

Reference to 'constituted on a democratic basis' could generally be interpreted as being confined to 'democratic principles' operating within the right of self-determination.[143] In practice, this would mean that this specific requirement would demand for independence to be declared fol-lowing a popular consultation at which a free and fair expression of the will of the people would be guaranteed.[144] The requirement of 'constituted on a democratic basis' would, arguably, not reach beyond the scope of the

---

[139]  See n 126, above.
[140]  EC Guidelines (1991), para 3.
[141]  See ch 1, 3.1.
[142]  EC Guidelines (1991), para 3.
[143]  *cf* ch 3, 7.
[144]  ibid.

statehood criterion which requires that a new state may not emerge in violation of the right of self-determination.[145]

However, the EC Guidelines do not make references to democracy exclusively in the context of the right of self-determination. While the document does not directly attempt to define the understanding of democracy, this understanding is expressed in the Charter of Paris, to which the EC Guidelines expressly refer.[146] The Charter of Paris for a New Europe was adopted on 21 November 1990 in the framework of the CSCE.[147] The document was adopted at the end of the Cold War and was signed by virtually all democratising (former) communist states in Europe, including the Soviet Union and the SFRY.[148]

The Charter's chapter entitled 'Human Rights, Democracy and Rule of Law', to which the EC Guidelines refer,[149] provides, inter alia:

> Democratic government is based on the will of the people, expressed regularly through free and fair elections. Democracy has its foundation respect for the human person and the rule of law. Democracy is the best safeguard of freedom of expression of all groups of society, and equality of opportunity for each person.[150]

Apart from using the terms 'democratic government' and 'democracy', this definition falls close to the definition of the right to political participation expressed in Article 21 of the UDHR[151] and Article 25 of the ICCPR.[152] As in these two elaborations, reference to elections in a multiparty setting

---

[145]   *cf* ch 1, 3.1.

[146]   There are also references made to the Final Act of Helsinki, with which the Conference on Security and Co-operation in Europe (CSCE) was established. However, dating back to 1975, this is a document that was drafted in the Cold War era. It does not invoke democracy or 'democratic principles' and deals with human rights within the boundaries of the UDHR and the two universal covenants (see the Final Act of Helsinki, (1975) 14 *International Legal Materials* 1292). The Charter of Paris, dating back to 1990, will thus be the most relevant document to determine the image of democracy as well as human rights standards in the EC Guidelines. An analysis of the Final Act of Helsinki will follow from the point of view of the commitment to peace expressed in this document. See ch 2, 3.3.3.

[147]   The Charter of Paris for a New Europe, with which the CSCE was transformed into the Organisation for Security and Cooperation in Europe (OSCE), was signed by the following states: France, Germany, Italy, the Soviet Union, the UK, the US, Canada, Belgium, the Netherlands, Poland, Spain, Sweden, Austria, Czechoslovakia, Denmark, Finland, Hungary, Norway, Switzerland, Greece, Romania, Turkey, Yugoslavia, Bulgaria, Ireland, Luxembourg, Portugal, Cyprus, the Holy See, Iceland, Liechtenstein, Malta, Monaco and San Marino (see www.osce.org/mc/39516). Later the following states also joined: Albania, Andorra, Armenia, Azerbaijan, Bosnia-Herzegovina, Estonia, Georgia, Kazakhstan, Kyrgyzstan, Latvia, the FRY, Macedonia, Moldova, Slovenia, Tajikistan, Turkmenistan, Ukraine and Uzbekistan (ibid.). Apart from Albania and Andorra, all of the states that have signed the Charter of Paris after 1990 are former republics of either the SFRY or of the Soviet Union.

[148]   ibid,

[149]   See n 29, above.

[150]   The Charter of Paris (1990) 3.

[151]   See ch 1, n 95.

[152]   See ch 1, n 96.

is omitted. However, Annex 1 of the Charter of Paris becomes much more specific with regard to the electoral method and, unlike the UDHR and the ICCPR, narrows the room for different interpretations. Indeed, Article 7 of Annex 1, inter alia, provides:

> To ensure that the will of the people serves as the basis of the authority of government, the participating States will
>
> . . .
>
> – respect the right of citizens to seek political or public office, individually or as representatives of political parties or organizations, without discrimination;
> – respect the right of individuals and groups to establish, in full freedom, their own political parties or other political organizations and provide such political parties and organizations with the necessary legal guarantees to enable them to compete with each other on a basis of equal treatment before the law and by the authorities;
>
> . . .
>
> – provide that no legal or administrative obstacle stands in the way of unimpeded access to the media on a nondiscriminatory basis for all political groupings and individuals wishing to participate in the electoral process.[153]

These references to a multiparty system and specific provisions for, rather than general reference to, free and fair elections go beyond the reach of 'democratic rights', which require a very restricted interpretation within the universal human rights instruments.[154] Indeed, with these provisions, the Charter of Paris clearly stipulates the implementation of the institutional requisites for multiparty democracy.

### 3.3.2  Human Rights in the EC Guidelines

Apart from references to some human rights within the definition of democratic standards, the Charter of Paris makes the respect of human rights a separate requirement and a number of civil and political rights are specifically mentioned, while references to economic, social and cultural rights are only general.[155] The Charter of Paris does not specifically invoke the right of self-determination, which is otherwise referred to in the Final Act of Helsinki. This reference essentially repeats the universal elaboration of the

---

[153] The Charter of Paris (1990), Annex 1, art 7.
[154] *cf* ch 1, 2.4.
[155] The Charter of Paris (1990) 3. The Charter thus invokes a number of civil and political rights and only makes a brief mention of the entire economic, social and cultural cluster, without naming those rights individually. On the other hand, the Final Act of Helsinki specifically invokes the freedom of thought, conscience, religion or belief, and rights of minorities, without further elaborations on the scope of these rights. Further, there is a general reference to civil, political, economic, social, cultural and other rights and freedoms. The Final Act of Helsinki (1975), ch VII, paras 1, 2 and 4.

common Article 1 of the ICCPR and the ICESCR,[156] while it also adds an important limitation on the right of self-determination, which is to be exercised 'in conformity with the purposes and principles of the Charter of the United Nations and with the relevant norms of international law, including those relating to territorial integrity of states'.[157] In other words, the Final Act of Helsinki affirms that the right of self-determination is not an entitlement to secession.[158]

It has been argued above that human rights in general have not been regarded as statehood criteria and that democracy as a political system (or type of government in general) has not had any role in the creation of states.[159] Yet the EC Guidelines, adopting the Charter of Paris, set a much higher bar and proclaimed general respect for human rights a recognition requirement.[160]

### 3.3.3  The EC Guidelines and a Commitment to Peace

A commitment to peace is expressed in the EC Guidelines and in the EC Declaration indirectly by a reference to the Final Act of Helsinki[161] and by specific references in the two documents regarding the situation in the disintegrating SFRY in 1991.[162] The scope of the requirement for new states to be committed to peace will be initially analysed through the understanding expressed in the Final Act of Helsinki. Subsequently, the scope of 'peace activism' in the EC Guidelines and in the EC Declaration will also be considered. The central question will be whether the commitment to peace as expressed in the two documents reaches beyond the legality requirement that a state cannot be established as a result of an unlawful use of force.[163]

With a view to reducing the Cold War tensions,[164] the Final Act of Helsinki was signed in 1975 by both Western and socialist states.[165] As already

---

[156]  The Final Act of Helsinki (1975), ch VII. For more on the right of self-determination and on the distinction between internal and external self-determination, see ch 3, 2.2.

[157]  ibid, para 1.

[158]  *cf* ch 3, 2.2.

[159]  See ch 1, 3.1.

[160]  *cf* n 126, above.

[161]  ibid.

[162]  ibid.

[163]  *cf* ch 1, 3.1.

[164]  For an outline of the OSCE history see http://www.osce.org/who/87.

[165]  The document was signed by the following states: Austria, Belgium, Bulgaria, Canada, Cyprus, Czechoslovakia, Denmark, Finland, France, the German Democratic Republic, the Federal Republic of Germany, Greece, the Holy See, Hungary, Iceland, Ireland, Italy, Liechtenstein, Luxembourg, Malta, Monaco, the Netherlands, Norway, Poland, Portugal, Romania, San Marino, Spain, Sweden, Switzerland, Turkey, the Soviet Union, the UK, the US and Yugoslavia. The following states also subsequently signed the document: Albania, Andorra, Armenia, Azerbaijan, Belarus, Bosnia-Herzegovina, Croatia, the Czech Republic, Estonia, Georgia, Kazakhstan, Latvia, Lithuania, FYR Macedonia, Montenegro, Slovenia, Tajikistan, Ukraine and Uzbekistan. With the exceptions of Albania, Andorra and the Czech Republic, all of these states emerged in the territories of the former SFRY and of the former Soviet Union. See http://www.osce.org/who/83.

argued, its references to human rights do not reach beyond the universal interpretation and reflect the Cold War compromise to accommodate competing interpretations of democracy and human rights standards.[166]

The first chapter of the Final Act of Helsinki deals with sovereign equality and respect for the rights inherent in sovereignty,[167] where it essentially subscribes itself to the provisions of Article 2 of the UN Charter.[168] In the chapter on refraining from the threat or use of force, the Final Act of Helsinki mutatis mutandis repeats Article 2(4) of the UN Charter.[169] But then, with regard to inviolability of boundaries, the Final Act of Helsinki continues:

> The participating States regard as inviolable all one another's frontiers as well as the frontiers of all States in Europe and therefore they will refrain now and in the future from assaulting these frontiers. Accordingly, they will also refrain from any demand for, or act of, seizure and usurpation of part or all of the territory of any participating State.[170]
>
> . . .
>
> The participating States will likewise refrain from making each other's territory the object of military occupation or other direct or indirect measures of force in contravention of international law, or the object of acquisition by means of such measures or the threat of them. No such occupation or acquisition will be recognized as legal.[171]

In the case of the unlawful use of force, existing states are protected from having their international personality extinguished.[172] The same protection applies when partial occupation of the territory of a state resulting from an unlawful use of force is at issue – in such a situation, international law would not recognise a shift of sovereignty.[173] Consequently, with regard to the existing states, the Final Act of Helsinki does not extend the scope of the prohibition of the use of force and its implications for the law of statehood any further than does the UN Charter and the practice of UN organs.[174] In other words, from the point of view of the prohibition of the use of force and the non-recognition of factual situations resulting from the illegal use of force, the Final Act of Helsinki did not bind the participating states to any higher standards than generally applicable international law does.

---

[166]  *cf* ch 1, 2.2.
[167]  The Final Act of Helsinki (1975), ch 1.a.1,
[168]  See the UN Charter, art 2.
[169]  The Final Act of Helsinki (1975), ch II, para 1. *cf* the UN Charter, art 2(4).
[170]  The Final Act of Helsinki (1975), ch 3,
[171]  ibid, ch IV, para 3.
[172]  See Crawford (n 1) 132, who argues that the prohibition of the use of force expressed in Article 2(4) of the UN Charter '[e]xtends to continuity of legal personality in the face of illegal invasion and annexation: there is a substantial body of practice protecting the legal personality of the State against extinction, despite prolonged lack of effectiveness'.
[173]  ibid.
[174]  *cf* ch 1, 3.1 and 1, 3.5.

The Final Act of Helsinki dealt with existing states and generally did not refer to the creation of new states,[175] while the EC Guidelines and the EC Declaration were documents applied to new state creations. The question thus arises how the provisions of the Final Act of Helsinki, in conjunction with specific provisions of the EC Guidelines, work in the law governing state creation.

The EC Guidelines provide that: 'The Community and its Member States will not recognize entities which are the result of aggression.'[176] With this requirement, the EC Guidelines follow the obligation to withhold recognition where an entity is created illegally.[177] Yet the EC Guidelines set further requirements on the basis of the prohibition of the use of force. The requirement of 'respect for the inviolability of all frontiers which can only be changed by peaceful means and by common agreement'[178] resembles the provisions of the Final Act of Helsinki on the inviolability of frontiers and the territorial integrity of states.[179] Such a requirement applied to entities which are not (yet) states presupposes the confinement of new international borders along the lines of internal boundaries in the case of the dissolution of a parent state. This is, however, a controversial issue and will be discussed later in this book[180]

Moreover, this requirement does not relate to the use of force within the entity itself in an attempt to create a new state[181] but to the use of force beyond the newly confined international borders. Indeed, the EC Guidelines not only refer to the entities which could become effective as a result of an illegal use of force but also to potential new states which could be involved in armed conflict in *other* newly created states. In such a situation, the question is not whether the entity itself is a result of an unlawful use of force,[182] but rather whether an entity resorts to an unlawful use of force *outside of its territory*. Such a requirement extends the scope of the legality of state creation, which demands that a state itself may not be created as the result of an unlawful use of force, yet does not associate

---

[175] It can be argued that it touches upon the question of new state creations indirectly in the chapter on self-determination by affirming that the right of self-determination is limited by the principle of the territorial integrity of states. Unlike the universal elaboration of the right of self-determination in the common Article 1 of the Covenants, the Final Act of Helsinki thus unequivocally adopts the distinction between internal and external modes of the exercise of the right of self-determination.

[176] EC Guidelines (1991), para 5.

[177] *cf* ch 1, 3.5.

[178] EC Guidelines (1991), para 3.

[179] See n 170, above.

[180] For more on the *uti possidetis* principle applied in the territory of the SFRY, *cf* ch 4, 2.2.

[181] Crawford (n 1) 135–35, who argues that: 'It is probably the case that the use of force by a non-State entity in exercise of a right of self-determination is legally neutral, that is, not regulated by international law at all (though the rules of international humanitarian law may well apply).'

[182] Later Republika Srpska and Republika Srpska Krajina became such entities, but they initially did not exist in the framework of the SFRY. See ch 2, 3.4.3 and 2, 3.4.4.

statehood with peaceful behaviour in general.[183] Non-recognition follow-ing a failure to meet the requirement for peaceful behaviour internation-ally falls outside of the scope of the *erga omnes* applicable obligation to withhold recognition.[184]

The EC Guidelines further set out requirements which are either broadly related to the commitment to peace, such as the 'acceptance of all relevant commitments with regard to disarmament and nuclear non-proliferation as well as to security and regional stability'[185] and the 'commitment to settle by agreement, including where appropriate by recourse to arbitration, all questions concerning State succession and regional disputes'.[186] The EC Declaration also demanded the support of 'the efforts of the Secretary General and the Security Council of the United Nations, and the continuation of the Conference on Yugoslavia'.[187] These requirements evidently fall beyond the statehood criteria and express some recognition requirements which are specifically associated with the situation in the SFRY at the end of 1991.

## 3.4  The EC Guidelines and EC Declaration in Action

### 3.4.1  *Background: The SFRY*

The SFRY was a federation of six republics[188] and two autonomous prov-inces.[189] It was established during the Second World War, on 29 November 1943, under the name of the Federal People's Republic of Yugoslavia,[190] following the Kingdom of Yugoslavia, initially named the Kingdom of Serbs, Croats and Slovenes, which was established in 1918.[191]

At the time of the dissolution, the 1974 SFRY Constitution was in force, which defined republics as states[192] and delimited internal boundaries,[193] whereas the 'federal organization relied heavily on the ethnic component'.[194] The 1974 Constitution adopted a distinction between 'nations' and 'nationalities'. The term 'nation' applied to the people

---

[183] See ch 1, 3.1.
[184] ibid, See also ch 1, 3.5.
[185] EC Guidelines (1991), para 4.
[186] ibid.
[187] EC Declaration (1991), para 3.
[188] The six republics were: Slovenia, Croatia, Bosnia-Herzegovina, Serbia, Montenegro and Macedonia. See the Constitution of the SFRY (1974), art 2.
[189] The two autonomous regions, Kosovo and Vojvodina, were otherwise part of broader Serbia but had their autonomous status rooted within the federal (not Serb) constitutional order. See ibid.
[190] Renamed the SFRY by the Constitution of 1963.
[191] *cf* ch 4, 3.2.6.
[192] Constitution of the SFRY (1974), art 3.
[193] ibid, art 5(1).
[194] Türk (n 113) 66.

attached to a certain republic and 'nationality' to the people attached to one of the two respective autonomous provinces.[195] The constitutional design was an implementation of (internal) self-determination:[196] federal units were given wide powers for the exercise of effective control over their respective territories[197] and even had some limited competencies in the conducting of foreign policy.[198] Such competencies were not confined to republics but were extended even to the two autonomous provinces.[199] These units also had representatives in the federal organs.[200] Such widely conceived autonomy within the federal constitution in many respects elevated the powers of the autonomous provinces to the level of powers vested in republics.

According to the preamble to the Constitution of the SFRY, only 'nations', ie, peoples attached to one of the republics, were entitled to the right of self-determination, and this right extended to cover even secession.[201] However, a specific constitutional provision enabling the exercise of the right to secession inherent in 'nations' was missing. It thus remains debatable whether nations (ie, peoples attached to certain republics) really had a right to secession under the federal constitution.

When the Badinter Commission dealt with the situation in the SFRY, the entitlement to secession, possibly stemming from the preamble to the 1974 Constitution, was not invoked. In its Opinion 1, the Commission held 'that the Socialist Federal Republic of Yugoslavia is in the process of dissolution'.[202] Such an opinion denied the position taken by Serbia, which argued that 'those Republics which have declared or would declare themselves independent or sovereign have seceded or would secede from the SFRY which would otherwise continue to exist'.[203] The Badinter Commission based its reasoning on the following arguments: four out of the six republics of the SFRY (Slovenia, Croatia, Bosnia-Herzegovina and Macedonia) had declared independence;[204] the 'composition and workings of the essential organs of the Federation . . . no longer meet the criteria of participation and representatives inherent in a federal state';[205] and 'an armed conflict between different elements of the federation had erupted [while the] authorities of the Federation and the Republics have shown themselves to be powerless to

---

[195] See the Constitution of the SFRY (1974), art 1.
[196] *cf* ch 3, 2.2.
[197] See the Constitution of the SFRY (1974), arts 268 and 273.
[198] ibid, art 271.
[199] ibid.
[200] ibid, art 291 (regulating the assembly), art 348 (regulating the federal government) and art 381 (regulating the constitutional court).
[201] ibid, preamble, General Principle I.
[202] The Badinter Commission, Opinion 1 (29 November 1991), para 3, reprinted in Trifunovska (n 29) 415.
[203] ibid, Introduction.
[204] ibid, para 3(a).
[205] ibid, para 3(b).

enforce respect for the succeeding ceasefire agreements concluded under the auspices of the European Communities or the United Nations Organization'.[206]

In its subsequent opinions, the Badinter Commission applied the *uti possidetis* principle in order to 'upgrade' the former internal boundaries to international borders.[207] As follows from the EC Declaration, only republics were considered to be eligible for independence.[208] Accordingly, autonomous provinces (Kosovo and Vojvodina) and subsequently created entities in the territory of the disintegrating SFRY, such as Republika Srpska in Bosnia-Herzegovina and Republika Srpska Krajina in Croatia, could not become states.[209] The application of *uti possidetis* in this non-colonial situation was very controversial and remains the subject of criticism.[210] This issue will be revisited at a later point.

### 3.4.2 *Slovenia*

On 25 June 1991, the Assembly of the Republic of Slovenia adopted the Foundational Constitutional Instrument on Sovereignty and Independence of the Republic of Slovenia and a separate Declaration on Independence. The preamble to the first instrument spelt out that 'the SFRY does not function as a state governed by the rule of law and allows grave violations of human rights, rights of peoples, as well as rights of republics and autonomous provinces'.[211]

The decision that the Republic of Slovenia should become an independent and sovereign state was adopted at a referendum, held on 23 December 1990, by a majority of 88.5 per cent of all those eligible to vote (92 per cent of those who voted) with four per cent in absolute figures expressly voting against it.[212]

After the adoption of the Brioni Agreement, Slovenia's declaration of independence was suspended for three months.[213] During the period of suspension, no compromise was found and no alternative arrangement within the framework of Yugoslavia developed. On 23 December 1991, the Assembly of the Republic of Slovenia adopted a new constitution

---

[206] ibid, para 3(c).

[207] The Badinter Commission, Opinion 2 (11 January 1992), reprinted in Trifunovska (n 29) 474.

[208] See n 128, above.

[209] The Badinter Commission, Opinion 3 (11 January 1992), reprinted in Trifunovska (n 29) 479.

[210] See ch 4, 2.2.

[211] The Foundational Constitutional Instrument on Sovereignty and Independence of the Republic of Slovenia (1991), preamble, para 3 (author's own translation). The Official Gazette of the Republic of Slovenia No 1/91-I (25 June 1991).

[212] See the Government of the Republic of Slovenia, Office of Information http://www.slovenija2001.gov.si/10years/path/chronology/.

[213] See n 102, above.

which implemented democratic institutions[214] and a chapter on human rights and fundamental freedoms.[215]

The Badinter Commission specifically dealt with the recognition of Slovenia in its Opinion 7. Applying the requirements from the EC Guidelines and the EC Declaration, the Commission made the following references with respect to democratic standards implemented in Slovenia:

> [T]he present Assembly was the outcome of elections held in April 1990, after which an Executive Council supported by six parties controlling a majority of the Assembly was formed. It should be noted that Article 81 of the new Constitution of 23 December 1991 provides for universal, equal and direct suffrage and the secret ballot. The Constitutional Act to give effect to the Constitution provides that the present Assembly will remain in place until the election of the new Parliament.[216]

The Badinter Commission further observed that Slovenia's '[r]espect for the provisions of the United Nations Charter, the Helsinki Final Act and the Charter of Paris is stated in the Declaration of Independence' and that with regard to:

> [T]he requirement that Slovenia's legal system should respect human rights, observe the rule of law and guarantee a democratic regime, the Republic's answers to the Commission's questionnaire cite a number of constitutional provisions which establish to the Commission's satisfaction that these principles will be acted upon . . . The Republic of Slovenia undertakes to accept international machinery for monitoring respect for human rights, including individual petitions to the European Commission of Human Rights.[217]

With regard to the requirement for the protection of ethnic groups and minorities, the Badinter Commission held that Slovenia's constitutional order guarantees 'a number of specific rights to the Italian and Hungarian minorities'.[218] The Opinion further analysed the provisions on human rights standards in Slovenia's Constitution and concluded that 'while the Republic of Slovenia . . . accepts the international machinery that has been set up to protect and monitor respect for human rights, the Constitution

---

[214] The Constitution of the Republic of Slovenia (1991), ch 4, arts 80–137. Chapter 4 of the 1991 Constitution introduced the model of parliamentary democracy with a merely ceremonial role of the president of the republic. This system replaced the previous 'Assembly model', usually adopted by socialist states, which, inter alia, foresees fusion of the legislative and executive branches. Consequently, in the previous constitutional order, the government acted as the Executive Council of the Assembly. The democratic elections in April 1990 were held to the socialist institutional design upon constitutional amendments which enabled a multiparty setting. See J Vidmar, *Democratic Transition and Democratic Consolidation in Slovenia* (Frankfurt, Peter Lang Verlag, 2008) 146–50.

[215] Constitution of the Republic of Slovenia (1991), ch 2, arts 14–65.

[216] The Badinter Commission, Opinion 7 (11 January 1992), para 1, reprinted in Trifunovska (n 29) 495.

[217] ibid, para 2(a).

[218] ibid, para 2(b).

of 23 December also institutes a Constitutional Court with jurisdiction to enforce respect for human rights and fundamental freedoms both in the law and in individual actions'. [219]

In the context of Slovenia's commitment to peace and resolving of the conflict in the territory of the SFRY, the Badinter Commission stated:

> The commitment of the Republic of Slovenia to respect the inviolability of territorial boundaries made in the Declaration of Independence is repeated in the application for recognition. The Republic's frontiers are delimited in Article 2 of the Basic Constitutional Charter of 25 June 1991 unchanged by reference to the existing frontiers.
>
> The Republic of Slovenia also stresses that it has no territorial disputes with neighbouring states or the neighbouring Republic of Croatia. [220]

The Badinter Commission ultimately held that 'the Republic of Slovenia satisfies the tests in the [EC] Guidelines and the [EC] Declaration'. [221]

From the reasoning of the Badinter Commission in Opinion 7, the following observations can be derived. First, the Commission did not pay much attention to the statehood criteria. Indeed, its reasoning was mainly based on the requirements expressed in the EC Guidelines, reaching beyond those criteria. Second, when assessing Slovenia's meeting of recognition requirements associated with democracy, protection of human rights and commitment to peace, the Badinter Commission based its reasoning on the institutional implementation of these requirements. Third, when the Badinter Commission examined Slovenia's implementation of a democratic political system, its approach was electoral-centric and did not go beyond the observation that democratic elections had been held and the next democratic elections were scheduled.

Slovenia was recognised by the EC Member States on 15 January 1992 and was admitted to the UN on 22 May 1992. [222] The Badinter Commission, however, subsequently held that Slovenia became a state on 8 October 1991, when the Brioni Agreement was terminated. [223]

### 3.4.3 *Croatia*

On 25 June 1991, the Croatian Parliament adopted the Declaration on Promulgation of a Sovereign and Independent Republic of Croatia. [224] The Declaration, inter alia, drew its legitimacy on the expressed will of the

---

[219]  ibid, para 3(a).
[220]  ibid, para 2(c).
[221]  ibid, para 4.
[222]  UN Doc A/RES/46/236 (22 May 1992).
[223]  The Badinter Commission, Opinion 11, para 4 (16 July 1993), reprinted in Trifunovska (n 29) 1017.
[224]  The Declaration on Promulgation of a Sovereign and Independent Republic of Croatia (1991). The Official Gazette of the Republic of Croatia No 31/1991 (25 June 1991).

people at a referendum, held on 19 May 1991.[225] At the referendum, 93 per cent of those who voted cast their votes in favour of independence.[226] The adoption of the Brioni Agreement suspended Croatia's declaration of independence for a period of three months.[227]

Because of the ethnic structure of its population, the case of Croatia was not as clear as that of Slovenia. A total of 12 per cent of the population of Croatia was of Serb ethnic origin[228] and opposed the declaration of independence.[229] Already prior to the referendum on the declaration of independence, Serbs in Croatia proclaimed that they no longer accepted Croatia's authority.[230] As a result, Kninska Krajina, an entity which sought union with Serbia, was established; however, the Serbian Parliament rejected such an arrangement.[231] With YNA support, Kninska Krajina became an entity in whose territory Croatia did not exercise effective control.[232] On 19 December 1991, the self-proclaimed parliament of Kninska Krajina declared independence and, referring to the EC Declaration, addressed a request for recognition as an independent state.[233] The Badinter Commission ignored the application and recognition was not granted by any state, not even by the Federal Republic of Yugoslavia (FRY). It was not until 1995 that Croatia established effective control over Kninska Krajina.[234]

The Badinter Commission dealt with the recognition of Croatia in its Opinion 5 delivered on 11 January 1992. Applying the EC Guidelines, the Commission found deficiencies in Croatia's meeting of minority protection standards:

---

[225]  ibid, art 2.

[226]  See Trifunovska (n 29) 299.

[227]  See n 102, above.

[228]  See D Raič, *Statehood and the Law of Self-Determination* (The Hague, Kluwer Law International, 2002) 349.

[229]  ibid, For more on the historical background of Serbian minority within Croatia, see ch 4, 3.2.6.

[230]  ibid.

[231]  ibid, 388. The exact reason why the Milošević-controlled Serbian parliament rejected a union with Kninska Krajina is unknown. The answer should probably be sought in the context of international pressure to stop the conflicts in both Croatia and Bosnia-Herzegovina and secret agreements between the Presidents of Croatia and Serbia. In 1993, the *New York Times* made the following observation: 'In Zagreb, Croatia's capital, Western diplomats say they suspect President Milosevic reached a secret understanding with President Franjo Tudjman of Croatia over territory [of Kninska Krajina] . . . No one seems sure of the substance of this agreement, but there is a suspicion in the Zagreb diplomatic corps that President Milosevic at least offered to force the Serbs in northern, western and southern Krajina to surrender in return for Croatia's giving him the separate eastern Krajina region, which directly abuts his territory.' See 'Conflict in the Balkans; Croatia's Serb Enclave Feels Betrayed', *New York Times* (9 May 1993), http://query.nytimes.com/gst/fullpage.html?res=9F0CE7DA1E3EF93AA35756C0A965958260&scp=1&sq=a%20plan%20for%20peace%20may%209%201993&st=cse.

[232]  Raič (n 228) 338.

[233]  ibid, 389.

[234]  ibid, 390.

[T]he Constitutional Act of 4 December 1991 does not fully incorporate all the provisions of the draft Convention of 4 November 1991, notably those contained in Chapter II, Article 2(c), under the heading 'Special status' [and] the authorities of the Republic of Croatia should therefore supplement the Constitutional Act in such a way as to satisfy those provisions.[235]

The Badinter Commission thus referred to the Draft Convention of the Conference on Yugoslavia (the so-called Carrington Draft Convention) from 4 November 1991, which, inter alia, adopts minority protection standards agreed upon in the agreement between Presidents Franjo Tuđman (Croatia), Slobodan Milošević (Serbia) and the Yugoslav Defence Minister Veljko Kadijević, brokered by the Netherlands' Minister of Foreign Affairs, Hans van den Broek, at The Hague on 4 October 1991.[236] The relevant chapter provides:

[A]reas in which persons belonging to a national or ethnic group form a majority, shall enjoy a special status of autonomy.

Such a status will provide for:

(a)  The right to have and show national emblems of that group;
(b)  The right to a second nationality for members of that group in addition to the nationality of the republic;
(c)  An educational system which respects the values and needs of that group;
(d)  (i)    A legislative body,
    (ii)   An administrative structure, including regional police force,
    (iii)  And a judiciary responsible for matters concerning the area, which reflects the composition of the population of the area;

. . .

Such areas, unless they are defined in part by an international frontier with a State not party to This Convention, shall be permanently demilitarized and no military forces, exercises or activities on land or in the air shall be permitted in those areas.[237]

As argued above, the Badinter Commission held that Croatia did not meet these standards and concluded that subject to this reservation:

[T]he Republic of Croatia meets the necessary conditions for its recognition by the Member States of the European Community in accordance with the Declaration on Yugoslavia and the Guidelines on the Recognition of New States in Eastern Europe and in the Soviet Union, adopted by the Council of the European Communities on 16 December 1991.[238]

---

[235]  The Badinter Commission, Opinion 5 (11 January 1992), para 3, reprinted in Trifunovska (n 29) 489.
[236]  UN Doc S/23169 (4 October 1991).
[237]  ibid, 39–40. *cf* also Caplan (n 117) 22, at n 30.
[238]  The Badinter Commission, Opinion 5 (11 January 1992), para 3, reprinted in Trifunovska (n 29) 489.

The Badinter Commission did not invoke the problem that Croatia did not exercise effective control over part of its territory (ie, in the territory of Kninska Krajina), although the EC Guidelines provide that 'the normal standards of international practice',[239] ie, statehood criteria, would be considered when recognition was to be granted. Nevertheless, despite this deficiency and despite the Badinter Commission's finding that Croatia did not sufficiently fulfil the required minority protection standards, the EC Member States granted recognition to Croatia on 15 January 1992[240] Admission to the UN followed on 22 May 1992.[241] The Badinter Commission subsequently held that Croatia, like Slovenia, became a state on 8 October 1991, which is the day on which the Brioni Agreement terminated. [242] Unlike in its reasoning in the case of Slovenia,[243] the Badinter Commission did not invoke Croatian democratic elections or make any other direct observations with regard to democracy in Croatia. Indeed, '[r]ecognition proceeded apace for Croatia despite some unanswered questions over . . . [President] Tudjman's methods of governance'.[244]

### 3.4.4 *Bosnia-Herzegovina*

Within the SFRY, Bosnia-Herzegovina was defined as a republic of three constitutive 'nations': Muslims, Serbs and Croats.[245] Most numerous were Muslims (43.7 per cent in 1991), followed by Serbs (31.3 per cent in 1991) and Croats (17.3 per cent in 1991).[246] Its diverse ethnic composition and the armed conflict that broke out made the recognition of Bosnia-Herzegovina an especially difficult issue.

On 15 October 1991, the Assembly of Bosnia-Herzegovina, in the absence of the representatives of Serbian nationality, adopted the Memorandum on Sovereignty of Bosnia-Herzegovina.[247] On 20 December 1991, Bosnia-

[239]  See n 118, above.

[240]  Crawford (n 1) 397.

[241]  UN Doc A/RES/46/238 (22 May 1992).

[242]  The Badinter Commission, Opinion 11 (16 July 1993), para 4, reprinted in Trifunovska (n 29) 1017.

[243]  See ch 2, 3.4.2.

[244]  Grant (n 110) 95.

[245]  Constitution of the Socialist Republic Bosnia and Herzegovina (1969), Article 1. The term 'Muslim' had an ethnic and not necessarily a religious connotation. In the times of the SFRY, the term 'Bosniak' was not in use, while the term 'Bosnian' was in politically correct language only used as an adjective, while it had a pejorative meaning if used as a noun to refer to the people of Bosnia.

[246]  In addition, 5.5 per cent of the inhabitants of Bosnia-Herzegovina declared themselves 'Yugoslavs' and 2.2 per cent invoked some other ethnic background: 1991 census, the Socialist Republic of Bosnia and Herzegovina. Due to the outbreak of the armed conflict in Bosnia-Herzegovina, the official results of the 1991 census were never published, but they are available at this unofficial website: http://josip.purger.com/other/bih/index.htm.

[247]  The Memorandum on Sovereignty of Bosnia-Herzegovina, the Official Gazette of the Socialist Republic of Bosnia and Herzegovina, No 32 (15 October 1991). The Memorandum was

Herzegovina addressed the application for recognition in accordance with the EC Declaration.[248]

The Badinter Commission, inter alia, held that:

[T]he current Constitution of the SRBH [Socialist Republic of Bosnia and Herzegovina] guarantees equal rights for 'the nations of Bosnia-Herzegovina – Muslims, Serbs and Croats – and the members of the other nations and ethnic groups living on its territory'.

The current Constitution of the SRBH guarantees respect for human rights, and the authorities of Bosnia-Herzegovina have sent the Commission a list of the laws in force giving effect to those principles; they also gave the Commission assurances that the new Constitution now being framed would provide full guarantees for individual human rights and freedoms.

The authorities gave the Commission an assurance that the Republic of Bosnia-Herzegovina had no territorial claims on neighbouring countries and was willing to guarantee their territorial integrity.[249]

The Badinter Commission thus saw no institutional deficiencies for the implementation of human rights standards. Direct references to democracy were not made 'and Bosnia received recognition . . . with doubts lingering over whether . . . [its] nascent institutions would function democratically'.[250] Democratic principles were nevertheless invoked in the context of the right of self-determination. This issue will be further discussed below.[251]

A referendum on independence, upon a specific request by the Badinter Commission,[252] was subsequently held between 29 February and 1 March 1992.[253] The referendum was boycotted by Bosnian Serbs,[254] while independence was supported by 63 per cent of all those eligible to vote (to which the boycotting Serbs also counted).[255] Bosnia-Herzegovina was recognised as a state by the EC Member States on 6 April 1992[256] and was admitted to the UN on 22 May 1992.[257]

The Badinter Commission subsequently held that Bosnia-Herzegovina became an independent state on 6 March 1992, the day when results of the

---

adopted at a night-meeting of the Assembly, which began on the previous day; therefore, it is sometimes dated 14 October 1991.

[248] The Badinter Commission, Opinion 4 (11 January 1992), reprinted in Trifunovska (n 29) 486.
[249] ibid, para 1.
[250] Grant (n 110) 195.
[251] See ch 3, 2.
[252] See ch 3, 7.2.3.
[253] See Crawford (n 1) 398.
[254] ibid.
[255] ibid.
[256] ibid.
[257] UN Doc A/RES/46/237 (22 May 1992).

referendum on independence were proclaimed.[258] This critical date for Bosnia-Herzegovina's becoming a state was also affirmed by the ICJ in the *Bosnia Genocide* case, in the context of the question of when Bosnia-Herzegovina became party to the Genocide Convention.[259]

The Badinter Commission and the recognising states did not find it problematic that large parts of Bosnia-Herzegovina were not under the effective control of the central government and therefore that the statehood criteria wrere not satisfied.[260] The question of popular consent was another problematic issue in Bosnia-Herzegovina. Although independence was supported at the referendum held prior to the international recognition of Bosnia-Herzegovina, in light of the boycott of one of its constitutive peoples, the quality of popular consent remains questionable. Two interpretations are possible regarding the question of why the boycott of the Serbian population was irrelevant: first, the majoritarian concept of democratic decision-making at the referendum prevailed; and, second, the exercise of the right of self-determination was limited by the previous internal boundary arrangement which prevented Bosnian Serbs from seeking the arrangement they preferred.[261] These two options will be addressed at a later point.

### 3.4.5 Macedonia

Macedonia held its referendum on independence on 8 September 1991. The decision for independence was upheld by 72.16 per cent of those eligible to vote (95 per cent of those who voted).[262] On 17 September 1991, the Declaration of Independence was proclaimed by Macedonia's Assembly.[263] On 20 December 1991, Macedonia sent a request for recognition in accordance with the EC Declaration.[264]

---

[258] The Badinter Commission, Opinion 11 (16 July 1993), para 6, reprinted in Trifunovska (n 29) 1017.

[259] The relevant reasoning of the ICJ reads: 'Whether Bosnia and Herzegovina automatically became party to the Genocide Convention on the date of its accession to independence on 6 March 1992, or whether it became a party as a result – retroactive or not – of its Notice of Succession of 29 December 1992, at all events it was a party to it on the date of the filing of its Application on 20 March 1993.' *Case Concerning Application of the Convention on the Prevention and Punishment of the Crime of Genocide (Bosnia and Herzegovina v Yugoslavia)* (Preliminary Objections) [1996] ICJ Rep 596 (the *Bosnia Genocide* case), para 23.

[260] See Crawford (n 1) 398.

[261] *cf* ch 4, 3.2.6.

[262] Trifunovska (n 29) 345. A total of 3.5 per cent of those who voted were expressly against independence. According to the 1991 census, major ethnicities populating Macedonia were as follows: Macedonians (65.3%), Albanians (27.73%), Turks (3.79%) and Serbs (2.09%): Macedonian census (1991), www.makedonija.info/republic.html.

[263] The Declaration on the Sovereignty and Independence of the Republic of Macedonia, 17 September 1991, reprinted in Trifunovska (n 29) 345–47.

[264] The Badinter Commission, Opinion 6 (11 January 1992), reprinted in Trifunovska (n 29) 491.

The Badinter Commission, inter alia, held that 'the Arbitration Commission also notes that on 17 November 1991, the Assembly of the Republic of Macedonia adopted a Constitution embodying the democratic structures and the guarantees for human rights which are in operation in Europe'.[265] The Commission further found that Macedonia had implemented an adequate institutional framework for minority rights protection[266] and showed adequate commitment to international peace[267] and the inviolability of borders.[268]

Much of the Badinter Commission's reasoning on Macedonia was dedicated to the latter's dispute with Greece over the name 'Macedonia'. Greece maintained (and still maintains) that use of the name 'Macedonia' implies territorial claims against Greece.[269] The Badinter Commission noted that Macedonia amended its constitution on 6 January 1992 and unequivocally renounced any territorial claims and interference into affairs of other states. It ultimately took the view:

> [T]hat the Republic of Macedonia satisfies the tests in the Guidelines on the Recognition of New States in Eastern Europe and in the Soviet Union and the Declaration on Yugoslavia adopted by the Council of the European Communities on 16 December 1991 [and] that the Republic of Macedonia has, moreover, renounced all territorial claims of any kind in unambiguous statements binding in international law; that the use of the name 'Macedonia' cannot therefore imply any territorial claim against another State.[270]

However, Greece was not willing to grant recognition to Macedonia under this name.[271] Despite an explicit recommendation by the Badinter Commission, Macedonia remained unrecognised by the EC Member States until 16 December 1993, and even then it was recognised under the compromise name of 'The Former Yugoslav Republic of Macedonia' (FYR Macedonia).[272] Prior to recognition by the EC, on 8 April 1993, the FYR Macedonia had already become a member of the UN.[273]

For more than a year, non-recognition of Macedonia, which had its origins in the EC's internal policy, had been virtually universalised as only Bulgaria, Turkey and Lithuania granted recognition, under its original

---

[265] ibid, para 3.
[266] ibid.
[267] ibid, para 1.
[268] ibid, para 4.
[269] *See Application of the Interim Accord of 13 September 1995 (The Former Yugoslav Republic of Macedonia v Greece)*, ICJ Rep 2011.
[270] The Badinter Commission, Opinion 6 (11 January 1992), para 4, reprinted in Trifunovska (n 29) 491.
[271] See M Craven, 'What's in a Name: The Former Yugoslav Republic of Macedonia and Issues of Statehood' (1995) 16 *Australian Yearbook of International Law* 199, 199–200.
[272] See Crawford (n 1) 398.
[273] UN Doc A/RES/47/225 (8 April 1993).

name, before the admission of the FYR Macedonia to the UN.[274] Non-recognition had an evidently political character, as Macedonia otherwise clearly met both the statehood criteria as well as other recognition requirements expressed in the EC Guidelines, and the legal duty to withhold recognition did not apply.[275] Moreover, Macedonia's former parent state no longer existed,[276] so this was not a case of unilateral secession and there was no applicable claim to territorial integrity which could stand as a barrier between the claim for statehood and its acquisition.

Nevertheless, the fact that Macedonia for some time remained virtually universally non-recognised does not mean that it was not a state during that period; rather, it was an example of political non-recognition. This follows even from the position of the EC. A good example is the Declaration on the Former Yugoslav Republic of Macedonia, which the EC and its Member States adopted on 1 and 2 May 1992. The Declaration expressed the willingness of the EC Member States 'to recognise that State [ie, Macedonia] as a sovereign and independent State, within its existing borders, and under a name that can be accepted by all parties concerned'.[277] The use of the term 'state' rather than, for example, 'entity' or 'republic' clearly implies that Macedonia's attributes of statehood were not in dispute; it was rather that the EC did not want to enter into relations with Macedonia under its constitutional name.[278] It also needs to be noted that in its Opinion 11, the Badinter Commission held that Macedonia became a state on 17 November 1991, the day when it adopted a new constitution which proclaimed Macedonia a sovereign state.[279]

### 3.4.6 The FRY

The two remaining former republics of the SFRY, Serbia and Montenegro, unified in the FRY and claimed continuity of the SFRY's international personality. This position was expressed in the Constitution of the FRY, which was promulgated on 27 April 1992. Article 2 defined the FRY as a state of Serbia and Montenegro,[280] while the preamble provided that the republics had unified on the grounds of the 'uninterrupted international personality of Yugoslavia'.[281]

---

[274] See R Rich, 'Recognition of States: The Collapse of Yugoslavia and the Soviet Union' (1993) 4 *EJIL* 36, 52.

[275] *cf* ch 1, 3.1 and 1, 3.5.

[276] See the Badinter Commission, Opinion 9 (4 July 1992), reprinted in Trifunovska (n 29) 637.

[277] Declaration on the Former Yugoslav Republic of Macedonia, Informal Meeting of Ministers of Foreign Affairs, Guimaracs, 1 and 2 May 1992, reprinted in C Hill and K Smith, *European Foreign Policy: Key Documents* (London, Routledge, 2000) 376.

[278] See also Craven (n 271) 207–18.

[279] The Badinter Commission, Opinion 11 (16 July 1993), para 5.

[280] Constitution of the FRY (1992), art 2.

[281] ibid, preamble (author's own translation).

The FRY's claim to the SFRY's international personality is evident from the submissions of both Serbia and Montenegro to the EC in response to the invitation to apply for recognition, as expressed by the EC Declaration. In his reply on 23 December 1991, Serbia's Foreign Minister recalled that Serbia acquired 'internationally recognized statehood at the Berlin Congress of 1878 and on that basis had participated in the establishment in 1918 of the Kingdom of Serbs, Croats and Slovenes which became Yugoslavia [and concluded that Serbia] is not interested in secession'.[282] Montenegro's Foreign Minister, in his response on 24 December 1991, also declined the EC's invitation to apply for recognition and recalled the international personality that Montenegro had prior to joining the Yugoslav state formations.[283]

The Badinter Commission, however, noted already in its Opinion 1 'that the Socialist Federal Republic of Yugoslavia is in the process of dissolution'.[284] Subsequently, the UN Security Council in its Resolution 757 specified that 'the claim by the Federal Republic of Yugoslavia (Serbia and Montenegro) to continue automatically the membership of the former Socialist Federal Republic of Yugoslavia (in the United Nations) has not been generally accepted'.[285] The Security Council further stated in Resolution 777:

> [T]he Federal Republic of Yugoslavia (Serbia and Montenegro) cannot continue automatically the membership of the former Socialist Federal Republic of Yugoslavia in the United Nations; and therefore recommends to the General Assembly that it decide that the Federal Republic of Yugoslavia (Serbia and Montenegro) should apply for membership in the United Nations and that it shall not participate in the work of the General Assembly.[286]

This recommendation was accepted by the General Assembly in its Resolution 47/1.[287]

The Badinter Commission referred to Resolution 757 when it found that 'the process of dissolution of the SFRY referred to in Opinion 1, from 29 November 1991, is now complete and that the SFRY no longer exists'.[288] In this context, the Commission concluded in its Opinion 9 that '[n]ew states have been created on the territory of the former SFRY and replaced it. All are successor states to the former SFRY'[289] and that it followed from the Security Council resolutions that the 'Federal Republic of Yugoslavia

[282] Rich (n 274) 47.
[283] ibid.
[284] The Badinter Commission, Opinion 1 (29 November 1991), para 3, reprinted in Trifunovska (n 29) 415.
[285] UN Doc S/RES/757, preamble (30 May 1992).
[286] UN Doc S/RES/777, para 1 (19 September 1992).
[287] UN Doc A/RES/47/1 (19 September 1992).
[288] The Badinter Commission, Opinion 8 (4 July 1992), para 4, reprinted in Trifunovska (n 29) 629.
[289] The Badinter Commission, Opinion 9 (4 July 1992), para 1, reprinted in Trifunovska (n 29) 637.

(Serbia and Montenegro) has no right to consider itself the SFRY's sole successor'.[290] Consequently, 'the SFRY's membership of international organizations must be terminated according to their statutes and . . . none of the successor states may thereupon claim for itself alone the membership rights previously enjoyed by the former SFRY'.[291] The Badinter Commission ultimately concluded in its Opinion 10:

> [T]he FRY (Serbia and Montenegro) is a new state which cannot be considered the sole successor to the SFRY . . . its recognition by the Member States of the European Community would be subject to its compliance with the conditions laid down by general international law for such an act and the joint statement and [EC] Guidelines.[292]

Nevertheless, the FRY continued to claim continuity with the international personality of the FRY and did not apply for membership of the UN before the end of the Milošević regime. It was thus admitted to the UN only on 1 November 2000.[293] While non-admission to the UN can be simply ascribed to the absence of an application for membership, the FRY's non-recognition remains more controversial. Since the FRY refused to seek recognition in accordance with the EC Declaration, it remained universally unrecognised. The EC recognition policy was thus universalised, just as in the case of Macedonia, although the circumstances were different.

This does not mean that the FRY was not treated as a state. Indeed, it appeared before the ICJ in the *Bosnia Genocide* case and the Court established that the case was admissible, although the FRY was universally non-recognised at that time.[294] Since the FRY did not emerge illegally and nor was a counterclaim for territorial integrity of a parent state applicable in this situation, there could be no doubt that the FRY was a state.

One circumstance also made the position of the FRY significantly different in comparison to other universally non-recognised states:

> [T]he FRY had the advantage of possession. The SFRY's foreign service had been progressively denuded of its non-Serbian or Montenegrin representatives and accordingly, the personnel in the Yugoslav missions abroad were by and large loyal to Belgrade and most accepted the FRY as the country they now represented.[295]

---

[290]  ibid, para 3.

[291]  ibid, para 4.

[292]  The Badinter Commission, Opinion 10 (4 July 1992), para 5, reprinted in Trifunovska (n 29) 639.

[293]  UN Doc A/RES/55/12 (1 November 2000). Some statements made by officials of the Republic of Serbia imply that Serbia still holds that it inherited the international personality of the former SFRY. When addressing the Security Council after Kosovo's declaration of independence, the President of Serbia, Boris Tadić, inter alia, made the following statement: 'Serbia, let me recall, is a founding State Member of the United Nations.' UN Doc S/PV.5838 (18 February 2008) 4.

[294]  The *Bosnia Genocide* case (n 259) 622, para 45.

[295]  Rich (n 274) 54.

As Rich further notes: 'In response many countries reserved their positions and stated that continuing dealings with FRY representatives were without prejudice to any eventual decision on the FRY's claim [to continuation of international personality of the SFRY]'.[296] However, 'the advantage of possession' gave the FRY the capacity to enter into relations with foreign states, which is otherwise a notable problem faced by non-recognised *states*.[297]

The non-recognition of the FRY was somewhat unusual because the FRY denied that there was any new state creation in its case.[298] Nor did other states deny that the FRY was a state; rather, their legal position was that it did not continue the international personality of the SFRY. The FRY was deemed to be a successor of rights and duties of the SFRY – but not the continuator – and non-recognition did not influence this question.

The Badinter Commission in its Opinion 11 held that the FRY became a state on 27 April 1992, the day when it adopted its constitution.[299] The UK, for example, recognised the FRY in 9 April 1996.[300] Its denying recognition for this long has been described as 'overtly political'.[301] It needs to be noted that recognition came after the FRY had signed the General Framework Agreement for Peace in Bosnia and Herzegovina which, inter alia, demanded a mutual recognition of the FRY and Bosnia-Herzegovina[302] and effectively terminated the FRY's direct military involvement in the armed conflict in Bosnia-Herzegovina.[303]

---

[296] ibid.

[297] The capacity to enter into relations with other states is a statehood criterion under the Montevideo Convention. Article 1 of the Montevideo Convention provides: 'The State as a person of international law should possess the following qualifications: (a) a permanent population; (b) a defined territory, (c) government; and (d) capacity to enter into relations with other states.' The Montevideo Convention on Rights and Duties of States, 165 LNTS 19 (1933), art 1. However, the last criterion is the most controversial one and is said to be a corollary of a sovereign and independent government, which exercises jurisdiction on the territory of the state. See H Charlesworth and C Chinkin, *The Boundaries of International Law* (Manchester, Manchester University Press, 2005) 132. As such, it is 'a consequence of statehood, not a criterion for it': Crawford (n 1) 61. Indeed, the criterion is self-fulfilling as non-state entities cannot enter into relations with foreign states on the same level as do states. They have the capacity to do so once they become states.

[298] This problem is also pointed out in Opinion 11 of the Badinter Commission: 'There are particular problems in determining the date of State succession in respect of the Federal Republic of Yugoslavia because that State considers itself to be the continuation of the Socialist Federal Republic of Yugoslavia rather than a successor State.' The Badinter Commission, Opinion 11 (16 July 1993), para 7.

[299] ibid, para 7, reprinted in Trifunovska (n 29) 1017.

[300] HC Deb 7 May 1996, col 89. See www.publications.parliament.uk/pa/cm199596/cmhansrd/vo960507/text/60507w19.htm.

[301] M Dixon, R McCorquodale and S Williams, *Cases and Materials in International Law* (Oxford, Oxford University Press, 2011) 163.

[302] The General Framework Agreement for Peace in Bosnia and Herzegovina, Article X (14 December 1995), http://www.ohr.int/dpa/default.asp?content_id=380.

[303] In this regard, the House of Commons Select Committee on Foreign Affairs later noted (in the context of the Kosovo crisis): 'The EU's "Declaration on Yugoslavia", adopted on 16 December 1991, required that all Yugoslav republics seeking recognition agree to accept

*3.4.7  State Creations, International Involvement and Democracy in the Territory of the SFRY: A Synthesis*

The statehood criteria played virtually no role in the process of the dissolution of the SFRY and were not systematically discussed in the reasoning of the Badinter Commission. Croatia and Bosnia-Herzegovina were universally considered to have become independent states, despite the fact that their governments clearly did not exercise effective control over large parts of their respective territories.

Macedonia did not have problems with satisfying the statehood criteria and recognition requirements expressed in the EC Guidelines, but remained unrecognised.[304] Nevertheless, the non-recognition of Macedonia was political and not an obligation under international law. As Macedonia's former parent state at that time no longer existed, there was no applicable counterclaim for territorial integrity that could have prevented it from acquiring statehood.[305] If one does not accept the extreme constitutive position,[306] Macedonia's statehood in the period of non-recognition cannot be contested.

Although in self-denial, the FRY was a new state.[307] Based on its claim for continuity of the international personality of the SFRY, the FRY did not seek recognition as foreseen by the EC Declaration.[308] Consequently, the Badinter Commission did not need to apply the EC Guidelines to this situation. Given its involvement in armed conflicts in Croatia[309] and Bosnia-Herzegovina,[310] atrocities in Kosovo[311] and the authoritarian nature of the

extensive provisions for safeguarding the rights of national minorities within their boundaries, including the granting of autonomy ("special status") to minorities forming a majority in the area where they lived. However, when in April 1996 the EU member states, including the United Kingdom, decided to extend recognition to Yugoslavia, they chose to ignore the requirement of autonomy for the Kosovo Albanians which earlier had been a central component of the EU's recognition policy. The EU merely noted at the time that improved relations between Yugoslavia and the international community would depend upon, inter alia, a "constructive approach" by Yugoslavia to the granting of autonomy for Kosovo. Again, achieving Milosevic's cooperation on Bosnia was given priority over exercising leverage on Kosovo.' HC Select Committee on Foreign Affairs, Fourth Report (23 May 2000), para 32, www.publications.parliament.uk/pa/cm199900/cmselect/cmfaff/28/2807.htm#note53. For more on Kosovo, see ch 4, 6.

[304] See ch 1, 3.1 and 2, 3.2.1. See also Rich (n 274) 57.

[305] *cf* ch 1, 3.4.

[306] Above an argument was made that recognition can have constitutive effects. However, this is so when it is not clear whether an entity meets the statehood criteria and/or there exists a competing claim to territorial integrity. Nor was this the case in the example of Macedonia. *cf* ch 1, 3.4.

[307] See ch 2, 3.4.6.

[308] *cf* n 128, above.

[309] See especially UN Doc S/RES/815 (30 March 1993), UN Doc S/RES/820 (17 April 1993), the latter implying Serbia's involvement in both Croatia and Bosnia-Herzegovina.

[310] See especially UN Doc S/RES/752 (15 May 1992), UN Doc S/RES/757 (30 May 1992), UN Doc S/RES/758 (8 June 1992), UN Doc S/RES/760 (18 June 1992).

[311] See ch 2, 6.

Milošević regime,[312] it is possible to speculate that the FRY would not have met the EC Guidelines standards associated with a commitment to international peace, human rights and democracy.[313] But the FRY was nevertheless a state.

While the legality requirements preclude a state creation where an effective entity is established as a result of an unlawful use of force or in denial of the right of self-determination,[314] the EC Guidelines have a broader scope: they demand peaceful behaviour in the international community in general[315] and adherence to a particular (ie, democratic) political system.[316] The FRY may have been involved in armed conflicts elsewhere, but it was not itself an entity created as a result of an illegal use of force. The duty of non-recognition was not owed *erga omnes*. The non-recognition of the FRY can be seen as merely political and not as a consequence of territorial illegality associated with the creation of the FRY. A counterclaim for territorial integrity was also inapplicable in this situation and thus there was no doubt that the FRY was a state. Indeed, it was shown that the FRY was internationally treated as one.[317] And in the absence of any other state in its territory, it is indeed questionable what else it could be.

The Badinter Commission expressly held that recognition is declaratory and did not perceive itself as a body which creates states. Such a perception is obvious from the reasoning in its Opinion 11 in which it was, inter alia, held that Slovenia and Croatia became states on 8 October 1991 (the day of the expiry of the EC-imposed moratorium on their respective declarations on independence),[318] Macedonia on 17 November 1991 (the day of the adoption of a new constitution),[319] Bosnia-Herzegovina on 6 March 1992 (the day of the proclamation of referendum results)[320] and the FRY on 27 April 1992 (the day of the adoption of a new constitution).[321] While these opinions reflect a declaratory understanding of recognition, they were made subsequently – in the context of state succession – and are somewhat problematic.[322]

---

[312] See N Miller, 'Serbia and Montenegro' in R Frucht (ed.), *Eastern Europe: An Introduction to the People, Lands, and Culture* (Santa Barbara, ABC CLIO, 2005) 552–64.

[313] See ch 2, 3.2.1.

[314] See ch 1, 3.1.

[315] See ch 2, 3.2.1.

[316] ibid.

[317] See ch 2, 3.4.6.

[318] The Badinter Commission, Opinion 11 (16 July 1993), para 4.

[319] ibid.

[320] ibid.

[321] ibid.

[322] In Opinion 11, the Badinter Commission dealt with questions of succession after the dissolution of the SFRY had been completed and for this purpose it had to establish critical dates on which the SFRY's former republics became independent states. See the Badinter Commission, Opinion 11 (16 July 1993), para 2.

When the Badinter Commission delivered its Opinion 11 on 16 July 1993, Slovenia and Croatia had already been recognised as independent states and were members of the UN.[323] On 16 July 1993, there also already existed the authority of the Badinter Commission's previous opinions holding that the SFRY was in the process of dissolution (Opinion 1)[324] and that this process was completed (Opinion 8).[325] Yet, on 8 October 1991, an authority holding that the process of dissolution was under way in the SFRY was absent. Moreover, such a finding was supported by the fact that four out of the SFRY's six constitutive republics had declared independence,[326] while on 8 October 1991, Bosnia-Herzegovina had not yet declared independence[327] and Macedonia's declaration was fairly recent.[328] The prevailing view on 8 October 1991 was that Slovenia and Croatia sought unilateral secession.[329] In such a circumstance, the acquisition of statehood is much more questionable and, arguably, may depend on recognition.[330]

On 8 October 1991, recognition was not certain. Caplan notes: 'As much as the Slovenes may have wished and hoped for EC recognition, it was really not until the EC Council of Ministers meeting of 16 December [1991] that they would be assured of it.'[331] As he continues, 'if one reads history of this period backwards from its final denouement, the uncertainty is less apparent'.[332] And this is what the Badinter Commission did when it subsequently held that Slovenia and Croatia became states on 8 October 1991 – it read history backwards. It was the opinion of the Badinter Commission, delivered only on 29 November 1991,[333] which established the universally accepted authority stating that the SFRY was in the process of dissolution. On 8 October 1991, the legal status of Slovenia and Croatia was, however,

---

[323]    See UN Doc A/RES/46/236 (22 May 1992) and UN Doc A/RES/46/238 (22 May 1992).

[324]    The Badinter Commission, Opinion 1 (29 November 1991), para 3.

[325]    The Badinter Commission, Opinion 8 (4 July 1992), para 4.

[326]    The Badinter Commission, Opinion 1 (29 November 1991), para 2.

[327]    Bosnia-Herzegovina declared independence on 15 October 1991. See the Official Gazette of the Socialist Republic of Bosnia-Herzegovina, No 32 (15 October 1991).

[328]    Macedonia declared independence on 17 September 1991. See the Declaration on the Sovereignty and Independence of the Republic of Macedonia, 17 September 1991, reprinted in Trifunovska (n 29) 345–47.

[329]    See Grant (n 110) 152–53, who argues that: 'Though the United States, the Soviet Union, and various West European states and organizations stated their disapproval of Croat and Slovene unilateral declarations of independence, Germany quickly began to suggest that it would extend recognition to the putative states. As early as August 7, 1991, the German government expressed support for the secessionists.' See also Raič (n 228) 352, who argues that on 8 October 1991, the people of Croatia possessed the right to secession based on the 'remedial secession' doctrine.

[330]    See *Reference re Secession of Québec* [1998] 2 SCR 217 (Supreme Court of Canada) (hereinafter the *Québec* case), para 155, where the Court argued that: 'The ultimate success of . . . [unilateral] secession would be dependent on recognition by the international community.'

[331]    Caplan (n 117) 105–06.

[332]    ibid, 104.

[333]    The Badinter Commission, Opinion 1 (29 November 1991).

at least ambiguous and it may well be that in the general perception they were actually not states.

The opinions of the Badinter Commission were not formally legally binding and were not entirely followed by the EC Member States.[334] Nevertheless, they importantly shaped state practice of the entire international community and, after such a finding of the Badinter Commission, it was not disputed that the SFRY was a case of dissolution. This view was adopted even by the Security Council.[335] As a consequence, the universally accepted legal position was that the international personality of the SFRY was extinguished[336] and thus there was no applicable claim to territorial integrity. In the absence of a competing claim to territorial integrity, international recognition was ultimately declaratory. It was thus not the act of recognition but the broader international political involvement which led to the emergence of new states.[337]

The dissolution of the SFRY was an internationalised political process which also comprehended an attempt to procure a democratic political system in the newly emerged states. In this regard, two general observations need to be made: first, the absence of democratic standards did not prevent former Yugoslav republics from becoming states; and, second, the Badinter Commission applied the requirements for democracy very loosely when discussing recognition. An exception is Slovenia, in which case the Commission discussed the implemented democratic standards at great length.[338] Democracy was broadly invoked in the opinion on Macedonia,[339] while it played virtually no role in the opinions dealing with Croatia and Bosnia-Herzegovina.

The Badinter Commission found significant deficiencies in Croatia's meeting of minority rights protection standards, but the EC Member States nevertheless granted recognition.[340] In the case of Bosnia-Herzegovina, the

---

[334] *cf* ch 2, 3.1.

[335] UN Doc S/RES/757 (30 May 1992) and UN Doc S/RES/777 (19 September 1992).

[336] Security Council Resolution 777, for example, takes the view that 'the state formerly known as the Socialist Federal Republic of Yugoslavia has ceased to exist': UN Doc S/RES/777, preamble, para 2.

[337] The constitutive effects of the EC's involvement in the state creations are captured in the following anecdote: 'At the second meeting with an EC foreign ministerial troika in Zagreb on 30 June [1991], where the EC negotiators were seeking a restoration of the status quo ante, De Michelis [the Foreign Minister of Italy] approached Rupel [the Foreign Minister of Slovenia] and assured him privately that Slovenia would not be forced to rejoin Yugoslavia: "You will be an independent state. Croatia, on the other hand is a more complicated issue, since its situation is different from yours. But you'll be free in three months. You just have to stick to your agreements."' Caplan (n 117) 102–03, quoting an interview with Slovenian Foreign Minister Dimitrij Rupel.

[338] See ch 2, 3.4.2.

[339] See ch 1, 4.5.

[340] See ch 2, 3.4.3. Croatia had later improved institutional provisions for the protection of minority rights (especially in regard to the protection of the Serb minority). See the Constitutional Act on Rights of National Minorities, the Official Gazette of the Republic of Croatia No 01-081-02-3955/2 (13 December 2002). However, it is still maintained that minority

Badinter Commission held that it was unclear whether the will of its peoples really favoured the creation of a separate state.[341] Although the Commission did not deal with democratic institutions, democratic principles were invoked in the context of the right of self-determination. Only after the overwhelming majority of all citizens supported the emergence of a separate state was recognition to Bosnia-Herzegovina granted by the EC and subsequently by the entire international community.[342] Yet the referendum was boycotted by Bosnian Serbs and support for independence, although widespread, ignored the wishes of one of the constitutive peoples.[343]

In sum, the emergence of new states in the territory of the SFRY confirms that state creation in contemporary international law is a political process and does not depend on meeting the statehood criteria. The dissolution of the federation was one of the possible interpretations of the developments in the SFRY in 1991, but was not the only one. When this interpretation was adopted by the Badinter Commission, it was universally followed by state practice. As soon as the federation no longer existed, there was no applicable counterclaim to territorial integrity and thus no doubt existed that the former republics had emerged as new states. It was also a political decision that *only* republics could become states, while it remains debatable whether the new international delimitation was a matter of law or policy. These issues will be further discussed below.

The international involvement in the dissolution of the SFRY reflects a general attempt at creating a democratic political system in the newly emerged states. But after the SFRY in the universal perception no longer existed, there was little room left for international interference in the choice of the political system in each of the newly emerged states. International considerations for democracy in the territory of the SFRY remained rather general, but nevertheless reflected a tendency which was further developed in the practice of some subsequent (internationalised) state creations.

---

rights in general and the rights of Serbs in specific remain inadequately protected in practice. In its 2008 report on Croatia, Amnesty International noted: 'The 1991–95 war continued to overshadow human rights in Croatia. Despite some progress in the investigation and prosecution of war crimes, impunity remained widespread for crimes allegedly committed by members of the Croatian Army and police forces. Minorities, including Roma and Croatian Serbs, suffered discrimination, including in economic and social rights. Of at least 300,000 Croatian Serbs displaced by the conflict, approximately 130,000 were officially recorded as having returned home.' Amnesty International, Croatia, Report 2008, www.amnesty.org/en/region/croatia/report-2008.

[341] See ch 2, 3.4.4.
[342] ibid.
[343] ibid.

## 4 THE INDEPENDENCE OF MONTENEGRO

As set out above, in 1992 Montenegro and Serbia founded the FRY.[344] The two republics of this federation enjoyed a significant degree of self-government,[345] but the FRY's constitution did not foresee a mechanism for secession. In the last period of the Milošević regime in the FRY, which came to an end in October 2000,[346] political forces favouring independence became more prominent in Montenegro.[347] Opinion polls suggested that, at the end of 2000, independence was supported by roughly 50 per cent of Montenegro's population and was expressly opposed by 25 per cent.[348] The other 25 per cent of Montenegro's population did not have an opinion on this question.[349] This was a notable difference in comparison to 1998, when independence was supported by only 25 per cent, rising to 30 per cent in 1999.[350] Despite the increasing support for independence, a significant share of the population and the influential political parties opposed the change of Montenegro's territorial status.[351]

Given the experience of armed conflict associated with the dissolution of the SFRY, the international community feared that pro-independence pressures could result in Montenegro's unilateral declaration of independence and could potentially lead to turmoil in Montenegro itself and broadly in the region. In response, the EU brokered a compromise between those who favoured independence and those who advocated a continued union with Serbia. In this context, it was noted that:

> The EU worked very hard to counter, or at least postpone, any prospect of Montenegrin independence, which is felt would have a negative spillover effect on Kosovo . . . Javier Solana, the EU's High Representative for Common Foreign and Security Policy, applied long and strong pressure on Montenegro's politicians to obtain their agreement to remain in an awkward construct with Serbia that permitted both republics de facto independence in nearly all spheres. In return they were promised they could engage in a more rapid EU accession process.[352]

[344] See ch 2, 3.4.6.
[345] Each of the two republics had its own constitution and significant powers in internal matters as well as some limited competencies in foreign policy. See the Constitution of the FRY (1992), arts 6 and 7.
[346] See 'Yugoslav Opposition Supporters Enter Parliament Building', *CNN* (5 October 2000), http://transcripts.cnn.com/TRANSCRIPTS/0010/05/bn.03.html.
[347] See 'Montenegro Reviews Yugoslavia Ties', *Associated Press* (18 June 1999), www.highbeam.com/doc/1P1-23210818.html.
[348] See 'Crnogorsko javno mnjenje uoči referenduma' (23 December 2000), www.aimpress.ch/dyn/pubs/archive/data/200012/01223-005-pubs-pod.htm.
[349] ibid.
[350] ibid.
[351] ibid.
[352] The International Crisis Group Briefing No 169, Montenegro's Independence Drive (7 December 2006) 1.

The result of a compromise was the adoption of a new constitution in February 2003, which crucially differed from the one previously in force. The Constitution, inter alia, renamed the FRY as the State Union of Serbia and Montenegro (SUSM)[353] and referred to its constitutive parts as 'states'.[354]

Compared to the federal arrangement of the FRY, the SUSM was a very loose federation with only a few federal organs which had severely restricted competencies.[355] Unlike the Constitution of the FRY, the Constitution of the SUSM provided for a clear constitutional mechanism to secede. Article 60 of the Constitution of the SUSM provided:

> After the end of the period of three years, member-states shall have the right to begin the process of a change of the status of the state or to secede from the State Union of Serbia and Montenegro.
>
> The decision on secession from the State Union of Serbia and Montenegro shall be taken at a referendum.
>
> In case of secession of the state of Montenegro from the State Union of Serbia and Montenegro, international documents referring to the Federal Republic of Yugoslavia, especially the United Nations Security Council Resolution 1244, shall only apply to the state of Serbia as a successor.
>
> The member-state which resorts to the right to secession shall not inherit the right to international personality and all disputes shall be solved between the successor-state and the seceded state.
>
> In case that both states, based on the referendum procedure, opt for a change of the state-status or independence, the disputable questions of succession shall be regulated in a process analogical to the case of the former Socialist Federative Republic of Yugoslavia.[356]

This Article indicates the transitional nature of the SUSM and reflects the fact that the creation of this state was a political compromise, and the political reality was clearly expressed: Article 60 evidently acknowledged that Montenegro (not Serbia) was the federal unit likely to seek independence.

At the referendum held on 21 May 2006, independence was supported by 55.53 per cent of those who voted in a turnout of 86.49 per cent of those eligible to vote.[357] Following this vote, the Montenegrin Parliament adopted

---

[353] Constitution of the SUSM (2003), art 1.

[354] ibid, art 2.

[355] The state union had only five common ministries: internal affairs, defence, international economic affairs, domestic economic affairs and human and minority rights. ibid, arts 40–45. The Constitution further specified that only the SUSM had the international personality, but at the same time allowed the federal units some competencies in foreign policy, even membership in those international organisations which do not prescribe statehood as a condition for membership. ibid, art 14.

[356] Constitution of the SUSM (2003), art 60 (author's own translation).

[357] 'Svet ministara državne zajednice Srbija i Crna Gora, Direkcija za informisanje' (24 May 2006), www.info.gov.yu/saveznavlada/list_detalj.php?tid=1&idteksta=15132.

the Declaration of Independence on 3 June 2006[358] and on 30 June 2006 Montenegro was admitted to the UN.[359] The referendum rules were subject to the political involvement of the EU and will be discussed further below.[360]

When the dissolution of the SFRY was in question, the EC became involved after Slovenia and Croatia respectively had already declared independence.[361] In the framework of the EC's involvement, the Badinter Commission held that the dissolution of the federation was under way in the SFRY rather than attempts at unilateral secession.[362] This opinion became the universally followed legal authority which made the claim to territorial integrity inapplicable. In the case of Montenegro, the EU became involved in the process of the dissolution of the FRY prior to Montenegro's declaration of independence. To prevent possible turmoil resulting from Montenegro's attempt at unilateral secession, the EU brokered a compromise which resulted in the transitional constitution of the SUSM. The constitution of this state established a clear mechanism for secession and even a formula for continuation of the SUSM's international personality.[363] The claim to territorial integrity was thus removed and Montenegro's secession was not unilateral.

As democratic institutions in Montenegro already existed,[364] international involvement in the state creation was not coupled with the implementation of a democratic political system. However, in the process of state creation, attempts were made to achieve a broader democratic

[358] Declaration of Independence of the Republic of Montenegro, the Official Gazette of the Republic of Montenegro, No 36/06 (3 June 2006).

[359] UN Doc A/RES/60/264 (28 June 2006).

[360] See ch 3, 7.7.

[361] See ch 2, 3.4.1.

[362] ibid.

[363] Article 60 obviously intends to regulate that Serbia is the 'continuator' of the State Union's international personality and Montenegro is a newly independent state. However, there is some ambiguity because Article 60 makes references to Serbia as the 'successor' rather than 'continuator'. Moreover, Article 60 also invokes analogy to state succession after the dissolution of the SFRY, where no state continued the international personality of the former federation. The question of whether Serbia was a successor or a continuator of the State Union's international personality arose in the commercial dispute of *Republic of Serbia v Imagesat International NV* [2009] EWHC 2853 (Comm). Justice Beatson made the following decision: 'Notwithstanding the terms of the fourth paragraph of Article 60 [of the Constitution of the SUSM] . . . the term "the successor state" in Article 60 cannot be read as a reference to "successor" in the narrow sense because of the contrast in the fifth paragraph between one "successor state" and one "newly independent state" and because that paragraph provides that the part of the State Union that breaks away "shall not inherit the right to legal personality" of the State Union' (ibid, para 137). Serbia should thus be seen as the continuator, although Article 60 imprecisely uses the term 'successor', which would mean that after Montenegro's secession, both states were in the same legal position. This clearly was not the case. Serbia, for example, continued the State Union's membership of the UN, while Montenegro applied for membership as a new state.

[364] The OSCE has observed presidential and parliamentary elections in Montenegro since 1997. All of the elections observed took place in a multiparty setting and were deemed to be reasonably free and fair. For more on this, see OSCE, 'Office for Democratic Institutions and Human Rights, Elections: Montenegro', www.osce.org/odihr-elections/20443.html.

legitimacy. This issue will be discussed in more detail later in this book. Montenegro is another example which proves that state creation is an outcome of a political process rather than a 'checklist fulfilment' of the statehood criteria. The independence arrangement was achieved on the basis of an EU-brokered political compromise via the rather peculiar constitutional arrangement of the SUSM and the pre-negotiated procedural standards that paved the way to independence.

## 5  INTERNATIONAL STATE-MAKING AND DEMOCRACY-MAKING IN EAST TIMOR

Thus far, it has been established that state creation in contemporary international law is a political process rather than an exercise in satisfying the statehood criteria. If this political process is completed successfully, the change of the legal status of a certain territory is internationally accepted. The internationalisation of the political process leading towards independence also brings along an attempt at creating democratic institutions in the new state. While the emergence of new democratic states is generally channelised through the practice of (some) states, two recent developments reflect attempts at the collective creation of new democratic states under UN auspices: East Timor and Kosovo. Both territories were put under the regime of international territorial administration under binding Security Council resolutions. In both cases, attempts were made under the auspices of the UN to implement democratic institutions and procure the consent of the parent states for independence. But the legal characteristics of these processes in the two situations are not entirely overlapping.

### 5.1  East Timor: Historical Background

The division of the Timor Island dates to the Portuguese and Dutch colonial conquests. The Portuguese first arrived on the island of Timor at the beginning of the sixteenth century.[365] In the early seventeenth century, their control over the island was challenged by the Dutch.[366] The history of foreign rule of East Timor has been thoroughly examined elsewhere.[367]

---

[365] See B Singh, *East Timor, Indonesia and the World: Myths and Realities* (Singapore, Singapore Institute of International Affairs, 1995) 2.

[366] ibid, 3.

[367] See generally ibid; H Krieger and D Rauschning, *East Timor and the International Community: Basic Documents* (Cambridge, Cambridge University Press, 1997); J Taylor, *East Timor: The Price of Freedom* (London, Zed Books, 1999); P Hainsworth and S McCloskey (eds), *The East Timor Question: The Struggle for Independence from Indonesia* (London, IB Tauris, 2000); I Martin, *Self-Determination in East Timor: The United Nations, the Ballot, and International Intervention* (Boulder, Lynne Rienner, 2001).

For the purposes of this book, it should suffice to recall that the Portuguese managed to strengthen their power in the eastern part of the island of Timor while the Dutch controlled the western part. The division was officially confirmed in a treaty initially concluded in 1848[368] and unequivocally accepted by both states in 1859.[369] The colonial boundary between the Dutch-controlled western part and the Portuguese-controlled eastern part of the island of Timor was finally determined by the Treaty of The Hague in 1913.[370] This delimitation now represents the international border between the Democratic Republic of Timor-Leste and Indonesia.[371]

The colonial possessions of the Netherlands in the Indonesian archipelago were lost at the end of the Second World War. Indonesia declared independence in 1945, which was acknowledged by the Netherlands in 1949.[372] Portugal, on the other hand, retained its colonial possessions until the democratic change in the 1970s.[373] In East Timor, the democratic change in Portugal led to the creation of three main political factions,[374] the rivalries between which led to a civil war.[375] After the outbreak of hostilities in 1975, the Portuguese administration left the island and, subsequently, two factions separately declared independence.[376] While the pro-independence faction claimed that East Timor had become an independent state, the pro-Indonesian faction maintained that East Timor had acquired independence from Portugal and entered into association with Indonesia.[377] On 7 December 1975, Indonesia occupied the territory, claiming 'to be effecting [*sic*] East Timorese self-determination'.[378] On 17 July 1976, the President of Indonesia promulgated an act which declared East Timor an Indonesian province.[379] In Indonesia's view, the people of East Timor consummated their right of self-determination 'through integration with Indonesia'.[380]

In Portugal's understanding, however, East Timor was not properly decolonised and, consequently, Portugal still regarded itself as its

---

[368] For more on this, see Singh (n 365) 6.

[369] ibid.

[370] See 'Chronology of East Timor', http://rmit.nautilus.org/publications/timor-cronology.html.

[371] See N Deeley, *The International Boundaries of East Timor* (Durham, International Boundaries Research Unit, 2001), especially 25–27. See also the *East Timor* case [1995] ICJ Rep, para 10.

[372] G Davison, 'Historical Reality and the Case of East Timor' in *International Law and the Question of East Timor* (Leiden, Catholic Institute for International Relations & International Platform of Jurists for East Timor, 1995) 18

[373] Singh (n 365) 7.

[374] Taylor (n 367) 23–25.

[375] Martin (n 367) 16.

[376] ibid.

[377] ibid.

[378] R Wilde, *International Territorial Administration: How Trusteeship and the Civilizing Mission Never Went Away* (Oxford, Oxford University Press, 2008) 179.

[379] Martin (n 367) 16.

[380] ibid, 16–17.

administering power.[381] Such positions were also expressed by the UN organs. The Security Council Resolution 384 called upon:

> [A]ll States to respect the territorial integrity of East Timor as well as the inalienable right of its people to self-determination in accordance with General Assembly resolution 1514 (XV); . . . the Government of Indonesia to withdraw without delay all its forces from the Territory [of East Timor]; the Government of Portugal as administering Power to co-operate fully with the United Nations so as to enable the people of East Timor to exercise freely their right to self-determination; [and urged] . . . all States and other parties concerned to co-operate fully with the efforts of the United Nations to achieve a peaceful solution to the existing situations and to facilitate the decolonization of the Territory.[382]

These views were reaffirmed by Security Council Resolution 389[383] and by a set of General Assembly resolutions.[384] East Timor remained on the list of Non-Self-Governing Territories[385] and 'Portugal continued to assert its formal ties to East Timor throughout the occupation, notably by bringing a case about East Timor against Australia to the ICJ in 1991'.[386]

## 5.2 Transition to Statehood and Democracy

In 1999, the new Indonesian leadership indicated that it would be willing to discuss the future legal status of East Timor.[387] On 30 August 1999, following an agreement between Indonesia and Portugal,[388] a referendum on the future status of the territory was held. At the referendum, which was supervised by the UN Mission,[389] the people of East Timor rejected an

---

[381] ibid, 17.

[382] UN Doc S/RES/384 (22 December 1975), paras 1–4. A similar view was previously expressed by UN Doc A/RES/3485 (XXX) (12 December 1975).

[383] UN Doc S/RES/389 (22 April 1976), especially paras 1 and 2.

[384] UN Doc A/RES/31/53 (1 December 1976); UN Doc A/RES/32/34 (28 November 1977); UN Doc A/RES/33/39 (13 December 1978); UN Doc A/RES/34/40 (21 November 1979); UN Doc A/RES/35/27 (11 November 1980); UN Doc A/RES/36/50 (24 November 1981).

[385] See Wilde (n 378) 179–80.

[386] ibid, 181. For more on the *East Timor* case, see I Scobbie, 'The Presence of an Absent Third: Procedural Aspects of the East Timor Case in *International Law and the Question of East Timor* (Leiden, Catholic Institute for International Relations & International Platform of Jurists for East Timor, 1995) 223–42; R Clark, 'The Substance of the East Timor Case in the ICJ' in *International Law and the Question of East Timor* (Leiden, Catholic Institute for International Relations & International Platform of Jurists for East Timor, 1995) 243–50; G Simpson, 'The Politics of Self-Determination in the Case Concerning East Timor' in *International Law and the Question of East Timor* (Leiden, Catholic Institute for International Relations & International Platform of Jurists for East Timor, 1995) 251–68.

[387] ibid.

[388] See ch 3, 7.6.

[389] See UN Doc S/RES/1236, especially paras 4, 8 and 9 (7 May 1999).

autonomy arrangement within Indonesia and set the course towards independence.[390] This decision led to an outbreak of violence initiated by Indonesian forces.[391] Subsequently, on 15 September 1999, the Security Council, acting under Chapter VII, adopted Resolution 1264, which, inter alia,

> Authorizes the establishment of a multinational force under a unified command structure, pursuant to the request of the Government of Indonesia conveyed to the Secretary-General on 12 September 1999, with the following tasks: to restore peace and security in East Timor, to protect and support UNAMET in carrying out its tasks and, within force capabilities, to facilitate humanitarian assistance operations, and authorizes the States participating in the multinational force to take all necessary measures to fulfil this mandate.[392]

On 25 October 1999, the Security Council, acting under Chapter VII, adopted Resolution 1272, with which it established 'a United Nations Transitional Administration in East Timor (UNTAET), which will be endowed with overall responsibility for the administration of East Timor and will be empowered to exercise all legislative and executive authority, including the administration of justice'.[393] Resolution 1272 in its preamble also reaffirmed 'respect for the sovereignty and territorial integrity of Indonesia'.[394]

Prior to the 'release' of East Timor to independence and the transfer of power from international territorial administration to the organs of the East Timorese state, the international administrative authority supervised the creation of democratic institutions.[395] Under the auspices of the UN, elections were held on 30 August 2001 and 91.3 per cent of those eligible to vote cast their votes.[396] On 15 September 2001, the Special Representative of the United Nations Secretary-General 'swore in the 88 members of the Constituent Assembly'.[397] On 20 September 2001, the Special Representative appointed a second transitional government, the members of which were all East Timorese, and the composition of the government reflected the outcome of the elections to the assembly.[398] The UN Secretary-General noted that this was 'the first time that the executive government [was] controlled by East Timorese, albeit under the overall authority of [the UN Secretary-General's] Special Representative'.[399]

---

[390] See ch 3, 7.6.
[391] ibid.
[392] UN Doc S/RES/1264, para 3 (15 September 1999).
[393] UN Doc S/RES/1272, para 1 (25 October 1999).
[394] ibid, para 12.
[395] UN Doc S/2001/436 (2 May 2001), paras 2–7; S/2001/983 (18 October 2001), paras 4–8.
[396] UN Doc S/2001/983 (18 October 2001), para 5.
[397] ibid.
[398] ibid, para 7.
[399] ibid.

On 28 November 2001, the Constituent Assembly adopted a resolution in which it expressed support for direct presidential elections.[400] The Special Representative determined that the presidential elections would take place on 14 April 2002.[401] On 22 March 2002, the text of the new Constitution was signed by members of the East Timorese political elite, religious leaders and representatives of the civil society.[402] It was determined that the Constitution would enter into force on 20 May 2002, which was the day foreseen for the proclamation of independence.[403]

East Timor's course to independence was also affirmed in Security Council Resolution 1338, which was adopted on 31 January 2001.[404] However, this resolution was not adopted under Chapter VII of the UN Charter and it cannot be said that it was creative of a new state. The resolution was rather an affirmation of the completion of the internationalised process which resulted in the emergence of a new state. East Timor declared independence on 20 May 2002[405] and was admitted to the UN on 27 September 2002.[406]

The Constitution of East Timor makes a number of specific references to a democratic political order. Section 1 of the Constitution provides: 'The Democratic Republic of East Timor is a democratic, sovereign, independent and unitary State based on the rule of law, the will of the people and the respect for the dignity of the human person.'[407] Section 6(c) provides that one of the fundamental objectives is: 'To defend and guarantee political democracy and participation of the people in the resolution of national problems.'[408] Besides these general references to democracy, a number of other operative articles enact specific provisions which leave no doubt that the electoral process in East Timor is organised along democratic lines in a multiparty setting. Section 7 expressly enacts universal suffrage and a multiparty political system,[409] sections 46 and 47 deal with the right to political participation and with the right to vote, respectively, within the elaboration of which a multiparty political system is expressly demanded,[410] and section 70 deals specifically with political parties and the 'right of opposition'.[411]

---

[400]    UN Doc S/2002/80 (17 January 2002), para 7.
[401]    ibid, See also UN Doc S/2002/432 (17 April 2002), para 7.
[402]    ibid, para 4.
[403]    ibid, paras 2 and 4.
[404]    UN Doc S/RES/1338 (31 January 2001).
[405]    See 'East Timor: Birth of a Nation', *BBC News* (19 May 2002) http://news.bbc.co.uk/2/hi/asia-pacific/1996673.stm.
[406]    UN Doc A/RES/57/3 (27 September 2002).
[407]    Constitution of the Democratic Republic of East Timor (2002), s 1(1).
[408]    ibid, s 6(c).
[409]    ibid, s 7.
[410]    ibid, ss 46 and 47.
[411]    ibid, s 70.

According to the Constitution, the Constitutive Assembly was transformed into the Parliament.[412] The Constitution specifically regulated elections of the Parliament[413] and of the President.[414] The political system, which was designed in East Timor under the auspices of the UN, is organised along democratic (procedural) lines. The international territorial administration thus not only guided East Timor towards independence but also through the process of democratic transition and building of democratic institutions.[415]

East Timor is another example which supports the position that states in international law do not emerge on the basis of meeting the statehood criteria or historic entitlement. Its claim for independence may have been stronger because it remained on the list of self-governing territories. Nevertheless, it did not become an independent state before an internationalised process procured Indonesia's consent. The implementation of a democratic political system was an integral part of this process. East Timor's transition to both democracy and statehood ran under the auspices of the UN. This is a prominent example of practice of an internationalised creation of a new democratic state in the post-Cold War era and of the implementation of democratic institutions under the legal framework of international territorial administration.

## 6  KOSOVO AS AN ATTEMPT AT THE INFORMAL COLLECTIVE CREATION OF A DEMOCRATIC STATE

One can certainly draw parallels between Kosovo and East Timor, but the main difference is that Serbia has not given consent for Kosovo's independence. The secession of Kosovo thus remains unilateral, but has attracted a large number of recognitions. Does this mean that Kosovo is a state? And what can Kosovo tell us about the contemporary law of statehood and the role of democracy in this legal framework?

---

[412]  ibid, ss 92–101.
[413]  ibid, s 93(1).
[414]  ibid, s 76(1).
[415]  cf J d'Aspremont, 'Post-Conflict Administrations as Democracy-Building Instruments' (2008) 9 *Chicago Journal of International Law* 1. Scepticism towards such an imposition was, however, expressed by East Timor's first President, Xanana Gusmao, in the following words: 'We are witnessing . . . an obsessive acculturation to standards that hundreds of international experts try to convey . . . we absorb [these] standards just to pretend we look like a democratic society and please our masters of independence. What concerns me is the noncritical absorption of [such] standards given the current stage of the historic process we are building.' Quoted in C Foley, *The Thin Blue Line: How Humanitarianism Went to War* (London, Verso, 2008) 141.

## 6.1 Background to the Kosovo Crisis

After the medieval Serbian state lost the Battle of Kosovo in 1389,[416] the territory came under Turkish rule.[417] In modern times, the Ottoman Turks lost control over Kosovo in 1912.[418] Kosovo came under the de facto authority of the Kingdom of Serbia, but, due to the outbreak of the First World War, no treaty was ever ratified between the Kingdom of Serbia and the Ottoman Empire on the ceding of Kosovo.[419] After the First World War, Kosovo became part of the newly created Kingdom of Serbs, Croats and Slovenes in 1918.[420] In the federal Yugoslav Constitution of 1946, Kosovo was formally defined as an autonomous province within the republic of Serbia,[421] although at that time it had no organs for the exercise of self-government.[422] The autonomous status was further expanded in the last Constitution of the SFRY from 1974, which established Kosovo's political organs that were necessary for the exercise of self-government.[423]

In 1989, with Milošević already firmly in power in Serbia,[424] Kosovo's autonomous status within the federation was suspended by extra-constitutional means.[425] On 7 September 1989, Albanian members of Kosovo's dissolved assembly met in a secret meeting and proclaimed the Constitutional Act of the Republic of Kosovo.[426] This was not a declaration of independence; the act adopted by this group aimed to create a republic of Kosovo within the framework of the SFRY.

The dissolution of the SFRY[427] resulted in a push by ethnic Albanians for Kosovo to become an independent state.[428] On 22 September 1991, the unofficial parliament of Kosovo Albanians proclaimed the Resolution on Independence and Sovereignty of Kosovo.[429] The decision was subsequently

[416] For more on the Battle of Kosovo, both fact and myth, see M Vickers, *Between Serb and Albanian: A History of Kosovo* (London, Hurst, 1998) 12–16; N Malcolm, *Kosovo: A Short History* (London, Macmillan, 1998) 58–80.

[417] See Vickers (n 416) 16–21.

[418] See Malcolm (n 416) 252.

[419] ibid, 264–65. In 1913, Albania became a state by the Treaty of London; however, Kosovo Albanians were left in Serbia against their will. For more on this, see Vickers (n 416) 5–6.

[420] See Malcolm (n 416) 266. This not only applied to the Kosovo Albanians but also to Albanians living in other parts of the Kingdom of Serbs, Croats and Slovenes (later called Yugoslavia).

[421] Constitution of the Federative Peoples' Republic of Yugoslavia (1946), art 2.

[422] Vickers (n 416) 146.

[423] Constitution of the SFRY (1974), art 2. See also the Constitution of the Socialist Autonomous Province of Kosovo (1974), translated in the Helsinki Committee for Human Rights in Serbia (1998), *Kosovo: Law and Politics, Kosovo in Normative Acts Before and After 1974*, especially 41 and 45 (hereinafter *Kosovo in Normative Acts*).

[424] ibid.

[425] For more on this, see *Kosovo in Normative Acts* (n 423) 49; Malcolm (n 416) 344.

[426] ibid, 347.

[427] For more on this, see ch 2, 3.4.1.

[428] See Vickers (n 416) 251.

[429] ibid.

confirmed at an unofficial referendum, held in secrecy between 26 and 30 September 1991.[430] Reportedly, 87 per cent of all those eligible to vote cast their votes at the referendum, with 99.87 per cent voting in favour of independence.[431] Following the referendum, the unofficial parliament declared independence on 19 October 1991.[432] Recognition was granted only by Albania.[433]

On 24 May 1992, elections for the informal Kosovo assembly were held and overwhelming support was given to the Democratic League of Kosovo.[434] The League supported a peaceful revolt against the oppression, tried to internationalise developments and created the parallel institutions of the putative Republic of Kosovo.[435] Meanwhile the actions against ethnic Albanians by Serbian forces continued. Writing in 1998, Noel Malcolm noted:

> To produce an adequate survey of the human rights abuses suffered by the Albanians of Kosovo since 1990 would require several long chapters in itself. Every aspect of life in Kosovo has been affected. Using a combination of emergency measures, administrative fiats and laws authorizing the dismissal of anyone who had taken part in one-day protest strike, the Serb authorities have sacked the overwhelming majority of those Albanians who had any form of state employment in 1990. Most Albanian doctors and health workers were also dismissed from the hospitals; deaths from diseases such as measles and polio have increased, with the decline in the number of Albanians receiving vaccinations. Approximately 6,000 school-teachers were sacked in 1990 for having taken part in protests, and the rest were dismissed when they refused to comply with a new Serbian curriculum which largely eliminated teaching of Albanian literature and history.[436]

In this environment, Kosovo Albanians not only organised parallel political institutions but also a parallel system of education and healthcare.[437] Kosovo became an entity of two parallel societies in which the majority population was discriminated against in virtually all segments of life due to its ethnic background.

In November 1995, the US sponsored 'peace talks' at Dayton, Ohio, which led to the settlement of the conflicts in Bosnia-Herzegovina and Croatia by the so-called Dayton Peace Accords.[438] It is argued that the disappointment that Kosovo was not included in this settlement became a

---

[430] ibid.

[431] ibid.

[432] ibid, 252.

[433] See Crawford (n 1) 408

[434] The Democratic League of Kosovo won 96 out of 130 seats in the underground parliament. See Vickers (n 416) 260.

[435] See Malcolm (n 416) 48.

[436] ibid.

[437] ibid.

[438] For more on the Dayton Peace Accords, see Crawford (n 1) 528–30. See also ch 2, 3.4.4.

turning point in the attitude of Kosovo Albanians towards the settlement of the Kosovo question.[439] After years of peaceful resistance by the Democratic League of Kosovo, the militant Kosovo Liberation Army (KLA) now emerged.[440] Serbian oppression escalated in response.[441] The situation in Kosovo was dealt with by Security Council Resolutions 1160,[442] 1199,[443] 1203[444] and 1239.[445] The first three of these were adopted under Chapter VII. The resolutions, inter alia, called for a political solution of the situation in Kosovo,[446] condemned the violence used by organs of the FRY as well as violent actions taken by Kosovo Albanians (the latter were called 'acts of terrorism')[447] and, affirming the territorial integrity of Serbia,[448] expressed support for 'an enhanced status of Kosovo which would include a substantially greater degree of autonomy and meaningful self-administration'.[449]

While violence in Kosovo continued, negotiations between the FRY and the Kosovo Albanians aiming for a political settlement began in February 1999 at Rambouillet, France.[450] On 23 February 1999, the Rambouillet Accords: Interim Agreement for Peace and Self-Government in Kosovo were drafted.[451] The document sought to establish conditions for the termination of hostilities in Kosovo[452] and foresaw meaningful self-

---

[439] See Vickers (n 416) 287, who argues that 'the Kosovars were both surprised and bitterly disillusioned by the outcome of the Dayton Agreement, which made no specific mention of Kosovo . . . It now became apparent to all that as long as there appeared to be relative peace in Kosovo, the international community would avoid suggesting any substantive changes.'

[440] See Vickers (n 416) 292–97.

[441] ibid, 297–300.

[442] UN Doc S/RES/1160 (31 March 1998).

[443] UN Doc S/RES/1199 (23 September 1998).

[444] UN Doc S/RES/1203 (24 October 1998).

[445] UN Doc S/RES/1239 (14 May 1999).

[446] See especially UN Doc S/RES/1160, paras 1, 2 and 5; UN Doc S/RES/1199, paras 3, 4 and 5; UN Doc S/RES/1203, paras 1, 2 and 5.

[447] See especially UN Doc S/RES/1160, paras 2–3; UN Doc S/RES/1199, paras 1–2; UN Doc S/RES/1203, paras 3–4.

[448] References to the territorial integrity of the FRY appear in the preambles of UN Doc S/RES/1160, para 7; UN Doc S/RES/1199, para 13; and UN Doc S/RES/1203, para 14. The preamble to UN Doc S/RES/ 1239, para 7, comprehends a more general reference to 'the territorial integrity and sovereignty of all States in the region'.

[449] UN Doc S/RES/1160, para 5.

[450] See Crawford (n 1) 557.

[451] See Interim Agreement for Peace and Self-Government in Kosovo (23 February 1999) (hereinafter the Rambouillet Accords), http://www.state.gov/www/regions/eur/ksvo_rambouillet_text.html. The draft was prepared by the Contact Group composed of the US, the UK, Russia, France and Italy. See E Herring, 'From Rambouillet to the Kosovo Accords: NATO's War against Serbia and its Aftermath' (2000) 4 *International Journal of Human Rights* 225, 225. Herring (at 226) further argues: 'The Contact Group proposal was effectively a NATO proposal as Russia was in many ways a dissenting voice within the Contact Group.' The Rambouillet Accords foresaw signatures by the FRY, Serbia and by representatives of the Kosovo Albanians. Signatures of the US, the EU and Russia were foreseen as witnesses. See the Rambouillet Accords, ch 8, art 2,

[452] See The Rambouillet Accords (1999), ch 8, art II, paras 1 and 2.

government for Kosovo based on democratic principles.[453] In this context, the Rambouillet Accords included a constitution for Kosovo,[454] which established self-governing organs with wide powers.[455] The document further foresaw a withdrawal of Serbian military and police forces from Kosovo[456] and NATO peacekeeping.[457] Importantly, the Accords stressed the territorial integrity of the FRY in both the preamble[458] and in the operative articles.[459]

The Rambouillet Accords foresaw a comprehensive arrangement for the exercise of the right of self-determination for the Kosovo Albanians, while avoiding the use of this term. At the same time, unequivocal references to the territorial integrity of the FRY excluded the possibility of secession. Despite the wide powers of the self-governing organs in Kosovo, clear links were established between those organs and their federal counterparts.[460] Kosovo was thus meant to be an entity with a high degree of self-government, but still legally anchored within the international borders of the FRY.

The Accords were signed by the representatives of the Kosovo Albanians on 18 March 1999, while the FRY and Serbia refused to sign.[461] Following this refusal, on 24 March 1999, NATO started a military campaign against the FRY.[462] A full discussion of the legality question of the NATO intervention is outside of the scope of this book. Suffice it here to recall that given the absence of the authorisation of the use of force in the relevant Security Council resolutions,[463] the NATO intervention is generally perceived to be in breach of the prohibition of the use of force elaborated in Article 2(4) of the UN Charter.[464]

[453] ibid, ch 8, art II, para 4.

[454] ibid, ch 1.

[455] See ibid (the organs established by the proposed Constitution were the Assembly (Article II), the President of Kosovo (Article III), the Government and Administrative Organs [Article IV] and the Judiciary (Article V)).

[456] ibid, ch 7, arts IV and VI.

[457] ibid, ch 7, arts I, para 1(a).

[458] ibid, preamble, para 4. The preamble to the Rambouillet Accords, inter alia, recalls 'the commitment of the international community to the sovereignty and territorial integrity of the Federal Republic of Yugoslavia'.

[459] ibid, ch 7, art I, para 1(a).

[460] See ibid, ch 1, art II, para 5(a)(ix). In regard to the powers of the Assembly, the proposed Constitution, inter alia, foresaw '[c]ooperating with the Federal Assembly, and with the Assemblies of the Republics, and conducting relations with foreign legislative bodies'. See also ibid, ch 1, Article III, para 2(vi); in regard to the powers of the President of Kosovo, the proposed Constitution, inter alia, foresaw '[m]eeting regularly with the Federal and Republic Presidents'.

[461] See Crawford (n 1) 557–58.

[462] See D Kritsiotis, 'The Kosovo Crisis and NATO's Application of Armed Force Against the Federal Republic of Yugoslavia' (2000) 49 *ICLQ* 330, 330.

[463] See UN Doc S/RES/1160; UN Doc S/RES/1199; UN Doc S/RES/1203; UN Doc S/RES/1239.

[464] See B Simma, 'NATO, the UN and the Use of Force: Legal Aspects' (1999) 10 *EJIL* 1, 10; A Cassese, '*Ex iniuria ius oritur*: Are We Moving Towards International Legitimation of

The end of hostilities between NATO and the FRY was achieved on 9 June 1999 by the signing of the Military Technical Agreement at Kumanovo, Macedonia.[465] The Agreement reaffirmed 'deployment in Kosovo under UN auspices of effective international civil and security presences' and noted that 'the UN Security Council is prepared to adopt a resolution, which has been introduced [Resolution 1244], regarding these presences'.[466] It foresaw a 'phased withdrawal of FRY forces from Kosovo to locations in Serbia outside of Kosovo'[467] and provided that:

> [T]he international security force ('KFOR') will deploy following the adoption of the UNSCR [United Nations Security Council Resolution] . . . and operate without hindrance within Kosovo and with the authority to take all necessary action to establish and maintain a secure environment for all citizens of Kosovo and otherwise carry out its mission.[468]

The Military Technical Agreement thus severely limited the sovereign powers of the FRY (Serbia) in Kosovo and adopted the spirit of the Rambouillet Accords.[469] It is possible to argue that, given the use of force against Serbia,[470] the latter was coerced into signing this Agreement. However, similar provisions were adopted and further developed by Resolution 1244.

## 6.2  Resolution 1244  and International Territorial Administration

The international territorial administration in Kosovo was established by Resolution 1244, which was adopted under Chapter VII of the UN Charter, on 10 June 1999.[471] The preamble to Resolution 1244, inter alia, reaffirms 'the commitment of all Member States to the sovereignty and territorial integrity of the Federal Republic of Yugoslavia and other states of the region, as set out in the Final Act of Helsinki and annex 2'.[472] Yet the reso-

---

Forcible Humanitarian Countermeasures in the World Community?' (1999) 10 *EJIL* 23, 24; C Chinkin, 'Kosovo: A "Good" or "Bad" War?' (1999) 93 *American Journal of International Law* 841, 844; Kritsiotis (n 462) 340.

[465] The Military-Technical Agreement between the International Security Force ('KFOR') and the Governments of the Federal Republic of Yugoslavia and the Republic of Serbia (9 June 1999), www.nato.int/kosovo/docu/a990609a.htm.
[466] ibid, art I, para 1.
[467] ibid, art II, para 2.
[468] ibid, art I, para 2. See also ibid, Appendix B.
[469] *cf* n 451, above.
[470] See n 464, above.
[471] UN Doc S/RES/1244 (10 June 1999). Resolution 1244 refers to the FRY, but now applies to Serbia. *cf* n 356, above.
[472] ibid, preamble, para 10.

lution's operative paragraphs created an effective situation in which the FRY exercised no sovereign powers in Kosovo.[473]

In accordance with Resolution 1244, the Special Representative of the Secretary-General promulgated a document which vested wide authority in the United Nations Interim Administration Mission in Kosovo (UNMIK). Section I of the regulation (entitled 'On the Authority of the Interim Administration in Kosovo') provides:

1. All legislative and executive authority with respect to Kosovo, including the administration of the judiciary, is vested in UNMIK and is exercised by the Special Representative of the Secretary-General.
2. The Special Representative of the Secretary-General may appoint any person to perform functions in the civil administration in Kosovo, including the judiciary, or remove such person. Such functions shall be exercised in accordance with the existing laws, as specified in section 3, and any regulations issued by UNMIK.[474]

Furthermore, Resolution 1244, inter alia, identifies 'promoting the establishment, pending a final settlement, of substantial autonomy and self-government in Kosovo'[475] and '[o]rganizing and overseeing the development of provisional institutions for democratic and autonomous self-government pending a political settlement, including the holding of elections'[476] as the main responsibilities of the international civil presence.

Drawing authority from Resolution 1244, the Special Representative promulgated a document entitled 'Constitutional Framework for Provisional Self-Government'.[477] The chapter on basic provisions of the Constitutional Framework provides for the institutional setting for the exercise of Kosovo's self-government,[478] enacts an electoral system based on democratic principles[479] and stipulates for the protection of human rights.[480]

---

[473] The resolution initially demanded 'that the Federal Republic of Yugoslavia put an immediate and verifiable end to violence and repression in Kosovo, and begin and complete verifiable phased withdrawal from Kosovo of all military, police and paramilitary forces according to a rapid timetable' (ibid, 1244, para 3). It allowed for the return of 'an agreed number of Yugoslav and Serb military personnel' (ibid, para 4) after the withdrawal. However, as follows from Annex 2, to which the commitment to territorial integrity expressed in the preamble refers, this return was merely symbolic (ibid, Annex 2, art 6) and the number of personnel was severely limited (ibid, Annex 2, note 2). The resolution further decided to deploy 'international civil and security presences' (ibid, para 5), requested 'the Secretary-General to appoint, in consultation with the Security Council, a Special Representative to control the implementation of the international civil and security presence' (ibid, para 6) and authorised 'Member States and relevant international organizations to establish the international security presence in Kosovo' (ibid, para 7).
[474] UNMIK/REG/1999/1 (25 July 1999), s 1.
[475] ibid, para 11(a).
[476] ibid, para 11(c).
[477] UNMIK/REG/2001/9 (15 May 2001) (hereinafter the Constitutional Framework).
[478] ibid, ch 1.
[479] ibid, ch 9.1.3.
[480] ibid, ch 3.

The Constitutional Framework also expresses the commitment of Kosovo's self-governing institutions 'through parliamentary democracy [to] enhance democratic governance and respect for the rule of law in Kosovo'.[481] It further provides that 'Kosovo shall be governed democratically through legislative, executive, and judicial bodies and institutions'[482] and enumerates the promotion and respect of the democratic principles among those principles, which shall be observed by the self-governing institutions.[483] The Special Representative of the UN Secretary-General thus promulgated a legal instrument which implemented democratic institutions.[484] The process of democratic transition in Kosovo was thus carried out under the auspices of the UN, which, as a universal organisation, thereby implemented a political system that is not universally accepted as the only legitimate one.

The democratic institutional design of the Kosovo self-governing organs under the Constitutional Framework was not without its flaws. While the institutions of self-government were vested with powers in the exercise of effective control over the territory of Kosovo which can be compared to those of the authorities of sovereign states, the Constitutional Framework foresaw an appointed supervisor of the democratic process, ie, the Special Representative of the UN Secretary General, to whom the self-governing organs remained subordinated.[485]

The Constitutional Framework did not foresee the organs of the FRY or Serbia having any authority over the decision-making of Kosovo's self-governing institutions. Thus, although Resolution 1244 states that the aim of the interim administration is that 'the people of Kosovo can enjoy substantial autonomy within the Federal Republic of Yugoslavia',[486] the effective situation in fact established Kosovo's autonomy within the interim administration. Indeed, 'UNMIK has assumed what is effectively (though not in name) the federal-type role of the Serb and FRY authorities, because these authorities failed to perform that role in the past'.[487] Kosovo thus became an internationally administered territory without being put under the international trusteeship system of Chapter XII of the UN Charter.[488]

---

[481]  ibid, preamble, para 7.

[482]  ibid, ch 1.1.4.

[483]  ibid, ch 2.b.

[484]  *cf* ch 1, 2.1.

[485]  The Constitutional Framework, ch 12.

[486]  UN Doc S/RES/1244, para 10. But see also W O'Neill, *Kosovo: An Unfinished Peace* (Boulder, Lynne Rienner, 2002) 30, especially the following observation: 'No one knew what the terms "substantial autonomy" and "meaningful self-administration" really meant. What united all Kosovo Albanians, regardless of their political party loyalties, was full independence from Serbia and what was left of the FRY. They did not want to hear about autonomy, however defined.'

[487]  Wilde (n 378) 595.

[488]  See M Bothe and T Marauhn, 'UN Administration of Kosovo and East Timor: Concept, Legality and Limitations of Security Council-Mandated Trusteeship Administration' in

While establishing international administration, Resolution 1244 did not define a future territorial status of Kosovo, but called for a political process leading towards a final settlement.[489] However, in this period of unclear future status, the international administration, which had been established to solve the governance problem, ended up 'affecting or creating a sovereignty problem'.[490] The political process aiming to lead towards a final settlement was thus greatly influenced by the unclear future status, the presence of international administration and the fact that Serbia had no sovereign powers in Kosovo.

## 6.3 Failed Attempts at Settlement of the Final Status

On 24 October 2005, the Security Council expressed its support for the commencement of a political process leading towards Kosovo's final status[491] and former Finnish President Martti Ahtisaari was appointed Special Envoy of the UN Secretary-General on Kosovo's status talks.[492]

After more than a year of unproductive negotiations, Special Envoy Ahtisaari recommended internationally supervised independence, with the continued presence of international territorial administration.[493] In a letter dated 26 March 2007, the Special Envoy observed that: 'Belgrade demands Kosovo's autonomy within Serbia, while Pristina will accept nothing short of independence.'[494] In his view, 'the negotiation's potential to produce any mutually agreeable outcome on Kosovo's status [was] exhausted'.[495] At the same time, eight years of governance in separation from Serbia created an irreversible reality and, according to Ahtisaari, Serbia could not regain any degree of control over Kosovo without the violent opposition of Kosovo Albanians.[496] The effective situation suggested that the only alternative to independence was the status quo. However, this option was also rejected by Ahtisaari, arguing that its uncertain status prevents Kosovo's democratic and economic development.[497]

Serbia and Russia rejected the Ahtisaari Plan and Russia made it clear that it would veto any draft Security Council resolution expressing support

---

C Tomuschat (ed.), *Kosovo and the International Community: A Legal Assessment* (The Hague, Kluwer Law International, 2001) 230–35.

[489] *cf* n 471, above.
[490] See Wilde (n 378) 605.
[491] UN Doc S/PRST/2005/51 (24 October 2005).
[492] See the Security Council Report, *Kosovo Historical Chronology* (hereinafter *Kosovo Historical Chronology*), www.securitycouncilreport.org/site/c.glKWLeMTIsG/b.2693009.
[493] UN Doc S/2007/168 (16 March 2007) (hereinafter the Ahtisaari Plan).
[494] ibid, para 2.
[495] ibid, para 3.
[496] ibid, para 7.
[497] ibid, para 4.

for Kosovo's independence.[498] As a result, the Ahtisaari Plan was not endorsed by the Security Council.

Another round of negotiations followed and Serbia proposed the so-called 'Åland Islands Model' for Kosovo,[499] which would be put in place for 20 years. Once again, it became clear that the Kosovo Albanians were not willing to accept anything but independence and the additional round of negotiations merely reaffirmed the observations of Special Envoy Ahtisaari – a mutual agreement on the future status of Kosovo was not achievable and thus the political process called for by Resolution 1244 failed.[500]

Officials of the US and of the EU soon expressed a general willingness to recognise Kosovo as an independent state.[501] Ultimately, Kosovo's declaration of independence on 17 February 2008 came as no surprise. Media reports in the weeks and days prior to the declaration suggest that it was coordinated between Kosovo officials, on the one hand, and part of the EU and the US, on the other.[502] It thus became obvious that part of the

[498] For more on this, see *Kosovo Historical Chronology* (n 492).

[499] 'Belgrade's Proposal Freezes Kosovo Status for 20 Years', *Tanjug* (20 November 2007), http://www.srbija-damask.org/Arapski/News.html. The so-called Åland Islands Model is summarised in the following terms: 'Serbia's sole jurisdiction in the case of Kosovo would be in the sphere of the foreign policy, control of the borders, protection of the Serb religious and cultural heritage. Serbia would solely be in charge of defence and this would not be applied in Kosovo . . . Kosovo would be solely in charge of its budget, economic policy, agriculture, the media, education, protection of the environment, youth, sports, fiscal policy, internal affairs, health care, energy, infrastructure and employment. Kosovo would independently elect and develop its institutions, and Serbia would not interfere in this. Kosovo would have legislative powers in the spheres of its sole jurisdiction and in other cases determined by the agreement. Serbia could not change and abolish laws in Kosovo, Kosovo would have executive powers, an independent and complete judicial system in charge of disputes in the sole jurisdiction of Kosovo and in other cases determined in the agreement. Belgrade's proposal calls for a transitional period under EU monitoring and the presence of international judges. In keeping with the example of Finland and the Aland Islands, in the case of Kosovo Serbia is the subject of international law and Kosovo is offered as its exclusive jurisdiction the negotiating of agreements with other states and international organizations. Kosovo prepares agreements in consultations with Serbia, while Belgrade formally signs the agreements along with the signature with Kosovo and Metohija.'

[500] Kosovo Troika Press Communiqué, the Baden Conference (28 November 2007), www.consilium.europa.eu/ueDocs/cms_Data/docs/pressData/en/declarations/97300.pdf.

[501] See 'Talks on Kosovo Hit a Dead End, Rice Says', *New York Times* (8 December 2007), http://query.nytimes.com/gst/fullpage.html?res=9F06E4DB1F3EF93BA35751C1A9619C8B 63&scp=94&sq=kosovo&st=nyt.

[502] See 'Here Comes Kosovo', *New York Times* (14 February 2008), www.nytimes. com/2008/02/14/opinion/14cohen.html?scp=57&sq=kosovo&st=nyt. See also the protocol drafted (in Slovene) by an official of the Slovenian Foreign Ministry after meeting with representatives of the United States Department of State on 24 December 2007 (in the first half of 2008 Slovenia held the Presidency of the Council of the EU), which leaked to the media (on file with author). The protocol proves that Kosovo's declaration of independence was coordinated between Kosovo's leaders on the one hand and the US and the EU on the other. The following notes are especially instructive: 'The prevailing view in the EU is that independence of Kosovo needs to be declared after the elections in Serbia (20 January [2008] and 3 February [2008]) . . . The session of the Kosovo Parliament, at which [the] declaration of independence would be adopted, should take place on Sunday, so RF [the Russian

international community decided to implement the Ahtisaari Plan with-out a Security Council resolution.

On 9 April 2008, Kosovo's Parliament adopted the Constitution of the Republic of Kosovo.[503] The Constitution affirms Kosovo's commitment to democracy in both the preamble[504] and in the operative articles,[505] and pro-claims that Kosovo 'is a democratic Republic based on the principle of separation of powers and the checks and balances among them'.[506] Apart from these generally expressed commitments, the Constitution establishes the institutions of a democratic political system. It provides for periodic elections of the parliament[507] and of the president,[508] and elections based on a secret ballot and on the proportionality electoral system.[509] There is no explicit reference to multiparty elections, yet the multiparty environment is implied in some of the provisions, such as those regulating the composition of the parliament,[510] the competencies of the president[511] and the formation of the government.[512]

However, the competencies of Kosovo's constitutional organs remain subordinated to the international territorial administration. Article 147 of the Constitution reads:

> Notwithstanding any provision of this Constitution, the International Civilian Representative shall, in accordance with the Comprehensive Proposal for the Kosovo Status Settlement dated 26 March 2007, be the final authority in Kosovo regarding interpretation of the civilian aspects of the said Comprehensive Proposal. No Republic of Kosovo authority shall have jurisdiction to review, diminish or otherwise restrict the mandate, powers and obligations.[513]

The Constitution thus not only accepts limits on Kosovo's sovereignty and on competencies of its constitutional organs but also unequivocally subscribes Kosovo to the Ahtisaari Plan.[514]

Federation] has no time to call for the meeting of the UNSC [United Nations Security Council]. In the mean time the first recognitions could already arrive . . . The United States . . . after Kosovar authorities declare independence, will be among the first to recognise Kosovo. The United States strives for recognition of Kosovo by as many non-EU states as possible. The United States is lobbying with Japan, Turkey, Arab states, that have showed readiness to recognise Kosovo without hesitation . . . The United States is currently drafting a constitution with Kosovars. The situation on the ground is favourable. The United States hopes that Kosovars are not going to lose self-confidence, as this could result in United States' loss of influence' (author's translation from Slovene, on file with author).

[503] Constitution of the Republic of Kosovo (2008).
[504] ibid, preamble, para 1.
[505] ibid, arts 1(1), 4, 7, 55(2) and 125.
[506] ibid, art 4(1).
[507] ibid, art 66.
[508] ibid, art 86.
[509] ibid, art 64.
[510] ibid.
[511] ibid, art 84(14).
[512] ibid, arts 95(1) and 95(5).
[513] ibid, art 147.
[514] *cf* n 493, above.

## 6.4  The ICJ's Advisory Opinion on Kosovo

On 8 October 2008, the United Nations General Assembly submitted a request for an Advisory Opinion from the ICJ on the unilateral declaration of independence of Kosovo. The question posed to the Court reads: 'Is the unilateral declaration of independence by the Provisional Institutions of Self-Government of Kosovo in accordance with international law?'[515] The question did not ask whether Kosovo was a state; whether recognition of Kosovo was lawful; and whether the Kosovo Albanians are a people for the purpose of the right of self-determination or even whether they have a 'right to remedial secession'.

In the Opinion of 22 July 2010, the Court drew a distinction between the question posed by the General Assembly and the question which was dealt with by the Supreme Court of Canada in the *Québec* case.[516] While the question in the *Québec* case specifically asked whether the organs of Québec had 'the right to effect the secession of Quebec from Canada unilaterally',[517] the ICJ noted that the question referred to it did not ask whether or not there existed a specific right vested in Kosovo in general or in the institutions of its self-government in particular to declare independence.[518]

The Opinion thus focused only on the question of whether or not the unilateral declaration of independence was *itself* in accordance with international law. In so doing, the Court identified three possible sources of illegality: (i) general international law; (ii) Resolution 1244; and (iii) the Constitutional Framework of Kosovo.[519]

With regard to general international law, the Court held that the unilateral character of a declaration of independence alone does not render such a declaration illegal.[520] In the Court's words:

> [T]he illegality attached to [some other] declarations of independence . . . stemmed not from the unilateral character of these declarations as such, but from the fact that they were, or would have been, connected with the unlawful use of force or other egregious violations of norms of general international law, in particular those of a peremptory character *(jus cogens)*.[521]

Thus, according to the ICJ, a declaration of independence may be illegal under *some circumstances*, but the unilateral character alone does not make it illegal.

---

[515] UN Doc A/RES/63/3 (8 October 2008).
[516] *Accordance with International Law of the Unilateral Declaration of Independence in Respect of Kosovo (Request for Advisory Opinion)*, Advisory Opinion, ICJ Rep 2010 (the *Kosovo Advisory Opinion*), para 55.
[517] Quoted in ibid, para 55.
[518] The *Kosovo Advisory Opinion*, para 56.
[519] ibid, para 78.
[520] ibid, para 81.
[521] ibid, para 81.

The Court further identified Resolution 1244 as the *lex specialis* which could potentially prohibit a unilateral declaration of independence. But, according to the Court, Resolution 1244, 'did not bar the authors of the declaration . . . from issuing a declaration of independence from the Republic of Serbia'.[522]

The formulation 'did not bar the *authors of the declaration*' seems to be very carefully chosen. Indeed, in the Court's view, independence was not declared by Kosovo's institutions of self-government, 'but rather [by] persons who acted together in their capacity as representatives of the people of Kosovo outside the framework of the interim administration'.[523] The Court thus left open a possibility that the prohibition was addressed to Kosovo's institutions of self-government, but, in light of the Court's finding on the informal identity of the authors of the unilateral declaration of independence, this question had become irrelevant.

It is also important to note that the Court did not build its argument entirely on its pronouncement on the identity of the authors of the declaration of independence. Discussing Resolution 1244 more broadly, the Court held that a prohibition of a declaration of independence cannot 'be derived from the language of the resolution understood in its context and considering its object and purpose. The language of Security Council resolution 1244 (1999) is at best ambiguous in this regard'.[524] According to the Court, the object and purpose of the resolution was the creation of the interim administration and not the final settlement of Kosovo's territorial status.[525] If this argument is accepted, the final settlement of the territorial status of Kosovo falls outside the purview of Resolution 1244 and therefore a unilateral declaration of independence is not prohibited, no matter who the authors of the Declaration were.

In relation to the possible illegality under the Constitutional Framework, the Court argued as follows:

> The Court has already held . . . that the declaration of independence of 17 February 2008 was not issued by the Provisional Institutions of Self-Government, nor was it an act intended to take effect, or actually taking effect, within the legal order in which those Provisional Institutions operated. It follows that the authors of the declaration of independence were not bound by the framework of powers and responsibilities established to govern the conduct of the Provisional Institutions of Self-Government. Accordingly, the Court finds that the declaration of independence did not violate the Constitutional Framework.[526]

In the context of the Constitutional Framework, the Court thus based its argument only on its prior pronouncement that the declaration

---

[522] ibid, para 119
[523] ibid, para 109.
[524] ibid, para 118.
[525] ibid, para 114.
[526] ibid, para 121.

of independence was not issued by Kosovo's institutions of self-government, but rather by a group of individuals.[527] Unlike in the context of Resolution 1244, the Court did not try to make a broader argument.

The ICJ's reasoning is not without its controversies, yet a thorough analysis of the Advisory Opinion is not the purpose of this book.[528] The Court ultimately concluded that 'the adoption of the declaration of independence of 17 February 2008 did not violate general international law, Security Council resolution 1244 (1999) or the Constitutional Framework. Consequently [the Court held that] the adoption of that declaration did not violate any applicable rule of international law'.[529] As pointed out earlier in the Opinion, these findings did not have any implications for the question of whether or not Kosovo is a state and whether or not recognition of Kosovo is allowed or prohibited under international law.[530]

## 6.5  Issues of Statehood and Recognition

In terms of the statehood criteria, one could question whether Kosovo meets the criterion of 'government'.[531] In the general interpretation of this criterion, it is not enough that a government merely exists; it also needs to be effective in the territory of the state in question as well as to have the capacity to act independently of any other government.[532] In this regard, the International Commission of Jurists held in the *Åland Islands* case that Finland did not become a sovereign state 'until the public authorities had become strong enough to assert themselves throughout the territories of that State without the assistance of foreign troops'.[533]

Kosovo's Declaration of Independence[534] and the subsequently adopted Constitution of the Republic of Kosovo[535] both subscribe Kosovo to the Ahtisaari Plan and to Resolution 1244. Kosovo thus legally accepted the

---

[527]  See n 523, above.

[528]  For more on this, see generally J Vidmar, 'The Kosovo Advisory Opinion Scrutinized' (2011) 24 *Leiden Journal of International Law* 355.

[529]  The *Kosovo Advisory Opinion*, para 122.

[530]  ibid, para 51.

[531]  See ch 1, 3.1.

[532]  See, for example, Aust (n 38) 136–37.

[533]  The *Åland Islands* case (1920) LNOJ Spec Supp. 3 (the International Committee of Jurists) 8–9. It is, however, questionable to what degree this decision has been followed in the subsequent practice of new state creations.

[534]  See n 499, above.

[535]  Kosovo's Parliament adopted the Constitution of the Republic of Kosovo on 9 April 2009. Article 147 of the Constitution provides: 'Notwithstanding any provision of this Constitution, the International Civilian Representative shall, in accordance with the Comprehensive Proposal for the Kosovo Status Settlement dated 26 March 2007, be the final authority in Kosovo regarding interpretation of the civilian aspects of the said Comprehensive Proposal. No Republic of Kosovo authority shall have jurisdiction to review, diminish or otherwise restrict the mandate, powers and obligations . . .'

continuous presence of the supreme international authority which imposes notable restraints on its sovereignty. It is therefore obvious that Kosovo does not have an independent government. Kosovo evidently has a government independent of Serbia, but what is required under the statehood criteria is a government independent of any other government and not only independent of a particular one.

One possibility would be to regard Kosovo as a protected state, with a status similar to that of Bosnia-Herzegovina.[536] However, there is one important difference between the two situations. Bosnia-Herzegovina accepted restraints on its sovereignty voluntarily, through the Dayton Accords in 1995,[537] when it was already a state and a member of the UN,[538] while it is highly questionable whether Kosovo accepted the restraints on its sovereignty voluntarily. It obviously had to accept them in order to comply with the pre-existing legal arrangement governing its territory. In addition, Kosovo's government is not effective in the entire territory of Kosovo.[539]

Non-effective entities have emerged as states before. In the age of decolonisation, the exercise of the right of self-determination was often regarded as more important than effectiveness.[540] Even in non-colonial situations, effectiveness considerations were not applied strictly when new states were created: Croatia and Bosnia-Herzegovina became states, although their governments did not exercise effective control over their respective territories.[541] As discussed at an earlier point in this book, in contemporary practice, states do not emerge by meeting the Montevideo criteria and can also emerge when they evidently do not meet them.[542]

In terms of the (il)legality of Kosovo's (attempt at) state creation, the potential illegality can be traced back to NATO's use of force.[543] Such an

---

[536] See the General Framework Agreement for Peace in Bosnia and Herzegovina (the Dayton Accords), art X (14 December 1995), http://www.ohr.int/dpa/default.asp?content_id=380. Created in the context of a violent attempt to dismember Bosnia-Herzegovina, the current federal arrangement is a compromise, brokered by the US. The parties to the Dayton Accords were the Republic of Bosnia-Herzegovina, the Republic of Croatia, the FRY and two newly created entities in Bosnia-Herzegovina: Republika Srpska and the Federation of Bosnia and Herzegovina. The Dayton Accords also implemented the institution of the High Representative, which severely limits the sovereign powers of the authorities of Bosnia-Herzegovina.

[537] For more on this, see Crawford (n 1) 528–30.

[538] Bosnia-Herzegovina became a member of the UN on 22 May 1992. See UN Doc A/RES/46/237 (22 May 1992). The Badinter Commission expressed the view that Bosnia-Herzegovina became a state on 6 March 1992: the Badinter Commission, Opinion 11 (16 July 1993), para 6. This critical date for Bosnia-Herzegovina's becoming a state was also affirmed by the ICJ: the *Bosnia Genocide* case (n 259).

[539] Kosovo's government does not exercise effective control over the predominantly Serb-settled northern parts of Kosovo. See, for example, 'Walking the Kosovo Tightrope', *The Guardian* (29 June 2009), www.guardian.co.uk/commentisfree/2009/jun/29/kosovo-eu-un-serbia.

[540] See M Shaw, *International Law* (Cambridge, Cambridge University Press, 2008) 205.

[541] See Raič (n 228) 398.

[542] See ch 1, 3.1.

[543] See n 464, above.

argument is not without its difficulties. According to the ICJ, Kosovo's declaration of independence was proclaimed by a group of individuals drawing their legitimacy from the legal framework created by Resolution 1244.[544] It is therefore difficult to accept that Kosovo's declaration of independence stems directly from the NATO intervention and that the obligation to withhold recognition applies *erga omnes*, as a consequence of a violation of *jus cogens*.[545] Resolution 1244 interrupts the legal link between the (illegal) use of force and the state creation. Even para 81 of the *Kosovo Advisory Opinion* suggests that Kosovo's (attempt at) unilateral secession cannot be attributed to the use of force or, more generally, to a violation of *jus cogens*.[546]

In light of references to the territorial integrity of the FRY (now Serbia),[547] it is arguable that a non-consensual state creation was prohibited under Resolution 1244. However, the ICJ rejected the view that Resolution 1244 prohibited a declaration of independence.[548] It remains questionable whether Resolution 1244 prohibits the recognition of Kosovo. States expressly denying recognition and states granting recognition do not have unitary answers to this question.[549] In some previous situations of non-recognition stemming from the illegality of a state creation, there existed specific resolutions of UN organs explicitly calling for non-recognition.[550] It remains unclear whether 'a binding resolution or decision of a UN body is necessary' for an obligation of non-recognition to be triggered,[551] but, nevertheless, 'such a resolution or decision makes the obligation definitive'.[552]

---

[544] See n 523, above.

[545] See J d'Aspremont, 'Regulating Statehood' (2007) 20 *Leiden Journal of International Law* 649, 663.

[546] The *Kosovo Advisory Opinion*, para 81.

[547] See n 472, above.

[548] See n 524, above.

[549] Consider Russia's view: 'The Russian Federation continues to recognize the Republic of Serbia within its internationally recognized borders. The 17 February declaration by the local assembly of the Serbian province of Kosovo is a blatant breach of the norms and principles of international law – above all of the Charter of the United Nations – which undermines the foundations of the system of international relations. That illegal act is an open violation of the Republic of Serbia's sovereignty, the high-level Contact Group accords, Kosovo's Constitutional Framework, Security Council resolution 1244 (1999) – which is the basic document for the Kosovo settlement – and other relevant decisions of the Security Council.' UN Doc S/PV.5839 (18 February 2008) 6. On the other hand, it was argued on behalf of the UK that: 'Resolution 1244 (1999) placed no limits on the scope of that status outcome, and paragraph 11 (a) of the resolution is clear that the substantial autonomy which Kosovo was to enjoy within the Federal Republic of Yugoslavia was an interim outcome pending a final settlement'. ibid, 18.

[550] See ch 1, 3.5.

[551] R McCorquodale, 'The Creation and Recognition of States' in S Blay, R Piotrowicz and BM Tsamenyi (eds), *Public International Law: An Australian Perspective* (Melbourne, Oxford University Press, 2005) 197

[552] ibid.

Non-recognition has been called for in a number of General Assembly resolutions[553] and there has been one instance where the Security Council acted under Chapter VII when it called for non-recognition: after Southern Rhodesia proclaimed itself a republic.[554] In some other instances, the Security Council issued non-Chapter VII resolutions, yet even when these resolutions were in question, virtually full compliance with the obligation to withhold recognition was achieved.

It needs to be noted that collective non-recognition has also been practiced 'in a number of other situations without a formal United Nations resolution to that effect'.[555] This suggests that states perceive themselves to be legally bound to withhold recognition in situations of illegal state creations even in the absence of resolutions of the UN organs explicitly calling for non-recognition. The added value of resolutions which explicitly call for non-recognition seems to be that they set out the reasons for non-recognition and leave little room for states to interpret the question of illegality of a state creation.

In the example of Kosovo, a specific resolution calling for non-recognition is absent. The interpretation of whether there exists an obligation to collectively withhold recognition under Resolution 1244 is left to states and there is no unitary answer to this question. The number of recognitions implies that at least 92 states believe that an obligation to withhold recognition does not apply under Resolution 1244.

An attempt was made to secure the approval of its parent state and confirm Kosovo's path to independence with a Security Council resolution. After this attempt failed, a group of states decided to implement the Ahtisaari Plan without Serbia's consent and/or a Security Council resolution.[556] Kosovo declared independence with the prior approval of a number of states, which also promised recognition in advance.[557] Unlike in a number of other post-Cold War situations, international involvement did not procure a consensual removal of the applicable counterclaim to territorial integrity; rather, a group of states granted recognition to an attempt at unilateral secession. With 92 recognitions to date,[558] recognition of Kosovo is widespread, but is far from universal.

---

[553] See ch 1, 3.5.
[554] See UN Doc S/RES/277 (18 March 1970).
[555] Crawford (n 1) 159
[556] See ch 2, 6.3.
[557] See n 502, above.
[558] See 'Who Recognized Kosova as an Independent State', www.kosovothanksyou.com.

## 6.6  Kosovo: An Attempt at the Collective Creation of a State and its Political System

Kosovo was put under international territorial administration because of the governance problem. This problem was not associated with the absence of democratic practices but with gross human rights violations and a grave humanitarian situation. The international territorial administration, whose actions are attributable to the UN,[559] implemented a democratic institutional design and thus carried out the process of democratic transition.[560] The situation in Kosovo was thus comparable to that in East Timor.[561] Yet, in the case of Kosovo, no negotiated solution on its future status was arrived at. Ultimately, Kosovo declared independence unilaterally. Although unilateral, independence was declared following the prior approval of a number of states, which also promised recognition in advance. But there was no approval of the parent state.

From the perspective of international law, unilateral secession is not per se illegal.[562] This also follows from para 81 of the *Kosovo Advisory Opinion*. It is very unlikely, though, that unilateral secession would result in a new state creation. In the UN Charter era, states tend to give preference to the observance of the principle of territorial integrity of other states. Despite the relatively high number of new state creations after the end of the Cold War, in this period no new state has managed to emerge unambiguously against a competing claim to territorial integrity by its parent state. It remains questionable whether Kosovo is an exception to this practice and whether parallels could be drawn to Bangladesh, which could be, arguably, characterised as an example of a successful unilateral secession in the UN Charter era.[563]

There exist doubts as to whether Kosovo meets the statehood criteria, but entities that did not satisfy them have become states before. Indeed, it was demonstrated earlier in this book that the question of whether or not an entity is a state cannot be reduced to the question of whether it objectively meets the statehood criteria.[564] Kosovo is an example which shows that states do not emerge as a matter of self-evident fact upon meeting the statehood criteria. Its statehood is neither self-evident nor a question of fact; it is a matter of legal status which remains ambiguous. Before the number of recognitions was granted, it was clear that Kosovo was not a state. This is now unclear and remains unclear even after the *Kosovo Advisory*

---

[559] See Bothe and Marauhn (n 488) 228.
[560] *cf* ch 2, 6.2.
[561] See ch 2, 5.
[562] See ch 1, 3.6.
[563] *cf* ch 3, 6.3.1.
[564] See ch 1, 3.1.

*Opinion*, where the ICJ avoided any reference in respect of Kosovo's legal status.[565]

Is Kosovo a state? If so, would it be a state without the recognitions that have been granted? If recognition is always declaratory, why should Kosovo be considered a state now if it was not after the declaration of independence in 1991?[566] The FRY's claim to territorial integrity existed then and Serbia's claim to territorial integrity exists now. The government which declared independence in 1991 was not the effective government of Kosovo.[567] The government which declared independence in 2008 was not an independent government of Kosovo.[568] Similar legal considerations to Kosovo's status of a state under international law therefore existed in 1991 as exist now. Notably, however, after the declaration of independence in 1991, recognition was granted only by Albania, while after the 2008 declaration of independence, recognition has been granted by 92 states.[569]

The most probable answer is that an informally practised collective recognition aimed to have the effects of a collective state creation. The problem, however, is that the new state creation is not acknowledged by the entire international community. To put it differently, if recognition has constitutive effects, are 92 recognitions enough for a state creation? How many and whose recognitions are in such circumstances necessary for an entity to be considered a state? On the other hand, whose and how many *withholdings* of recognition are necessary for an entity *not* to be considered a state? Is Kosovo a state because it has been recognised by 92 states or is it not a state because it has been recognised *only* by 92 states? No doubt, this dilemma well illustrates the problem of the constitutive theory, yet it also illustrates the shortcoming of the declaratory theory. It is precisely the high number of recognitions which led to the situation in which Kosovo's legal status is at least ambiguous.

It is possible to make an objection that Kosovo is a misuse of the act of recognition for the purpose of an attempt at state creation,[570] or even that recognition was granted on political and not legal grounds. Such arguments are not persuasive. Indeed, recognition is always a political act which is, however, capable of having legal consequences.[571] Only an obligation to withhold recognition may be required by law,[572] while the

---

[565] The ICJ specifically observed that the question posed to the Court did 'not ask whether or not Kosovo has achieved statehood': the *Kosovo* Advisory Opinion, para 51.

[566] The unofficial parliament of the Kosovo Albanians issued a declaration of independence on 22 September 1991. See M Weller, *Contested Statehood: Kosovo's Struggle for Independence* (Oxford, Oxford University Press, 2009) 39.

[567] See ch 2, 6.2.

[568] See ch 2, 6.1.

[569] See n 558, above.

[570] *cf* C Warbrick, 'States and Recognition in International Law' in M Evans (ed), *International Law*, 2nd edn (Oxford, Oxford University Press, 2006) 262.

[571] *cf* ch 1, 3.2.

[572] ibid.

decision on whether or not recognition would be granted is a matter of policy.

It was shown above that international law does not prohibit unilateral secession and actually presupposes that the ultimate success of an attempt at unilateral secession 'would be dependent on recognition by the international community'.[573] Moreover, the obligation to withhold recognition is not triggered by the unilateral character of a claim to independence.[574] It thus follows that where an entity does not emerge illegally,[575] nothing precludes foreign states from granting recognition. Granting recognition to an attempt at unilateral secession is then neither illegal nor extra-legal under international law. If recognition of an attempt at unilateral secession is granted universally, the political act of recognition may well create a new state.

This mode of state creation requires that recognition is virtually universal and may effectively be seen as a tool of collective state creation. If recognition of an attempt at collective state creation is not virtually universal, the legal status of the entity in question will remain ambiguous and may only be clarified over time. Such an ambiguity is a consequence of the concept of the state in international law. Statehood is a legal status and not an objective fact. As such, it can sometimes be ambiguous.

The creation of Kosovo as a state is a political process that has not been entirely completed and the statehood criteria in this process are virtually irrelevant. Initially, the international involvement tried to procure Serbia's consent and when this did not yield any results, an attempt was made through 'constitutive recognition'. In this political process, the democratic institutions were also implemented under UN auspices. Yet UN organs did not confirm Kosovo's path to independence. At the same time, some recognising states find democratic development a factor that may legitimise Kosovo's secession. These arguments will be further considered below when the doctrine of remedial secession is discussed.[576] The commitment to a democratic political system is also expressed in Kosovo's Constitution, which was also subject to internationalised drafting.

Kosovo is not only an example of an internationalised political transition to statehood but also an attempt at an internationalised creation of a new *democratic* state.

---

[573] The *Québec* case (n 330), para 155.
[574] See ch 1, 3.2.
[575] For discussion on illegal entities, see ch 1, 3.4.
[576] See ch 3, 6.

## 7 CONCLUSION

The post-Cold War practice confirms that new states do not emerge auto-matically upon meeting the statehood criteria.[577] In order to emerge as a state, an entity needs to overcome the hurdle of a competing claim to ter-ritorial integrity.[578] This is achieved (or not) in a political process.

In a number of post-Cold War situations, new states emerged as a mat-ter of domestic consensus. Ethiopia consented to the secession of Eritrea and waived its claim to territorial integrity by recognising Eritrea as an independent state. Sudan consented to South Sudan's independence in the peace agreement and implemented constitutional provisions which enabled South Sudan's path to independence. The federations of the Soviet Union and Czechoslovakia were dissolved on the basis of domestic political processes. In the absence of an applicable claim to territorial integrity and, indeed, in the absence of a parent state, there could be no doubt that the former republics of these federations had become inde-pendent states.

In other situations, new states emerged upon international involve-ment. In the SFRY, the legal position of the Badinter Commission achieved internationally what in the Soviet Union and Czechoslovakia had been achieved domestically and consensually – the international personality of the federation was extinguished through international practice and, as soon as the parent state no longer existed, its former republics emerged as independent states.

East Timor and Montenegro were ultimately consensual secessions; East Timor emerged as a new state following the prior consent of Indonesia, while Montenegro seceded from the SUSM in accordance with domestic constitutional provisions. However, the political process which led to the parent states' consent in these two situations was internationalised. The consent for East Timor's independence was procured by UN involvement, while the EU brokered negotiations between Serbia and Montenegro which ultimately led to the transitional constitutional arrangement of the SUSM.

Kosovo is a contested situation; as such, it proves that statehood is not a matter of an objective fact, but rather a politically-realised legal status.[579] It is not contested whether or not the territory of Kosovo exists as a fact; instead, it is contested whether or not this territory has the international legal status of an independent state. Recognition has been granted by more than 90 states, yet Serbia, Kosovo's parent state, has not consented to its independence. Serbia's claim to territorial integrity is thus widely disregarded, but widespread recognition created ambiguity rather than

---

[577] *cf* ch 1, 3.6.
[578] See ch 1, 3.4.
[579] *cf* ch 2, 6.6.

settled Kosovo's legal status.[580] It is possible that the legal status would only be clarified over time, if Kosovo, through the practice of states and UN organs, became universally accepted as a state.

Such an ambiguity is precisely a consequence of the concept of the state and the nature of state creation in contemporary international law. Statehood is a legal status which is achieved in a political process. Sometimes it can be unclear whether this process has been successfully completed and whether a new legal status has been created.

In the post-Cold War period, considerations for democracy as a political system also became an integral part of the political process leading to independence, but this does not mean that a new state must be a democracy in order to be a state. Democracy is not a requirement under the international law of statehood which could prevent an entity from becoming a state; however, the same can be said of the traditional statehood criteria. The analysed practice clearly demonstrates that the non-meeting of these criteria does not necessarily prevent an entity from becoming a state. Yet the role of democracy in international law should not be reduced to questions of whether democracy is a statehood criterion or recognition requirement, or whether the international law of statehood allows for the creation of a non-democratic state.

Such a focus would require considering whether democracy is on the *checklist* of the statehood criteria which can objectively tell us whether or not an entity is a state. The emergence of a new state is, however, not a checklist-based fact but a political *process* governed by certain legal requirements. In this political process, an independence-seeking entity needs to overcome the hurdle of a competing claim to territorial integrity by its parent state. In the absence of the parent state's consent, overcoming this hurdle may become a matter of internationalised action.[581] Where this is the case, recent practice demonstrates that a democratic political system will be internationally enacted in the foundational legal instruments of the new state. Democracy is thus one of the considerations in the political process of state creation, as are the statehood criteria, but neither democracy nor the statehood criteria determine the emergence or non-emergence of a new state in contemporary international law. One can say that in the contemporary law of statehood, democracy is as equally relevant or irrelevant as the Montevideo Convention.

This chapter was concerned with the role of democracy as a political system in the process of state creation. The next chapter turns to the right of self-determination and demonstrates the difference between the requirement for democracy as a political system and the international legal requirement for a state creation to be a *democratic process*.

[580] ibid.
[581] *cf* ch 2, 3.4.

# 3

# *Democratic Aspects of the Right of Self-Determination*

## 1  INTRODUCTION

T HE IDEA OF a government that is representative of its people is the underlying principle of both democracy and the concept of self-determination. It originates in Enlightenment political theory and dates to the American and French Revolutions of 1776 and 1789, respectively. Both events 'marked the demise of the notion that individuals and peoples, as subjects of the King, were objects to be transferred, alienated, ceded, or protected in accordance with the interests of the monarch. The core of the principle lies in the American and French insistence that the government be responsible to the peoples'.[1]

Democracy is seen as a synonym for self-determination only in the Western European and American tradition,[2] while '[i]n Central and Eastern Europe . . . the notion of self-determination was based primarily on the Nineteenth-Century phenomenon of nationalism'.[3] Therefore, from the beginning of its modern appearance, self-determination had two possible scopes of operation: in one view it dealt with the internal political organisation of states, yet in another it could create new states. This dualism was also reflected in the later development of this political principle and human right.

In the early twentieth century, the idea of self-determination featured prominently in the work of US President Woodrow Wilson, for whom self-determination was virtually a synonym for democracy.[4] The aftermath of the First World War, however, led President Wilson to expand the concept of self-determination to include external effects.[5] Yet the internal

---

[1] A Cassese, *Self-Determination of Peoples: A Legal Reappraisal* (Cambridge, Cambridge University Press, 1995) 11.

[2] T Musgrave, *Self-Determination and National Minorities* (Oxford, Oxford University Press, 1997) 2.

[3] ibid.

[4] Cassese (n 1) 19.

[5] ibid.

(democratic) and external (state-creating) aspects seemed to contradict each other and were difficult to implement in practice.[6]

In the era of the League of Nations, self-determination was not considered to be a positive rule of international law and remained a political principle.[7] Its codification as a human right came in the UN Charter era.[8] It is generally accepted in international legal scholarship that self-determination is not an absolute human right and as such it is subject to limitations.[9] One important limitation on this right is the principle of the territorial integrity of states.[10] Outside of colonialism, the right of self-determination will normally be consummated in its internal mode.[11] It was the internal scope of operation, encompassing the requirement for a representative government, which again linked self-determination and democracy and, in the view of some governments and commentators, effectively turned the right of self-determination into a 'right to democracy'.[12]

This chapter considers the links between self-determination and democracy and questions whether democratic elections are a necessary and / or sufficient requirement for the internal exercise of the right of self-determination. It clarifies the scope of the concept of governmental representativeness in the framework of the right of self-determination and argues that the influence of the right to political participation on the right of self-determination is not to be interpreted too broadly. Subsequently, the chapter turns to the external exercise of the right. It makes an argument that secession is never an entitlement under international law, not even when the doctrine of remedial secession is in question. However, it demonstrates that when new states are created, the operation of the right of self-determination requires that some democratic principles be

[6] See M Pomerance, 'The United States and Self-Determination: Perspectives on the Wilsonian Conception' (1976) 70 *American Journal of International Law* 1, 17

[7] The *Åland Islands* case (1920) LNOJ Spec Supp 3 (the International Committee of Jurists) 5.

[8] See ch 3, 2.1.

[9] See R McCorquodale, 'Self-Determination: A Human Rights Approach' (1994) 43 *ICLQ* 857, 875–76.

[10] See the Declaration on Principles of International Law Concerning Friendly Relations and Co-operation Among States in Accordance with the Charter of the United Nations (hereinafter the Declaration on Principles of International Law), UN Doc A/RES/2625 (24 October 1970) 121, annex, principle 5, para 7.

[11] See *Reference re Secession of Québec* (1998) 2 SCR 217 (Canada) (the *Québec* case), para 126.

[12] The government of West Germany argued in 1988 that 'the exercise of the right to self-determination required the democratic process'. GAOR, A/C.3/43/SR.7 (13 October 1988) 16, para 76. The government of India argued in 1996 that: 'The internal aspects of self-determination . . . includes [*sic*] the right of people to choose their own form of government and the right to democracy and they do not and cannot include the right of a fraction of the people to secede.' UN Doc CCPR/C/76/Add.6 (17 July 1995), para 32. For an express association of human rights and democracy, see P Thornberry, 'The Democratic or Internal Aspect of Self-determination with Some Remarks on Federalism' in C Tomuschat (ed.), *Modern Law of Self-Determination* (Dordrecht, Martinus Nijhoff, 1993) 120. See also S Wheatley, *Democracy, Minorities and International Law* (Cambridge, Cambridge University Press, 2005) 135–36.

followed. In this context, the procedures and legal effects of independence referenda will be analysed.

## 2 SELF-DETERMINATION: DEVELOPMENT, DEMOCRATIC PEDIGREE AND LIMITATIONS

### 2.1 Self-Determination and its Democratic Pedigree: The Political Principle of Self-Determination in the Twentieth Century

At the beginning of the twentieth century, the principle of self-determination featured prominently in the writings of two important political and intellectual figures, Lenin and Woodrow Wilson. As the former was the leader of the Socialist Revolution in Russia and the latter the US President, these two champions of self-determination had different ideological underpinnings for advancing self-determination and consequently also differing interpretations of the scope and objective of this principle.

Writing in 1916, Lenin wrote that 'victorious socialism must necessarily establish a full democracy and, consequently, not only introduce full equality of nations but also realise the right of the oppressed nations to self-determination, i.e. the right to free political separation'.[13] Lenin thus paired self-determination with democracy, yet these thoughts need to be looked at through the prism of his ideological background. Indeed, for Lenin, self-determination was not a synonym for a democratic political system but a synonym for secession, which he saw as a last resort to end the nationalist oppression taking place in non-socialist societies.[14]

Lenin's argument in favour of the Treaty of Brest-Litovsk[15] further confirmed that in his understanding, self-determination was subordinated to the benefit of the socialist revolution. This peace settlement included substantial transfers of the territories of Poland, Lithuania, Latvia, Estonia and Belarus to Germany, thus denying self-determination to the populations of these territories.[16] Yet Lenin saw the Treaty of Brest-Litovsk as crucially important for advancing the socialist revolution, arguing that socialism had priority over the respect for self-determination.[17]

---

[13] VI Lenin, *Questions of National Policy and Proletarian Internationalism* (Moscow, Foreign Languages Publishing House, year of publication unknown) 135.

[14] D Raič, *Statehood and the Law of Self-Determination* (The Hague, Kluwer Law International, 2002) 186.

[15] The Treaty of Brest-Litovsk was signed between Russia and the Central Powers on 3 March 1918 and brought about a separate peace between these belligerents in the First World War. See G Freund, *Unholy Alliance: Russian-German Relations from the Treaty of Brest-Litovsk to the Treaty of Berlin* (London, Chatto & Windus, 1957) 1–33.

[16] ibid,

[17] Cassese (n 1) 18, quoting Lenin's article in *Pravda* on 21 February 1918.

Although in Lenin's understanding self-determination was merely a tool for furthering the Socialist Revolution, the ideological attachment of the Soviet Union to self-determination played an important role in codifying it as a human right in the UN Charter era.[18] It is therefore somewhat paradoxical that '[s]elf-determination enjoys a "democratic" label in spite of the fact that it was the former Eastern Bloc nations that played the most significant role in developing and promoting self-determination following World War II, usually in the face of great reluctance from Western democracies'.[19]

While Leninist self-determination originated in socialist political theory, President Wilson built his ideas of self-determination on liberal premises. Indeed, '[f]or the US president, self-determination was the logical corollary of popular sovereignty, it was synonymous with the principle that governments must be based on "the consent of the governed"'.[20] The Wilsonian concept of 'self-government'[21] was initially developed for internal purposes and its meaning was that 'peoples of each State be granted the right freely to choose State authorities and political leaders'.[22] The understanding of self-government (ie, self-determination)[23] was not only rooted in democratic political theory but was actually a synonym for a democratic political system. It was the experience of the First World War which led President Wilson also to ascribe an external connotation to the concept of self-government.[24]

The external implications of the right of self-determination were reflected in the Fourteen Points speech, which President Wilson delivered in the US Congress on 8 January 1918.[25] In this speech, Wilson stipulated the key criteria for drawing new borders in Europe, which would follow ethnic lines, respect the will of the people in regard to in which state they wanted to live and facilitate economic development of the peoples of Europe. Consequently, in Wilson's understanding, self-determination also became a right of oppressed European peoples to create their own states.

But the original internal (ie, democratic) meaning and external (ie, state-creating) implications could not be easily reconciled. The idea of self-determination 'implied the right of a population to select its own form of

---

[18]  ibid, 19.

[19]  R Miller, '*Self-Determination* in International Law and the Demise of Democracy' (2003) 41 *Columbia Journal of Transnational Law* 601, 612.

[20]  Cassese (n 1) 19.

[21]  It is argued that Wilson publicly used the term 'self-determination' for the first time in his public appearance on 11 February 1918, which was about a month after he delivered the Fourteen Points speech. His preferred term until then was 'self-government'. See Pomerance (n 6) 2.

[22]  Cassese (n 1) 19.

[23]  *cf* n 21, above.

[24]  ibid.

[25]  'President Woodrow Wilson's Fourteen Points', Yale Law School, the Avalon Project http://avalon.law.yale.edu/20th_century/wilson14.asp.

government, yet, on the other hand, it also suggested that self-government must be a *continuing* process and must therefore be synonymous with the *democratic* form of government'.[26] Wilson thus presumed that the people's choice of government would always be a democratic government.[27] This, however, implies interference with other peoples' choice of political system and thus a violation of rather than support for self-determination. Wilson's understanding of self-determination was thus paradoxical.

Wilsonian self-determination was criticised for such inconsistencies, as was Wilson himself for departing from this principle in the post-First World War peace settlement. Indeed, 'Wilson had proclaimed national self-determination as though it were an absolute principle',[28] yet the aftermath of the First World War showed that it had to be reconciled with the principle of the territorial integrity of states.[29]

## 2.2 The Territorial Integrity Limitation: The Link between Internal Self-Determination and Democracy

In the era of the League of Nations, self-determination remained merely a political principle; its codification as a human right came in the UN Charter era. The right of self-determination is elaborated in the common Article 1 of the International Covenant on Civil and Political Rights (ICCPR) and the International Covenant on Social, Economic and Cultural Rights (ICSECR).[30] Furthermore, this right 'has been declared in other international treaties and instruments [and] is generally accepted as customary international law'.[31] As a human right, self-determination is subject to the same limitations as most human rights:

> [T]he right of self-determination is not an absolute right without any limitations. Its purpose is not directly to protect the personal or physical integrity of individuals or groups as is the purpose of the absolute rights and, unlike the absolute rights, the exercise of this right can involve major structural and institutional changes to a State and must affect, often significantly, most groups and individuals in that State and beyond that State. Therefore, the nature of the right does require some limitations to be implied on its exercise.[32]

These limitations are designed to protect the rights of everyone, 'not just those seeking self-determination'.[33]

---

[26] Pomerance (n 6) 17 (emphasis in original).
[27] Miller (n 19) 619.
[28] Raič (n 14) 189.
[29] Pomerance (n 6) 22.
[30] International Covenant on Civil and Political Rights (ICCPR) and International Covenant on Economic, Social and Cultural Rights (ICESCR), art 1.
[31] McCorquodale (n 9) 858.
[32] ibid, 875–76.
[33] ibid, 876.

In the process of decolonisation, 'the only territorial relationship to be altered was that with the metropolitan power. Achieving independence . . . did not come at the expense of another sovereign state's territory or that of an adjacent colony'.[34] Only the colonial exercise of the right of self-determination usually resulted in the emergence of former colonial territories as independent states,[35] while outside of colonialism the right collides with the principle of the territorial integrity of states and will only exceptionally result in a new state creation.[36]

The principle of the territorial integrity of states is elaborated upon in the Declaration on Principles of International Law:

> Nothing in the foregoing paragraphs shall be construed as authorizing or encouraging any action which would dismember or impair, totally or in part, the territorial integrity or political unity of sovereign and independent States conducting themselves in compliance with the principle of equal rights and self-determination of peoples as described above and thus possessed of a government representing the whole people belonging to the territory without distinction as to race, creed or colour.[37]

This provision has been referred to as the 'safeguard clause'[38] and while it represents 'a shift in the tone of self-determination, from the Soviet-sponsored emphasis on external self-determination to the Western-sponsored emphasis on internal self-determination',[39] a reversed reading of the 'safeguard clause' might also imply an external dimension of this right. Indeed, it could be interpreted that a state which does not have a government that represents 'the whole people belonging to the territory without distinction as to race, creed or colour'[40] may, possibly, not have a right to avail itself of the principle of territorial integrity.[41] In other words, in such circumstances, external self-determination may be legitimised.

The inverted reading of the 'safeguard clause' has been invoked as one of the foundations of the so-called remedial secession doctrine, which will

---

[34] G Fox, 'Self-Determination in the Post-Cold War Era: A New Internal Focus' (1994–95) 16 *Michigan Journal of International Law* 733, 736.

[35] A reference to the right of self-determination was made in the Declaration on the Granting of Independence to Colonial Countries and Peoples: 'All peoples have the right to self-determination; by virtue of that right they freely determine their political status and freely pursue their economic, social and cultural development.' UN Doc A/RES/1514 (14 December 1960) 66, para 2. In the process of decolonisation, colonies could opt for: (i) emergence as a sovereign independent state; (ii) free association with an independent state; or (iii) integration with an independent state. UN Doc A/RES/1541 (15 December 1960) 19, principle VI.

[36] The *Québec* case (n 11), para 126.

[37] The Declaration on Principles of International Law (n 10).

[38] See Crawford, *The Creation of States in International Law* (Oxford, Oxford University Press, 2006) 118–21.

[39] Miller (n 19) 623.

[40] ibid.

[41] See Crawford (n 38) 119.

be considered below.[42] At this point the chapter turns to the 'safeguard clause' in order to consider how governmental representativeness is qualified in the context of the right of self-determination, when consummated internally.

In one view, the 'safeguard clause' is one of the links between the right of self-determination and democracy: 'The "democratic" aspect of self-determination is present in muted form, through the idea of representation in the Declaration on Principles [on International Law], and by an indeterminate "connection" with human rights.'[43] If democracy presupposes a multiparty political system, these premises lead to the conclusion that the right of self-determination, when exercised internally, requires a multiparty political system. This chapter will now consider whether the operation of the right of self-determination can be stretched this far. Three main questions will be considered: (i) whether the 'safeguard clause' defines governmental representativeness in terms of multiparty elections; (ii) whether the right of self-determination requires a multiparty political system through the interdependence of human rights, most notably through the impact of the right to political participation; and (iii) whether multiparty electoral procedures automatically lead to the realisation of the right of self-determination.

### 3 SELF-DETERMINATION, GOVERNMENTAL REPRESENTATIVENESS AND MULTIPARTY DEMOCRACY

It follows from the 'safeguard clause' that the operation of the right of self-determination requires a representative government. A definition of such a government is not straightforward and attempts have been made to link it to democratic electoral procedures.[44] One writer argued: 'Is it not a mockery of self-determination to say that an oppressive dictatorship "represents" the whole people?'[45] The term 'oppressive dictatorship' is not easy to define, but in the context of a democratic interpretation of the right of (internal) self-determination, it is often understood as a government whose authority is not validated by a democratic electoral process.[46] However, even if one assumes that such governments do not reflect the will of the people, it is questionable whether non-democratic governments breach the right of self-determination prima facie, ie, solely by not adhering to democratic electoral procedures.

---

[42] See ch 3, 6.
[43] Thornberry (n 12) 120.
[44] See ch 3, 2.1.
[45] A Rosas, 'Internal Self-Determination' in C Tomuschat (ed.), *Modern Law of Self-Determination* (Dordrecht, Martinus Nijhoff, 1993) 238.
[46] See T Franck, 'The Emerging Right to Democratic Governance' (1992) 86 *American Journal of International Law* 46, 46–52.

## 3.1  The Scope of Governmental Representativeness in the 'Safeguard Clause'

The Declaration on Principles of International Law defined governmental representativeness in terms of 'race, colour or creed'.[47] After the end of the Cold War, the Vienna Convention and Programme in Action essentially repeated the 'safeguard clause' from the Declaration on Principles of International Law, but defined a representative government as the one 'representing the whole people belonging to the territory without distinction of any kind'.[48] Although the qualification 'without distinction of any kind' appears to be broad, the fact that it was made in the context of the right of self-determination imposes significant restrictions on the scope of its applicability.

The right of self-determination only applies to peoples.[49] Therefore, the identities determining the governmental representativeness for the purpose of the right of self-determination cannot be extended beyond the identities relevant for the existence of a separate people. This leads to the problem of distinguishing between those groups who qualify as a people and those who do not.

Investigating the events in East Pakistan in 1972, the International Commission of Jurists made the following remark with regard to the concept of 'people':

> If we look at the human communities recognized as peoples, we find that their members usually have certain characteristics in common, which act as a bond between them. The nature of the more important of these common features may be [historical, racial or ethnic, cultural or linguistic, religious or ideological, geographical or territorial, economic, quantitative]. This list . . . is far from exhaustive . . . [A]ll the elements combined do not necessarily constitute proof: large numbers of persons may live together within the same territory, have the same economic interests, the same language, the same religion, belong to the same ethnic group, without necessarily constituting a people. On the other hand, a more heterogeneous group of persons, having less in common, may nevertheless constitute a people.
>
> To explain this apparent contradiction, we have to realize that our composite portrait lacks one essential and indeed indispensable characteristic – a characteristic which is not physical but rather ideological and historical: a people begin to exist only when it becomes conscious of its own identity and asserts its will to exist . . . the fact of constituting a people is a political phenomenon, that the right of self-determination is founded on political considerations and that the exercise of that right is a political act.[50]

[47] See n 37, above.
[48] The Vienna Declaration and Programme of Action A/CONF.157/23 (12 July 1993), para 2.
[49] See ICCPR and ICESCR, Article 1.
[50] International Commission of Jurists, Events in East Pakistan (International Court of Justice Secretariat, 1972) 49.

Similar criteria and caveats accompanying these criteria were invoked in the document entitled 'Final Report and Recommendations of an International Meeting of Experts on the Further Study of the Concept of the Right of People for UNESCO'.[51] The following criteria were specifically invoked: (a) a common historical tradition; (b) racial or ethnic identity; (c) cultural homogeneity; (d) linguistic unity; (e) religious or ideological affinity; (f) territorial connection; and (g) common economic life.[52]

Although not of direct legal relevance, these references give some suggestion as to what criteria shall be applied when considering whether a group qualifies as a people and is thus a beneficiary of the right of self-determination. These criteria are not entirely clear, as well as non-comprehensive and subjective,[53] but they nevertheless show that the affiliation in terms of party politics is not an identity which could suggest the existence of a separate people and is thus not relevant for the purpose of the exercise of the right of self-determination. Indeed, one cannot plausibly claim that members or voters of the Labour Party in the UK constitute a people and are thus beneficiaries of the right of self-determination.

The fact that governmental representativeness is not defined in terms of political parties also follows from the practice of UN organs. In the above-discussed situation of Southern Rhodesia, the General Assembly called for the participation of all political parties;[54] however, this needs to be looked at in the light of the exclusion of black, ie, colour/race-based, political parties from the process of the drafting of the constitution.[55] The international response was thus confined to the violation of the right of self-determination stemming from racial discrimination and not from the absence of a multiparty political system. In the resolutions dealing with the South African Homelands, violation of the right of self-determination also originated in racial discrimination and not in an absence of democratic electoral practices.[56]

The link between racial discrimination and the denial of the right of self-determination was also expressed by Security Council Resolution 417 on apartheid rule in South Africa,[57] in which the Security Council expressed grave concern 'over reports of torture of political prisoners and the deaths of a number of detainees, as well as the mounting wave of repression against individuals, organizations and the news media',[58] reaffirmed 'its

---

[51] UNESCO, International Meeting of Experts on Further Study of the Concept of the Rights of Peoples, Final Report and Recommendations, SHS-89/CONF.602/7 (22 February 1990), para 22.
[52] ibid, para 22(1).
[53] See generally Musgrave (n 2) 154–67.
[54] See ch 1, 3.5.3.
[55] See UN Doc S/RES/202 (6 May 1965), preamble.
[56] See ch 1, 3.5.4.
[57] UN Doc S/RES/417 (31 October 1977).
[58] ibid, preamble, para 3.

recognition of the legitimacy of the struggle of the South African people for the elimination of *apartheid* and racial discrimination'[59] and affirmed 'the right to the exercise of self-determination by all the people of South Africa as a whole, irrespective of race, creed or colour'.[60] The Security Council then condemned 'the South African racist regime for its resort to massive violence and repression against the black people, who constitute the great majority of the country, as well as all other opponents of *apartheid*'[61] and expressed 'its support for, and solidarity with, all those struggling for the elimination of *apartheid* and racial discrimination and all victims of violence and repression by the South African racist regime'.[62]

Although Security Council Resolution 417, inter alia, makes references to political violence and to all opponents of apartheid, which can also be associated with the freedom of expression of South African whites and not only with the right of self-determination and the prohibition of racial discrimination of South African blacks, it is obvious that the scope of this resolution is the prohibition of racial discrimination and not a political opinion, broadly understood. Indeed, the Security Council's response to the apartheid regime in South Africa was triggered by racial discrimination and not by the lack of democratic electoral practices.

The situations outlined above show a close-knit relationship between the right of self-determination and the prohibition of racial discrimination. It follows from the wording of Article 1 of the International Convention on the Elimination of All Forms of Racial Discrimination (ICERD) that racial discrimination is to be interpreted as virtually any kind of discrimination based on identities which, inter alia, suggest the existence of a separate people.[63] But the collective responses to situations in which non-representative governments were universally proclaimed to be in breach of the right of self-determination do not suggest that governmental representativeness could be understood in terms of party politics or in any other way beyond the identities relevant for the existence of a separate people.[64]

[59]  ibid, preamble, para 5 (emphasis in original).

[60]  ibid, preamble, para 6.

[61]  ibid, para 1 (emphasis in original).

[62]  ibid, para 2 (emphasis in original).

[63]  See Article 1 of the International Convention on the Elimination of All Forms of Racial Discrimination, where racial discrimination is defined as 'any distinction, exclusion, restriction or preference based on race, colour, descent, or national or ethnic origin'. *cf* nn 50 and 51, above.

[64]  *cf* ch 1, 3.5.3, 1, 3.5.4, 2, 3.4 and 2, 6.

### 3.2  Self-Determination, Representativeness and Non-democratic Governments

Thus far, it has been shown that the practice of states and UN organs affirms that breaches of the right of self-determination do not stem from an absence of a democratic (multiparty) political system. This subsection will go further and will consider the collective practice which explicitly shows that even governments which are not an outcome of a multiparty electoral process may be considered to be legitimate and representative of their peoples.

The Declaration on Principles of International Law was adopted in 1970, in the time of the Cold War. It can be presumed that the socialist states at that time would not have supported the Declaration if this elaboration meant to bind them to a multiparty electoral system. To reinforce the universality of the Declaration, the UK and the US, at the time of drafting, clearly expressed that the term 'representative government' did not presuppose any particular political system. On behalf of the UK, it was stated that '[t]he use of the word "representative" . . . was not intended to mean that only one system of government properly met the criterion [of representativeness]'.[65] Similarly, in the context of the meaning of the term 'representative government', the representative of the US stated that his government 'understood that the Charter, as originally conceived, did not impose upon Members of the United Nations the duty to adopt a certain type of government'.[66] Hence, at the time of drafting of the Declaration on Principles of International Law, there was a unanimous perception that the term 'representative government' was not exclusively associated with the multiparty political system and that the 'safeguard clause' could not be interpreted to require multiparty elections.

The view that the legitimacy of a government and the territorial integrity of a state – as elaborated in the 'safeguard clause' – do not depend on adherence to a democratic political system also stems from the post-Cold War practice of the UN organs. The Security Council has expressed its support for the restoration of democratically elected governments in some coup situations, such as Haiti and Sierra Leone,[67] while in non-coup situations it has never denied legitimacy to non-elected governments on democracy considerations. Security Council resolutions dealing with Kuwait and

---

[65] GAOR, Special Commission on Friendly Relations, A/AC.125/SR.69 (1967) 9 (4 December 1967).

[66] GAOR, Special Commission on Friendly Relations, A/AC.125/SR.92, 133 (21 December 1968).

[67] See UN Doc S/RES/940 (31 July 1994) (Haiti) and UN Doc S/RES/1132 (8 October 1997) (Sierra Leone). See generally J d'Aspremont, 'Responsibility for Coups in International Law (2010) *Tulane Journal of International & Comparative Law* 451.

Afghanistan are good examples of the fact that governmental legitimacy in international law is not linked to a democratic political process.

After the Iraqi occupation of Kuwait in 1990, which coincided with the end of the Cold War, the Security Council, acting under Chapter VII of the UN Charter, affirmed the territorial integrity of Kuwait. The Security Council expressed its determination 'to bring the invasion and occupation of Kuwait by Iraq to an end and to restore the sovereignty, independence and territorial integrity of Kuwait'.[68] The Security Council also proclaimed the government of Kuwait to be the legitimate government of that state by holding that 'Iraq so far has failed to comply with paragraph 2 of resolution 660 (1990) and has usurped the authority of the legitimate Government of Kuwait'[69] and 'as a consequence, [decided] to take . . . measures . . . to restore the authority of the legitimate Government of Kuwait'.[70]

It should be noted that Kuwait was an example of the violation of territorial integrity by a breach of Article 2(4) of the UN Charter. Nevertheless, the Security Council established that Kuwait's ousted government was the only legitimate government of this state. This was established despite the fact that the government of Kuwait was not known for its adherence to democratic practices and despite its record of gross human rights violations.[71]

In relation to the Taliban government in Afghanistan, the Security Council denied legitimacy to the Taliban government in representing the entire people of Afghanistan.[72] The reasoning was based on grave human rights violations and threats to international peace. The Security Council expressed its support for a change of government and held that a new government should be 'broad-based . . . multi-ethnic and fully representative of all the Afghan people'.[73] These criteria can be closely associated with the identities

---

[68]  UN Doc S/RES/661 (6 August 1990), preamble.

[69]  ibid, para 1.

[70]  ibid, para 2.

[71]  Consider the following observation: 'The human rights situation in Kuwait prior to the [Iraqi] invasion was not a good one. The National Assembly (dissolved by the Emir of Kuwait in 1986, during the Iran-Iraq war, citing concerns that national security was being compromised by open debate) remained dissolved in 1990, although the war ended in 1988. The ruling al-Sabah family continued in 1990 to resist calls to restore parliamentary rule and to relax the severe restrictions imposed on constitutionally guaranteed freedom of expression and assembly. It continued to rule by decree, to tolerate torture, and to permit the secret trial of security cases by special tribunals whose decisions were not subject to appeal.' Testimony of Andrew Whitley, Before the House Foreign Affairs Committee, Human Rights in Iraq and Iraqi-Occupied Kuwait Middle East Watch, 8 January 1991, www.hrw.org/reports/1991/IRAQ91.htm. See generally also S Ghabra, 'Democratization in a Middle Eastern State: Kuwait' (1994) 3 *Middle East Policy* 102.

[72]  UN Doc S/RES/1267 (15 October 1999); UN Doc S/RES/1333 (19 December 2000); UN Doc S/RES/1378 (14 November 2001).

[73]  UN Doc S/RES/1378 (14 November 2001), preamble. It is also notable that some relevant Security Council resolutions expressed concern over discrimination against women and girls under the Taliban regime in Afghanistan, but no reference was made to either democracy or multiparty elections. See UN Doc S/RES/1267 (15 October 1999), preamble, para 3 and UN Doc S/RES/1333 (2000), preamble, para 13.

relevant for the existence of a separate people. But the resolutions, which declared the Taliban government to be non-representative of the people of Afghanistan, did not qualify governmental representativeness in terms of (democratic) electoral procedures.[74]

As a general principle, the Security Council has acknowledged that governmental representativeness in international law does not (necessarily) come from a democratic electoral process. International law will not automatically regard a non-democratic government as non-representative of its peoples. The only exception might be coup governments, which overthrow democratically elected ones.[75]

The fact that even a non-democratic state is capable of having a government representative of its peoples was implied by the Badinter Commission in the case of the SFRY. In Opinion 1, in which it ultimately established that the SFRY was in the process of dissolution,[76] the Commission stated: 'The composition and workings of the essential organs of the Federation, be they the Federal Presidency, the Federal Council, the Council of the Republics and the Provinces, the Federal Executive Council, the Constitutional Court or the Federal Army, *no longer meet* the criteria of participation and representativeness inherent in a federal state.'[77] The Badinter Commission thus implied that prior to Serbia's usurpation of the federal organs,[78] these organs were representative of the peoples of the SFRY. This was so although the post-holders in these organs were not elected according to democratic electoral practices.[79]

Also instructive in this context is the example of Kosovo. The government of Slobodan Milošević in Yugoslavia and Serbia may have violated the right of self-determination of the Kosovo Albanians,[80] but there exists no support for a claim that it violated the right of self-determination of the Serbs and/or the Montenegrins. Indeed, its undemocratic character cannot be interpreted to mean a prima facie violation of the right of self-determination of all peoples in its territory. The lack of democracy in Yugoslavia did not automatically constitute a violation of the right of self-determination of the Kosovo Albanians.

[74] See ch 1, 2.3.3.
[75] ibid.
[76] The Badinter Commission, Opinion 1 (29 November 1991), para 3, reprinted in S Trifunovska, *Yugoslavia through Documents: From its Creation to its Dissolution* (Dordrecht, Martinus Nijhoff, 1994) 415.
[77] ibid, para 2(c) (emphasis added).
[78] See J Dugard and D Raič, 'The Role of Recognition in the Law and Practice of Secession' in M Kohen (ed.), *Secession: International Law Perspectives* (Cambridge, Cambridge University Press, 2006) 126.
[79] Elections in the SFRY were indirect and not multiparty. For details on this, see Constitution of the SFRY (1974) Articles 282–312 (Assembly), 313–32 (Presidency) and 346–62 (the Federal Executive Council).
[80] See ch 2, 6.

These examples show that governmental representativeness for the purpose of the right of self-determination is not qualified in terms of democratic electoral procedures or the existence of a multiparty political system. In turn, this leads to the question of how the right of self-determination is consummated in its internal mode. Federalism is argued to be an exemplary arrangement for this purpose.[81] A federal arrangement can indeed vest significant powers in subunits of a state, even some attributes of statehood.[82] Two caveats apply. First, not all federations are arrangements for the exercise of the right of self-determination. There exist states with federal units, the populations of which do not qualify as peoples, and the right of self-determination is thus not applicable. Austria, for example, is a federal state, but the respective populations of its federal units clearly do not constitute separate peoples. Second, even non-federal states can adopt mechanisms for the protection of the right of self-determination and even have clearly delimited self-determination units. Such an example is the UK, which 'may not be a federal system, but it is a union state built in 1707 upon the union of two established, or at least incipient, national societies'.[83]

Furthermore, when the right of self-determination is realised within self-governing subunits of a state, 'customary and treaty law on *internal* self-determination [do not] provide guidelines on the possible distribution of power among institutionalized units or regions'.[84] International law does not prescribe how exactly the right of self-determination is to be consummated internally and '[t]he exercise of this right can take a variety of forms, from autonomy over most policies and laws in a region or part of a State . . . to a people having exclusive control over only certain aspects of policy'.[85]

It is not the purpose of this book to identify possible arrangements for the internal exercise of the right of self-determination and to set the minimum threshold of governmental representativeness in the context of this right.[86] Rather, this section shows that governmental representativeness

---

[81] Y Dinstein, 'The Degree of Self-Rule of Minorities in Unitarian and Federal States' in C Brölmann, R Lefeber and M Zieck (eds), *Peoples and Minorities in International Law* (Dordrecht, Martinus Nijhoff, 1993) 223–24.

[82] See D Harris, *Cases and Materials on International Law* (London, Sweet & Maxwell, 2010) 98.

[83] S Tierney, *Constitutional Law and National Pluralism* (Oxford, Oxford University Press, 2006) 112.

[84] Cassese (n 1) 332 (emphasis in original).

[85] McCorquodale (n 9) 864.

[86] Consider the following definition of a representative government in the context of the right of self-determination: 'A minimum requirement seems to be that the claim to representativeness by a non-oppressive government is not contested or challenged by (part of) the population. Thus, the notion of "representativeness" assumes that government and the system of government is not imposed on the population of a State, but that it is based on the

for the purpose of the right of self-determination cannot be interpreted beyond the identities relevant for the existence of a separate people. The practice of states and UN organs confirms that even governments which do not claim office through democratic electoral procedures can be representative of their respective peoples.

4  THE RIGHT OF SELF-DETERMINATION, POLITICAL PARTICIPATION AND CHOICE OF POLITICAL SYSTEM

## 4.1  Self-Determination and Political Participation

While the concept of a representative government operating within the right of self-determination does not prescribe one particular political system, it remains questionable whether the interdependence of human rights has such an effect. This section will give a specific consideration to the interdependence between the right of self-determination and the right to political participation. It will be considered whether the link between the right to political participation and the right of self-determination results in a requirement for states to hold multiparty elections. Subsequently, the section will address the question of whether a multiparty political system leads to an automatic realisation of the right of self-determination.

One exemplary expression of interdependence between the right of self-determination and other human rights is captured in the statement of the West German representative in the General Assembly in 1988:

> The right of self-determination had far broader connotations than simply freedom from colonial rule and foreign domination. Article 1 [of the ICCPR and ICESCR] . . . defined the right of self-determination as the right of all peoples freely to determine their political status and freely to pursue their economic, social and cultural development. The question as to how peoples could freely determine their status was answered in Article 25 [of the ICCPR] . . . The right of self-determination was indivisible from the right of the individual to take part in the conduct of public affairs, as was very clearly stated in Article 21 of the Universal Declaration of Human Rights. The exercise of the right to self-determination required the democratic process which, in turn, was inseparable from the full exercise of such human rights as the right to freedom of thought conscience and religion; the right of freedom of expression; the right of peaceful assembly and of association; the right to take part in cultural life; the right to liberty and security of person; the right to move freely in one's country

---

consent or assented by the population and in that sense is representative of the will of the people regardless of the forms or methods by which the consent or assent is freely expressed.'
Raič (n 14) 279.

and to leave any country, including one's own, as well as to return to one's country.[87]

This statement not only holds that the right of self-determination is interdependent with other human rights, it also implies that the exercise of this right requires adherence to some democratic standards. Particular attention was paid to Article 25 of the ICCPR, which elaborates the right to political participation. This interpretation has also been given support among writers. In one such view: 'The right of peoples to self-determination, taken with the rights of citizens to political participation, creates an obligation for the 150-plus States parties to the [ICCPR] to both introduce and maintain democratic forms of government.'[88] Wheatley leaves no doubt that a democratic form of government, inter alia, presupposes multiparty elections.[89] Consequently, the interdependence between the right of self-determination and the right to political participation leads to an obligation to hold elections in a multiparty setting.

Such an interpretation presupposes that Article 25 of the ICCPR requires multiparty elections. In contrast to this, chapter one of this book demonstrates that the democratic interpretation of Article 25 is not generally accepted in contemporary international law, not even in the post-Cold War era.[90] Furthermore, the 'democratic interpretation' of the interdependence between the right of self-determination and the right to political participation exceeds the interpretation of the interdependence between these two rights, as provided by the Human Rights Committee (HRC) in its General Comment 25:

> The rights under article 25 are related to, but distinct from, the right of peoples to self-determination. By virtue of the rights covered by article 1 (1), peoples

---

[87] GAOR, A/C.3/43/SR.7 (13 October 1988) 16, para 76. More recently, the German Constitutional Court wed the right of self-determination and multiparty democracy in the *Treaty of Lisbon Decision*. The Court, inter alia, argued: 'The right to vote establishes a right to democratic self-determination, to free and equal participation in the state authority exercised in Germany and to compliance with the principle of democracy including the respect of the constituent power of the people.' The *Treaty of Lisbon Decision*, BVerfG, 2 BvE 2/08 (English version) (30 June 2009), para 208. The Court continued: 'The right to equal participation in democratic self-determination (democratic right of participation), to which every citizen is entitled, can . . . be violated by the organisation of state authority being changed in such a way that the will of the people can no longer effectively form within the meaning of Article 20.2 of the Basic Law and the citizens cannot rule according to the will of a majority.' ibid, para 210. This statement refers to Article 20(2) of the German Basic Law, which reads: 'All state authority is derived from the people. It shall be exercised by the people through elections and other votes and through specific legislative, executive, and judicial bodies.' This reasoning well illustrates the German understanding of the relationship between the right of self-determination and the right to political participation. Yet this understanding cannot be universalised, as it is not based on international human rights law, but on German constitutional law. Indeed, the Court was concerned with the right to vote under Article 20(2) of the German Basic Law and not under Article 25 of the ICCPR.
[88] Wheatley (n 12) 136.
[89] ibid, 143–44.
[90] See ch 1, 2.2.

have the right to freely determine their political status and to enjoy the right to choose the form of their constitution or government. Article 25 deals with the right of individuals to participate in those processes which constitute the conduct of public affairs.[91]

General Comment 25 thus interprets the interdependence more narrowly, without suggesting that under the influence of Article 25 of the ICCPR, the right of self-determination requires a particular form of government. Indeed, the General Comment affirms that 'peoples have the right to freely determine their political status'. This does not suggest that peoples are only allowed to choose one particular political system.

## 4.2 Self-Determination: Realisation of the Right through Democratic Elections?

An exemplary association of the right of self-determination with democratic electoral procedures can be found in the following statement of the UK government:

> [T]he right of self-determination in the United Kingdom itself is exercised primarily through the electoral system . . . The British system of parliamentary government is sustained by an electorate casting its votes in free and secret ballots at periodic elections which offer a choice between rival candidates, usually representing organised political parties of different views . . . All elections in Northern Ireland continue to produce an overall majority of the electorate voting for Unionist policies, i.e. continuing as part of the United Kingdom.[92]

In this perception, the right of self-determination is exercised through the electoral system. The UK did not claim that democratic electoral practices are the only means for the exercise of the right of self-determination, but that the electoral system per se leads to consummation of the right of self-determination. The association of the right of self-determination with the electoral system is rather problematic:

> As well as the difficulty in principle of expecting elections to be able to show the wishes of the people . . . the United Kingdom electoral system is particularly problematic as there is no proportional representation electoral system [apart from local and EU elections]. It has a 'first-past-the-post' electoral system, where the winner of a constituency seat is the person who polls the most votes, however few, which means that the winner of the election may very often not reflect the views of the majority of voters. There is an additional difficulty with

---

[91] HRC, General Comment 25, para 2.
[92] The Third Report of the United Kingdom to the Human Rights Committee at paras 18–20, quoted in R McCorquodale, 'Negotiating Sovereignty: The Practice of the United Kingdom in Regard to the Right of Self-Determination' (1996) 66 *British Yearbook of International Law* 283, 309.

a 'first-past-the-post' system if it is the sole means to determine the wishes of the people of Northern Ireland because of the divided nature of its society.[93]

One of the problems with the UK's proclamations lies in the specific features of its electoral system. The HRC stated in its General Comment 25 that the right to political participation does not impose any particular electoral system on a state; however, it stressed the need that an electoral system enables the equality of votes and does not discriminate against any group.[94] In the UK, groups exist which qualify as peoples for the purpose of the right of self-determination and the electoral system alone does not provide for their representation.

Furthermore, the claim that electoral democracy per se leads to the exercise of the right of self-determination is problematic in general, not only in connection with anomalies of a particular electoral system. The electoral process can lead to 'tyranny of the majority', ie, to dominance of the majority people over a numerically inferior people.[95] Indeed:

> Although, theoretically, in a Western-style representative democracy the entire population is entitled to participate in the elections of representatives who, in their turn, participate in the political decision-making process on behalf of the population, this does by no means mean that this form of governance is automatically a sufficient *guarantee* for genuine respect for the right of internal self-determination of a people which constitutes a numerical minority within a State.[96]

This is especially the case when political parties are organised along ethnic or religious lines and parties of a numerically superior people have access to a much broader electoral base and wider representation. If no other mechanisms limit the power of the majority,[97] the democratic electoral process can lead to the violation, not the fulfilment, of the right of self-determination.

Another problem of the association of the right of self-determination with the electoral process is the complexity of voters' decision-making in the voting booth. Indeed:

> [T]o rely on elections as the primary means of determining . . . free and genuine wishes [of the people of a territory] is fraught with difficulty. It is impossible to prove from election results on what particular issues a voter casts her/his vote, when there will invariably be other issue or issues besides self-determination which are raised during an election campaign.[98]

---

[93] ibid, 310.

[94] UN HRC, General Comment 25, para 21.

[95] For more on the problem of majoritarian democracy and the right of self-determination, see Miller (n 19) 634–44.

[96] Raič (n 14) 280 (emphasis in original).

[97] For more on mechanisms for the prevention of the 'tyranny of the majority' in democratic states, see Wheatley (n 12) 144–47.

[98] McCorquodale (n 92) 304.

In other words, voting for a certain party does not imply that a voter agrees with the entire programme of the party. Indeed, it cannot be presumed that a vote for a party that puts secession on its agenda implies a vote for secession. For example, at the 2011 Scottish elections, the Scottish National Party (SNP) came out as the strongest party in the Scottish Parliament by winning 69 out of 129 seats.[99] While the SNP puts independence of Scotland on its political agenda,[100] it cannot be assumed that all votes for the SNP are automatically votes for Scottish independence. Likewise, it cannot be assumed that all votes for parties other than the SNP are votes against Scottish independence.

In sum, the right of self-determination cannot be consummated through the existence of a democratic, multiparty electoral system alone. What is more, in the absence of an adequate mechanism for the protection of numerically inferior peoples, a democratic electoral system can lead to the violation and not the fulfilment of the right of self-determination.

### 5 DEMOCRACY AND THE EXERCISE OF THE RIGHT OF SELF-DETERMINATION IN ITS INTERNAL MODE

The elaboration of the principle of territorial integrity originally qualified a representative government as one that does not discriminate against its people based on race, creed or colour.[101] This qualification is now understood broadly and covers all identities relevant for the existence of a separate people. However, as the right of self-determination only applies to peoples, the qualification of a representative government in the context of this right does not cover identities other than those constituting a separate people. For this reason, the requirement for a representative government cannot be extended to mean non-discrimination based on an affiliation with political parties.

A representative government can also be a government which is not an outcome of multiparty elections. Indeed, the drafting of the Declaration on Principles of International Law expressly shows that the requirement for a representative government was not meant to interfere with the specific choice of a political and/or electoral system. The practice of UN organs shows that this attitude has not changed in the post-Cold War period. Furthermore, despite the absence of a democratic political system and multiparty electoral procedures, the Badinter Commission implied that the SFRY was representative of all of its peoples prior to Serbia's

---

[99] See 'Scotland Elections', *BBC News* (1 May 2011), www.bbc.co.uk/news/special/election2011/overview/html/scotland.stm.

[100] See www.snp.org/node/240.

[101] See n 10, above.

usurpation of the federal organs.[102] This suggests that even states which do not adhere to multiparty electoral practices can have a government that is representative of their peoples.

With regard to the 'democratic nature' of the right of self-determination stemming from the interdependence of human rights, it was demonstrated that such an understanding would require an interpretation that universal human rights instruments bind state parties to holding multiparty elections. Such a view was rejected by the ICJ in the *Nicaragua* case.[103] In the post-Cold War era, references to democracy were made in many General Assembly resolutions, but all of them carefully avoid a proclamation that elections need to take place in a multiparty setting.[104] Instead, the relevant resolutions commonly affirm that the choice of a political system remains a domestic matter for states. It is far from settled in international law that the right to political participation, either under Article 25 of the ICCPR or under customary international law, requires multiparty elections.[105] Therefore, the interdependence between this right and the right of self-determination cannot result in an obligation to hold multiparty elections.

The analysis in this chapter has also demonstrated that a multiparty electoral process by itself cannot guarantee respect for the right of self-determination and does not mean a per se fulfilment of this right. Indeed, the electoral process can lead to a situation of a tyranny of the majority. Furthermore, party politics is not an adequate channel for the implementation of self-determination standards, as programmes of political parties cover a wide range of issues and not only those associated with the right of self-determination.[106]

## 6 THE 'SAFEGUARD CLAUSE' AND REMEDIAL SECESSION

For the study of the right of self-determination, the 'safeguard clause' in the Declaration on Principles of International Law is also relevant because its inverted reading suggests that a state which does not possess 'a government representing the whole people belonging to the territory without any distinction' is not entitled to invoke the principle of territorial integrity when limiting the right of self-determination. The inverted reading gives rise to the remedial secession doctrine.[107] This section will consider

[102] See ch 2, n 205.
[103] See ch 1, n 108.
[104] See ch 1, 2.3.2.
[105] See ch 1, 2.4.
[106] See n 98, above.
[107] For a detailed account of the academic support for remedial secession, see A Tancredi, 'A Normative "Due Process" in the Creation of States through Secession' in M Kohen (ed.), *Secession: International Law Perspectives* (Cambridge, Cambridge University Press, 2006) 176.

both the doctrine and state practice relevant for this doctrine and will clarify its normative position in contemporary international law.

## 6.1 The Theory of Remedial Secession

Perhaps the most prominent judicial pronouncement which gives rise to the theory of remedial secession is that of the Supreme Court of Canada in the *Québec* case. The Court affirmed that there exists no right to unilateral secession in international law. However, this statement was not unqualified:

> The recognized sources of international law establish that the right to self-determination of a people is normally fulfilled through internal self-determination – a people's pursuit of its political, economic, social and cultural development within a framework of an existing state. A right to external self-determination (which in this case potentially takes the form of the assertion of a right to unilateral secession) arises in only the most extreme of cases and, even then, under carefully defined circumstances.[108]

Reference to 'the most extreme cases', which may justify a unilateral secession, is to be read against the background of the provision on self-determination and territorial integrity, which is expressed in the Declaration on Principles of International Law, ie, the 'safeguard clause'.[109] The Supreme Court of Canada seems to have upheld the inverted reading of the 'safeguard clause' by arguing: 'The other clear case where a right to external self-determination accrues [apart from colonial situations] is where a people is subject to alien subjugation, domination or exploitation outside a colonial context.'[110] But the Court also pronounced that these circumstances were not met in the case of Québec[111] and the pronouncement remained an obiter dictum.

In the case of *Loizidou v Turkey*, before the European Court of Human Rights, Judges Wildhaber and Ryssdal argued:

> In recent years a consensus has seemed to emerge that peoples may also exercise a right to self-determination if their human rights are consistently and flagrantly violated or if they are without representation at all or are massively under-represented in an undemocratic and discriminatory way. If this description is correct, then the right to self-determination is a tool which may be used to re-establish international standards of human rights and democracy.[112]

---

[108] *The Quebec case*, para 126.
[109] See n 10, above.
[110] The *Québec* case (n 11), para 133.
[111] ibid, para 135.
[112] *Loizidou v Turkey* (1997) 23 EHRR 244, 535 (Judge Wildhaber concurring, joined by Judge Ryssdal).

The two concurring Judges did not make a reference to secession. Yet this omission is not too significant: the right of self-determination is applicable to all peoples[113] and there is no need for this to be specifically affirmed in a concurring opinion. The exercise of the right of self-determination in a form of secession is a different issue and the context suggests that this is what Judges Wildhaber and Ryssdal had in mind. Their concurring opinion obviously adopts the remedial secession argument and accepts the possibility of secession in situations where peoples are oppressed by and/or are not adequately represented within the political structures of their parent states.

The support for remedial secession in jurisprudence is thus limited to an obiter dictum and to a concurring opinion of two judges, while no judicial body has accepted secession as an entitlement in any particular case. The doctrine nevertheless has some support among writers. The main argument of the academic proponents is well-captured by Buchanan:

> If the state persists in serious injustices toward a group, and the group's forming its own independent political unit is a remedy of last resort for these injustices, then the group ought to be acknowledged by the international community to have the claim-right to repudiate the authority of the state and to attempt to establish its own independent political unit.[114]

The academic proponents of remedial secession thus tend to see secession as a 'qualified right',[115] which is triggered by oppression. At the same time, it is an exceptional solution and is the last resort for ending the oppression.[116]

Summers rightfully observes that most writers express their support for remedial secession rather cautiously by claiming that such a right 'perhaps' or 'possibly' exists, or by giving a circular reference to 'a number of commentators', without taking a firm stance on whether this right exists or not.[117] Shaw further argues that a theory based on an inverted reading of the 'safeguard clause' is rather problematic:

> Such a major change in legal principle cannot be introduced by way of an ambiguous subordinate clause, especially when the principle of territorial integrity has always been accepted and proclaimed as a core principle of international law, and is indeed placed before the qualifying clause in the provision in question.[118]

[113] See n 30, above.

[114] A Buchanan, *Justice, Legitimacy, and Self-Determination* (Oxford, Oxford University Press, 2004) 335. For a thorough account of the academic support for remedial secession, see Tancredi (n 107) 176.

[115] Raič (n 14) 323.

[116] In this part, academic writings follow early speculation on the possibility of a shift of sovereignty as a last resort, which appeared in the question of the Aaland Islands. The *Aaland Islands* case (1920) LNOJ Spec Supp 3 (the International Committee of Jurists) 21.

[117] J Summers, *Peoples and International Law: How Nationalism and Self-Determination Shape a Contemporary Law of Nations* (Leiden, Martinus Nijhoff, 2007) 347.

[118] M Shaw, 'Peoples, Territorialism and Boundaries' (1997) 8 *European Journal of International Law* 478, 483.

In essence, judicial decisions and academic writings on remedial secession do not provide for sufficient evidence suggesting that in international legal doctrine, remedial secession is a universally accepted entitlement of oppressed peoples. Nevertheless, the underlying idea of remedial secession, that is, ending the oppression directed against a certain people, can still influence the recognition policies of some states. In turn, it will now be considered how remedial secession can have effects through the act of recognition.

## 6.2 The Effects of Remedial Secession through Recognition

The absence of a right to unilateral secession does not imply that such an act is illegal. Indeed, 'secession is neither legal nor illegal in international law, but a legally neutral act the consequences of which are regulated internationally'.[119] Even the 'safeguard clause' says that the disruption of territorial integrity is not 'authorised' or 'encouraged', but it does not say it is prohibited.[120] In the UN Charter era, it is thus very unlikely that an attempt at unilateral secession would result in a new state creation, but such an outcome is not excluded. In the *Quebec* case, the Supreme Court of Canada pronounced:

> The ultimate success of . . . a [unilateral] secession would be dependent on recognition by the international community, which is likely to consider the legality and legitimacy of secession having regard to, amongst other facts, the conduct of Québec and Canada, in determining whether to grant or withhold recognition.[121]

This position of the Supreme Court of Canada suggests that: (i) the success of a unilateral secession depends on international recognition; and (ii) the conduct of the parent state towards the independence-seeking entity will be considered very important when states decide on granting recognition. It thus implies that remedial secession could be given effect through recognition and falls close to Shaw's argument that 'recognition may be more forthcoming where the secession has occurred as a consequence of violations of human rights'.[122]

Any argument suggesting that recognition could create states needs to be taken with caution, as it could be problematic in light of the general perception in contemporary international law that recognition is a declaratory and not a constitutive act.[123] However, an argument was set out in chapter one that acknowledging the constitutive effects of the act of recognition in such

---

[119] Crawford (n 38) 390.
[120] *cf* n 10, above.
[121] The *Québec* case (n 11), para 155.
[122] Shaw (n 118) 483.
[123] See ch 1, 3.4.

circumstances is not the same as saying that non-recognised states cannot exist as states;[124] Rather, it is that the universal recognition of an attempt at unilateral secession would have the effect of a collective state creation.[125] In the end, remedial secession is still an attempt at unilateral secession, whereas oppression may make a claim for independence more legitimate.

There exists an important limitation on giving effect to remedial secession via recognition. While in a situation of oppression, foreign states might be more willing to grant recognition to unilaterally declared independence,[126] no circumstances make recognition an international legal obligation.[127] The actual position of remedial secession in international law may therefore be that, as a consequence of oppression, the parent state's claim to territorial integrity becomes weaker and foreign states may decide to recognise the secession-seeking entity, thus deciding not to observe the territorial integrity of the parent state. But remedial secession is not an entitlement of oppressed peoples and oppression creates no obligation for third states to grant recognition.

## 6.3  Remedial Secession and State Practice

### 6.3.1  *The East Pakistan (Bangladesh) Precedent*

In 1947, Pakistan was created 'out of the provinces of the British India and the Indian states with majority Muslim population'.[128] Its territory was geographically divided into two parts, which were separated by around 1,000 miles of Indian territory. In East Pakistan, most of the population spoke Bengali, a language not spoken in West Pakistan, while '[t]he only aspect of social life which the two populations shared was that of Islam'.[129] East Pakistan 'had suffered relatively severe and systematic discrimination from the central government based in Islamabad'.[130]

At the general Pakistani elections in December 1970, the Awami League, an autonomy-seeking East Pakistani party, won 167 out of 169 seats allo-

[124]  ibid.

[125]  See ch 2, 6.

[126]  See Buchanan (n 114) 335, who argues that where oppressed peoples try to create their own state, their parent state's 'right to territorial integrity no longer encompasses the area in question, because the injustices the state has perpetrated have voided its claim to a part of the state's territory'. At the same time, Buchanan (ibid) is aware that in international law as it currently stands, this 'does not imply that states are obliged to recognize the entity in question as a . . . state'.

[127]  R McCorquodale, 'The Creation and Recognition of States' in S Blay, R Piotrowicz and BM Tsamenyi (eds), *Public International Law: An Australian Perspective* (Melbourne, Oxford University Press, 2005) 193. See also ch 1, 3.2.

[128]  A Pavković and P Radan, *Creating New States: Theory and Practice of Secession* (Aldershot, Ashgate, 2007) 103.

[129]  ibid, 104.

[130]  Crawford (n 38) 140.

cated to the eastern part of the state in the Pakistani Parliament. This result meant a solid majority in the 313-seat Pakistani Parliament. In response to the dominance of the Awami League, the central government suspended the Parliament and introduced a period of martial rule in East Pakistan, 'which involved acts of repression and even possibly genocide and caused some ten million Bengalis to seek refuge in India'.[131]

On 17 April 1971, the Awami League proclaimed the independence of East Pakistan.[132] At that time, East Pakistani guerrilla forces were already in armed conflict with Pakistani armed forces.[133] On 3 December 1971, India intervened in support of East Pakistan, fighting Pakistani armed forces on both the eastern and western sides. On 17 December 1971, Pakistani armed forces surrendered and India declared a ceasefire on the western side. On 6 December 1971, India recognised the independence of Bangladesh.[134] With help of Indian forces, the Awami League exercised substantial control over the territory of Bangladesh. Within weeks, Bangladesh was explicitly recognised by 28 states. Recognition by Pakistan was granted on 22 February 1974.[135]

While the case of Bangladesh may serve as an argument in support of remedial secession, other interpretations may also be plausible. It may well be that 'the withdrawal of the Pakistan Army after the ceasefire on 16 December 1971 merely produced a *fait accompli*, which in the circumstances other States had no alternative but to accept'.[136] Although Pakistan had already withdrawn from the eastern part by the end of 1971, the legal status of Bangladesh remained ambiguous for two years. It was not until recognition of Bangladesh was granted by Pakistan that universal recognition followed. Bangladesh was only admitted to the UN on 17 September 1974.[137] It is therefore not a clear example in support of the remedial secession theory. Indeed, it is obvious that the international community did not see secession as an entitlement and Bangladesh became universally recognised only after Pakistan had given consent to its independence.

The episode with Bangladesh also confirms the nature of state creation as a political process. One can say that between 1971 and 1974, its legal status was ambiguous. Reading history backwards, an argument can be made that the status of Bangladesh had to be clarified. But this is easy to say from today's perspective when we know that Bangladesh *is* a state. If one were asked in 1972, it would only be possible to answer that there was ambiguity with regard to its legal status. And this ambiguity is a consequence of the nature of statehood in international law: it is a legal status

---

[131] ibid, 141.
[132] Pavković and Radan (n 128) 102.
[133] ibid.
[134] Crawford (n 38) 141.
[135] ibid.
[136] ibid, 393.
[137] ibid. See also GA Res 3203 (XXIX) (17 September 1974).

achieved in a political process, not an objective fact.[138] As states do not emerge automatically and self-evidently, oppression did not directly lead to Bangladesh's statehood. International acceptance was required for this state creation. It may well be that the political process and the international acceptance of independence were triggered by the oppression, but the latter did not have any *direct* legal implications for statehood.

### 6.3.2 Other Possible Examples of Remedial Secession

The remedial secession argument has also been advanced in relation to the dissolutions of the SFRY and the Soviet Union. In one such argument:

> After the recognition by the international community of the disintegration as unitary States of the Soviet Union and Yugoslavia, it could now be the case that any government which is oppressive to peoples within its territory may no longer be able to rely on the general interest of territorial integrity as a limitation on the right of self-determination.[139]

It is questionable whether the remedial secession argument was really acknowledged by the international community in these two situations.

Although the political situation in the Soviet Union in 1991 was rather complicated,[140] from the legal point of view, the dissolution of the Soviet Union was a consensual act supported by all republics, including Russia.[141] The remedial secession argument could only be plausible with regard to the Baltic States, which achieved independence prior to the dissolution of the Soviet Union.[142] Such an argument stems from the suppression of their independence, which resulted from the Ribbentrop-Molotov Pact.[143] When the Baltic States were accepted to UN membership, '[i]ndividual Member States [of the UN] emphasised that, since the independence of the Baltic States had been unlawfully suppressed, they had the right of self-determination'.[144] Yet, as pointed out in this chapter, the right of self-determination does not mean a 'right to unilateral secession' and even in the example of the Baltic States, the applicability of the right of self-determination did not automatically result in secession.[145] In the end, the secession of the Baltic States was consensual, with the approval of the Soviet Union.[146]

---

[138] See ch 1,.3.4.
[139] McCorquodale (n 92) 880.
[140] For more on this, see ch 2, 2.1.
[141] ibid.
[142] ibid.
[143] See ch 2, 2.1, n 4.
[144] Crawford (n 38) 394.
[145] ibid, 395.
[146] See ch 2, 2.1.

In the case of the SFRY, it is argued that both Slovenia and Croatia were initially examples of an attempt at unilateral secession which later resulted in the dissolution of the parent state.[147] Both republics advanced remedial secession arguments. Slovenia's reference to this doctrine, however, only appears in the preamble to the Foundational Constitutional Instrument on Sovereignty and Independence of the Republic of Slovenia. A section of the preamble states: '[T]he SFRY does not function as a state governed by the rule of law and allows grave violations of human rights, rights of peoples, as well as rights of republics and autonomous provinces.'[148]

This preambular proclamation suggests that Slovenia only made a political assertion to remedial secession and did not claim to have any legal rights under this doctrine. On the other hand, Croatia's claim to remedial secession had a much more prominent legal quality. When declaring independence, Croatia referred to Article 140 of its Constitution,[149] which provides:

> The Republic of Croatia shall remain a constitutive part of the SFRY until a new agreement of the Yugoslav republics is achieved or until the Assembly of the Republic of Croatia decides otherwise. Shall an act or procedure of a federal body or of a body of another republic or province member of the federation constitute a violation of territorial integrity of the Republic of Croatia, or *shall she be brought into an unequal position in the federation*, or shall her interests be threatened, the organs of the Republic shall, stemming from the right of self-determination and the sovereignty of the Republic of Croatia, affirmed by this Constitution, deliver necessary decisions, regarding the protection of sovereignty and interests of the Republic of Croatia.[150]

Importantly, Article 140 did not declare that Croatia had a 'right to secession' by virtue of the right of self-determination alone; rather, its claim to independence was qualified by a reference to its 'unequal position in the federation'. Croatia notably adopted the language of remedial secession, yet it is debatable whether this argument was really accepted by the international community.

The attempts at unilateral secession played an important role in the process of the dissolution of the SFRY, which proves that 'secession and dissolution are not mutually exclusive'.[151] Indeed, the Badinter Commission based its opinion in which it established that the SFRY was in the process of

---

[147] Dugard and Raič (n 78) 123–30.
[148] The Foundational Constitutional Instrument on Sovereignty and Independence of the Republic of Slovenia (1991), preamble, para 3 (author's own translation), *Official Gazette of the Republic of Slovenia*, No 1/91-I (25 June 1991).
[149] The Constitutional Decree of the Assembly of the Republic of Croatia on Sovereignty and Independence of the Republic of Croatia, *Official Gazette of the Republic of Croatia*, No 31/1991 (25 June 1991).
[150] The Constitution of the Republic of Croatia (1990), art 140, emphasis added (author's own translation).
[151] ibid, 128.

dissolution on the fact that three out of its six constituent republics had already declared independence and that, due to Serbia's usurpation of federal organs, the federation was no longer functioning.[152] As this implies that the SFRY was no longer representative of its peoples, in the interpretation of Dugard and Raič, Opinion 1 of the Badinter Commission adopts the remedial secession doctrine.[153] But such an argument is not without its difficulties, as the Badinter Commission expressly held that dissolution, not unilateral secession, was at work.[154] This view was subsequently affirmed by the state practice and the practice of UN organs.[155]

Another example where the remedial secession argument was advanced is Kosovo. When Kosovo declared independence on 17 February 2008,[156] the Declaration of Independence made reference to 'years of strife and violence in Kosovo, that disturbed the conscience of all civilised people'[157] and expressed its gratitude that 'in 1999 the world intervened, thereby removing Belgrade's governance over Kosovo and placing Kosovo under United Nations interim administration'.[158] It declared Kosovo to be 'a democratic, secular and multi-ethnic republic, guided by the principles of non-discrimination and equal protection under the law',[159] welcomed 'the international community's continued support of . . . democratic development through international presences established in Kosovo'[160] and stated that 'independence brings to an end the process of Yugoslavia's violent dissolution'.[161]

These proclamations in the Declaration of Independence may come close to remedial secession arguments, but such an explanation is not without its difficulties. Indeed, if remedial secession is understood as the last resort for ending oppression,[162] this argument could only have been accepted if Kosovo had declared independence in 1999. It is difficult to see how secession in 2008 ended any oppression. At the time of the Declaration, Kosovo had been governed independently of Serbia for almost nine years.

The real difficulty with Kosovo was expressed by Martti Ahtisaari, the Special Envoy of the UN Secretary-General, who wrote in his report:

> For the past eight years, Kosovo and Serbia have been governed in complete separation. The establishment of the United Nations Mission in Kosovo

---

[152]  See n 76, above. See also Dugard and Raič (n 78) 125–26.

[153]  See Dugard and Raič (n 78), 130.

[154]  See Badinter Commission, Opinion 1 (29 November 1991), reprinted in Trifunovska (n 76) 415.

[155]  See ch 2, 3.7.

[156]  See Assembly of Kosovo, Kosovo Declaration of Independence, www.assembly-kosova.org/?cid=2,128,1635.

[157]  ibid, preamble, para 7.

[158]  ibid, preamble, para 8.

[159]  ibid, para 2.

[160]  ibid, para 5.

[161]  ibid, para 10.

[162]  *cf* n 114, above.

(UNMIK) pursuant to resolution 1244 (1999), and its assumption of all legislative, executive and judicial authority throughout Kosovo, has created a situation in which Serbia has not exercised any governing authority over Kosovo. This is a reality one cannot deny; it is irreversible. A return of Serbian rule over Kosovo would not be acceptable to the overwhelming majority of the people of Kosovo. Belgrade could not regain its authority without provoking violent opposition. Autonomy of Kosovo within the borders of Serbia – however notional such autonomy may be – is simply not tenable.[163]

It is not the purpose of this chapter to determine whether the irreversible reality caused by Resolution 1244 can justify Kosovo's secession, yet the Ahtisaari Report suggests that the reasoning behind the declaration of independence was not grounded in the remedial secession theory. Nevertheless, Kosovo has been recognised by 92 states.[164] In their recognition texts, many states recalled the oppression from before the adoption of Resolution 1244.[165] Yet these references were not made in the context of the remedial secession doctrine. Instead, some states invoked the *sui generis* character of the Kosovo situation, which was determined by the legal regime created by Resolution 1244.[166] References to prior developments were made in order to clarify the origins of the invoked special circumstances. Remedial secession was also referred to in some of the pleadings before the ICJ in the *Kosovo Advisory Opinion*,[167] yet the Court did not consider these arguments and avoided commenting on whether Kosovo could support the case for remedial secession.

If remedial secession is understood as an entitlement, the practice of non-colonial state creation shows that there is no clear support for this doctrine in state practice. The secession of East Pakistan may well have ended oppression, but it is questionable whether the remedial secession argument was actually given an effect. Similarly, while some states may have decided to recognise Kosovo because they saw no alternative to Kosovo's independence, this is not enough to make a plausible argument in favour of remedial secession. Kosovo's declaration of independence in 2008 simply was not the last resort for the *ending of oppression*. South Sudan's independence followed on from the peace agreement aimed at stopping a civil war and bringing a grave humanitarian situation to an

---

[163] UN Doc S/2007/168 (16 March 2007), para 7.

[164] See 'Who Recognized Kosova as an Independent State', www.kosovothanksyou.com.

[165] See recognition of the US, http://2001-2009.state.gov/secretary/rm/2008/02/100973.htm; recognition of Australia, http://www.foreignminister.gov.au/releases/2008/fa-s034_08.html; recognition of Germany (on file with author); and recognition of the United Kingdom (on file with author).

[166] ibid.

[167] See Pleadings of Albania, ICJ Verbatim Record, CR 2009/26 (2 December 2009), paras 2–15; and the UK, ICJ Verbatim Record, CR 2009/32 (10 December 2009), paras 29 and 30. Interestingly, Russia did not argue against the concept of remedial secession as such; it only held that it is not applicable in the situation of Kosovo. See ICJ Verbatim Record, CR 2009/30 (8 December 2009), paras 19–22.

end,[168] but the path to independence was rooted in a clear constitutional provision and consent of the parent state.[169] Due to its consensual nature, the independence of South Sudan was not a matter of the exercise of a remedial right under international law.

The cases of the Soviet Union and of the SFRY provide examples of dissolutions. Although the dissolution of the SFRY started as a chain of secessions, it was universally accepted that the international personality of the SFRY was extinguished. In such a circumstance, new states emerge in the absence of a claim to territorial integrity by a parent state. Ultimately, the mode of state creation is not secession, and where there is no secession, there can be no remedial secession. This also applies to the dissolution of the Soviet Union, which was consensual.

The concept of remedial secession does not lead to any legal rights and duties. But it can be accommodated within the political reasoning of states when they take a decision on whether to grant recognition to a secession-seeking entity. Since recognition is a political act with legal consequences,[170] oppression could still have implications for the legal status of a territory and its statehood. Oppression can initiate the political process which could ultimately lead to statehood, yet it does not have any *direct* implications for the legal status of a territory.

Although the remedial secession doctrine may operate through recognition, there is no evidence that 'oppression' as the qualifying criterion of remedial secession would be associated with the absence of democratic (electoral) practices in a certain state. Indeed, remedial secession is a doctrine founded on the 'safeguard clause' and it was shown above that governmental representativeness in the context of the 'safeguard clause' is not to be associated with governmental representativeness in the context of democratic political theory. It also follows from practice that where remedial secession arguments could be possibly advanced, these were not associated with a claim to democratisation. Indeed, remedial secession is rather understood as the last resort to end gross and systematic breaches of human rights. It was argued in chapter one of this book that respect for human rights is not the same as the implementation of democratic (electoral) practices.[171]

It also needs to be noted that in the *Québec* case, the Supreme Court of Canada made an additional argument that secession may possibly become a right 'when a people is blocked from the meaningful exercise of the right to self-determination internally'.[172] Yet this was also an *obiter dictum* and the Court's language was ambiguous. And even if this doctrine were

[168] See ch 2, 2.4.
[169] ibid.
[170] McCorquodale (n 127) 193. *cf* also ch 1, 3.2.
[171] See ch 1, 2.2.
[172] The *Québec* case (n 11), para 134.

accepted, it was shown above that the denial of internal self-determination cannot be qualified as the absence of a democratic political system.[173]

While the right of self-determination is not to be associated with democracy as a political system and the absence of a democratic political system does not create a remedial right to secession, this is not to say that the process of state creation is not governed by some democratic principles. These operate within the right of self-determination and will be considered in turn.

## 7  DEMOCRATIC PRINCIPLES AND EXTERNAL EXERCISE OF THE RIGHT OF SELF-DETERMINATION

In the *Western Sahara Advisory Opinion*, the ICJ set the standard that 'the application of the right of self-determination requires a free and genuine expression of the will of the peoples concerned'.[174] As discussed above, outside of the colonial context, the right of self-determination does not equal a 'right to independence'.[175] Thus, popular support in favour of independence will not necessarily create a new state. Combining the contemporary doctrine on self-determination and the *Western Sahara Advisory Opinion*, 'a free and genuine expression of the will of the peoples concerned' may be seen as a necessary, albeit not sufficient, requirement for a new state creation.

The requirement for a popular consultation is not absolute. In the *Western Sahara Advisory Opinion*, the ICJ also acknowledged the existence of 'special circumstances' in which a 'consultation [is] totally unnecessary'.[176] It remains to be clarified which circumstances are considered 'special', so that the consultation requirement can be dispensed with. This section thus considers whether the practice of non-colonial new state creations confirms the standard which follows from the general rule and exception established by the ICJ in *Western Sahara*: the operation of the right of self-determination requires an expression of the will of the peoples before the legal status of a territory may be altered, save for exceptional circumstances.[177]

As expressions of the will of the people, popular consultations, usually formalised by referenda, have been a co-traveller of self-determination since the appearance of this principle in modern democratic political thought.[178] Popular consultations for determining the legal status of

---

[173] See ch 3, 3 and 3, 4.
[174] *Western Sahara Advisory Opinion*, ICJ Rep 1975, para 55.
[175] See ch 3, 2.
[176] *Western Sahara Advisory Opinion* (n 174), para 59.
[177] See n 174, above.
[178] *cf* ch 3, 2.

territories were already held in the aftermath of the French Revolution.[179] After the First World War, under the influence of US President Woodrow Wilson and his concept of self-determination,[180] several referenda on the future legal status of European territories took place under the auspices of the League of Nations.[181] In the UN Charter period, self-determination became a positive rule of international law and was codified as a human right.[182] The operation of this right initially resulted in the process of decolonisation. In this period, popular consultations 'came to be the stock-in-trade of the United Nations in situations involving accession to independence, association, or integration of colonies and non-self-governing territories'.[183] This book is, however, concerned with post-1990 state creations which occurred outside of the process of decolonisation. In this part, it will clarify how the requirement expressed in the *Western Sahara Advisory Opinion* is qualified in contemporary international law and in the practice of post-1990 state creations, occurring outside of the process of decolonisation.

In principle, the section is only concerned with independence referenda where new states eventually emerged. An exception is the situation of Québec. Although the attempt at secession by Québec was not successful, the reasoning in the *Québec* case[184] and the writings of qualified authors on the matter provide important clarifications regarding the role of popular consultations in situations of new state creations and the standards that need to be observed in order for such consultations to be considered 'free and genuine expressions of the will of the people'. Although in Canada these standards were implemented with a specific situation in Québec in mind, it will be argued that they nevertheless have universal validity. Subsequent chapters are then concerned with the legal significance of the expression of the will of the people and procedural standards followed at independence referenda in successful post-1990 state creations.

---

[179]   ibid.

[180]   For more on the Wilsonian concept of self-determination, see generally R Baker and W Dodd (eds), *War and Peace: Presidential Messages, Addresses, and Public Papers* (New York, Harper, 1927).

[181]   H Brady and C Kaplan, 'Eastern Europe and the Former Soviet Union' in D Butler and A Ranney (eds), *Referendums Around the World: The Growing Use of Direct Democracy* (Washington DC, AEI Press, 1994) 175.

[182]   See n 30, above.

[183]   Miller (n 19) 630. See also Y Beigbeder, *International Monitoring of Plebiscites, Referenda and National Elections: Self-Determination and Transition to Democracy* (Dordrecht, Martinus Nijhoff, 1994) 91.

[184]   The *Québec* case (n 11), para 126.

## 7.1 Québec: Attempts at Secession and Popular Consultation

### 7.1.1 *Background to the* Québec *case*

At the 1976 elections in the Province of Québec, the Parti Québécois (PQ) became the strongest political party in the Province.[185] On the political agenda of the PQ was the state sovereignty of Québec, a Canadian province in which the majority of the population is French-Canadian.[186] On 20 May 1980, a referendum was held on a mandate to the government of Québec to negotiate a new agreement with the rest of Canada, which would lead to Québec's sovereignty, while economic ties with Canada would be maintained. The English version of the referendum question reads as follows:

> The Government of Québec has made public its proposal to negotiate a new agreement with the rest of Canada, based on the equality of nations; this agreement would enable Québec to acquire the exclusive power to make its laws, administer its taxes and establish relations abroad in other words sovereignty and at the same time, to maintain with Canada an economic association including a common currency; any change in political status resulting from these negotiations will be submitted to the people through a referendum; on these terms, do you agree to give the Government of Québec the mandate to negotiate the proposed agreement between Québec and Canada?[187]

At a turnout of 85.61 per cent of all those eligible to vote, the mandate to the government of Québec to negotiate with the rest of Canada on the sovereignty of Québec was rejected by 59.56 per cent of the valid votes cast.[188]

After another electoral success of the PQ in 1994, the Draft Bill Respecting the Sovereignty of Québec was tabled at the Québec National Assembly.[189] The Draft Bill foresaw Québec's declaration of independence and authorisation of the government of Québec to negotiate a new economic association with Canada.[190] According to the Draft Bill, sovereignty could only be proclaimed upon the approval of the population of Québec expressed at a referendum.[191]

---

[185] P Dumberry, 'Lessons Learned from the Quebec Secession Reference before the Supreme Court of Canada' in M Kohen (ed.), *Secession: International Law Perspectives* (Cambridge, Cambridge University Press, 2006) 418.
[186] A Bayefsky, *Self-Determination in International Law: Quebec and Lessons Learned* (The Hague, Kluwer Law International, 2000) 5.
[187] Reprinted in Dumberry (n 185) 418.
[188] See Le Directeur général des élections du Québec, at http://www.electionsquebec.qc.ca/english/provincial/media/referendums.php?n=2.
[189] See Dumberry (n 185) 419.
[190] ibid. See also Draft Bill Respecting the Sovereignty of Québec, Articles 1 and 2, at www.solon.org/misc/referendum-bill.html.
[191] ibid, Article 16.

Subsequently, another independence referendum was held on 30 October 1995. The question posed at the second referendum reads: 'Do you agree that Québec should become sovereign, after having made a formal offer to Canada for a new economic and political partnership, within the scope of the Bill respecting the future of Québec and of the agreement signed on 12 June 1995?'[192] At a turnout of 95.52 per cent of all those eligible to vote, the proposal was rejected by 50.58 per cent of the votes cast.[193]

Prior to the referendum, a Québec resident challenged the legality of the Draft Bill and the referendum at the Superior Court of Québec.[194] After his motion was denied, he filed another, revised, action in 1996.[195] Although the referendum results were already known, the Canadian federal government intervened and referred the matter to the Supreme Court of Canada.[196]

The Supreme Court of Canada dealt with questions of whether Québec has a right to unilateral secession under the Constitution of Canada and/ or under international law.[197] As already argued, the Court established that there exists no such right and confirmed that the right of self-determination would normally be consummated in its internal mode.[198] At the same time, unilateral secession is not prohibited under international law and the ultimate success of such secession would depend on international recognition.[199] At this point, it needs to be considered in more detail what role the Court ascribed to popular consultation in the context of the attempt at unilateral secession.

### 7.1.2 The Québec Case and the Effects of Popular Consultation

The Supreme Court of Canada established in the *Québec* case that a democratic decision in favour of secession does not result in a 'right to secession'. At the same time, such a will of the people cannot be ignored:

> The democratic principle . . . would demand that considerable weight be given to a clear expression by the people of Québec of their will to secede from Canada, even though a referendum, in itself and without more, has no direct legal effect, and could not in itself bring about unilateral secession.[200]

[192] Reprinted in Dumberry (n 185) 420.
[193] ibid.
[194] ibid.
[195] Details on this issue are beyond the scope of this book. For more on this, see Dumberry (n 185) 421–22; Bayefsky (n 186) 10–12.
[196] Bayefsky (n 186) 12.
[197] The *Québec* case (n 11), Introduction, para 2.
[198] See n 11, above.
[199] See n 121, above.
[200] ibid, para 87.

The Court went on to argue that to accept:

> [T]hat a clear expression of self-determination by the people of Québec would impose no obligations upon the other provinces or the federal government . . . would amount to the assertion that other constitutionally recognized principles necessarily trump the clearly expressed democratic will of the people of Québec.[201]

According to the Court, in such a circumstance, an obligation would be put on both Québec and Canada to negotiate a future constitutional arrangement for Québec. In this context, the Court stressed that:

> No negotiations could be effective if their ultimate outcome, secession, is cast as an absolute legal entitlement based upon an obligation to give effect to that act of secession in the Constitution. Such a foregone conclusion would actually undermine the obligation to negotiate and render it hollow.[202]

The Court thereby defined the duty to negotiate very loosely. Yet, as one commentator has observed, 'it is clear that it should not solely consist of the "logistical details of secession"'.[203] The Court did not discuss any possible arrangements that would indicate an outcome of such negotiations, nor did it address the problem of a situation in which Québec would accept nothing short of independence, while Canada would be unwilling to accept such a demand.[204]

Nevertheless, according to the Supreme Court of Canada, the principle of democracy is not an absolute principle and 'cannot be invoked to trump' other constitutional principles.[205] In the context of Canadian constitutional law, the following principles were identified: federalism, democracy, constitutionalism, the rule of law and respect for minorities.[206]

The Court also gave special consideration to the problem of a tyranny of the majority, to which procedural adherence to democratic decision-making may lead:

> Although democratic government is generally solicitous of [fundamental human rights and individual freedoms] there are occasions when the majority will be tempted to ignore fundamental rights in order to accomplish collective goals more easily or effectively. Constitutional entrenchment ensures that those rights will be given due regard and protection.[207]

The problem of a tyranny of the majority is a well-known problem of democratic decision-making and modern definitions of democracy have

---

[201] ibid, para 91.
[202] ibid.
[203] Dumberry (n 185) 429.
[204] *cf* ch 3, 2.2.
[205] The *Québec* case (n 11), para 91.
[206] ibid, para 33.
[207] ibid, para 74.

adopted some mechanisms for the protection of minorities.[208] Indeed, 'centuries of philosophical debate over, and political experimentation with, the majority principle have led to the protected status of the minority as much as to the authoritative status of the majority in Western democracies'.[209] In the context of the right of self-determination, decision-making regarding a change of the legal status of a territory thus cannot be merely a matter for the majority and its preference.

When unilateral rather than pre-negotiated, ie, consensual, secession is at issue, the *Québec* case confirms the standard that a successful referendum does not lead to a 'right to secession', but is one of the factors that might legitimise a secessionist claim. As follows from the *Québec* case, minority protection standards would also play an important role in determining the legitimacy of a secessionist claim. The *Québec* case thus reflects the view that the right of self-determination is not an absolute human right and, as such, is limited by other human rights, which include the right of self-determination of other peoples.[210] However, when the will of the people favours independence, the *Québec* case also suggests that such a will cannot be ignored. Now it needs to be considered how the requirement for a 'free and genuine expression of the will of the people' was qualified in the situation of Québec.

### 7.1.3 *The Québec Situation and the Clarification of Popular Consultation Standards*

The Supreme Court of Canada stated in the *Québec* case that '[t]he referendum result, if it is to be taken as an expression of the democratic will, must be free of ambiguity both in terms of the question asked and in terms of the support it achieves'.[211] In the Canadian context, the requirement of 'free of ambiguity' and the issue of negotiations for the determination of the future status of an independence-seeking federal unit were subsequently addressed by the Clarity Act (2000). According to this Act, ambiguity could stem from the referendum question itself or from the required majority which is considered to be representative of the will of the people. With regard to the referendum question, the Clarity Act provides:

---

[208] For more on the protection of minorities within the democratic constitutional order and safeguards against a tyranny of the majority, see A Lijphart, *Democracies: Patterns of Majoritarian and Consensus Government in Twenty-One Countries* (New Haven, Yale University Press, 1984) 187–96.

[209] Miller (n 19) 637.

[210] *cf* n 9, above.

[211] The *Québec* case (n 11), para 87.

[A] clear expression of the will of the population of a province that the province cease to be part of Canada could not result from

(*a*) a referendum question that merely focuses on a mandate to negotiate without soliciting a direct expression of the will of the population of that province on whether the province should cease to be part of Canada; or

(*b*) a referendum question that envisages other possibilities in addition to the secession of the province from Canada, such as economic or political arrangements with Canada, that obscure a direct expression of the will of the population of that province on whether the province should cease to be part of Canada.[212]

It is evident that the Clarity Act was drafted with 1980 and 1995 referenda questions in Québec in mind, which were both formulated in a way that they implied a future economic association with Canada.[213] Furthermore, the referendum question in 1980 did not ask voters directly on independence but on a mandate for the government of Québec to negotiate on a new arrangement with the rest of Canada, which would lead to independence.[214] Although the requirement for clear referendum questions reflects specific issues previously experienced with the referenda question in Québec, they nevertheless have universal validity. Indeed, unclear or even misleading referenda questions cannot be considered 'free and genuine expressions of the will of the people', as required by the standard established in the *Western Sahara Advisory Opinion*.[215] It remains to be determined below, when referenda questions in situations of post-1990 new state creations will be examined, to what degree the Clarity Act standard can be universalised.

Another procedural requirement of independence referenda mentioned by the Clarity Act is a clear winning majority. The Clarity Act invoked the following elements relevant for the achievement of a clear majority at independence referenda: (i) the size of the majority of valid votes cast in favour of the secessionist option; (ii) the percentage of eligible voters voting in the referendum; and (iii) any other matters or circumstances it considers to be relevant.[216]

The required majority was not expressed quantitatively. It remains unclear whether a majority of all valid votes cast would be perceived as an expression of the will of the people or whether a more qualified majority would be required (eg, a majority of all those eligible to vote). As follows from the Clarity Act, the required majority may be situation-specific and no universally prescribed standard can be imposed. In this context it

---

[212] Clarity Act (29 June 2000), art 1, para 3, at http://laws-lois.justice.gc.ca/eng/acts/C-31.8/page-1.html.
[213] See nn 187 and 192, above.
[214] See n 187, above.
[215] *Western Sahara Advisory Opinion* (n 174), para 55.
[216] Clarity Act, art 2, para 2.

needs to be recalled that the expressed will of a people does not lead to a self-executing secession of a province, but merely gives a mandate to a provincial government to negotiate with the federal government. This is specifically reaffirmed in the Clarity Act.[217]

In the Québec situation, where consultation is to be understood as part of a broader process of negotiations for a future constitutional arrangement, a firmly prescribed majority is not necessary. This is different where consultation may lead to a self-executing secession with the approval of a parent state. In such circumstances, clear referendum rules need to be established in order to avoid ambiguity. A good example of such a situation is Montenegro.[218]

In sum, the *Québec* case takes a clear position that self-determination is not an absolute human right. Outside of colonial situations, the will of the people in favour of independence will not create a new state, but a free and genuine expression of the will of the people in favour of independence cannot be ignored and creates a duty to negotiate the future status of the secession-seeking entity. In order for an expression of the will of the people to be considered free and genuine, the referendum question and the winning majority need to be free of ambiguity. The referendum question needs to relate to independence directly and not only implicitly. But the winning majority is not determined quantitatively; this will depend on the circumstances. The chapter now turns to the legal relevance of independence referenda in the practice of successful post-1990 state creations. It considers the procedural standards developed at these referenda and argues how these standards relate to the background of the Québec situation.

## 7.2  Popular Consultation Standards in the Territory of the SFRY

It follows from chapter two that it was not the will of the people (expressed at independence referenda) which would directly create new states in the territory of the SFRY; rather, it was the universally accepted international legal position that the SFRY no longer existed which was crucial for the emergence of new states. But independence referenda nevertheless played an important role in the process of dissolution. The following subsections demonstrate that the Badinter Commission paid significant attention to the referenda. The legal effects of the referenda in the SFRY will now be analysed and the procedural standards evaluated in a comparative perspective.

---

[217]  ibid, art 3.
[218]  See ch 3, 7.7.

### 7.2.1 Slovenia

The referendum on Slovenia's independence was held on 23 December 1990[219] and was regulated by the Plebiscite on the Sovereignty and Independence of the Republic of Slovenia Act, adopted by Slovenia's Assembly on 21 November 1990.[220] The Act prescribed the following referendum question: 'Shall the Republic of Slovenia become a sovereign and independent state?'[221] It also specified that: 'The decision that the Republic of Slovenia becomes an independent state shall be adopted if supported by the majority of all those eligible to vote.'[222]

The decision in favour of independence was adopted by a majority of 88.5 per cent of all those eligible to vote (92 per cent of those who voted), with four per cent of all those eligible to vote expressly voting against it.[223] The expression of the will of the people on Slovenia's independence was clear from the points of view of both the clarity of the question asked and the majority in its support.

On 25 June 1991, the Assembly of the Republic of Slovenia adopted the Declaration of Independence.[224] When discussing the recognition of Slovenia, the Badinter Commission noted that Slovenia's independence was supported at a referendum with an absolute majority and that negotiations on the future internal arrangement within the SFRY were unsuccessful.[225] The Commission thus resorted to the same logic as was later applied in the *Québec* case: the nearly unanimous vote for independence in Slovenia did not create a new state, but such a will of the people could not be ignored. After all other solutions had been exhausted, independence became more feasible, but nevertheless it was not considered to be an entitlement. Recognitions by the EC Member States followed on 15 January 1992 and Slovenia was admitted to the UN on 22 May 1992.[226]

### 7.2.2 Croatia

On 25 April 1991, the President of Croatia issued the Decree on the Call for Referendum on Independence of the Republic of Croatia.[227] The Decree

---

[219] The Plebiscite on the Sovereignty and Independence of the Republic of Slovenia, *Official Gazette of the Republic of Slovenia*, No 44-2102/1990 (2 December 1990) (on file with the author).

[220] ibid.

[221] ibid, art 2 (author's own translation).

[222] ibid, art 3 (author's own translation).

[223] See 'Od plebiscita do samostojnosti' ['From the Plebiscite to Independence'], available in Slovene at http://www.slovenija2001.gov.si/10let/pot/kronologija.

[224] The Declaration of Independence of the Republic of Slovenia (25 June 1991), available in Slovene at www.uradni-list.si/dl/vip_akti/1991-01-0007.pdf.

[225] The Badinter Commission, Opinion 7, para 1, reprinted in Trifunovska (n 76) 495.

[226] UN Doc A/RES/46/236 (22 May 1992). See ch 2, 3.2.

[227] The Decree on the Call for Referendum on Independence of the Republic of Croatia, *Official Gazette of the Republic of Croatia*, No 21 (2 May 1991) (on file with the author).

set the date of the referendum to be 19 May 1991.[228] Two choices were offered at the referendum:

1.  Do you agree that the Republic of Croatia, as a sovereign and independent state which guarantees the cultural autonomy and all civil liberties of Serbs and members of other nationalities in Croatia, shall enter into an association of sovereign states together with other republics (according to the suggestion of the Republic of Croatia and the Republic of Slovenia for solving of the state crisis in the SFRY)?
2.  Do you agree that the Republic of Croatia shall remain in Yugoslavia as a unitary federal state (according to the suggestion of the Republic of Serbia and the Socialist Republic of Montenegro for solving of the state crisis in the SFRY)?[229]

Unlike Slovenia's straightforward question,[230] the Croatian referendum question was somewhat ambiguous. It is thus questionable whether the Croatian question would pass the standard set by the Clarity Act in Canada, which states that the referendum results are relevant only if they are free of ambiguity.

In the Québec context, Article 1(3) of the Clarity Act specifies that the referendum question cannot be perceived as free of ambiguity if it: (i) merely consults on the beginning of negotiations for a future legal status of a territory rather than on secession itself; and/or (ii) envisages other possibilities of association with its parent state and thus obscures the real question.[231] The Croatian referendum question did both. A possible loose association was a matter to be negotiated with other republics and was not a pre-negotiated arrangement that was tested at a referendum. Furthermore, the question on the actual independence of Croatia was only implied in the first choice and to some degree was obscured within a broader question. Indeed, the wording of the referendum question actually suggests a situation in which Croatia at that time would already be a sovereign and independent state, and its population was given a choice to join a loose association of former Yugoslav states. This was not the case on 19 May 1991 when the referendum was held.

Nevertheless, it is questionable whether the Canadian standards can be transplanted to the situation in Croatia in 1991. The referendum question makes a reference to the Croatian and Slovenian proposal at that time, according to which the SFRY would transform itself into a loose association of independent states.[232] It is questionable whether the political elites in Croatia and Slovenia really believed that such an association was feasible.[233]

---

[228]   ibid, art 2.
[229]   ibid, art 3 (author's own translation).
[230]   *cf* n 221, above.
[231]   See n 212, above.
[232]   Pavković and Radan (n 128) 147.
[233]   ibid.

Due to the internal political situation in the SFRY and the reactions of the international community[234] to the aspirations of Croatia and Slovenia to become independent states, the proposal aimed to express the independence agenda in a milder form. The Croatian referendum question should be read with this proposal in mind. Hence, the ambiguously-worded question on independence at the Croatian referendum should be ascribed to the political situation; but there was no doubt among the population of Croatia that they were deciding on independence. Such a perception was implicitly confirmed by the Serb population of Croatia, who boycotted the referendum out of opposition to Croatia's path to independence.[235] For them, no doubt existed that the Croatian referendum was a referendum on independence, despite the ambiguously worded questions.

To specify the majority required for ascertaining the will of the people at the referendum, the Decree on the Call for Referendum on Independence of the Republic of Croatia adopted the referenda rules spelled out in Article 87 of the Constitution of the Republic of Croatia:[236] 'At a referendum, a decision is taken by the majority of voters who cast votes, under the condition that majority of the eligible to vote cast their votes at the referendum.'[237] The required majority was thus less demanding than was the case in Slovenia, where a majority of all those eligible to vote was required.[238] The majority of all those eligible to vote was, however, easily achieved. At a turnout of 83.56 per cent of all those eligible to vote, 94.17 per cent of votes were cast in favour of independence.[239] In absolute shares, this means that independence of Croatia was supported by 78.69 per cent of all those eligible to vote.

In its Opinion 5, the Badinter Commission noted that it took the referendum results from 19 May 1991 into account,[240] while the boycott of the referendum by the Serb population was not discussed. The Commission was obviously ready to accept that the Croatian Serbs were outvoted by the Croat majority. At the same time, it insisted on the implementation of adequate mechanisms for the protection of minority rights before Croatia

[234] See L Cohen, *Broken Bonds: Yugoslavia's Disintegration and Balkan Politics in Transition* (Boulder, Westview, 1995) 217–22, who argues that the international community at that time opposed the independence of Croatia and Slovenia.
[235] See Raič (n 14) 349, who argues that 12 per cent of the population of Croatia was of Serb ethnic origin and opposed the declaration of independence. Already prior to the referendum on the declaration of independence, Serbs in Croatia proclaimed that they no longer accepted Croatia's authority (ibid). As a result, an entity called Kninska Krajina was established which sought union with Serbia; however, the Parliament of Serbia rejected such an option (ibid, 388).
[236] The Decree on the Call for Referendum on Independence of the Republic of Croatia (n 227), preamble.
[237] Constitution of the Republic of Croatia (1990), art 87, para 2 (author's own translation).
[238] See n 222, above.
[239] See 'A Short Summary of Croatian History', available (in Croatian) at www.andrija-hebrang.com/povijest.htm#nastanak.
[240] The Badinter Commission, Opinion 5, point 4, reprinted in Trifunovska (n 76) 489.

could be recognised as an independent state.[241] Such a standard is mutatis mutandis similar to the one later established by the Clarity Act in Canada, which provides that no secession may occur if, inter alia, sufficient minority rights protection standards in the secession-seeking territory are not implemented.[242] This requirement may be interpreted as a safeguard against the tyranny of the majority which can follow decision-making based on majoritarian principles.

Despite the Badinter Commission's finding that Croatia did not sufficiently fulfil the required minority protection standards, the EC Member States granted recognition to Croatia on 15 January 1991.[243] Croatia was admitted to the UN on 22 May 1992.[244]

### 7.2.3 *Bosnia-Herzegovina*

Bosnia-Herzegovina declared independence on 14 October 1991,[245] but the Badinter Commission held that the will of the people (or, perhaps, of the peoples) of Bosnia-Herzegovina was unclear, ie, had not been ascertained. The reasoning behind such a conclusion was (also) obviously rooted in the political activities of the Serbian population of Bosnia-Herzegovina (eg, the attempt at secession by Republika Srpska).[246] The Badinter Commission referred to the three ethnic groups constituting Bosnia-Herzegovina as 'peoples' and not to a people of Bosnia-Herzegovina.[247] Furthermore, it expressly held that the right of self-determination applies to the Serbian populations in Bosnia-Herzegovina and in Croatia, respectively.[248] It thus follows that the right of self-determination applies to all three constitutive ethnic groups of Bosnia-Herzegovina, but the Badinter Commission also explicitly noted that the applicability of the right of self-determination did not grant the Serbian population of Bosnia-Herzegovina the right to found its own state.[249]

In order to ascertain the will of the people in Bosnia-Herzegovina, the Badinter Commission suggested a referendum.[250] A referendum was not proclaimed as the only means of the expression of the will of people (or peoples); however, the Badinter Commission did not specify what other

[241] ibid, para 3.
[242] Clarity Act, art 2.3.
[243] Crawford (n 38) 397.
[244] UN Doc A/RES/46/238 (22 May 1992).
[245] The Badinter Commission, Opinion 4 (11 January 1992), para 3, reprinted in Trifunovska (n 76) 486.
[246] ibid, especially paras 3 and 4.
[247] The Badinter Commission, Opinion 4, reprinted in Trifunovska (n 76) 486.
[248] The Badinter Commission, Opinion 2 (11 January 1992), reprinted in Trifunovska (n 76) 474.
[249] The Badinter Commission, Opinion 4, reprinted in Trifunovska (n 76) 486.
[250] ibid, para 4.

means could also be acceptable.[251] On 27 January 1992, the Assembly of Bosnia-Herzegovina adopted the Decree on the Call of the Republic's Referendum for Affirming of the Status of Bosnia and Herzegovina.[252] The referendum question reads: 'Do you support sovereign and independent Bosnia-Herzegovina, a state of equal citizens, peoples of Bosnia-Herzegovina – Muslims, Serbs, Croats and people of other nationalities who live in Bosnia-Herzegovina?'[253]

The referendum question was thus clear, although it notably avoided wording such as: 'Do you agree with the creation of Bosnia-Herzegovina as an independent state?' The omission of a more specific wording probably needs to be ascribed to the fact that, at the request of the Badinter Commission, the referendum was held after Bosnia-Herzegovina had already declared independence and after the Commission had already held that the SFRY was in the process of dissolution.[254] In the perception of its central government, Bosnia-Herzegovina at that time already existed as an independent, although non-recognised, state.[255] Such a perception also follows from the title of the Decree calling for a referendum, which expressly suggests affirming and not determining the status of Bosnia-Herzegovina. The most plausible explanation may be that the central government did not want the referendum question to imply that Bosnia-Herzegovina was not a state at the time of the referendum.

To prescribe the referendum rules, the Act on Referenda of the Socialist Republic of Bosnia-Herzegovina from 1977 was used.[256] This Act foresaw decision-making with a majority of all valid votes cast and without any special guarantees to the constitutive peoples of Bosnia-Herzegovina that they would not be outvoted by the other two constitutive peoples.[257] The referendum on the independence of Bosnia-Herzegovina was boycotted

---

[251] The Badinter Commission, Opinion 4, para 4. The Badinter Commission held: '[T]he Arbitration Commission is of the opinion that the will of the peoples of Bosnia-Herzegovina to constitute [Bosnia-Herzegovina] as a sovereign and independent State cannot be held to have been fully established. This assessment could be reviewed if appropriate guarantees were provided by the Republic applying for recognition, possibly by means of a referendum of all citizens of [Bosnia-Herzegovina] without distinction, carried out under international supervision.'

[252] The Decree on the Call of the Republic's Referendum for Affirming of the Status of Bosnia and Herzegovina, *Official Gazette of the Republic of Bosnia and Herzegovina*, No 2 (27 January 1992) (on file with the author).

[253] ibid, art 3.

[254] For more details on this, see ch 2, 3.1.

[255] It needs to be recalled that the Badinter Commission held that Bosnia-Herzegovina became a state on the date when referendum results were declared. The same critical date for Bosnia-Herzegovina's becoming a state was also adopted by the ICJ in the *Bosnia Genocide* case. See *Case Concerning Application of the Convention on the Prevention and Punishment of the Crime of Genocide (Bosnia and Herzegovina v Yugoslavia)* (Preliminary Objections) [1996] ICJ Rep 596 (the *Bosnia Genocide* case), para 23.

[256] The Act on Referenda of the Socialist Republic of Bosnia-Herzegovina, *Official Gazette of the Socialist Republic of Bosnia and Herzegovina*, No 29/77 (1977) (on file with the author).

[257] ibid, art 28.

by the Serb population, while the Bosnian Muslims and the Bosnian Croats overwhelmingly supported an independent state of Bosnia-Herzegovina. The result was that 63 per cent of all those eligible to vote did so in favour of independence.[258] The boycotting Serb population (31.3 per cent of the entire population of Bosnia-Herzegovina) counted in the mathematical total of 100 per cent.[259] The referendum results were nevertheless deemed to be an expression of the will of the people in favour of independence.

The Bosnian Serbs were thus outvoted and, although they were bearers of the right of self-determination, were not given a chance to seek an arrangement which they preferred. Indeed, the Badinter Commission held that they could only consummate the right of self-determination in its internal mode.[260] One possible explanation is that the majoritarian understanding of democratic decision-making prevailed. While the right of self-determination is, in general, virtually confined to consummation in its internal mode,[261] it is significant that Bosnia-Herzegovina was a new state creation and one of its constitutive peoples was unified in this state arrangement against its wishes and without its consent. However, such an outcome cannot be only ascribed to the majoritarian principles of democratic decision-making, as the *uti possidetis* principle was also applied by the Badinter Commission.[262] The relevance of the limitations imposed on the will of the people by the previous internal boundary arrangement will be discussed in the next chapter.

Bosnia-Herzegovina was recognised as a state by the EC Member States on 6 April 1992[263] and was admitted to the UN on 22 May 1992.[264]

### 7.2.4 *Macedonia*

Macedonia held its independence referendum on 8 September 1991.[265] The referendum question reads: 'Are you in favour of an independent Macedonia with a right to enter into a future association of sovereign states of Yugoslavia?'[266] Similarly to the Croatian referendum question, the Macedonian also mentioned a possibility of a loose association of sov-

---

[258] For more on the declaration of independence of Bosnia-Herzegovina and its subsequent recognition as an independent state, see ch 2, 3.4.

[259] ibid.

[260] The Badinter Commission, Opinion 2 (11 January 1992), reprinted in Trifunovska (n 76) 474.

[261] See n 37, above.

[262] See ch 4, 2.

[263] See ch 2, 3.4.

[264] UN Doc A/RES/46/237 (22 May 1992).

[265] The Badinter Commission, Opinion 6 (11 January 1992), para 4, reprinted in Trifunovska (n 76) 491.

[266] See, for example, Ден што веднаш стана историја [Den shto vednash stana istorija], the author's own translation of the referendum question, at http://star.dnevnik.com.mk/default.aspx?pbroj=1349&stID=2147477716.

ereign states in the territory of the SFRY. However, unlike the Croatian question, the Macedonian referendum question unequivocally asked the voters on independence, though the question was not as clear as it was in Slovenia.[267] An argument can be made that the possibility of a new Yugoslav association – an association of sovereign states – to some degree also obscured the real question and it is debatable whether it would pass the 'clarity test' set out in the Canadian Clarity Act.[268] A possible interpretation is that the political elite sought approval on two different issues: (i) the independence of Macedonia; and (ii) a mandate to negotiate Macedonia's entry into a possible loose Yugoslav association, premised on the sovereignty of its member states. If this was the purpose of the referendum question, it should have been expressed in two separate questions in order not to be ambiguous.

A majority of 72.16 per cent of all those eligible to vote supported independence[269] and Macedonia declared independence on 17 September 1991.[270] The Badinter Commission held that Macedonia had implemented relevant minority protection mechanisms and dedicated most of its reasoning to Macedonia's misunderstanding with Greece over its name, and called for Macedonia's unequivocal renouncing of its territorial claims towards Greece.[271] Despite an explicit recommendation by the Commission to grant recognition, Macedonia remained unrecognised by the EC Member States until 16 December 1993, and even then it was recognised under the compromise name 'The Former Yugoslav Republic of Macedonia' (FYR Macedonia).[272] Prior to recognition by the EC, on 8 April 1993, the FYR Macedonia had already become member of the UN.[273]

### 7.2.5 The Absence of a Referendum in the FRY

Although it was a new state, it was only at the end of the Milošević regime in 2000 that the FRY itself acknowledged this fact, most notably by applying for membership of the UN.[274] In these circumstances, no consultation was held either in Serbia or in Montenegro on the question of whether the population of these two republics approved the creation of the FRY. Instead, the view that there was no new state creation was expressed in the preamble to the Constitution of the FRY from 1992, which claimed the FRY's continuity with the international personality of the SFRY.[275]

---

[267] See n 221, above.
[268] See n 212, above.
[269] Trifunovska (n 76) 345.
[270] The Badinter Commission, Opinion 6, para 5, reprinted in Trifunovska (n 76) 491.
[271] ibid.
[272] See Crawford (n 38) 398.
[273] UN Doc A/RES47/225 (8 April 1993).
[274] The FRY was admitted to the UN by UN Doc A/RES/55/12 (1 November 2000).
[275] The Constitution of the FRY (1992), preamble.

The example of the FRY points out some contradictions of the EC's involvement in the dissolution of the SFRY. While the Badinter Commission held that the SFRY was in the process of dissolution,[276] the EC Guidelines invited its constitutive republics to opt for recognition as independent states.[277] Yet the EC Guidelines and the Badinter Commission did not address the problem of those republics which might not want to become independent states. The problem is that the parent state, according to the Badinter Commission, no longer existed and thus the alternative to independence was not a continued status within the SFRY but an association in a new state formation – in this case, the FRY. Such an association would, however, also require the approval of the peoples in question.

Nevertheless, this was a problem only in Serbia and in Montenegro, where no significant independence movements existed at that time, while the problem in Bosnia-Herzegovina was only theoretical. The referendum on independence in Bosnia-Herzegovina was held after the EC Declaration had already invited the Yugoslav republics to opt for recognition as independent states and after the Badinter Commission already held that the SFRY was in the process of dissolution.[278] This was not the case in Slovenia, Croatia and Macedonia, where referenda were held and independence was declared before the adoption of the EC Guidelines and before the Badinter Commission delivered its first opinion.[279] In theory, if the population of Bosnia-Herzegovina rejected the independence option at the referendum, this would not be a proper expression of the will of the people to join the newly created FRY. Given the fact that the SFRY no longer existed, there was no other choice left.[280]

The fact that there was no referendum on association held in Serbia and in Montenegro cannot per se be deemed a violation of the right of self-determination. Indeed, the Badinter Commission's opinion on Bosnia-Herzegovina can be interpreted in a way that referendum is one means to ascertain the will of the people, but is not the only one.[281] In addition, the standard set by the ICJ in the *Western Sahara Advisory Opinion* allows for circumstances in which popular consultations may not be necessary.[282] In the absence of significant independence movements at that time, there can be little doubt that the Serbs and the Montenegrins favoured the associa-

---

[276] The Badinter Commission, Opinion 1 (29 November 1991), reprinted in Trifunovska (n 76) 415.

[277] See ch 2, 3.2.1.

[278] See ch 2, 3.1.

[279] See ch 2, 3.7.

[280] In the example of Bosnia-Herzegovina, necessary caveats apply, as one of its constitutive peoples opposed independence and demanded either independence or continuation in association with Serbia and Montenegro. See ch 2, 3.4.

[281] ibid.

[282] *cf* n 174, above.

tion. The FRY was also an unusual example as its government denied that it was a new state.


## 7.3 The Demise of the Soviet Union and Popular Consultations

In the context of the Soviet Union, it is necessary to consider two separate issues: independence referenda in the Baltic States and the referenda which took place in the political turmoil leading to the Minsk Agreement.[283] It will be argued that these referenda had little influence on the dissolution dynamic.


### 7.3.1  The Baltic States

At a referendum held on 9 February 1991 in Lithuania, the question was: 'Are you for the independent and democratic state of Lithuania?'[284] Notably, the referendum in Lithuania took place after independence had already been declared.[285] Furthermore, Lithuania's Constitution adopted the view that Lithuania was not a new state creation but had continuity with its international personality prior to the suppression of its independence.[286] The referendum question needs to be looked at in this context. Indeed, as it was worded, it did not imply that Lithuania was a new state creation.

At a turnout of 84.4 per cent, 90.5 per cent supported independence;[287] in absolute shares, this translates to 76.4 per cent of all those eligible to vote. Independence was expressly opposed by 5.5 per cent of all those eligible to vote.[288] The share of ethnic Russians in Lithuania amounted to approximately 20 per cent.[289] The results show that even assuming that all ethnic Lithuanians voted in support of independence, there was no unanimous opposition of the ethnic Russian minority on this question.

Referenda in Estonia and in Latvia were held on the same day (3 March 1991). In Estonia, the referendum question read: 'Do you want restoration of the Independence of the Republic of Estonia?'[290] The question thus implied Soviet Union's illegal occupation of Estonia and the view that

---

[283] See ch 2, 2.1.
[284] See 'Lithuania Votes Overwhelmingly for Independence from Moscow', *New York Times* (10 February 1991), http://query.nytimes.com/gst/fullpage.html?res=9D0CE1D61E3 DF933A25751C0A967958260.
[285] *cf* ch 2, 2.1.
[286] I Ziemele, *State Continuity and Nationality: The Baltic States and Russia: Past Present and Future as Defined by International Law* (Leiden, Martinus Nijhoff, 2005) 38–41.
[287] Brady and Kaplan (n 181) 193.
[288] R Taagepera, *Estonia: Return to Independence* (Boulder, Westview, 1993) 194.
[289] ibid.
[290] ibid, 193.

Estonia's independence from the interwar period would be restored. Estonia would thus not be a new state creation. It remains controversial whether such a view is supported by international law.[291] Nevertheless, the referendum question was free of ambiguity and left no doubt that an affirmative answer would be a vote for Estonia's independence.

The outcome was 77.7 per cent of votes cast in favour of independence, at a turnout of 83 per cent of all those eligible to vote.[292] Independence was thus supported by 64.5 per cent of all those eligible to vote and was expressly opposed by 17.7 per cent of all those eligible to vote.[293] The share of ethnic Russians in Estonia amounted to approximately 39 per cent.[294] These figures imply that independence was not unanimously rejected by the ethnic Russian minority.

The referendum question in Latvia read: 'Do you support the democratic and independent statehood of the Republic of Latvia?'[295] Similarly to that of Lithuania, the referendum question did not imply that Latvia was (necessarily) a new state creation. The independence of Latvia was supported by 73.7 per cent of those who voted at a turnout of 87.6 per cent.[296] Of all those eligible to vote, 64.6 per cent supported independence, while 21.6 per cent explicitly voted against it.[297] The share of ethnic Russians in Latvia amounted to approximately 48 per cent, which means that Latvia's independence was not unanimously disputed by the Russian minority.[298]

The questions asked at the referenda in the Baltic States (republics) were determined by their legal positions, according to which they were not new state creations, due to the illegal Soviet occupation. Although the referenda questions did not unequivocally consult on new state creations, they nevertheless consulted on support for independence. At the same time, the winning majorities were clear and the results also suggest that the Russian-speaking minorities were not outvoted by the majority vote. Popular support for independence, however, did not create new states. Indeed, international recognition and UN membership followed only after the Soviet Union had given its consent to independence. It is also significant that Lithuania declared independence 11 months before it held the referendum on independence, yet the Soviet Union and the international community accepted Lithuanian independence only after the will of the people had been ascertained.

---

[291]  See ch 2, 2.1.
[292]  Taagepera (n 288) 193.
[293]  ibid.
[294]  ibid.
[295]  Ziemele (n 286) 34.
[296]  ibid.
[297]  Taagepera (n 288) 194.
[298]  ibid.

It is notable that the referenda questions in Lithuania and Latvia made references to 'democratic statehood'. This phrasing implies that the goal of independence was also to pursue a democratic political system, which was not feasible within the structures of the Soviet state. Indeed, the Baltic States implemented democratic institutions. However, this is not to say that the claim for the independence of Lithuania and Latvia was more legitimate than that of Estonia simply because the latter did not mention democracy in the referendum question. 'Democratic statehood' in the two referenda questions does not have any direct legal significance; it may be seen as a symbolic contrast to the Soviet Union and a reflection of the democratic zeitgeist at the end of the Cold War.

### 7.3.2  The Establishment of the CIS and Independence Referenda

The dissolution of the Soviet Union was an outcome of the rather complicated political situation in this federation. The decisive development was a power contest between the Soviet leader Mikhail Gorbachev and the then already-elected President of Russia, Boris Yeltsin.[299] The failed putsch attempt of a group of Soviet officials in August 1991 further weakened Gorbachev and the federal organs, and strengthened Yeltsin and his agenda to undermine the federation.[300] In the post-putsch environment of a virtually non-functioning federation and with the former Baltic republics having been recognised as independent states, 'independence for the republics [was] essentially a matter of declaring it'.[301]

Independence was initially not on the agenda of the political leadership in all of the Soviet republics. Yeltsin's primary goal was to undermine Gorbachev's power and not to disrupt the Soviet Union;[302] the latter was a side-effect of the primary goal. Meanwhile, the Ukrainian leadership, faced with a strong pro-independence movement, only co-opted independence ideas at the end of 1990.[303] In the Central Asian republics, the political elites initially opposed the referendum on the future of the Soviet Union,[304] but 'once it became clear it would occur, they sought a way to co-opt nationalist sentiment'.[305] Nevertheless, 'up until the very last minute . . . almost all of Central Asia's leaders maintained hope that the Union could be saved'.[306] In many republics, independence was not a result of

---

[299] S Kotkin, *Armageddon Averted: The Soviet Collapse* (Oxford, Oxford University Press, 2001) 103.
[300] For a detailed account of the situation, see ibid.
[301] Brady and Kaplan (n 181) 192.
[302] Kotkin (n 299) 104.
[303] ibid, 105.
[304] *cf* nn 317–20, below.
[305] Brady and Kaplan (n 181) 194.
[306] Kotkin (n 299) 40.

secessionist activities, but rather an outcome of the political developments in the Soviet Union. Therefore, for the most part, 'it was not nationalism *per se*, but the structure of the Soviet state . . . that proved fatal to the USSR'.[307]

Faced with opposition from anti-reform Party hardliners, the demands of the groups seeking democratisation, secessionist claims by some republics and Yeltsin's attempt to usurp the Soviet state institutions and put them in the service of Russia, Gorbachev called for an all-Union referendum on the future of the Soviet Union[308] in order 'to obtain the authority he needed to keep the Soviet Union intact'.[309]

The all-Union referendum was held on 17 March 1991[310] and the question read: 'Do you consider necessary the preservation of the Union of Soviet Socialist Republics as a renewed federation of equal sovereign republics, in which the rights and freedoms of an individual of any nationality will be fully guaranteed?'[311] The required majority for the preservation of the Soviet Union to be voted for was 50 per cent of those who voted,[312] while other referendum rules were somewhat unclear and the results were open to different interpretations 'so that success could be claimed for a variety of different outcomes'.[313] It was not specified what the consequences of a negative answer would be, either by the entire population of the Soviet Union or by a single republic. Furthermore, the question did not specify how the federation would be renewed or imply what would be the new constitutional arrangement.

The referendum proposal was not unanimously accepted by the Soviet republics and approaches towards the referendum question were not uniform. The referendum was boycotted by six out of the 15 republics: Armenia, Estonia, Georgia, Latvia, Lithuania and Moldova.[314] Estonia, Latvia and Lithuania also held referenda on independence prior to 17 March 1991, when the all-Union referendum was scheduled.[315] Armenia organised a separate independence referendum after this date.[316] Of those Soviet republics which did not boycott the all-Union referendum, special referenda on independence prior to the dissolution of the Soviet Union on 8 December

---

[307]   ibid, 106.
[308]   Brady and Kaplan (n 181) 187.
[309]   ibid.
[310]   ibid, 186.
[311]   ibid, 187.
[312]   See Taagepera (n 288) 193.
[313]   Brady and Kaplan (n 181) 188.
[314]   ibid.
[315]   *cf* n 310, above.
[316]   At the Armenian referendum held on 21 September 1991 (announcing it before the all-Union referendum was scheduled), independence was supported by 99.3 per cent of those who voted, at a turnout of 95.1 per cent: Brady and Kaplan (n 181) 193.

1991 were held in Turkmenistan[317] and Ukraine.[318] On 29 December 1991, when the Soviet Union had already been dissolved, special referenda on independence were also held in Azerbaijan and Uzbekistan.[319] In three Soviet republics (Kazakhstan, Kirghizia and Uzbekistan), no specific referenda on independence were held, but the question of the all-Union referendum was modified to imply the possible creation of a sovereign state.[320] In Russia, the all-Union referendum question was also modified, but it did not ask on independence.[321] In Moldova, neither the all-Union referendum (in any of its variations) nor specific independence referendum was ever held.[322]

Independence referenda in the Soviet Union were held in the complicated political circumstances of a virtually non-functioning federation. The all-Union referendum on the future of the Soviet Union put forward

[317] In Turkmenistan, the independence referendum was organised on 26 October 1991. The referendum question on independence was presented along with 'a vaguely worded question about support for the domestic and foreign policy of the president of the Supreme Soviet of Turkmenistan': Brady and Kaplan (n 181) 201. Independence, along with the question on foreign and domestic policies, was supported by 97.4 per cent of those who voted at a turnout of 94.1 per cent (ibid).

[318] The referendum on the independence of Ukraine was held on 1 December 1991. The referendum question read: 'Do you support the Act of the Declaration of the Independence of Ukraine?' At a turnout of 84.18 per cent, 90.32 of votes cast were in favour of independence. This means that 76.03 per cent of all those eligible to vote supported an independent Ukraine. See *The Ukranian Weekly* (8 December 1991), at http://www.ukrweekly.com/archive/pdf3/1991/The_Ukrainian_Weekly_1991-49.pdf.

[319] Independence referenda in Azerbaijan and Uzbekistan were held subsequently, after the Soviet Union had already been dissolved. In the absence of any other option, the independence of Azerbaijan was confirmed by 99.6 per cent of those who voted at a turnout of 95.3 per cent of all those eligible to vote: Brady and Kaplan (n 181) 193. The independence of Uzbekistan was confirmed by 98.2 per cent of those who voted at a turnout of 94 per cent of all those eligible to vote (ibid).

[320] In Kazakhstan, Kirghizia and Uzbekistan, the all-Union referendum was modified to imply the creation of a sovereign state. The referendum questions in Kirghizia and Uzbekistan read: 'Do you consider it necessary the preservation of the Union of Soviet Socialist Republics as a renewed federation of equal sovereign states, in which the rights and freedoms of an individual of any nationality will be fully guaranteed?': Brady and Kaplan (n 181) 194. The referendum question in Kazakhstan read: 'Do you consider it necessary to maintain the USSR as a union of sovereign states of equal rights?' (ibid). Although these questions did not directly ask on independence, the shift from 'republics' to 'states' is notable. In Kazakhstan, the turnout was 88.2 per cent, while 94.1 per cent of valid votes were affirmative to the question asked (and implying independence) (ibid, 190–91). In Kirghizia, the turnout was 92.9 per cent and the answer was affirmative by 94.6 per cent of those who cast their votes (ibid). In Uzbekistan, the turnout was 95.4 per cent and the answer was affirmative by 93.7 per cent of those who cast their votes (ibid, 193). Unlike Kazakhstan and Kirghizia, Uzbekistan also held a special referendum on independence, which eventually took place after the Soviet Union had already been transformed into the CIS.

[321] In Russia, the original question of the all-Union referendum was not modified, but was supplemented with a question on the popular election of the president of Russia. At the referendum, the answer to the original question of the all-Union referendum was affirmative by 71.3 per cent of those who cast their votes, at a turnout of 75.4 per cent of registered voters (ibid). The question on the popular election of the Russian president was supported by 69.9 per cent of those who cast their votes (ibid, 194).

[322] Brady and Kaplan (n 181) 193.

an ambiguous question. Given the political circumstances, some republics modified this question to imply independence and some republics held separate independence referenda. In the confusing political situation, referenda rules were also confusing. Yet the dissolution of the Soviet Union was an outcome of internal political developments, in which the independence referenda did not play a decisive role. In the absence of any other choice, the referenda (usually with overwhelming majorities) merely confirmed the emergence of new states.

## 7.4 The Absence of a Referendum in Czechoslovakia

The dissolution of Czechoslovakia was negotiated among, at that time already elected, political elites[323] and was a result of different views on the internal organisation of the common state and the inability to reconcile these views.[324] In the negotiated settlement, Czechoslovakia ceased to exist on 31 December 1992.[325] On 1 January 1993, the Czech Republic and Slovakia were proclaimed independent states,[326] both of which were admitted to the UN on 19 January 1993.[327]

Czechoslovakia was a clear example of consensual dissolution and the existence of the two new states was not subject to any controversy. This was so despite the fact that the consent of the people for the alteration of the legal status of the territory was not unequivocally given. It was indeed unclear whether the people of either federal unit supported the creation of separate Czech and Slovak states. Not even the fact that the political leaders who carried out the dissolution were democratically elected changes this consideration. Indeed, as argued above, general elections are not a suitable channel for consultation of the will of the people in respect of self-determination.[328]

The legal status of the territory of Czechoslovakia was changed without ascertaining the will of the people. The emergence of two new states was simply a fait accompli, which the international community was willing to accept. It is at least debatable whether such a fait accompli creates 'special circumstances' which make a popular consultation dispensable.

---

[323] The first post-communist multiparty parliamentary elections in Czechoslovakia took place on 8 and 9 June 1990. Elections were held to the federal assembly and both assemblies of the constitutive republics. For more on this, see 'Czechoslovakia: Parliamentary Elections', at www.ipu.org/parline-e/reports/arc/2084_90.htm.

[324] See ch 2, 2.2.

[325] See Crawford (n 38) 402.

[326] ibid.

[327] UN Doc A/RES/47/221 (19 January 1993) (Czech Republic); UN Doc A/RES/47/222 (19 January 1993) (Slovakia).

[328] McCorquodale (n 92) 304.

## 7.5  The Independence Referendum in Eritrea

In the environment of a consensual secession, ie, with the approval of Ethiopia, the UN-observed independence referendum in Eritrea[329] was unambiguous from the point of view of both the question asked as well as popular support. The referendum question reads as follows: 'Are you in favour of Eritrea becoming an independent, sovereign State?'[330] At a turn-out of 93.9 per cent, a total of 99.8 per cent of the votes cast were in favour of independence.[331] Independence was thus supported by 94.06 per cent of all those eligible to vote. Due to the consensual nature of the new state creation, international recognition followed promptly. Eritrea was admitted to the UN on 28 May 1993, roughly a month after the holding of a referendum on independence.[332]

## 7.6  The Independence Referendum in East Timor under the Auspices of the UN

The independence referendum in East Timor was also held under the auspices of the UN, but the role of the UN in East Timor was much more complex than in Eritrea. Indeed, the referendum was part of the broader international effort to settle the territorial status of East Timor and the role of the UN in the independence referendum was not limited to the status of an observer.

On 5 May 1999, the Agreement between the Republic of Indonesia and the Portuguese Republic on the Question of East Timor was concluded.[333] The Agreement comprehended a document entitled 'A Constitutional Framework for a Special Autonomy for East Timor', which provided for the autonomy of East Timor within Indonesia,[334] but also foresaw a consultation of the people of East Timor on the autonomy arrangement. The consultation was conducted under the auspices of the UN.[335]

The popular consultation on the acceptance of the autonomy arrangement or its rejection, which would lead to independence, was further affirmed by Resolution 1246 of the UN Security Council.[336] Neither the

---

[329]  ibid. See also UN Doc A/RES/47/230 (28 May 1993).

[330]  See 'Elections in Eritrea', at http://africanelections.tripod.com/er.html.

[331]  ibid.

[332]  UN Doc A/RES/47/230 (28 May 1993).

[333]  I Martin, *Self-Determination in East Timor: The United Nations, the Ballot, and International Intervention* (Boulder, Lynne Rienner, 2001) 15–34.

[334]  ibid.

[335]  The Agreement between the Republic of Indonesia and the Portuguese Republic on the Question of East Timor, Articles 1–6. UN Doc S/1999/513 (5 May 1999).

[336]  UN Doc S/RES/1246 (11 June 1999), para 1.

Agreement nor Resolution 1246 specified the required majority or the exact referendum question. Nor was the required majority specified in the Agreement Regarding the Modalities for the Popular Consultation of the East Timorese through a Direct Ballot, which was also concluded between Indonesia and Portugal on 5 May 1999.[337]

As follows from the Agreement between Indonesia and Portugal, the interpretation of the referendum results was left to the Secretary-General. Some guidelines on standards adopted by the Secretary-General in regard to the referendum rules follow from the Report of the Secretary-General on the Question of East Timor from 5 May 1999:

> Article 6 of the Agreement [from 5 May 1999] provides . . . that, should the popular consultation result in a majority of the East Timorese people rejecting the proposed special autonomy, the Government of Indonesia would take the constitutional steps necessary to terminate Indonesia's links with East Timor, thus restoring under Indonesian law the status that East Timor held prior to 17 July 1976, and that the Governments of Indonesia and Portugal would agree with the Secretary-General on arrangements for a peaceful and orderly transfer of authority in East Timor to the United Nations, which would then initiate a process enabling East Timor to begin a transition towards independence.[338]

Reference to the 'majority of the East Timorese people'[339] could, perhaps, be interpreted as support for the more demanding majority of all those eligible to vote and not the less-demanding majority of all valid votes cast. Such a conclusion cannot be straightforward.

Two referendum questions were formulated by the Agreement Regarding the Modalities for the Popular Consultation:

> Do you accept the proposed special autonomy for East Timor within the Unitary State of the Republic of Indonesia?
>
> Do you reject the proposed special autonomy for East Timor, leading to East Timor's separation from Indonesia?[340]

The referendum questions were clear and unambiguous. Yet, in light of the somewhat undefined majority that determines the will of the people, if the Secretary-General's reference to the 'majority of the East Timorese people'[341] is interpreted as a requirement for the majority of all people eligible to vote, it is unclear what would have happened if neither of the two options received the required support. In the absence of any other possibility, the Secretary-General would probably need to declare the

---

[337] The Agreement Regarding the Modalities for the Popular Consultation of the East Timorese through a Direct Ballot (5 May 1999), UN Doc S/1999/513 (5 May 1999), Annex 2.
[338] The Question of East Timor: Report of the Secretary-General, UN Doc A/53/951; S/1999/513 (5 May 1999), para 2.
[339] ibid.
[340] The Agreement Regarding the Modalities for the Popular Consultation of the East Timorese through a Direct Ballot (n 337), para B.
[341] See n 339, above.

winning option to be the one which received the majority of all valid votes cast.

Nevertheless, the ambiguity associated with the required majority did not prove to be a problem in practice. The people of East Timor rejected the autonomy arrangement and supported the course to independence with 78.5 per cent of the votes cast, at a turnout of 98.6 per cent.[342] This means that independence was supported by 77.4 per cent of all those eligible to vote in East Timor.

The decision in favour of independence led to an outbreak of violence, which was initiated by Indonesian forces.[343] Subsequently, the Security Council, acting under Chapter VII, adopted Resolutions 1264 and 1272, which, inter alia, authorised 'the establishment of a multinational force'[344] and established 'a United Nations Transitional Administration in East Timor (UNTAET) . . . endowed with overall responsibility for the administration of East Timor and . . . empowered to exercise all legislative and executive authority, including the administration of justice'.[345] In the subsequent Resolution 1338, East Timor's course towards independence was affirmed.[346] Thus, the political process in East Timor led to internationally pre-determined (UN-sponsored) independence. East Timor declared independence on 20 May 2002[347] and was ultimately admitted to the UN on 27 September 2002.[348]

## 7.7  The Independence Referendum in Montenegro and EU Involvement

It was argued above that Montenegro declared independence in a political process marked by the considerable involvement of the EU and via the creation of the State Union of Serbia and Montenegro (SUSM).[349] The Constitution of this state provided for a clear mechanism for secession, elaborated in Article 60 of the Constitution.[350] The Article, inter alia, provided that '[t]he decision on secession from the State Union of Serbia and Montenegro shall be taken at a referendum'.[351]

The referendum rules again became the subject of EU involvement. The EU imposed the Independence Referendum Act, which required for

---

[342]  See Crawford (n 38) 561.

[343]  ibid.

[344]  UN Doc S/RES/1264, para 3 (15 September 1999).

[345]  UN Doc S/RES/1272, para 1 (15 October 1999).

[346]  UN Doc S/RES/1338 (31 January 2001). Notably, this Resolution was not adopted under Chapter VII of the UN Charter.

[347]  See 'East Timor: Birth of a Nation', *BBC News* (19 May 2002), http://news.bbc.co.uk/2/hi/asia-pacific/1996673.stm.

[348]  UN Doc A/RES/57/3 (27 September 2002).

[349]  See ch 2, 4.

[350]  See ch 2, n 356.

[351]  Constitution of the SUSM (2003), Article 60 (author's own translation).

secession to be confirmed by a majority of 55 per cent of votes cast, under the condition of participation of at least 50 per cent of all those eligible to vote plus one vote.[352] The required majority was probably based on the opinion polls, which suggested that approximately half of the population supported independence while a relatively large share of the population determinedly opposed it.[353] The referendum question was unambiguous: 'Do you agree that the Republic of Montenegro becomes an independent state with a full international legal personality?'[354]

At the referendum held on 21 May 2006, independence was supported by 55.53 per cent of those who voted at a turnout of 86.49 per cent of all those eligible to vote.[355] As the referendum results show, the support for independence barely met the EU-imposed 55 per cent requirement. The threshold was thus described as a political gamble as it would be quite possible that the result would fall in the 'grey zone' between 50 and 55 per cent.[356] In such a circumstance:

> Montenegro's government would have been legally unable to declare independence. At the same time it would have viewed the referendum result as a mandate to further weaken the State Union. The unionists would have viewed the result as a victory and demanded immediate parliamentary elections and closer ties with Belgrade.[357]

The EU feared that the 'unionists' would boycott the referendum and would thus endanger its democratic legitimacy.[358] The referendum formula, however, gave the union advocates reasonable hope that independence would not get sufficient support in a popular vote and thus motivated them to mobilise their supporters to take part in the vote. By avoiding either a boycott of the 'unionists' or victory of the independence option with a narrow majority of, in theory, merely a vote over 50 per cent, the referendum was given broader democratic legitimacy. Yet it was a politically risky endeavour.

The example of Montenegro also proves that the question of a relevant majority for a consultation to be considered an expression of the will of the people does not need to be limited to the choice between a majority of all those eligible to vote and a majority of all (valid) votes cast, but a situation-specific majority may be considered to be representative of the will

---

[352] The Act on Referendum on State-Legal Status of the Republic of Montenegro, *Official Gazette of the Republic of Montenegro*, No 12/06 (2 March 2006), art 6.

[353] See ch 2, 4.

[354] The Act on Referendum on State-Legal Status of the Republic of Montenegro (n 352), art 5 (author's own translation).

[355] Skupština Republike Crne Gore (24 May 2006), at http://www.skupstina.me/index.php?strana=fiksna&id=401

[356] International Crisis Group, Briefing No 42, Montenegro's Referendum (30 May 2006) 6.

[357] ibid.

[358] ibid, 2.

of the people. It is also important to note that Montenegro was an example of secession expressly permitted under the constitution of its parent
state. Referendum results in favour of independence directly resulted in
the creation of a new state and, for this reason, the required majority had
to be explicitly defined. Nevertheless, it needs to be pointed out that in
absolute shares, Montenegrin independence was supported by 48.02 per
cent of all those eligible to vote. If, for example, the Slovenian standard of
the majority of all people eligible to vote were applied,[359] Montenegro
would have been unable to declare independence.

## 7.8 The Independence Referendum in South Sudan

It has been established in an earlier chapter that the 2005 Comprehensive
Peace Agreement as well as the Interim National Constitution of the
Republic of Sudan defined Southern Sudan as a self-determination unit and
regulated a six-year interim period in which the vote on the future legal
status of the territory was to take place.[360] The referendum question was
first indicated in the Interim Constitution by providing that the people of
Southern Sudan shall either '(a) confirm unity of the Sudan by voting to
sustain the system of government established under the Comprehensive
Peace Agreement and this Constitution, or (b) vote for secession'.[361] The referendum rules were subsequently specified by the Southern Sudan
Referendum Act of 31 December 2009.[362]

This Act repeats the general references to self-determination and the
independence referendum, previously invoked in the Comprehensive
Peace Agreement and the Constitution.[363] It further repeats the referendum choice provided for by the Constitution, that is, either '[c]onfirma-
tion of the unity of the Sudan by sustaining the form of government
established by the Comprehensive Peace Agreement and the Constitution,
or [s]ecession'.[364]

Article 41 of the Act specifies the referendum rules and makes specific
provisions for the requirement quorum as well as the winning majority:

(2) The Southern Sudan Referendum shall be considered legal if at least (60%)
of the registered voters cast their votes.

. . .

---

[359] See n 222, above.
[360] See ch 2, 2.4.
[361] ibid, art 222(2).
[362] Southern Sudan Referendum Act (2009), http://saycsd.org/doc/SouthernSudan
ReferendumActFeb10EnglishVersion.pdf.
[363] ibid, art 4.
[364] ibid, art 6.

(3) . . . the referendum results shall be in favour of the option that secures a simple majority (50% +1) of the total number of votes cast for one of the two options, either to confirm the unity of the Sudan by maintaining the system of government established by the Comprehensive Peace Agreement or to secede.[365]

The referendum ballot was clear and simple; in accordance with the Constitution and the Southern Sudan Referendum Act, it provided for two options: 'unity' or 'secession'.[366] At a referendum held between 9 and 15 January 2011, the option for secession was given the overwhelming support of 98.83 per cent of those who voted, at a turnout of 97.58 per cent.[367]

The referendum rules were thus clear in terms of both the question and the winning majority. Moreover, Article 66 of the Southern Sudan Referendum Act specified that the referendum decision shall be binding:

The option approved by the people of Southern Sudan by a majority of 50% + 1 of valid votes cast in the referendum in accordance with the present Act, shall supersede any other legislation and shall be binding to all the State bodies as well as all citizens of Southern and Northern Sudan.[368]

The 'right to independence' of the people of Southern Sudan was created by the referendum rules and the arrangement is thus somewhat similar to that of Montenegro. The will of the people and the underlying domestic legislation were respected by the central government and, after the declaration of independence on 9 July 2011, South Sudan became an independent state.[369]

## 7.9 The Absence of a Referendum in Kosovo

A popular consultation in Kosovo took place in September 1991 as part of the underground political activities of the Kosovo Albanians.[370] Due to its unofficial character, it is possible to challenge the legal significance of this referendum. No independence referendum was held prior to the declaration of independence in 2008, ie, in the period of the legal regime created by Security Council Resolution 1244. However, despite these possible procedural objections, there exists no doubt that independence is the wish of virtually all the ethnic Albanians in Kosovo and thus of roughly 90 per

[365] ibid, art 41.
[366] For the referendum ballot, see 'A Southern Sudan Referendum Ballot', at www.flickr.com/photos/usaidafrica/5386993117.
[367] See 'South Sudan Backs Independence – Results', *BBC News* (7 February 2011), at http://www.bbc.co.uk/news/world-africa-12379431
[368] Southern Sudan Referendum Act (2009), art 66.
[369] See ch 2, 2.4.
[370] See ch 2, 6.1.

cent of Kosovo's population.[371] This was even affirmed in the report of the Special Representative of the UN Secretary-General:

> A return of Serbian rule over Kosovo would not be acceptable to the over-whelming majority of the people of Kosovo. Belgrade could not regain its authority without provoking violent opposition. Autonomy of Kosovo within the borders of Serbia – however notional such autonomy may be – is simply not tenable.[372]

Kosovo's independence is most commonly contested on the questions of whether the declaration of independence violated Resolution 1244 and whether the duty to withhold recognition applied, while the absence of a formal popular consultation has not been held to be a problematic aspect of Kosovo's declaration of independence. By the pronouncement that '[t]he adoption of . . . [Kosovo's] declaration [of independence] did not violate any applicable rule of international law',[373] even the ICJ implicitly took a stance that in this particular situation the declaration of independence without a formal popular consultation does not lead to a violation of any norm of international law.

Indeed, in Kosovo, the will of the people is obvious and formal popular consultation may not be considered necessary. It is also likely that an independence referendum would result in ethnic violence. A plausible argument can be made that in Kosovo, 'special circumstances' in the sense of the *Western Sahara Advisory Opinion* exist in which a formal referendum is not necessary for the ascertainment of the will of the people.

## 7.10 Procedural Standards at Independence Referenda Summarised

In the *Western Sahara Advisory Opinion*, the ICJ stated that the operation of the right of self-determination requires a free and genuine expression of the will of the people before the legal status of a territory may be altered. The will of the people is normally expressed at referenda. If a referendum is to be considered a proper expression of the will of the people, both the question asked and the winning majority need to be free of ambiguity. This follows from the Canadian Clarity Act and from the reasoning of the

---

[371] The 2011 Census in Kosovo was not comprehensive as it did not include the northern part, which is predominantly settled by ethnic Serbs. In 2001,however, the percentage of the Albanian population in Kosovo amounted to 88 per cent and the Serb population to approximately 7 per cent. According to some estimates, the shares have changed to 92 per cent of Albanians and 4 per cent of Serbs. See the Provisional Institutions of Self-Government, Ministry of Environment and Spatial Planning, available at http://enrin.grida.no/htmls/kosovo/SoE/popullat.htm.

[372] UN Doc S/2007/168 (16 March 2007) (the Ahtisaari Plan), para 7.

[373] *Accordance with International Law of the Unilateral Declaration of Independence in Respect of Kosovo (Request for Advisory Opinion)*, Advisory Opinion, ICJ Rep 2010 (the *Kosovo Opinion*), para 122.

Badinter Commission, but this requirement also has universal validity. Indeed, ambiguous referenda questions and ambiguous majorities cannot lead to free and genuine expressions of the will of the people.

In the post-1990 practice of independence referenda, questions have been put forward which attract some doubt as to whether they really were unambiguous. However, the requirement of 'free of ambiguity' is not universally qualified and will depend on political and general societal circumstances. As a matter of general principle, the referendum question needs to consult on independence directly (not merely implicitly) and should not obscure the issue of independence within a broader question.

The determination of an unambiguous majority is also situation-specific, as in different situations different majorities may lead to the legitimacy of the decision-making. The example of Montenegro shows that the choice of a prescribed majority is not limited to the choice between a simple majority of all votes cast and a more qualified majority of all those eligible to vote. Furthermore, in the post-1990 referenda practice, the requirement of a majority of all those eligible to vote is rare and was unequivocally demanded only at the independence referendum in Slovenia. Nevertheless, the post-1990 referenda practice shows that a majority of all those eligible to vote is often (though not always) achieved, even when it is not explicitly demanded.

Despite the importance of the expression of the will of the people before the legal status of a territory may be altered, in the *Western Sahara Advisory Opinion*, the ICJ held that there are exceptional circumstances in which a consultation is not necessary. Such circumstances may exist where the will of people(s) is obvious and is not subject to any controversy. The declaration of Kosovo's independence has been challenged on several grounds,[374] yet the absence of a referendum is not deemed to be problematic and it is not disputed that independence is the will of virtually all the Kosovo Albanians. Even the ICJ's advisory opinion on Kosovo suggests, albeit implicitly, that the absence of popular consultation does not render Kosovo's declaration of independence illegal under international law.[375]

The FRY was also created without prior popular consultation. This state creation was, however, unusual because the government of the FRY denied that it was a new state.[376] This is a clear example of 'special circumstances' in which the absence of a referendum is not deemed to be a problem. There is indeed little doubt that the federation was the preferred solution of the Serbs and the Montenegrins. It is also important to recall that a referendum is not necessarily the only means of ascertaining the will of the people. This was implied by the Badinter Commission in its

---

[374] See ch 2, 6.
[375] See ch 2, 6.4.
[376] See ch 2, 3.6.

opinion on Bosnia-Herzegovina. However, the Badinter Commission did not specify what other possibilities could also be acceptable.

The absence of a referendum in the situation of the dissolution of Czechoslovakia may be seen as more problematic, as the will of the people was at least ambiguous (if actually not in favour of a continued federal arrangement). The fact that the dissolution was negotiated by the elected political leaders of both constitutive parts does not resolve the issue because general elections cannot be seen as a replacement for a popular consultation on the issues of self-determination. Yet the emergence of two new states in the territory of Czechoslovakia was not contested and the emergence of two new states as an outcome of a domestic political process was promptly acknowledged by the international community.

## 8 CONCLUSION

The development of the principle of self-determination in its modern meaning was closely associated with democratic political theory, most notably in the ideas of representative government in the period of the Enlightenment and in the writings of US President Wilson. However, self-determination only had a democratic pedigree in the Western European and American contexts. Elsewhere, it was instead understood as a collective struggle of peoples against their subordination to other peoples. Self-determination is commonly invoked in the context of demands for independence. The codification of self-determination as a human right in the UN Charter era adopted the peoples approach to self-determination, while no specific political system is prescribed for its realisation.

As a non-absolute human right, the right of self-determination is limited by other human rights, including the right of self-determination of other peoples. In non-colonial situations, the right of self-determination also clashes with the principle of the territorial integrity of states. Two modes of the exercise of this right need to be distinguished: internal and external.

It is generally accepted in international legal scholarship that the right of self-determination would normally be consummated in its internal mode. The internal mode of this right inspired some to argue that the right of self-determination effectively works as a 'right to democracy'.[377] Such arguments stem from the requirement for a representative government, expressed in the elaboration of the principle of territorial integrity in the Declaration on Principles of International Law, and from the interdependence of human rights.

---

[377] *cf* ch 3, 2.

However, the right of self-determination only applies to peoples and thus the qualification of a representative government in the context of this right does not cover identities other than those constituting a separate people. The requirement for a representative government cannot be extended to mean non-discrimination based on an affiliation with political parties. Moreover, a representative government can also be a government which is not an outcome of multiparty elections. Indeed, the drafting of the Declaration on Principles of International Law shows that the requirement for a representative government was not meant to interfere with the specific choice of a political and/or electoral system. Not even the post-Cold War practice of the UN organs has changed this standard. Despite the absence of a democratic political system and multiparty electoral procedures, the Badinter Commission implied that the SFRY was representative of all of its peoples prior to Serbia's usurpation of the federal organs.[378] This confirms that even those states which do not adhere to multiparty electoral practices can have governments that are representative of their peoples.

With regard to the 'democratic nature' of the right of self-determination stemming from the interdependence of human rights, this chapter has showed that such an understanding would require an interpretation that universal human rights instruments bind state parties to holding multiparty elections. Such a view was rejected by the ICJ in the *Nicaragua* case.[379] In the post-Cold War era, references to democracy were made in many General Assembly resolutions, but all of them carefully avoid a proclamation that elections need to take place in a multiparty setting.[380] Instead, the relevant resolutions commonly affirm that the choice of a political system remains a domestic matter for states. It is far from settled in international law that the right to political participation, either under Article 25 or the ICCPR or customary international law, requires multiparty elections.[381] Thus, the interdependence between this right and the right of self-determination cannot result in an obligation to implement a particular political system or electoral method.

While the right of self-determination does not necessarily require a democratic political system, it requires for some democratic principles to be followed in the process of state creation. This does not mean that the absence of a democratic political system and multiparty elections creates a 'right to secession'. Rather, this chapter has demonstrated that outside of the colonial framework, the will of the people in favour of independence is not enough for a state creation, but, at the same time, a shift of sovereignty may not occur without popular support.

---

[378] See n 77, above.
[379] See ch 2, n 108.
[380] See ch 2, 2.3.2.
[381] ibid,

As stated by the Supreme Court of Canada, the democratically expressed will of the people in favour of independence puts an obligation on both sides to negotiate a future arrangement, but does not pre-determine an outcome.[382] This confirms the interpretation developed in this book that state creation in contemporary international law is a political process which aims to remove the applicable claim to territorial integrity of the parent state. This process is governed by certain legal rules and this chapter has demonstrated that some democratic principles operate within these rules.

Save for exceptional circumstances, the will of the people in favour of independence is expressed by democratic vote at referenda. Yet international law prescribes no universal referenda rules. Within the legal framework, where an expression of the will of the people does not automatically create a new legal situation (ie, a new state), a precise regulation of referenda rules is not necessary. However, the operation of the right of self-determination requires that the expression of the will of the people is free and genuine. In order to achieve these qualities, the referendum question and the winning majority need to be unambiguous. What is unambiguous is not universally qualified. Such a qualification remains situation-specific. The referenda results are, then, considered in the political process which may or may not lead to independence.

At the same time, the political process leading to independence may result in a legally binding referendum on independence, as was the case in Montenegro, South Sudan and, with some difficulties, perhaps also in East Timor. In such circumstances, the referenda results need to be very specific and the legal arrangement must contain a clear formula for secession. A comparison of the referenda rules in these situations shows that the prescribed thresholds for success are situation-specific.

Thus, the democratic expression of the will of the people in the context of the right of self-determination is not absolute. This chapter has demonstrated how it may be limited by the principle of the territorial integrity of states. A democratic expression of the will of the people does not create a state, but may become an important consideration in the political process (potentially) leading to independence of an entity. At the same time, the concept of governmental representativeness adopted in the elaboration of this principle in the Declaration on Principles of International Law is not to be understood as a call for a particular political system or electoral model. The next chapter turns to the limitations on the will of the people imposed by the previously existing internal boundary arrangement delimiting newly emerged states.

---

[382] See n 201, above.

# 4

# The Delimitation of New States and Limitations on the Will of the People

## 1 INTRODUCTION

T HE PREVIOUS CHAPTER showed that the right of self-determination, and the will of the people operating within this right, collide with the principle of territorial integrity as well as with other human rights, including the right of self-determination of other peoples and minority rights.[1] The right of self-determination is thus only exceptionally exercised in its external mode, but it may be exercised in this mode if the political process so determines.

When new states are created, a question also arises of how a territorial unit is determined in which a people exercises the right of self-determination in its external mode. In this context, it needs to be considered how the previously existing internal territorial arrangement within a parent state can limit the will of a people when new states are created. As Crawford argues, the rules of international law pertaining to the confinement of the borders of new states are one of the non-democratic features of international law, but 'may well serve other values'.[2]

The general legal position is that new state creations do not affect existing international borders. This follows from the Vienna Convention on the Law of Treaties,[3] the Vienna Convention on Succession of States in Respect of Treaties[4] and the jurisprudence of the ICJ.[5] Yet the establish-

---

[1] See ch 1, 3.4 and 3, 2.2.

[2] J Crawford, *The Creation of States in International Law* (Oxford, Oxford University Press, 2006) 153.

[3] See the Vienna Convention on the Law of Treaties, art 62(2a). Notably, the ICJ has held that Article 62 codified customary international law. See *Case Concerning the Gabčíkovo-Nagymaros Project (Hungary/Slovakia)*, ICJ Rep 1997, 64, para 104.

[4] See the Vienna Convention on Succession of States in Respect of Treaties, art 11. This article, inter alia, provides that a succession of states does not affect 'a boundary established by a treaty'.

[5] The standard that the delimitation, established by a treaty, is permanent regardless of the later fate of that treaty was confirmed in the *Case Concerning the Temple of Preah Vihear (Cambodia v Thailand)*, ICJ Rep 1962, 34, where the ICJ argued that: 'In general, when two countries establish a frontier between them, one of the primary objects is to achieve stability and finality. This is impossible if the line so established can, at any moment, and on the basis of a continuously available process, be called in question, and its rectification claimed,

ment of borders between the former units of a parent state or between a newly independent state and the remainder of its former parent state is much more controversial.

In the process of decolonisation, new international borders were confined by the *uti possidetis* principle. The post-1990 era, however, saw a number of new states emerge outside of the colonial context. These new state creations resulted from both consensual and non-consensual dissolutions of federations,[6] as well as from consensual secessions.[7] There has also been one partially successful attempt at unilateral secession.[8]

Where new states emerged consensually, new international delimitations were mutually agreed upon and commonly formalised in either bilateral or multilateral treaties.[9] Non-consensual state creations are, however, much more problematic, as outside of the process of decolonisation, no right to independence is applicable.[10] As was established in the previous chapter, an entity may nevertheless emerge as an independent state against the wishes of its parent state if this emergence is universally accepted by the international community.[11]

The mode of state creation in such a circumstance excludes the possibility of formalisation of the new international border through a treaty. It seems that international acceptance of the emergence of a new state will not only determine the state creation but will also confine its new international borders.[12] In the legal framework where new states do not emerge automatically, but rather in a political process which creates legal consequences, the boundary arrangement of the new state could also become a negotiable part of this process.

---

whenever any inaccuracy by reference to a clause in the parent treaty is discovered. Such a process could continue indefinitely, and finality would never be reached so long as possible errors still remained to be discovered. Such a frontier, so far from being stable, would be completely precarious.' The standard was even more unequivocally affirmed in the *Case Concerning the Territorial Dispute (Libyan Arab Jamahiriya/Chad)*, ICJ Rep 1994, 37, para 73, where the ICJ argued: 'A boundary established by treaty . . . achieves a permanence which the treaty itself does not necessarily enjoy. The treaty can cease to be in force without in any way affecting the continuance of the boundary . . . [W]hen a boundary has been the subject of agreement, the continued existence of that boundary is not dependent upon the continuing life of the treaty under which the boundary is agreed.'

  [6] The Soviet Union and Czechoslovakia are examples of consensual dissolutions of federations. See ch 2, 2.1 and 2, 2.2. The SFRY is an example of a non-consensual dissolution of a federation. See ch 2, 3.
  [7] Eritrea (see ch 2, 2.3), East Timor (see ch 2, 5) and Montenegro (see ch 2, 4) may be regarded as consensual state creations in the post-1990 era.
  [8] Kosovo is an example of a non-consensual attempt at unilateral secession which has attracted a significant number of international recognitions. See ch 2, 6.
  [9] See the examples of the Soviet Union (see ch 2, 2.1) and Czechoslovakia (see ch 2, 2.2).
  [10] *Reference re Secession of Québec* (1998) 2 SCR 217 (Canada) (the *Québec* case), para 112.
  [11] ibid, para 155.
  [12] See n 197, below.

In the context of the dissolution of the SFRY, the Badinter Commission applied the *uti possidetis* principle to delimit the newly emerged states.[13] The application of this colonial principle in a non-colonial situation remains controversial,[14] but the standard of 'upgrading' the former internal boundaries to the status of international borders in the territory of the SFRY was nevertheless accepted in the practice of states and the UN organs.[15] Moreover, such a standard was also affirmed by mutual agreements where consensual state creations were at issue.[16] The standard of confining new international delimitation along the lines of previously existing internal boundaries thus seems to have notable support in the practice of post-1990 state creations. Yet this practice also shows that, unlike in colonial situations, not just any internal boundary has the potential to become an international border.

This chapter considers the importance of the previously existing internal boundary arrangement within the parent state for the determination of new international borders and argues that the delimitation in new post-1990 state creations cannot be ascribed to the operation of the *uti possidetis* principle. In turn, it explains why in all successful post-1990 state creations, even in the absence of a presumption of *uti possidetis*, certain internal boundaries were nevertheless 'upgraded' to the status of international borders and why the will of the people tends to be disregarded in this process.

## 2 THE CREATION OF NEW STATES AND THE *UTI POSSIDETIS* PRINCIPLE

### 2.1 The Development of *Uti Possidetis*

The modern meaning of *uti possidetis* is captured in the following dictum of the Chamber of the ICJ in the *Frontier Dispute* case:

---

[13] The Badinter Commission, Opinion 2 (11 January 1992), reprinted in S Trifunovska, *Yugoslavia through Documents: From its Creation to its Dissolution* (Dordrecht, Martinus Nijhoff 1994) 474.

[14] See, eg, S Ratner, 'Drawing a Better Line: *Uti Possidetis* and the Borders of New States' (1996) 90 *American Journal of International Law* 590; M Pomerance, 'The Badinter Commission: The Use and Misuse of the International Court of Justice's Jurisprudence' (1998–99) 20 *Michigan Journal of International Law* 31; P Radan, 'Post-Secession International Borders: A Critical Analysis of the Opinions of the Badinter Arbitration Commission' (2000) 24 *Melbourne University Law Review* 50; R McCorquodale and R Pangalangan, 'Pushing Back the Limitation of Territorial Boundaries' (2001) 12 *EJIL* 867.

[15] All the former republics of the SFRY eventually received universal recognition as states and are members of the UN. The international community thus implicitly also accepted the 'upgrading' of internal boundaries to the status of international borders.

[16] See the examples of the Soviet Union, Czechoslovakia, Eritrea, East Timor and Montenegro.

The essence of the principle lies in its primary aim of securing respect for the territorial boundaries at the moment when independence is achieved. Such territorial boundaries might be no more than delimitations between different administrative divisions of colonies all subject to the same sovereign. In that case, the application of the principle of *uti possidetis* resulted in administrative boundaries being transformed into international frontiers in the full sense of the term.[17]

The Chamber of the ICJ further argued that: '[T]he principle of *uti possidetis* freezes the territorial title; it stops the clock but does not put back the hands.'[18]

In the moment of gaining independence, *uti possidetis* thus confined international borders along arbitrarily drawn colonial boundaries which took little account of local identities and were never intended to be international borders.[19] Despite the arbitrariness of colonial boundaries, the Chamber of the ICJ in the *Frontier Dispute* case held that *uti possidetis* 'is a firmly established principle of international law where decolonization is concerned'.[20] The Chamber of the ICJ also held that in the context of decolonisation, *uti possidetis* has become a principle of customary international law applicable beyond Latin America, where it was initially developed.[21]

The position of the Chamber of the ICJ that *uti possidetis* forms a part of customary international law remains controversial. Was the application of *uti possidetis* in the process of decolonisation required by a specific norm of international law or was it only 'a policy decision in order to avoid conflicts during decolonization'?[22] This question falls beyond the scope of the present book.[23] What is important here is that *uti possidetis* was referred to in order to confine international borders along colonial boundaries, regardless of the origin of these boundaries. Whether as a policy choice or as a customary norm, the 'upgrading' of colonial boundaries to international borders was deemed to be necessary in order to prevent the decolonised territories

---

[17] *Case Concerning the Frontier Dispute (Burkina Faso/Mali)*, ICJ Rep 1986, 566, para 23.

[18] ibid, para 30.

[19] See Ratner (n 14) 595. See also *Land, Island and Maritime Frontier Dispute case (El Salvador v Honduras)*, ICJ Rep 1992, 387, para 43.

[20] *Case Concerning the Frontier Dispute (Burkina Faso/Mali)*, ICJ Rep 1986, 565, para 20.

[21] ibid, para 21.

[22] Ratner (n 14) 598. See also H Ghebrewebet, *Identifying Units of Statehood and Determining International Boundaries* (Frankfurt, Peter Lang 2006) 76–77, who argues that: 'The necessary element for the establishment of customary law, *opinio juris* is lacking . . . Neither the Latin American republics nor the African states considered themselves bound to adopt the *uti possidetis* principle in delimiting their new international boundaries. Rather, they eventually agreed to adopt a *status quo* policy for reasons of expedience and convenience in the interests of peace and security.'

[23] For more on this, see Ghebrewebet (n 22) 9–80; S Lalonde, *Determining Boundaries in the Conflicted World: The Role of Uti Possidetis* (Montreal, McGill-Queens University Press, 2002) 24–60, 103–37.

from becoming *terra nullius* situations and to minimise the conflicts between the new states emerging in the process of decolonisation.[24]

## 2.2 The Application of *Uti Possidetis* Outside of the Process of Decolonisation

Although traditionally associated with decolonisation, arguments have been made that *uti possidetis* has been applied even in situations of the emergence of new states not resulting from decolonisation. In the context of dealing with the crisis in the SFRY, the Badinter Commission resorted to *uti possidetis* in order to 'upgrade' internal boundaries between federal republics to the status of international borders. In its Opinion 3, the Commission stated:

> Except where otherwise agreed, the former boundaries become frontiers protected by international law. This conclusion follows from the principle of respect for the territorial *status quo* and, in particular, from the principle of *uti possidetis*. *Uti possidetis*, though initially applied in settling decolonization issues in America and Africa, is today recognized as a general principle, as stated by the [Chamber of the ICJ in the *Frontier Dispute* case].[25]

At this point, the Badinter Commission quoted a fragment of para 20 of the *Frontier Dispute* case:

> [*Uti possidetis*] is not a special rule which pertains solely to one specific system of international law. It is a general principle, which is logically connected with the phenomenon of the obtaining of independence, wherever it occurs. Its obvious purpose is to prevent the independence and stability of new states being endangered by fratricidal struggles . . .[26]

This position of the Badinter Commission is highly controversial. The context of para 20 of the *Frontier Dispute* case implies that the reference to *uti possidetis* as 'a general principle' is to be understood as an argument stating that the principle is not limited to decolonisation in Latin America; rather, it is a generally applicable principle in the context of *decolonisation*. Furthermore, the remark that 'there is no need, for the purposes of the present case, to show that [*uti possidetis*] is a firmly established principle of international law where decolonization is concerned'[27] is a strong indication of the 'colonial scope' of the reference to the *uti possidetis* principle in

---

[24] G Abi-Saab, 'Le principe de l'*uti possidetis* son rôle et ses limites dans le contentieux territorial international' in M Kohen (ed.), *Promoting Justice, Human Rights and Conflict Resolution through International Law* (Dordrecht, Martunus Nijhoff, 2007) 657, 657–58.

[25] The Badinter Commission, Opinion 3 (11 January 1992), reprinted in Trifunovska (n 13) 479.

[26] *Case Concerning the Frontier Dispute (Burkina Faso/Mali)*, ICJ Rep 1986, 565, quoted in the Badinter Commission, Opinion 3.

[27] *Case Concerning the Frontier Dispute (Burkina Faso/Mali)*, ICJ Rep 1986, 565, para 20.

the *Frontier Dispute* case. Lastly, the omitted line at the end of the Badinter Commission's quote of the *Frontier Dispute* case refers to 'the challenging of frontiers following the withdrawal of the *administering power*'.[28] The reference to 'administering power' is also a clear indication that the Chamber of the ICJ had decolonisation in mind.

Therefore, nothing in the reasoning of the Chamber of the ICJ in the *Frontier Dispute* case suggests that the *uti possidetis* principle would apply in situations other than those dealing with decolonisation.[29] In fact, the applicability of the *uti possidetis* principle was unequivocally limited to decolonisation. The Badinter Commission's application of the *uti possidetis* principle outside of this context was clearly underpinned by selective quoting of the *Frontier Dispute* case. With such foundations, Opinion 3 of the Badinter Commission is a rather weak authority when it is referred to in order to prove a doctrinal acceptance of the applicability of *uti possidetis* outside of the process of decolonisation.

In its Opinion 3, the Badinter Commission did not specifically invoke all boundaries in the former SFRY, but only the contested ones: 'The boundaries between Croatia and Serbia, between Bosnia-Herzegovina and Serbia, and possibly other adjacent independent states may not be altered except by agreement freely arrived at.'[30] The Commission obviously took into account the armed conflict taking place in Croatia and Bosnia-Herzegovina at that time and applied the *uti possidetis* principle in order to bring these two states and their boundaries under the protection of Article 2(4) of the UN Charter.[31]

The reason for the Badinter Commission's application of *uti possidetis* was evidently an attempt at peace activism. In this attempt, its objective was to confine new international borders along previously existing internal boundaries, whereas it obviously believed that this could only be done if *uti possidetis* were applied. This reasoning leads to two questions: first, whether 'upgrades' of internal boundaries to international borders are only possible under the *uti possidetis* presumption; and, second, whether internal boundaries within the SFRY and in other non-colonial state creations are reminiscent of colonial delimitations, so that *uti possidetis* is the

---

[28] ibid (emphasis added).

[29] One author has proposed a middle way between the colonial and non-colonial application of *uti possidetis*, arguing that the reasoning of the Chamber of the ICJ 'makes it clear that [*uti possidetis*] is applicable specifically where a nation has been subjected to colonial, or *colonial-like* rule and should not be imposed in other situations'. D Luker, 'On the Borders of Justice: An Examination and Possible Solution to the Doctrine of *Uti Possidetis*' in R Miller and R Bratspies (eds), *Progress in International Law* (Dordrecht, Martinus Nijhoff, 2008) 166 (emphasis added). This argument is also problematic, as it is unclear where the reasoning of the Chamber of the ICJ left open a possibility for the application of *uti possidetis* in 'colonial-like' situations. Rather, it is obvious that the reasoning refers only to colonialism.

[30] The Badinter Commission, Opinion 3 (11 January 1992), reprinted in Trifunovska (n 13) 479.

[31] Ratner (n 14) 614.

appropriate principle to be invoked. These questions will be addressed in subsequent sections.

## 2.3 Non-colonial Situations: Internal Boundaries and International Borders

It has been established that in the process of decolonisation, *uti possidetis* was able to 'upgrade' any colonial boundary to the status of an international border, regardless of the origin of the 'upgraded' boundary.[32] This section deals with internal boundaries outside of colonialism. It argues that not all internal boundaries are reminiscent of colonial delimitation and new international delimitation in such circumstances is not reminiscent of the process of decolonisation, where *uti possidetis* was applied.

An 'upgrade' of internal boundaries to international borders can be problematic because internal boundaries are not established for the same purposes as international borders. Indeed, '[t]he core functional distinction between international borders and internal administrative boundaries lies in a critical antinomy: governments establish interstate boundaries to separate states and peoples, while they establish or recognize internal boundaries to unify and effectively govern a polity'.[33] For this reason, internal administrative boundaries are not necessarily capable of determining the territory of a potentially independent state.[34]

While it is true that internal boundaries are not established for the same purpose as are international borders, one also needs to take into account that not all internal boundaries have been established for the same purposes and that they may also have different origins. As Shaw notes:

> In some cases [internal boundaries] . . . are of relatively little importance; in others, such as is the case with federal states, they are of considerable significance. In many instances, such administrative borders have been changed by central government in a deliberate attempt to strengthen central control and weaken the growth of local power centres. In other cases, borders may have been shifted for more general reasons of promoting national unity or simply as a result of local pressures. In some states, such administrative borders can only be changed with the consent of the local province or state (in the subordinate sense) or unit. In some cases, internal lines are clear and of long standing. In others, they may be confused, of varying types and inconsistent.[35]

While some internal boundaries may be established for pure administrative purposes, others have a strong historical pedigree and even delimit

---

[32] See n 17, above.
[33] Ratner (n 14) 602.
[34] ibid,
[35] M Shaw, 'Peoples, Territorialism and Boundaries' (1997) 8 *EJIL* 478, 489.

self-determination units. Not all internal boundaries are merely administrative lines, reminiscent of colonial delimitation. The internal organisation of a multiethnic state, composed of delimited subunits, may be an
arrangement for the exercise of the right of self-determination in its internal mode.[36] Federalism is one such possibility, although this is not always
the case.[37]

Moreover, the historical roots of an internal boundary do not necessarily
constitute a self-determination unit. Borders between English counties
have a long history,[38] but the population of, for example, Oxfordshire
clearly does not constitute a people for the purpose of the right of
self-determination. On the other hand, the internal boundary between
England and Scotland is not merely administrative. Not only does it have
a strong historical pedigree, there also exists no doubt that the right of self-
determination is applicable to the Scottish people and that Scotland is a
self-determination unit.[39] In the case of the potential independence of
Scotland, the international border of this state would be easy to ascertain.[40]

For some internal boundaries, it is rather difficult to imagine how they
could become international borders. A hypothetical creation of an independent state of Oxfordshire, delimited along its present internal boundary of an English county, would be reminiscent of *uti possidetis* applied in
the context of decolonisation. It is very unlikely that Oxfordshire would
ever become an independent state. In some other situations, a claim for an
'upgrade' of other internal boundaries to international borders may be
much more plausible. Scotland's claim for an 'upgrade' of its internal
boundary with England to the status of an international border could
hardly be reminiscent of the process of decolonisation and of *uti possidetis*.
The question is what makes Scotland-type boundaries different from
Oxfordshire-type boundaries and, consequently, which internal boundaries are potentially capable of becoming international borders.

As the right of self-determination is central for a plausible independence
claim,[41] the answer needs to be sought in its context. Arguably, a group of

---

[36]  See ch 3, 2.2.
[37]  See ch 3, 3.2.
[38]  For more on the background on English counties, see 'A Vision of Britain through Time',
www.visionofbritain.org.uk/types/level_page.jsp?unit_level=4.
[39]  Consider the following argument: 'Scotland is a curious example of a sub-state national
society in that, on the one hand, it is a former nation-state, indeed one of the oldest in Europe,
but on the other, it is difficult to attribute points of clear objective distinction in terms of
language, religion or ethnicity between Scotland and England . . . Scotland's claim to societal
discreteness is, therefore, largely based upon the historical development of indigenous institutions of civic and public life which emerged when Scotland was an independent state and
which, to some extent, survived the Union of Parliaments with England in 1707.' S Tierney,
*Constitutional Law and National Pluralism* (Oxford, Oxford University Press, 2006) 71.
[40]  It would be the border in existence prior to the 1707 Union of Parliaments with England.
[41]  Strictly speaking, the applicability of the right of self-determination is not a precondition
for a new state creation. Yet peoples (who are beneficiaries of the right of self-determination)
will more plausibly make a claim for their own state. The right of self-determination is also

people to whom the right of self-determination does not apply cannot make a plausible claim for secession from their parent state.[42] It is unlikely that their claim would trigger a political process possibly leading towards independence. As follows from the wording of the right of self-determination, this right only applies to peoples.[43] A claim for 'upgrading' internal boundaries to international borders will be much more plausible where such boundaries delimit a self-determination unit, ie, a territory populated by a distinct people, which is separate from either the rest of a parent state or from other self-determination units within a parent state. Yet not even the 'self-determination approach' entirely resolves the question of which internal boundaries may eventually become international borders. This problem will be considered in the next section.

## 3 THE NATURE AND RELEVANCE OF INTERNAL BOUNDARIES IN THE POST-1990 PRACTICE OF NEW INTERNATIONAL DELIMITATION

This section is concerned with the relevance of internal boundaries and the importance of the latest internal boundary arrangement in the post-1990 practice of the confinement of new international borders. It will consider the pedigree of the 'upgraded' internal boundaries – whether these are colonial-like arbitrarily drawn lines or whether they generally delimit historically realised self-determination units.

The analysis will begin with Québec. Although it did not emerge as an independent state, the question of borders was discussed along with other questions dealing with the possibility of secession. The opinions of jurists may provide some guidelines on the legal doctrine concerning the process of 'upgrading' an internal boundary to an international border in the case of an emergence of a new state. The section will then turn to the practice of successful post-1990 state creations. It will argue that the Badinter Commission's non-colonial application of *uti possidetis* was not followed in subsequent practice. Consequently, the Commission's reference to this principle will be revisited in light of post-1990 practice. An argument will be made that the Commission had good reasons to confine new international borders along the previously existing internal boundaries, yet this was not a matter of *uti possidetis*. The section will also try to answer why the latest internal boundary arrangement has nevertheless been given significant prominence in the relevant practice.

central in the doctrine of remedial secession, which follows from an inverted reading of the elaboration of territorial integrity in the Declaration on Principles of International Law. See ch 3, 6.

[42] There is no explicit legal definition of a people. For some guidelines on this, see ch 3, 3.1.

[43] International Covenant on Civil and Political Rights (ICCPR) and International Covenant on Economic, Social and Cultural Rights (ICESCR), art 1.

## 3.1 The Québec Situation and its Significance for the Determination of International Borders

In the *Québec* case,[44] the Supreme Court of Canada made no direct references to the question of borders. Arguably, the view that Québec could, possibly, become an independent state in its present provincial boundaries was implied in the observation that the ultimate success of a unilateral secession would depend on recognition by the international community.[45] Since this observation refers to the entire territory of Québec and not only to one part of it, it may be interpreted in such a way that international recognition could lead to Québec's statehood in its provincial boundaries.[46]

Success of a unilateral secession in the UN Charter era is unlikely. The question of Québec's boundaries therefore also needs to be addressed in light of consensual secession, which could be an outcome of negotiations on the future legal status of Québec.[47] Three major questions need to be asked in this context: (i) could Québec become an independent state within its present provincial borders or should earlier boundaries become relevant?; (ii) does the duty to negotiate a future legal status include a duty to negotiate future international borders?; and (iii) could Québec become an independent state despite the wish of its minorities to remain in an association with Canada?

In the Québec Report,[48] it was stated that Québec's provincial borders are guaranteed by Canadian constitutional law, while after a possible achievement of independence, its borders would be protected by the principle of territorial integrity, which is firmly established in international law.[49] A question arises as to whether the borders protected by international law would be those presently determined by Canadian constitutional law. In this regard, the Québec Report established that: 'From a strictly legal perspective, since the attainment of independence is an instantaneous occurrence, there can be no intermediate situation in which other rules would apply. Furthermore, recent precedents have demonstrated that the principle of *uti possidetis juris* can be transposed to the present case.'[50] To this, the Québec Report added: '[I]f the territorial limits

---

[44] For the background to this, see ch 3, 7.1.
[45] The *Québec* case (n 10), para 155.
[46] See Radan (n 14) 56.
[47] *cf* ch 3, 7.1.
[48] The Territorial Integrity of Québec in the Event of the Attainment of Sovereignty (hereinafter the Québec Report), http://english.republiquelibre.org/Territorial_integrity_of_ Quebec_in_the_event_of_the_attainment_of_sovereignty. The Report was prepared in 1992 for the Québec Department of International Relations. Its authors were Thomas Franck, Rosalyn Higgins, Malcolm Shaw, Alain Pellet and Christian Tomuschat.
[49] ibid, ch 2.1.
[50] ibid.

of Québec were to be altered between now and the date of any future sovereignty . . . the borders of a sovereign Québec would not be its present boundaries (nor would they inevitably be those prevailing at the time of the formation of the Canadian Federation in 1867).'[51]

The Québec Report thus takes a view that the critical date for the 'upgrading' of internal boundaries to international borders is the moment of the gaining of independence. According to this doctrine, previous territorial arrangements do not matter. The Québec Report also invoked the *uti possidetis* principle, which was referred to by the Badinter Commission in the case of the dissolution of the SFRY.[52] However, it was established above that the applicability of the *uti possidetis* principle in non-colonial situations remains controversial and that its application by the Badinter Commission provides for a rather weak authority.[53]

The Québec Report further strengthened its position on the question of the critical date for determination of international borders by holding that '[a] particular problem arises in respect of the territories ceded to Québec by the Federation in 1912'.[54] With regard to these territories, the Québec Report concluded that only the latest territorial arrangement within a parent state is relevant.[55] At this point, the reasoning also gives an idea of the position of the newly created minorities within a new state. It follows from the Québec Report that such minorities have neither a veto power regarding the question of secession from a parent state nor the right to secession from the newly created state (but neither would their secession be prohibited by international law). It should be recalled, however, that secession is not an entitlement under international law and states do not emerge automatically. The status of minorities may be part of the negotiation process prior to a potential agreement on independence.[56]

The government of Canada did not accept that only the last internal boundary arrangement would be relevant for the potential international delimitation of Québec.[57] It held that internal boundaries may automatically become international borders in a case of dissolution (eg, the example of the SFRY), but not in a case of secession.[58] In this view, without a presumption of the inviolability of previous internal boundaries, a non-

---

[51] ibid, ch 2.2.

[52] See the Badinter Commission, Opinion 3 (11 January 1992), reprinted in Trifunovska (n 13) 479.

[53] See ch 4, 2.2.

[54] The Québec Report, ch 2.12. See also the Act to extend the Boundaries of the Province of Québec (1912), art 2(c), quoted in the Québec Report, ch 2.12.

[55] The Québec Report, ch 2.14.

[56] *cf* ch 3, 7.1.

[57] Statement of Stéphane Dion, Federal Minister of Intergovernmental Affairs in a Letter to the Premier of Québec, 11 August 1997, quoted in P Radan, 'The Borders of a Future Independent Québec: Does the Principle of *Uti Possidetis Juris* Apply?' (1997) 4 *Australian International Law Journal* 200, 201.

[58] ibid.

consensual dissolution results in chaos as it is not clear who is the sovereign of a certain territory. This is not a problem with consensual secessions as the parent state does not cease to exist and remains sovereign in the territory seeking secession until this territory emerges as an independent state. In the UN Charter era, it is very unlikely that this would happen without the parent state's consent.

The position of the government of Canada leads to the question of whether negotiations on future international borders may be made a part of the negotiation process on a potential consensual secession. According to Pellet, 'negotiations on Québec's borders are possible but are not obligatory'.[59] Pellet further notes that the Supreme Court of Canada in the *Québec* case 'has not ruled out the possibility that the issue of Québec's boundaries might be the subject of future negotiations [as] nothing in the Court's ruling precludes negotiations between the Parties dealing with the issue of Québec's borders'.[60] However, he concludes that international law imposes no obligation to negotiate future international borders.[61] A counter-argument was made that if this were the case, Québec would automatically become an independent state within its present internal boundaries and would have no reason to negotiate its future borderline with Canada.[62]

This argument does not take into account that under contemporary international law, Québec could not become a state automatically and, therefore, it could not automatically take its present delimitation out of Canada. Territorial rearrangements are always possible as a result of negotiations before new states emerge. It is possible that the entity would be offered a solution with narrower boundaries and such a 'latest internal arrangement' would then become a new international border. Since the creation of a state is a political process, such solutions are certainly possible. This was also affirmed in Opinion 3 of the Badinter Commission.[63] When potential independence becomes a matter of political negotiations, it is not difficult to imagine that borders could also become part of these negotiations. When a secession-seeking entity is presented with the dilemma of having either independence within narrower borders or no independence at all, it is not possible to predict for which option such an entity would opt. State practice in respect of this question is not developed.

---

[59] A Pellet, 'Avis juridique sommaire sur le projet de loi donnant effet à l'exigence de clarté formulae par la Cour suprême du Canada dans son avis sur le Renvoi sur la sécession du Québec' quoted in English translation in S Lalonde, 'Québec's Boundaries in the Event of Secession' (2003) 7 *Macquarie Law Journal* 129, 137.

[60] ibid.

[61] ibid.

[62] C Hilling, 'Débats' in O Corten, B Delcourt, P Klein and N Levrat (eds), *Démembrements d'États et délimitations territoriales: L'uti possidetis en question(s)* (Brussels, Bruylant, 1999) 445.

[63] The Badinter Commission, Opinion 3 (11 January 1992), reprinted in Trifunovska (n 13) 479.

It follows from the *Québec* case and from the Québec Report that the latest internal boundary arrangement within a parent state will form a strong base for the determination of a new international border. In the circumstances of a successful unilateral secession or of a non-consensual dissolution, it is virtually impossible to implement any other border arrangement. But the success of a unilateral secession in the UN Charter era is very unlikely and therefore it is also unlikely that the secession-seeking entity would, without any negotiations, emerge as an independent state delimited along its former internal boundaries. When a new state creation is consensual, the new international borders are, in principle, negotiable, yet it may well be that the last internal boundary arrangement will still be very important. This issue will be further discussed in relation to the practice of successful post-1990 state creations.

## 3.2 Post-1990 State Creations and the Practice of Border-Confinement

This subsection considers the practice of new international delimitation in successful post-1990 state creations. It is concerned with the confinement of new international borders in the processes of dissolutions of multi-ethnic federations (the Soviet Union, Czechoslovakia and the SFRY), the consensual creations of the independent states of Eritrea, East Timor and Montenegro, and, ultimately, Kosovo's unilateral secession. It will be argued that this practice gave significant prominence to the latest internal boundary arrangement and is thus compatible with the doctrine stemming from the Québec situation, but cannot be ascribed to the operation of *uti possidetis*.

### 3.2.1 *International Delimitation in the Territory of the Former Soviet Union*

Despite the ambiguity associated with the legal status of the Ribbentrop-Molotov Pact, it was widely (albeit for the most part tacitly) accepted by the international community that Estonia, Latvia and Lithuania were not independent states but Soviet republics.[64] It also needs to be recalled that they did not become members of the UN before the Soviet Union consented to their independence.[65] This implies that the Baltic States may ultimately be regarded as state creations with the consent of the parent state.

Upon the achievement of independence in 1991, Lithuania promptly accepted its delimitation along the lines of the latest internal boundary arrangement within the Soviet Union.[66] Estonia and Latvia contested part

---

[64] See ch 2, 2.1.
[65] ibid.
[66] P van Elsuwege, 'State Continuity and its Consequences: The Case of the Baltic States (2003) 16 *Leiden Journal of International Law* 377, 386.

of their borderlines with Russia, which were subject to territorial rearrangements in the Soviet era.[67] Initially they both insisted that the present international borders were the international borders in existence prior to the suppression of independence.[68] Russia, by contrast, claimed that the international borders were confined along the lines established by the last internal territorial arrangement in the Soviet Union. In the border treaty, concluded in 2007 by the Russian Federation and the Republic of Latvia, the Russian view prevailed.[69] The new international border was confined along the lines of the most recent internal boundary, but no reference to *uti possidetis* was made. The treaty has been ratified by the legislatures of both Latvia[70] and Russia.[71]

A similar treaty between Estonia and Russia has not entered into force. Estonia initially insisted on delimitation along the lines from the interwar period, established by the Peace Treaty of Tartu in 1920.[72] In 2005, however, a treaty on delimitation between Estonia and Russia was signed, which did not re-establish the border from 1920, but introduced 'only minor changes to the . . . border that was established when the Soviet Union occupied the Baltic states after World War II'.[73] The Estonian Parliament ratified the new border treaty, but in the process of ratification, it also included a preambulary reference to the Peace Treaty of Tartu. Russia strongly opposed any such reference, which could imply that the minor modifications were to be associated with the borderlines in the interwar period and, as a consequence, refused to ratify the treaty.[74]

The signed, but not ratified, border treaty between Russia and Estonia nevertheless shows a tendency that the most recent internal boundary arrangement (albeit with minor modifications) will form a strong base for the determination of new international borders. Furthermore, the border treaty between Russia and Latvia, which has entered into force, is entirely in line with the standard proposed in the Québec Report: in the case of secession, the most recent internal boundaries are those which would

[67] See 'Russia Spurns Estonia Border Deal', *BBC News* (27 June 2005), http://news.bbc.co.uk/2/hi/europe/4626141.stm.

[68] ibid, See also The Republic of Latvia and the Russian Federation Treaty On the State Border of Latvia and Russia (8 June 2006), at http://www.mfa.gov.lv/en/policy/bilateral-relations/4542/Russia/Treaty/. The Latvian Constitution expressly provided that the disputable territory was part of the Republic of Latvia.

[69] ibid.

[70] See 'Latvia Ratified Border Treaty with Russia', *Kommersant* (17 May 2007), www.kommersant.com/p-10733/r_500/border_treaty.

[71] See 'State Duma Ratifies Border Treaty with Latvia', *Kommersant* (5 September 2007), www.kommersant.com/p-11344/r_500/Border_Latvia_ratify.

[72] Peace Treaty of Tartu, Article 3, LNTS Vol 1, 1922, 51–71. See also van Elsuwege (n 66) 385.

[73] 'Russia/Estonia, Milestone Border Treaty Signed', *Radio Free Europe* (18 May 2005), http://en.wikisource.org/wiki/Treaty_of_Peace_between_Russia_and_Estonia.

[74] See 'Russia Withdraws from Border Treaty with Estonia', *Euractiv Network* (5 September 2005), www.euractiv.com/en/foreign-affairs/russia-withdraws-border-treaty-estonia/article-143852.

become international borders.[75] Nevertheless, different outcomes of (political) negotiations are possible and also permissible under international law.

As already argued, after the Baltic States (re)gained independence, the Soviet Union initially continued in existence but was subsequently transformed into the Commonwealth of Independent States (CIS) by the Minsk Agreement and the Alma Ata Protocol, both of which were signed in December 1991.[76] The former Soviet republics thus became independent states under international law.[77]

With regard to the question of borders, Article 5 of the Minsk Agreement provides: 'The High Contracting Parties acknowledge and respect each other's territorial integrity and the inviolability of existing borders within the Commonwealth.'[78] In addition to the Alma Ata Protocol, the Alma Ata Declaration was adopted, in which the newly independent states declared that they recognise and respect 'each other's territorial integrity and the inviolability of existing borders'.[79] The inviolability of borders was later affirmed even in the Charter of the CIS.[80]

While the internal boundaries of the Soviet republics were 'upgraded' to the status of international borders, the boundaries of autonomous republics (ie, subunits of the republics) were not.[81] Although the founding documents of the CIS expressly invoked rights of the newly created minorities,[82] no special provision was made which would give them a right to secession and the creation of a new state or merger with another state.

The new international delimitation was challenged by several ethnic groups in the territory of the CIS and the post-1991 era has seen a significant number of (violent) secessionist attempts. Abkhazia and South Ossetia

---

[75] See n 48, above.
[76] For more on this, see ch 2, 2.1.
[77] ibid,
[78] Minsk Agreement, art 5(1).
[79] Alma Ata Declaration, 31 ILM 147 (1992), para. 3.
[80] CIS Charter, art 3.
[81] The following Autonomous Soviet Socialist Republics (ASSRs) existed when the Soviet Union was transformed into the CIS in 1991: within Azerbaijan: Nakhchivan ASSR; within Georgia: Abkhaz ASSR, Adjar ASSR; within Russia: Bashkir ASSR, Buryat ASSR, Chechen-Ingush ASSR, Chuvash ASSR, Dagestan ASSR, Kabardino-Balkar ASSR, Kalmyk ASSR, Karelian ASSR, Komi ASSR, Mari ASSR, Mordovian ASSR, Northern Ossentian ASSR, Tatar ASSR, Tuva ASSR, Udmurt ASSR, Yakut ASSR; within Ukraine: Crimean ASSR; within Uzbekistan: Karakalpak ASSR. See the Constitution of the Soviet Union (1977), Article 85. On the other hand, the Soviet Secession Law, which was never implemented in practice, foresaw that in the event that a republic opted for independence, it would not necessarily keep its borders, as peoples in autonomous republics would be consulted separately. See the Law on Procedures for Resolving Questions Related to the Secession of Union Republics from the USSR, Article 3, reprinted in H Hannum, *Documents on Autonomy and Minority Rights* (Philadelphia, University of Pennsylvania Press, 1996) 753–60.
[82] Minsk Agreement, arts 2 and 3; Alma Ata Declaration, para 2.

have attempted to break away from Georgia,[83] Chechnya from Russia,[84] Nagorny-Kharabakh from Azerbaijan[85] and Gagauzia from Moldova.[86] Despite some recognitions, none of these entities has acquired sovereignty under international law or has merged with another state.[87] Up to the present day, no change of the principle encompassed in the Minsk Agreement and in the Alma Ata Protocol has been accepted under international law; international delimitation in the territory of the former Soviet Union runs exclusively along the former internal boundaries of the Soviet republics. This is not to say that consensual rearrangements or emergences of new states would not be allowed, but in the absence of a political process yielding such an effect, international law stands on the presumption of the territorial status quo.

The 'upgrade' of internal boundaries to the status of international borders in the founding documents of the CIS has been interpreted as a formal acceptance on the part of the former Soviet republics 'that *uti possidetis juris* would be a valid solution' to territorial disputes between them'.[88] The interpretation that the new international delimitation in the territory of the Soviet Union was a consequence of the operation of *uti possidetis* even appears in the Report of the EU Fact-Finding Mission investigating the armed conflict in Georgia in 2008.[89] Such arguments are problematic.

The *uti possidetis* argument in the Report of the Fact-Finding Mission has weak doctrinal foundations, as it uncritically refers to the Badinter Commission's opinion that this principle is applicable beyond the process of decolonisation.[90] The arguments in favour of Soviet *uti possidetis* also ignore the fact that no single reference to this principle appears in the Minsk Agreement, the Alma Ata Declaration, the Alma Ata Protocol, the Charter of the CIS or in any other document relevant for the dissolution of the Soviet Union. It is difficult to imagine that a reference to it was omitted accidentally.

In the absence of any specific reference to the principle, the argument in favour of Soviet *uti possidetis* obviously presumes that wherever an internal boundary becomes an international border, such an 'upgrade' is a consequence of the operation of *uti possidetis*. This argument does not differentiate between internal boundaries of different kinds and the fact that not all

---

[83] Crawford (n 2) 403. See also Council of the European Union, Report of the Independent Fact-Finding Mission on the Conflict in Georgia (2009), www.ceiig.ch/Report.html (hereinafter the Report of the Fact-Finding Mission).

[84] Crawford (n 2) 403.

[85] ibid.

[86] ibid.

[87] ibid.

[88] E Hasani, '*Uti Possidetis Juris:* From Rome to Kosovo' (2003) 27 *Fletcher Forum of World Affairs* 85, 92.

[89] The Report of the Fact-Finding Mission, 143.

[90] ibid.

internal boundaries are colonial-like administrative lines.[91] Yet the Soviet Union was one example where internal boundaries of different kinds existed, while only boundaries of one kind were 'upgraded' to the status of international borders.[92]

The internal organisation of the Soviet Union was, at least formally, conceived as an arrangement for the internal exercise of the right of self-determination of its peoples.[93] While it may well be that the right of self-determination of the peoples in the Soviet Union was violated in practice, Soviet federalism attached the constitutive peoples of the federation to their respective territorial units, some of which even had a previous history of being independent states.[94] Due to arbitrary territorial rearrangements within the Soviet Union, many boundaries of these units may rightfully be considered to have been unjust.[95] They were nevertheless delimitations between different self-determination units, which were not without any historical pedigree.

The former Soviet republics did not agree to 'upgrade' all internal boundaries to the status of international borders, but only those delimiting the republics (ie, constitutionally recognised self-determination units). The Report of the Fact-Finding Mission interpreted this as an acknowledgement of *uti possidetis* and argued: 'Under *uti possidetis,* not only former administrative borders are transformed into state borders, but also territorial sub-units remain part of the newly independent state.'[96] But the fact that only the boundaries of republics were 'upgraded' to the status of international borders actually proves the opposite.

It seems that what mattered for the new international delimitation in the territory of the Soviet Union was not the mere existence of an internal boundary; indeed, autonomous republics were also internally delimited territorial units, but did not become states. What mattered was the fact

---

[91] *cf* n 33.

[92] See Ratner (n 14) 594, for an argument that in the process of decolonisation, boundaries of various kinds were upgraded to the status of international borders: 'The Latin American boundaries were derived from various sorts of Spanish governmental instruments setting up hierarchical and other units such as provinces, *alcaldías, mayores, intendencias,* court (*audiencia*) districts, Captaincies-General, and Vice-Royalties.' See also the *Land, Island and Maritime Frontier Dispute case* (*El Salvador v Honduras*), ICJ Rep 1992, 387, para 43. In the non-colonial situation of the Soviet Union, on the other hand, only internal boundaries of one kind (ie, those of the republics) were 'upgraded' to the status of international borders. Hierarchically lower internal boundaries existed, but these did not become international borders.

[93] See Constitution of the Union of Soviet Socialist Republics, Article 70: 'The Union of Soviet Socialist Republics is an integral, federal, multinational state formed on the principle of socialist federalism as a result of the free self-determination of nations and the voluntary association of equal Soviet Republics.' Reprinted in Hannum (n 81) 745.

[94] J Castellino, *International Law and Self-Determination* (The Hague, Martinus Nijhoff, 2008) 118.

[95] ibid, 118–19.

[96] The Report of the Fact-Finding Mission, 154.

that the internal boundaries delimited a constitutionally defined self-determination unit. In the Soviet context, only republics were territorial units of this kind and thus became independent states. Yet under the colonial *uti possidetis* presumption, an 'upgrade' of other internal boundaries to the status of international borders would be equally plausible.[97] Indeed, what mattered in the process of decolonisation was a mere existence of *a* boundary. What matters in non-colonial situations is the *pedigree of the boundary* and not only its existence.

The mutual agreement of the former Soviet republics on the new international delimitation does not resemble the colonial *uti possidetis* principle (not even implicitly), according to which any boundary is capable of becoming an international border. Rather, it affirms that in non-colonial situations, a plausible claim to independence can only be made by a territorial unit whose population qualifies as a people for the purpose of the right of self-determination. Consequently, only internal boundaries of such units are capable of becoming international borders. The case of the dissolution of the Soviet Union also affirms that where the exact boundaries of historically realised self-determination units have been subject to change, the latest internal boundary will be considered very important when new international borders are confined.[98]

### 3.2.2  The Czech–Slovak International Delimitation

The creation of the Czech and Slovak Republics is an example of the consensual dissolution of the previous state.[99] The border between the two newly created states was determined by the Treaty on the General Delimitation of the Common State Frontiers, signed on 29 October 1992.[100] According to this Treaty, the internal boundary between the two constituent parts of Czechoslovakia became the international border between the Czech and Slovak Republics.[101] Like the Minsk Agreement in the case of the dissolution of the Soviet Union, the Czech–Slovak delimitation treaty made no reference to *uti possidetis*.

---

[97] Angelet points out that *uti possidetis* in non-colonial situations cannot apply because territorial units at different levels of internal organisation make claims to independence. Unlike in colonial situations, *uti possidetis* cannot answer the question of which of these units may become independent states and which may not. N Angelet, 'Quelques observations sur le principe de l'uti possidetis à l'aune du cas hypothétique de la Belgique' in O Corten, B Delcourt, P Klein and N Levrat (eds), *Démembrements d'États et delimitations territoriales: L'uti possidetis en question(s)* (Brussels, Bruylant, 1999) 204. The answer to this question is to be sought in the context of the right of self-determination and not within the context of *uti possidetis*.

[98] *cf* n 51, above.

[99] See E Stein, *Czechoslovakia: Ethnic Conflict, Constitutional Fissure, Negotiated Breakup* (Ann Arbor, University of Michigan Press, 1997) 45; Crawford (n 2) 402.

[100] See Shaw (n 35) 500.

[101] ibid.

The internal boundary within Czechoslovakia had a strong historical pedigree. It originated in the internal division within the Austro-Hungarian monarchy. Czechs were linked to the Austrian part of the monarchy while Slovaks were linked to the Hungarian part.[102] Thus, the '[e]stablishment of the border between the present-day Czech and Slovak Republics is . . . more plausibly associated with the historical pedigree of that line rather than with the line's later status as an internal administrative subdivision of the former Czechoslovakia'.[103] The new international border was therefore confined along the boundary delimiting two historically firmly established self-determination units, which was not reminiscent of arbitrarily drawn colonial lines.

### 3.2.3 *Colonial Pedigree, Non-colonial Situation: Eritrea*

As an Italian colony, Eritrea was an entity separate from Ethiopia and was federated with the latter in 1952.[104] In the 1952 federal Constitution, Eritrea was a self-governing unit. This status was suspended by the central government of Ethiopia in 1962.[105] Upon Eritrea's consensual secession from Ethiopia,[106] the border between colonial Eritrea and Ethiopia was re-established.[107] Because of some contested parts of the border, an armed conflict between Ethiopia and Eritrea broke out.[108] A peace agreement was signed in December 2000 and included provisions for the establishment of three dispute settlement bodies, including the Eritrea–Ethiopia Boundary Commission, which delivered its decision on 13 April 2002. [109] The Eritrea–Ethiopia Boundary Commission[110] noted that '[t]he parties [Ethiopia and Eritrea] agree that a neutral Boundary Commission composed of five members shall be established with a mandate to delimit and demarcate the colonial treaty border based on pertinent colonial treaties [concluded

---

[102]  See M Anderson, *Frontiers: Territory and State Formation in the Modern World* (Cambridge, Polity Press, 1997) 73.

[103]  T Bartoš, '*Uti Possidetis. Quo Vadis?*' (1997) 18 *Australian Yearbook of International Law* 37, 83.

[104]  See M Haile, 'Legality of Secessions: The Case of Eritrea' (1994) 8 *Emory International Law Review* 479, 482–87. See also UN Doc A/RES/390 (V) A (2 December 1950).

[105]  See Crawford (n 2) 402.

[106]  ibid.

[107]  See C Gray, 'The Eritrea/Ethiopia Claims Commission Oversteps its Boundaries: A Partial Award?' (2006) 17 *EJIL* 699, 701.

[108]  ibid.

[109]  ibid, 703.

[110]  The Commission was chaired by Elihu Lauterpacht. Other members were: Bola Adesumbo Ajibola, W Michael Reisman, Stephen Schwebel and Arthur Watts. See the Eritrea–Ethiopia Boundary Commission, ch 1, 1.1. www.un.org/NewLinks/eebcarbitration/EEBC-Decision.pdf.

between Ethiopia and Italy] (1900, 1902 and 1908) and applicable international law'.[111]

The example of Eritrea is different from most situations of border determinations in Africa. Indeed, '[f]or the first time the principles of the intangibility of African frontiers and opposition to secession were breached, but in a way which conformed to the basis of the other African frontiers – the colonial frontier was restored.'[112] Although the colonial boundary was restored, Eritrea clearly was not a matter of decolonisation.[113] Thus, the establishment of its historical borders, albeit of colonial origin, cannot be ascribed to the *uti possidetis* principle.[114] Notably, the decision of the Eritrea–Ethiopia Boundary Commission makes no reference to this principle.

### 3.2.4  *Colonial Pedigree, Non-colonial Situation: East Timor*

The border between East Timor and Indonesia was determined according to the colonial delimitation between the Portuguese and Dutch possessions on Timor Island.[115] Since East Timor remained on the list of non-self-governing territories after Indonesia's occupation,[116] it can be argued that it was properly decolonised when it declared independence in 2002.[117]

---

[111]  ibid, ch 1, 1.2., para 2. See also R Goy, 'L'indépendence de l'Érythrée' (1993) 39 *Annuaire français de droit international* 337, 350. It should be noted that despite the prior agreement of both parties that they would accept the decision of the Boundary Commission, Ethiopia continues to oppose the delimitation decided on by the Commission in some disputed areas. In its view, the Commission's decision, which awards some disputed areas under Ethiopian control to Eritrea, is 'totally illegal, unjust and irresponsible'. It thus proposes 'that the Security Council set up an alternative mechanism to demarcate the contested parts of the boundary in a just and legal manner'. UN Doc S/2003/1186 (19 December 2003), Annex I, para 10. The implementation of the Commission's decision was called for by the Security Council in Resolutions 1586 and 1622. Neither resolution was adopted under Chapter VII of the UN Charter. See UN Doc S/RES/1586 (14 March 2005) and UN Doc S/RES/1622 (13 September 2005). For more on this, see Gray (n 107) 707–10. See also generally M Shaw, 'Title, Control, and Closure? The Experience of the Eritrea–Ethiopia Boundary Commission' (2007) 56 *ICLQ* 755.

[112]  Anderson (n 102) 87.

[113]  Eritrea was decolonised when it was federated with Ethiopia. It should be recalled that the decolonisation process did not only foresee an emergence as an independent state but also a merger with another state. See UN Doc A/RES/1541 (15 December 1960), principle VI.

[114]  Shaw takes a different view (to some extent) and suggests that the delimitation between Ethiopia and Eritrea was about 'determining the *uti possidetis* line': Shaw (n 111) 776. Yet this is to accept that the *uti possidetis* principle is also applicable in situations which are not a matter of decolonisation.

[115]  B Singh, *East Timor, Indonesia and the World: Myths and Realities* (Singapore, Singapore Institute of International Affairs, 1995) 6. See also N Deeley, *The International Boundaries of East Timor* (University of Durham, International Boundaries Research Unit, 2001) 25–27. The territory of East Timor was also affirmed in the *Case Concerning East Timor (Portugal v Australia)*, ICJ Rep 1995, 95, para 11.

[116]  See R Wilde, *International Territorial Administration: How Trusteeship and the Civilizing Mission Never Went Away* (Oxford, Oxford University Press, 2008) 179–80.

[117]  See 'East Timor: Birth of a Nation', *BBC News* (19 May 2002), http://news.bbc.Co.uk/2/hi/asiapacific/1996673.stm. See also UN Doc S/RES/1338 (31 January 2001).

One could thus potentially posit that the delimitation of East Timor was a matter of *uti possidetis*. Yet the real question was not East Timor's independence from Portugal but its independence from Indonesia, which was not a matter of decolonisation, at least not in the traditional understanding of colonialism in the sense of European possessions of overseas territories.[118] The delimitation has a colonial pedigree, yet East Timor also constitutes a self-determination unit, populated by a people with a distinct identity, whose independence was not a matter of decolonisation.

The mode of state creation of East Timor was secession with the approval of the parent state.[119] Consequently, even the pattern of the determination of the international border was that of 'upgrading' the former internal boundary, where such a boundary had a strong historical pedigree and delimited a self-determination unit. Although the historical pedigree of this boundary was colonial, the delimitation of East Timor cannot be ascribed to the *uti possidetis* principle.

### 3.2.5 Colonial Pedigree, Non-colonial Situation: South Sudan

The basis for the new international border between Sudan and South Sudan in 2011 was the pre-independence North/South line, as it existed on 1 January 1956 (the day when Sudan became an independent state).[120] This is also the line to which Sudan referred in its recognition text of South Sudan: 'The Republic of Sudan announces that it recognises the Republic of South Sudan as an independent state, according to the borders existing on 1 January 1956.'[121]

South Sudan, in contrast, invokes an exception to the 1956 boundary. Article 1(2) of Part I of the Provisional Constitution of South Sudan provides:

> The territory of the Republic of South Sudan comprises all lands and air space that constituted the three former Southern Provinces of Bahr el Ghazal, Equatoria and Upper Nile in their boundaries as they stood on January 1, 1956, and the Abyei Area, the territory of the nine Ngok Dinka chiefdoms transferred from Bahr el Ghazal Province to Kordofan Province in 1905 as defined by the Abyei Arbitration Tribunal Award of July 2009.

As indicated in the South Sudanese constitutional provision, in 1905 the Abyei Area was transferred from a southern to a northern province. The

---

[118] For more on the problem of the narrow understanding of colonialism, see L Buchheit, *Secession: The Legitimacy of Self-Determination* (New Haven, Yale University Press, 1978) 18.

[119] See generally UN Doc S/1999/513 (5 May 1999). See also I Martin, *Self Determination in East Timor: The United Nations, the Ballot, and International Intervention* (Boulder, Lynne Rienner, 2001) 15–34.

[120] See the Comprehensive Peace Agreement, the Abyei Protocol (26 May 2004), www.sd. undp.org/doc/CPA.pdf. The Abyei Protocol, arts 1.4 and 8.3.

[121] See 'South Sudan Counts Down to Independence', *BBC News* (8 July 2011), www.bbc. co.uk/news/world-africa-14077511.

Abyei Protocol, which is included in the Comprehensive Peace Agreement,[122] defined the territory 'as the area of the nine Ngok Dinka chiefdoms transferred to Kordofan in 1905'.[123] The Protocol also foresaw a separate referendum to determine the area's future status, either within the northern or southern part,[124] and further specified: 'The January 1, 1956 line between north and south will be inviolate, except as agreed above.'[125]

A separate referendum on the legal status of the Abyei Area never took place. This was due to disagreements between the North and South on determining the population eligible to take part in the vote.[126] The Protocol also established the Abyei Boundary Commission in order 'to define and demarcate the area of the nine Ngok Dinka Chiefdoms transferred to Kordofan in 1905, referred to herein as [the] Abyei Area'.[127]

The Abyei Boundary Commission (ABC) defined the Abyei Area and delivered its report on 14 July 2005.[128] The central government of Sudan strongly disagreed with the ABC and refused to accept its findings. Subsequently, on 7 July 2008, the government of Sudan and the Sudan's People Liberation Movement/Army signed the Arbitration Agreement by way of which they referred the question of the Abyei Area to the Permanent Court of Arbitration (PCA), under the PCA Optional Rules for Arbitrating Disputes between Two Parties of Which Only One is a State.[129] The question referred to the arbitration was whether the ABC exceeded its mandate given in the Abyei Protocol.[130] If the mandate were not exceeded, the arbitral tribunal was authorised to proclaim the finding of the ABC as being final;[131] if the ABC exceeded its mandate, the Arbitral Tribunal was authorised to 'make a declaration to that effect, and shall proceed to define (i.e. delimit) on [the] map the boundaries of the area of the nine Ngok Dinka chiefdoms transferred to Kordofan in 1905, based on the submissions of the Parties'.[132]

---

[122] *cf* ch 2, 2.4.
[123] The Abyei Protocol, art 1.1.2.
[124] ibid, art 1.3.
[125] ibid, art 1.4.
[126] See 'SPLM's Amum Says Abyei Referendum Must Happen or President Should Transfer Region to South', *Sudan Tribune* (13 January 2011), www.sudantribune.com/SPLM-s-Amum-says-Abyei-referendum.37596.
[127] The Abyei Protocol, art 5.1.
[128] See the PCA in the matter of an arbitration before a tribunal constituted in accordance with Article 5 of the Arbitration Agreement between the Government of Sudan and the Sudan People's Liberation Movement/Army on delimiting Abyei Area, Final Award (22 July 2009), www.pca-cpa.org/showfile.asp?fil_id=1240 (hereinafter the *Abyei* Arbitration), para 122.
[129] The *Abyei* Arbitration, paras 1, 2 and 3.
[130] ibid, para 6(a).
[131] ibid, para 6(b).
[132] ibid, para 6(c).

The Arbitral Tribunal, inter alia, held that 'the ABC Experts did not provide sufficient reasoning with respect to essential elements of the decision, namely the determination of the eastern and western boundary lines of the Abyei Area'.[133] The Arbitral Tribunal thus partly overruled the ABC's findings, ie, declared the Western and Eastern boundaries as not being drawn in compliance with the ABC's mandate, and proceeded with determining the Western and Eastern boundaries of the Abyei area, pursuant to Article 2(c) of the Arbitration Agreement.[134]

The Arbitral Tribunal noted that there were no useful maps from 1905 to indicate the delimitation of the Abyei Area[135] and proceeded by considering oral statements and anthropological writings which located the area historically populated by the Ngok Dinka people.[136] It ultimately defined the Abyei Area within boundaries much narrower if compared to the previous ABC finding.[137]

The central government of Sudan refuses to accept the incorporation of the Abyei Area in the newly created Southern Sudanese state, not even in the narrower borders, and insists on the full re-establishment of the 1956 boundary.[138] The dispute over the new international border is very complex, not only politically but also legally.

The re-established 1956 boundary has a colonial pedigree. However, the colonial *uti possidetis* line could apply automatically only if North and South Sudan became two separate states on 1 January 1956. This was not the case and the emergence of South Sudan as an independent state is not a matter of decolonisation; as demonstrated above, this is rather a situation of a consensual emergence of a new state outside the colonial context.

The practice of state creations shows that new international borders are drawn along the lines of the most recent internal boundary arrangement.[139] The relevance of the 1956 boundary is therefore not in its colonial pedigree; rather, it is relevant because it was adopted by the internal legal regime of 2005.[140] Since the 2005 boundary is the latest internal boundary regime, the 1956 boundary is legally relevant *only* to the extent to which it was adopted in the 2005 internal arrangement.

The latest internal boundary arrangement did not fully adopt the 1956 line; it acknowledged the Abyei Area exception,[141] albeit not by determining its legal status but rather by creating a mechanism for its determination – a

---

[133]  ibid, para 708.
[134]  ibid, para 712.
[135]  ibid, para 713.
[136]  ibid, paras 717–44.
[137]  ibid, para 770.
[138]  *cf* ch 2, 2.4.
[139]  See n 98, above.
[140]  See n 121, above.
[141]  See nn 121–25, above.

popular consultation.[142] The consultation never took place.[143] Moreover, the ABC and the Arbitral Tribunal were asked to determine the Abyei Area geographically; they were not asked to determine its legal status. As a consequence, the Area is now determined geographically, but with the referendum still outstanding, its legal status remains undetermined. With South Sudan becoming an independent state, the internal boundary dispute became a dispute over international delimitation.

There can be no automatic presumption of re-establishment of the 1956 boundary, since this was not the latest internal boundary arrangement within Sudan. At the same time, this does not mean that the Abyei Area necessarily belongs to South Sudan. The final international delimitation can only be determined by a referendum in the Abyei Area held in accordance with the Abyei Protocol.[144]

### 3.2.6 Re-examining the Application of Uti Possidetis and Border-Drawing in the Territory of the SFRY in Light of Post-1990 State Practice

The example of the SFRY is more complex than other situations discussed in this section. The dissolution was not a treaty-based consensual process; rather, it was a consequence of a chain of secessions and of a constitutional breakdown of the federation which led the Badinter Commission to proclaim that the SFRY was in the process of dissolution.[145] In order to determine the new international borders, the Badinter Commission applied the *uti possidetis* principle.[146]

As outlined above, many commentators have criticised the Badinter Commission's application of *uti possidetis* in the territory of the SFRY. In addition, some also see the internal boundaries established within the SFRY to be unfit for becoming international borders and, as such, reminiscent of boundaries established in colonial situations. In one such view, 'in the SFRY, municipal borders were drawn by the Communist Party's Politbureau, taking little account of ethnic factors'.[147]

The argument that the internal boundaries in the SFRY were colonial-like administrative lines is not accurate and it is arguable that the determination of new international borders in the territory of the former SFRY, despite reference to *uti possidetis*, did not differ from subsequent practice in post-1990 state creations, where no references to this principle were made.

---

[142] See n 126, above.
[143] ibid.
[144] See n 124, above.
[145] The Badinter Commission, Opinion 1 (29 November 1991), para 3, reprinted in Trifunovska (n 13) 415.
[146] See ch 4, 2.2.
[147] Bartoš (n 103) 87. See also M Kreća, *The Badinter Arbitration Commission – A Critical Commentary* (Belgrade, Jugoslovenski pregled, 1993) 12–14.

It has been established that the practice of post-1990 state creations shows that internal boundaries are capable of becoming international borders where they delimit historically firmly established self-determination units. In order to establish whether the internal boundaries within the SFRY had the potential to become international borders in the absence of *uti possidetis* presumption, their historical pedigree needs to be considered.

The first common state of Southern Slavs was the Kingdom of Serbs, Croats and Slovenes, which was created on 1 December 1918.[148] Slovenia and Croatia previously did not exist as independent states; the territories settled by the Slovenes and the Croats, respectively, were part of the Habsburg monarchy.[149] The Kingdom of Serbia had existed as an independent state since the Congress of Berlin in 1878,[150] but not all Serbs lived within the territory of this state. The former Habsburg territories of Vojvodina, Bosnia-Herzegovina and Croatia were also populated by significant shares of ethnic Serbian population.[151] However, the establishment of the Kingdom of Serbs, Croats and Slovenes unified the Serb population in a common state. The new Kingdom included the territory of Montenegro, which was otherwise also recognised as an independent state at the Congress of Berlin in 1878,[152] and Bosnia-Herzegovina, which was previously not a state but a separate unit within the Habsburg monarchy with borders likewise confirmed at the Congress of Berlin.[153]

The Kingdom of Serbs, Croats and Slovenes was unified under the King of Serbia and created as a multiparty electoral democracy,[154] while it was initially not defined whether the new Kingdom would be a federal or a unitary state.[155] Since a numerous population of Serbs lived outside of the frontiers of the former Kingdom of Serbia, the entire Serb population could not be federated within a single federal unit. Serbia was thus disinclined towards a federal arrangement. On the other hand, the Slovenes and the Croats feared Serbian centralism and demanded a federated state. In the end, the Serbian majority within the parliament enacted the unitary Constitution of 1921.[156] The Constitution 'was a reflection of the official

---

[148] Radan (n 14) 136.

[149] S Pavlowitch, *Yugoslavia* (London, Ernest Benn, 1971) 42–43.

[150] ibid, 44.

[151] L Cohen, *Broken Bonds: Yugoslavia's Disintegration and Balkan Politics in Transition* (Boulder, Westview, 1995) 14.

[152] Pavlowitch (n 149) 44.

[153] At the Congress of Berlin, Bosnia-Herzegovina was 'entrusted to Austro-Hungarian administration' (ibid, 44). It was formally annexed by Austria-Hungary in 1908 (ibid, 48). In historical documents, Bosnia was first mentioned in the tenth century and in the twelfth century even existed as an independent state. For more on this, see O Ibrahimagić, *Državno-pravni razvitak Bosne i Hercegovine* (Sarajevo, Vijeće kongresa bošnjačkih intelektualaca, 1998) 7–11.

[154] See Pavlowitch (n 149) 59–64.

[155] Radan (n 14) 138.

[156] ibid.

view that the Serbs, Croats and Slovenes were three tribes of one unified nation, namely the Yugoslavs'.[157] The strong ideology of a unitary 'Yugoslav people' was also evident in the proclamation of the official language, which was 'Serbo-Croato-Slovene',[158] a language which linguistically does not exist. In this respect, one commentator noted:

> According to the constitution adopted in 1921, the new state expressed the political will of the single 'three-named Serbo-Croatian-Slovenian people', who allegedly spoke a single 'Serbo-Croatian-Slovenian language'. Although an ethnic alliance composed of three different 'tribes' was theoretically mandated to govern the country, the reality of power and rule was a centralized unitary kingdom, with state authority concentrated in Belgrade.[159]

As a consequence of centralisation and of an attempt to establish a unitary 'Yugoslav people', the 1922 ministerial decree established the internal boundaries of 33 districts which did not follow ethnic lines.[160] Such a division was satisfactory for the Serbs but was opposed by the Slovenes and the Croats, due to it being set arbitrarily and not delimiting their respective historical territories.[161] Internal clashes in the Kingdom continued and on 6 January 1929 the King dissolved the parliament and introduced his personal dictatorship, claiming that this was necessary in order 'to preserve the unity of the state and its peoples'.[162] At that time, the Kingdom of Serbs, Croats and Slovenes was also officially renamed the Kingdom of Yugoslavia.[163] In 1931, the King promulgated a new unitary constitution, which divided the Kingdom into nine administrative units called *banovina*. In some situations, these units came closer to historically delimited ethnic boundaries (eg, the unit called *Dravska banovina* followed the historically delimited territory of Slovenes), but this was not always the case.[164]

During the Second World War, in 1943, the second Yugoslavia (later known as the SFRY) was established by leaders of the partisan movement led by Josip Broz-Tito.[165] The new state was defined as a federation and the borders of its federal units were established by the Presidency

---

[157] ibid.

[158] Constitution of the Kingdom of Serbs, Croats and Slovenes (1921), Article 3.

[159] Cohen (n 151) 14. *cf* Shaw (n 35) 489, who argues that in some circumstances, 'administrative borders have been changed by central government in a deliberate attempt to strengthen central control and weaken the growth of local power centres'. It can be argued that this was the case in the Kingdom of Serbs, Croats and Slovenes.

[160] Radan (n 14) 138.

[161] ibid.

[162] ibid.

[163] See J Lampe, *Yugoslavia as History: Twice there was a Country* (Cambridge, Cambridge University Press, 2000) 159.

[164] See Cohen (n 151) 18 (map).

[165] For more on this, see Lampe (n 163) 197–228.

of the Anti-Fascist Council of the National Liberation of Yugoslavia[166] on 24 February 1945:[167]

> This decision relied largely on older historical borders, both as they existed in interwar Yugoslavia and in the former Austro-Hungarian and Ottoman Empires. In many respects the decision accepted borders that coincided with, either exactly or approximately, the borders claimed by the various nationalist movements of the nineteenth and early twentieth century.[168]

Ultimately, boundaries of no historical pedigree only had to be drawn between Slovenian and Croatian parts of the former Zone B of the Free Territory of Trieste,[169] between Croatia and Vojvodina (the former Habsburg territory with a majority Serb population)[170] and between Serbia and Macedonia.[171] In these situations, the ethnic compositions of the territories were taken into account and geographical boundaries (eg, rivers) were used for the purpose of delimitation.[172] In the end, the boundary between Slovenia and Croatia (apart from the short part within the former Zone B of the Free Territory of Trieste) followed the former division between the Austrian and Hungarian parts of the Habsburg (dual) monarchy.[173] Croatia and Serbia only bordered in Vojvodina, where ethnic and geographical principles were used for the exact delimitation.[174] Bosnia-Herzegovina was re-established along the lines determined at the Congress of Berlin,[175] which originated in the delimitation of the medieval Bosnian state and of the Bosnian entity within the Ottoman Empire.[176] Both Serbia and Montenegro were generally re-established along their pre-First World War international borders.[177] The only notable exception to the rule of boundaries of historical pedigree was Macedonia, which was part of the Kingdom of Serbia before the First World War.[178] In order to determine its boundaries, the lines of *Vardarska banovina*, a unit within the Kingdom of Yugoslavia, were taken into account, although they were

[166] At the time, the Anti-Fascist Council of the National Liberation of Yugoslavia was the provisional legislature. See Pavlowitch (n 149) 175.

[167] Radan (n 14) 149.

[168] ibid.

[169] For more on the Free Territory of Trieste, see Crawford (n 2) 553.

[170] Radan (n 14) 151.

[171] ibid.

[172] ibid.

[173] See Pavlowitch (n 149) 43. The Hungarian-Croatian compromise of 1868 assigned Croatia the status of a separate unit linked to the Hungarian crown (ibid,).

[174] See Radan (n 14) 151.

[175] ibid.

[176] See Ibrahimagić (n 153) 9–26.

[177] ibid, The exceptions were Kosovo and Vojvodina, which were not part of the Kingdom of Serbia but formally came under Serbian sovereignty in the time of the Kingdom of Serbs, Croats and Slovenes. See N Malcolm, *Kosovo: A Short History* (London, Macmillan, 1998) 264–66.

[178] For more on the creation of the Macedonian republic and recognition of Macedonian ethnicity, see Pavlowitch (n 153) 198–204.

narrower and followed ethnic division lines between the Serbs and the Macedonians.[179] An autonomous province of Kosovo was also established within its historical borders.[180]

Unlike the administrative units within the Kingdom of Yugoslavia, which resembled the arbitrariness of colonial boundary drawing, the federal units of the SFRY were not created along arbitrary lines but followed boundaries of a historical pedigree, often even former international borders.

Federalism and drawing internal boundaries along the lines of borders of historical pedigree also re-created the problem of Serbs settled outside of the boundaries of Serbia. However, this was not a problem originally created by the internal boundary arrangement within the SFRY but a problem inherited from the past. Furthermore, the internal boundaries in the SFRY did not create (or try to create) new ethnic identities within artificially defined territorial arrangements, but merely took into account the historically realised identities which the constitutional arrangement of the Kingdom of Yugoslavia disregarded and (unsuccessfully) tried to create a common Yugoslav ethnic identity.[181] Different identities were expressly recognised by the 1974 Constitution of the SFRY, which did not promote the idea of a common Yugoslav ethnicity, but rather created a federal arrangement which enabled the peoples of Yugoslavia to exercise the right of self-determination in its internal mode and vested wide powers within the republics.[182]

When the SFRY disintegrated, the internal boundaries 'upgraded' to international borders were thus not random, colonial-like boundaries (as would have been the case had the internal boundaries within the Kingdom of Yugoslavia become international borders), but for the most part were historically firmly established borders between groups of peoples with

---

[179] Radan (n 14) 151–52.

[180] For more on the historical background to Kosovo and its borders, see Malcolm (n 177) 58–80.

[181] *cf* n 159, above. The last reliable census in the SFRY dates from 1981 (the next one in 1990 was already heavily influenced by the crisis in the federation and was subject to some organized boycotts). The ethnic composition in the 1981 census was as follows: Serbs (36.3 per cent), Croats (19.7 per cent), Muslims (7.9 per cent), Slovenes (7.8 per cent), Macedonians (6.0 per cent), Albanians (5.8 per cent), Yugoslavs (5.4 per cent), Montenegrins (2.6 per cent) and Hungarians (2.3 per cent). Other ethnic identities included Italians, Roma, Turks, Slovaks, Bulgarians, Romanians and Germans. What is significant is that most of the population identified itself along ethnic lines. In this perception, individuals belonged to one of the constitutive peoples of the SFRY and only a small percentage of barely over five per cent identified itself with a common Yugoslav identity. The 1981 Census in the SFRY, *Popis stanovništva, domaćinstava i stanova u 1981. godini* (Belgrade, Savezni zavod za statistiku, 1983).

[182] The 1974 Constitution defined republics as states (art 3) and proclaimed borders of the republics inviolable without consent of the republic (art 5(1)), empowered republics to adopt their own legislation applicable only in their respective territories and to exercise effective control in their territories (art 268) and gave republics powers to conduct their own foreign policies, subject to limitation by the general framework of the federal foreign policy (art 271).

different ethnic identities. Thus, the Badinter Commission should not be criticised for 'upgrading' the internal boundaries to international borders. Indeed:

> Any attempted ethnic reconfiguration of the Former Yugoslavia on a totally free-for-all basis . . . would most likely have produced an even worse situation than that which did occur . . . The absence of [the] *uti possidetis* presumption would leave in place as the guiding principle only effective control or self-determination. To rely on effective control as the principal criterion for the creation of international boundaries would be to invite the use of force as the inexorable first step . . . Self-determination is a principle whose definition in this extended version is wholly unpredictable. Precisely which group would be entitled in such situations to claim a share of a territory? [183]

In other words, it is not possible to accept that in situations of non-consensual dissolutions, all borders are in flux and that the previously existing internal boundary arrangement could be changed by effective possession. This would be a call for ethnic cleansing. Instead, drawing borders along historically well-established boundaries, which separate peoples with different identities, seems to be a reasonable alternative. The Badinter Commission did what was later consensually achieved in Czechoslovakia.[184] It is, however, incorrect to term this process *uti possidetis*. The use of this term 'implied that the [SFRY] was a *quasi*-colonial administrative entity, namely, a party totally alien to the constituent nations of the old state'.[185] Besides the doctrinal question of whether this principle applies outside of colonial situations,[186] its colonial origin also implies the confinement of international borders along arbitrarily drawn internal boundaries. It has been shown in this section that this was not the case in the SFRY.

### 3.2.7 Montenegro

After the dissolution of the SFRY, Montenegro initially continued in the union with Serbia in the state formation called the Federal Republic of Yugoslavia (FRY). In 2003, the FRY was transformed into the State Union of Serbia and Montenegro (SUSM). In 2006, Montenegro declared independence.[187] The mode of state creation was consensual; indeed, secession was expressly allowed under Article 60 of the Constitution of the SUSM.[188]

---

[183] Shaw (n 177) 502.

[184] See ch 4, 3.2.2.

[185] C Antonopoulos, 'The Principle of *Uti Possidetis* in Contemporary International Law' (1996) 49 *Revue hellenique de droit international* 29, 84.

[186] See ch 4, 2.3.

[187] See Declaration of Independence of the Republic of Montenegro, *Official Gazette of the Republic of Montenegro*, No 36/06 (3 June 2006).

[188] Constitution of the SUSM (2003), art 60.

Article 60 also stipulated for Serbia's continuity of the international personality of the SUSM. Serbia also continues the membership of the SUSM of the UN.

The border between Serbia and Montenegro was firmly established in Article 5 of the Constitution of the SUSM: 'The border between state-members shall not be altered unless there exists mutual consensus of both sides.'[189] Montenegro's borders were identical to those in the FRY, those in the SFRY and, with some minor changes, those of the Montenegrin state recognised at the Congress of Berlin in 1878.[190]

When Montenegro acquired independence in accordance with Article 60 of the Constitution of the SUSM, its new international delimitation was not a matter of *uti possidetis*. This principle was not mentioned in any of the founding documents of the new Montenegrin state. Even more importantly, Montenegro's new international border was actually an old one and was not reminiscent of colonial delimitation. Indeed, it had a strong historical pedigree of delimiting a self-determination unit and previously already had the status of being an international border.

### 3.2.8 Kosovo

As in the territory of the Soviet Union, in the territory of the SFRY, not all internal boundaries became international borders, but only those delimiting federal republics.[191] It is notable that under the Constitution of the SFRY, only republics were defined as self-determination units, while the two autonomous provinces, Kosovo and Vojvodina, were considered to be the self-governing units of the Albanian and Hungarian ethnic minorities.[192] The reason that Kosovo's boundary was not elevated to the status of an international border in 1991 can be ascribed to the fact that under the SFRY's constitutional arrangement, the Kosovo Albanians were not bearers of the right of self-determination and Kosovo was not considered to be a separate constitutional self-determination unit (ie, it was not a federal republic).

The second half of the 1990s saw an escalation of ethnic conflict, which led to the intervention of NATO and the establishment of an international territorial administration under a Chapter VII Resolution of the UN Security Council.[193] The international territorial administration was established in the entire territory of Kosovo.[194] In one view, the UN Security Council

---

[189] ibid, art 5(3) (author's own translation).
[190] *cf* ch 2, 3.4.6.
[191] *cf* ch 4, 3.2.1.
[192] See the Constitution of the SFRY arts 1, 2 and 3. See also R Rich, 'Recognition of States: The Collapse of Yugoslavia and the Soviet Union' (1993) 4 *EJIL* 36, 39.
[193] See UN Doc S/RES/1244 (10 June 1999).
[194] ibid, especially paras 5, 6 and 7. See also UNMIK/REG/1999/1 (25 July 1999).

Resolution 1244 thus acknowledged the applicability of *uti possidetis* in Kosovo.[195] This interpretation is not convincing.

The problems are not only in that Resolution 1244 does not mention *uti possidetis* or that Kosovo is a non-colonial situation; indeed, even if one accepted the non-colonial application of *uti possidetis*, the *sine qua non* for its application would still be a state creation. Although interpretations of Resolution 1244 may differ significantly, there is one point on which universal consensus exists: between 10 June 1999 (when Resolution 1244 was adopted) and 17 February 2008 (when independence was declared), Kosovo was not a state.[196] And since there was no new state creation at issue when Resolution 1244 was adopted, the latter could not apply *uti possidetis* in Kosovo.

Resolution 1244 only established the international territorial administration in the territory of Kosovo, within its historically realised boundaries. These are also the boundaries which have been, upon Kosovo's declaration of independence, recognised by 92 states as borders of the independent state of Kosovo. As was held in the *Québec* case, the success of unilateral secession ultimately depends on recognition.[197] This also implies that recognition acknowledges the 'upgrading' of former internal boundaries to international borders. In the view of the 92 recognising states, Kosovo is thus a state within its historical borders. Notably, no recognising state made a reference to *uti possidetis*.

It is also of significance that, in the process of negotiations on Kosovo's future status, the division of the territory was never seriously discussed. This is somewhat surprising as Serbia has hinted that it would be potentially willing to accept the partition of Kosovo.[198] The division of Kosovo could be used as one of the options which would make a consensual state creation (albeit within narrower borders) more likely.

Although it remains controversial as to whether Kosovo has emerged as an independent state, this example nevertheless confirms the practice of new state delimitations in the post-1990 era: where previous internal boundaries delimit historically established self-determination units, the new international border will be confined along these lines. Although negotiations on the future international border are in principle not excluded, there exists no relevant state practice. While Kosovo is perhaps one example where such practice could develop, this has not happened.

---

[195] Hasani (n 88) 94.

[196] The dispute relates to the question of whether Resolution 1244 prohibited the emergence of Kosovo as a state. Yet no one contends the fact that with Resolution 1244 Kosovo became independent.

[197] The *Québec* case (n 10), para 155.

[198] See 'Serbia's President Considers Kosovo Division', *High Beam Research* (30 September 2008), http://www.highbeam.com/doc/1A1-D93H20HO0.html.

## 4 CONCLUSION

When dealing with the SFRY, the Badinter Commission resorted to *uti possidetis* in order to justify the 'upgrading' of internal boundaries to international borders. The application of this principle outside of the process of decolonisation was doctrinally underpinned by selective quoting of the Chamber of the ICJ in the *Frontier Dispute* case. So underpinned, the Badinter Commission's extension of *uti possidetis* beyond the process of decolonisation can hardly serve as an authority to be referred to in future situations. The non-colonial applicability of *uti possidetis* has very weak doctrinal foundations and a reference to it did not appear in any documents which are legally relevant for subsequent state creations and the delimitation of new states.

Relevant practice nevertheless shows that when new states are created, the previous internal boundary arrangement cannot be disregarded. Indeed, all new states created in the post-1990 period were delimited along previous internal boundaries, either by a formal agreement in the case of consensual state creations or by the subsequent acceptance of states and UN organs in the case of non-consensual ones. It has been shown that this was not the consequence of the operation of *uti possidetis* – indeed, if *uti possidetis* applied outside of colonialism, the pedigree of the 'upgraded' boundary would not matter – but the practice of post-1990 state creations shows that it *does* matter what kind of a unit the boundary delimits.

Unlike the process of decolonisation, the practice of post-1990 state creations shows that not just any internal boundary may potentially become an international border, but only those boundaries that have a strong historical pedigree of delimiting self-determination units. In the practice of post-1990 state creations, most new international borders have had a previous history as international borders, borders between empires or ethnic-based internal boundaries within empires. Not even the SFRY was an exception to this pattern, but the situation there was more complicated due to the non-consensual nature of its dissolution.

Thus, when new international borders were confined in the post-1990 practice, it was not the importance of internal boundaries per se which was relevant for 'upgrading' to international borders; what was important was the historical pedigree of these boundaries and the fact that they delimited historically established self-determination units.

A well-known difficulty with the concept of self-determination was once captured in the following words: 'On the surface [the idea of self-determination] seemed reasonable: let the people decide. It was in fact ridiculous because the people cannot decide until somebody decides who are the people.'[199] In the process of decolonisation, *uti possidetis* decided who the people are. In so doing, the principle imposed 'identities on the various inhabitants of former colonies'.[200]

Outside of decolonisation, it was not the new international delimitation which decided who the peoples are for the purpose of the right of self-determination, nor did the new international delimitation try to create new identities. In the practice of post-1990 state creations, the identities of separate peoples already existed and the internal boundaries did not delimit colonial-like entities. It was thus the pedigree of a historically real-ised self-determination unit and not *uti possidetis* which confined new international borders in the practice of post-1990 state creations.

The new international borders also created new minorities and many of these borders are contested as being unjust and drawn against the will of the people. But one needs to keep in mind that mono-ethnic 'nation states', the borders of which everyone perceives to be just, do not exist in reality. And, for this reason, one cannot expect that such states could be newly created. When new states are created, international law does not exclude modifications of the previously existing internal boundaries. One needs to keep in mind that state creation is a political process leading to a legal status. A new boundary arrangement may become a part of this process.

The practice of post-1990 state creations nevertheless shows that where these boundaries delimit historically realised self-determination units, the new international borders will be confined along these lines. Where internal boundaries were subject to recent alterations, the latest internal boundary arrangement will be the most relevant one for the determination of a new international border. But states in contemporary international law do not emerge automatically. For this reason, not even their internal boundaries are automatically upgraded to the status of international borders as soon as the statehood criteria are met. In principle, the exact delimitation of a new state could become a part of the political process (potentially) lead-ing toward statehood. But international practice to this effect remains undeveloped.

---

[199] I Jennings, *The Approach to Self-Government* (Cambridge, Cambridge University Press, 1956) 55–56.

[200] A Rosen, 'Economic and Cooperative Post-Colonial Borders: How Two Interpretations of Borders by the ICJ May Undermine the Relationship between *Uti Possidetis* and Democracy' (2006) 25 *Penn State International Law Review* 207, 212.

# 5

# *Democratic Statehood: Conclusions*

## 1 DEMOCRACY AND STATEHOOD:
### AN ANALYSIS FROM TWO PERSPECTIVES

T HE EARLY 1990s were not only marked by the demise of the
socialist/communist social, political and economic model but also
by the emergence of a number of new states in the territories of the
Soviet Union and the SFRY.[1] The impact on international law of the political developments at the end of the Cold War came from two perspectives.
Some scholars argued that the alleged global switch to democracy should
have an impact on the interpretation of the rules of international law governing the rights and duties of *existing* states.[2] However, in contemporary
international law, democracy cannot be seen as an ongoing requirement
for having the full attributes of statehood.

At the same time, the post-Cold War era of democratisation shaped the
practice of states and UN organs in relation to the emergence of *new states*.[3]
This practice has been the main focus of the present book. An argument
has been developed that the emergence of a new state needs to be seen as
a *process* which requires adherence to some legality-based requirements
and the principles of democratic decision-making. This process of creating new states *democratically* should not be conflated with democracy as a
political system. But in the post-Cold War era, the practice is also emerging of parallel internationalised creations of states and democratic political systems in newly emerged states.

This chapter offers conclusions on the post-Cold War practice of the
emergence of new states and argues how this practice has reshaped the
contemporary international law of statehood.

## 2 THE EMERGENCE OF NEW STATES IN POST-COLD WAR PRACTICE

In post-Cold War practice, modes of state creation were not unitary and
where the initial consent of the parent state was not achieved, international

---

[1] See ch 2, 2.1 and 2, 3.
[2] See ch 1, 2.3.
[3] See ch 2, 3, 2, 5 and 2, 6.

involvement focused on securing such consent. The dissolutions of the Soviet Union[4] and Czechoslovakia[5] were consensual. The secessions of Eritrea from Ethiopia[6] and South Sudan from Sudan[7] were also consensual, although marked by specific circumstances of lengthy armed conflicts. Where domestic political consensus existed, the new legal fact of the emergence of new states was merely acknowledged by the international community. In the absence of such a consensus, the state creations of East Timor, Montenegro and Kosovo were subject to international involvement.

International involvement in the territorial statuses of East Timor and Kosovo was channelled through the UN Security Council. In both instances, human rights abuses led to the establishment of international territorial administration and the loss of effective control of the respective parent states over the territories of East Timor and Kosovo.[8] Such arrangements were put in place by the Security Council, acting under Chapter VII of the UN Charter.[9]

In both East Timor and Kosovo, the international territorial administration, whose actions are attributable to the UN,[10] implemented democratic institutions and sponsored multiparty elections.[11] The UN, as a universal organisation, thus formally enacted a political system which is not universally perceived as the only legitimate one.[12]

The legal arrangements for international territorial administration established in East Timor and Kosovo influenced the question of sovereignty over these two territories.[13] In East Timor, international involvement led to Indonesia's consent to holding a referendum on independence, which was conducted under the auspices of the UN.[14] East Timor's path to independence was ultimately affirmed by a subsequent Security Council resolution which was not adopted under Chapter VII of the UN Charter.[15]

---

[4] See ch 2, 2.1.

[5] See E Stein, *Czechoslovakia: Ethnic Conflict, Constitutional Fissure, Negotiated Breakup* (Ann Arbor, University of Michigan Press, 1997); J Crawford, *The Creation of States in International Law* (Oxford, Oxford University Press, 2006) 402.

[6] See M Haile, 'Legality of Secessions: The Case of Eritrea' (1994) 8 *Emory International Law Review* 479; Crawford (n 5) 402.

[7] See ch 2, 2.4.

[8] See ch 2, 6.

[9] See UN Doc S/RES/1244 (Kosovo); UN Doc S/RES/1272 (East Timor).

[10] See M Bothe and T Marauhn, 'UN Administration of Kosovo and East Timor: Concept, Legality and Limitations of Security Council-Mandated Trusteeship Administration' in C Tomuschat (ed.), *Kosovo and the International Community: A Legal Assessment* (The Hague, Kluwer Law International, 2001) 228.

[11] See ch 2, 5, and 2, 6.

[12] ibid.

[13] See R Wilde, *International Territorial Administration: How Trusteeship and the Civilizing Mission Never Went Away* (Oxford, Oxford University Press, 2008) 605.

[14] See ch 2, 5.

[15] See UN Doc S/RES/1338 (31 January 2001).

In Kosovo, international involvement did not lead to Serbia's consent to independence and no Security Council resolution was passed which would affirm Kosovo's path to independence (against the wishes of its parent state). But independence was nevertheless proposed at the international level by the Special Envoy of the UN Secretary-General, Martti Ahtisaari.[16] The Ahtisaari Plan, inter alia, suggested that the absence of statehood hindered Kosovo's democratic development. Since democratic institutions had already been established by international territorial administration, Special Envoy Ahtisaari thus implied that Kosovo's democracy could not be consolidated without statehood.[17]

In the absence of Serbia's consent, from the legal point of view, Kosovo's secession was unilateral.[18] As identified by the Supreme Court of Canada in the *Québec* case, the success of a unilateral secession ultimately depends on recognitions, while the recognising states take legality and legitimacy criteria into consideration when they decide whether to grant recognition.[19] Thus, when unilateral secession is at issue, recognition by definition has constitutive effects. The democratic legitimacy of secession may be considered by foreign states when deciding whether to grant recognition, but such legitimacy does not create a legal entitlement to unilateral secession.

The creation of the state of Montenegro resulted from the involvement of the EU. The EU sponsored the transformation of the FRY into a transitional state formation, the State Union of Serbia and Montenegro (SUSM), the constitution of which explicitly allowed for secession, foresaw the holding of a referendum and even solved the problem of state succession and the continuity of international personality in advance.[20] Yet the referendum rules at that time remained undefined by the constitution.

Prior to holding a popular consultation, the EU also imposed the referendum rules,[21] which were designed to provide for the democratic legitimacy of the decision-making. The 55 per cent threshold obviously sought to avoid decision-making with a very narrow majority and gave reasonable hope to both sides of winning the referendum.[22] A democratic political system was not imposed, as the institutions of procedural democracy had already been implemented in Montenegro.[23]

On the basis of this practice, the legal framework for the emergence of new states in contemporary international law needs to be reconsidered.

---

[16] See ch 2, 6.3.
[17] UN Doc S/2007/168 (16 March 2007) (the Ahtisaari Plan), para 7.
[18] See ch 2, 6.3.
[19] *Reference re Secession of Québec* (1998) 2 SCR 217 (Canada) (the *Québec* case), para 155.
[20] The Constitution of the State Union of Serbia and Montenegro (2003), art 60.
[21] See International Crisis Group Briefing No 42 (30 May 2006) 6.
[22] See ch 2, 4.
[23] ibid.

## 3 CONTEMPORARY INTERNATIONAL PRACTICE AND THE LEGAL STATUS OF THE STATEHOOD CRITERIA

Acquiring statehood is not an international legal entitlement. Existing states are protected by the principle of territorial integrity. While this principle does not generate an absolute prohibition of secession, the consequence of its operation is that states cannot emerge automatically as a matter of objective fact; they can only emerge in the legal circumstances where the claim to territorial integrity is either overcome or becomes inapplicable. This section considers what implications this practice has for the law of statehood and how democracy relates to the traditional concepts in this area of international law.

### 3.1 State Creation as a Political Process of Overcoming a Counterclaim to Territorial Integrity

A consequence of the principle of territorial integrity is that the burden of moving the territorial status quo lies on the independence-seeking entity. This is a rather difficult task and only very rarely is it successful. The emergence of new states in contemporary international law has thus become a political process of overcoming the hurdle of a counterclaim to territorial integrity.

This book has identified the following modes of overcoming this hurdle: (i) waiver of the claim by the parent state; (ii) consensual extinction of the parent state; (iii) international involvement which either leads to a non-consensual extinction of the parent state or procures the latter's waiver of the claim to territorial integrity; and (iv) recognition of an attempt at unilateral secession which may have constitutive effects. All of these modes are signified by a political process which can be either primarily domestic, internationalised or a combination of both.

The least controversial modes are the parent state's waiver and consensual extinction. International involvement leading to non-consensual dissolution and thus the extinction of the predecessor state is more controversial than consensually achieved statehood. In principle, where dissolution is at issue, the legal personality of the state is extinguished and in the absence of a parent state, there is no applicable counterclaim for territorial integrity. In the absence of such a claim, there is no barrier between the entity's argument for independence and the acquisition of statehood (except where the emergence of a new state would have been as a result of territorial illegality).

The situation is relatively clear where dissolution is consensual. Where it is not, the outcome becomes dependent on international responses. The only clear example of non-consensual dissolution is the SFRY, where the Badinter Commission's legal position that dissolution, rather than attempts at unilateral secession, were at work was universalised and adopted even by the Security Council. The Badinter Commission's interpretation of the events in the SFRY in 1991 as being indicative of dissolution was one possible interpretation, but was not the only one. However, this is the one which became universally followed in the practice of states and UN organs. Non-consensual dissolution as a mode of removal of the claim to territorial integrity is thus fraught with difficulty: the international personality of the parent state, and thus the applicable claim to territorial integrity, can only be removed if the legal position of non-consensual dissolution is universally endorsed by the international community through the practice of states and UN organs.

The problem of universal acceptance by the international community is even more prominently present in the theory and practice of the international acceptance of a unilateral declaration of independence. International law does not prohibit granting recognition to an entity which declares independence unilaterally. And despite the general perception in contemporary international law of recognition being a declaratory rather than a constitutive act, it is doctrinally accepted that a state may be constituted by recognition and collective recognition could have the effect of a collective state creation. This conclusion needs to be accompanied by a caveat: it is unclear how many and whose recognitions are necessary for a state to be deemed as having been constituted through recognition.

## 3.2 The Obsolete Concept of Premature Recognition and the Legal Relevance/Irrelevance of the Montevideo Criteria

In light of the conceptions of the state advanced in this book, it appears somewhat odd that the modern theory of statehood still refers to the concept of 'premature recognition', whereby states are precluded from granting recognition to an entity that has not met the Montevideo criteria.[24] In such circumstances, recognition is said to offend against the territorial integrity of the state in whose territory a new state is trying to emerge.[25]

This explanation is essentially based on the assumption of 'state as effectiveness'.[26] Its underlying reasoning is that recognition offends

---

[24] See M Shaw, *International Law*, 5th edn (Cambridge, Cambridge University Press, 2008) 460–61.

[25] *cf* R Jennings and A Watts, *Oppenheim's International Law*, 9th edn (Harlow, Longman, 1992) 143, who argue that granting recognition before the Montevideo criteria have been met offends against the territorial integrity of the existing state.

[26] *cf* ch 1, 3.3.

against territorial integrity as long as the entity has not met the Montevideo criteria. As soon as these criteria are met, territorial integrity is no longer offended. This reasoning implies that at the moment of meeting the statehood criteria, the entity emerges as a new state and is no longer under the sovereignty of its (former) parent state, so the territorial integrity of that state can no longer be offended. It has been demonstrated in this book that in contemporary international law, this is not the case; this is not how new states emerge in the UN Charter period and outside of decolonisation.

Even if entities are effective, there is still a presumption of the territorial integrity of their parent states and such entities do not necessarily become states. Recognition then nevertheless offends against territorial integrity, but this does not mean that recognition in such circumstances is illegal.

The concept of premature recognition also leads to paradoxes, such as that of Bosnia-Herzegovina. This state is often used as an example of a relatively recent instance of premature recognition. However, when the international recognition of Bosnia-Herzegovina was extended in 1992, it had already been internationally accepted that the predecessor state, the SFRY, no longer existed. It is true that the central government of Bosnia-Herzegovina did not control large parts of the territory.[27] However, in the absence of any other state in that territory, it is unclear against whose territorial integrity recognition of Bosnia-Herzegovina actually offended. Bosnia-Herzegovina did not meet the Montevideo criteria, but, after the SFRY no longer existed, the only plausible explanation was that it was a state, unless one is prepared to accept that it was a *terra nullius* and could be subject to conquest.[28] So, despite ineffectiveness, recognition could not be premature as the predecessor state that could claim territorial integrity no longer existed and, at the same time, international law no longer allows *terra nullius* situations. The difficult issue here was instead the new international delimitation.

The concept of premature recognition is essentially based on the rejected presumption that states emerge automatically and self-evidently upon meeting the Montevideo criteria. Moreover, the concept does not take into account the importance of the claim to territorial integrity in the contemporary international law of statehood. For these reasons, it is of little relevance in present-day situations when statehood does not depend on meeting or not meeting the Montevideo criteria.

---

[27] Shaw (n 24) 461, who argues that the central government of Bosnia-Herzegovina was not in effective control of the entire territory of the new state.

[28] As Shaw argues elsewhere: 'Any attempted ethnic reconfiguration of the Former Yugoslavia on a totally free-for-all basis . . . would most likely have produced an even worse situation than that which did occur.' M Shaw, 'Peoples, Territorialism and Boundaries' (1997) 8 *EJIL* 478, 502.

Ultimately, these conclusions lead to the question of the legal status of the statehood criteria under contemporary international law. It seems to be generally accepted that these criteria form a part of customary international law, but in light of the findings in this book, such an assumption may be problematic.

The norms of customary international law need to be precisely that – legal norms. Are the statehood criteria legal norms of a prescriptive quality? If they were, they would need to have (at least some of) the following effects: (i) entities would become states by meeting the statehood criteria; (ii) entities that do not meet them would not become states; (iii) the recognition of entities that do not meet the statehood criteria would be prohibited; and (iv) the recognition of entities that meet the statehood criteria would be mandatory.

None of the above is true in contemporary international law. What is, then, the normative value of the statehood criteria? It appears that they are, at best, policy guidelines rather than legal norms. Indeed, the fact that states grant recognition even where the statehood criteria *are not* met and withhold it where they *are* met indicates that state practice does not accept that statehood would depend on the Montevideo criteria. These criteria do not produce any direct legal effects. To some degree, they can only influence the international practice of acceptance or non-acceptance of claims for independence.

## 3.3  Democracy in the Contemporary Theory of Statehood

In post-Cold War practice, the internationalised processes of state creation have also led to international impositions of democratic political systems in the newly created states, or at least to attempts at such impositions. This led some writers to argue that a new state in contemporary international law needs to be democratic.[29] Others have objected by arguing that democracy is not a statehood criterion, that is, not an addition to the Montevideo criteria.[30] The first statement is exaggerated and the second one is wrongly focused.

The international imposition of democratic institutions is only possible where state creation becomes an internationalised political process. The international preference of creating new democratic states clearly follows

---

[29] See A Peters, 'Statehood after 1989: "Effectivités" between Legality and Virtuality' in J Crawford and S Nouwen (eds), *Select Proceedings of the European Society of International Law* (Oxford, Hart Publishing, 2012) 171, who argues that 'a territorial entity which did not come about in a democratic procedure and which does not seek to establish democratic government structures would not qualify as a state'.

[30] See J Crawford, *The Creation of States in International Law* (Oxford, Oxford University Press, 2006) 150–55.

from the post-Cold War practice. At the same time, nothing in this practice indicates that the emergence of a non-democratic state would be prohibited, that is, illegal, in the same way as states may not emerge in violation of *jus cogens*. After the Minsk Agreement and the Alma Ata Protocol, the former Soviet republics emerged as independent states, regardless of how undemocratic the governments many (or most) of them were.[31]

Democracy is not a legality requirement for state creation and nor is it an addition to the Montevideo criteria. But despite not being on the 'Montevideo list', democracy should not be labelled as irrelevant. Namely, not even the Montevideo criteria are a 'legal checklist' that would tell whether or not an entity is a state; these criteria only *influence* the political process leading towards statehood, but so does democracy. Where the process of state creation is internationalised, a multilateral attempt is made to guide the entity to both meeting the statehood criteria and to implementing a minimum threshold of institutional democracy. At the same time, states can emerge even if they are undemocratic. However, they can also emerge if they do not meet the Montevideo criteria. Democracy in contemporary international law is therefore as equally relevant or irrelevant as the Montevideo criteria.

## 4 THE OPERATION OF AND LIMITS ON DEMOCRATIC PRINCIPLES WITHIN THE RIGHT OF SELF-DETERMINATION

Thus far, this chapter has considered the internationalised practice of creation of new democratic states. It was shown that this practice does not indicate that the creation of a non-democratic state would be illegal, just as it is not illegal to create or recognise a state which does not meet the Montevideo criteria. However, both democracy and Montevideo are important considerations in the political process that leads to a changed legal status of a territory. This section turns to the concept of creating new states *democratically*. It will be argued that international law requires for state creation to be a democratic process. But democratic principles in this process are not absolute and they should not be conflated for democracy as a political system.

### 4.1 Democracy and the Qualification of 'Representative Government'

The principles of self-determination and modern democratic political theory have (partly) overlapping origins and draw their ideals from

---

[31] See ch 2, 2.1.

the American and French Revolutions.[32] The underlying idea of both is that a government must be representative of its people.[33] The qualification of a representative government for the purpose of the right of self-determination under international law cannot be seen as identical to the qualification of a representative government within democratic political theory.

In the UN Charter era, self-determination is codified as a human right.[34] The drafting history of this specific right in the ICCPR and the ICESCR shows that self-determination as a human right is not to be understood through the prism of a democratic political system. One author cautions about the paradox that 'it was the former Eastern Bloc nations that played the most significant role in developing and promoting self-determination following World War II, usually in the face of great reluctance from Western democracies'.[35] It can also be assumed that socialist states would not have ratified the Covenants if they meant to bind the state parties to implementing a multiparty political system.[36]

The right of self-determination only applies to peoples.[37] For this reason, the qualification of a representative government can only be defined in the context of identities which define a separate people. There is no precise legal definition of a people in international law and the old remark still holds true: 'On the surface [the idea of self-determination] seemed reasonable: let the people decide. It was in fact ridiculous because the people cannot decide until somebody decides who are the people.'[38]

It has not been the purpose of this book to find a definition of a people. Rather, this book showed that in the process of decolonisation, a territorial approach was used to create identities of separate peoples, but this was not the case outside of colonialism.[39] The absence of a definition of a people does not mean that the entire concept is in limbo. Relevant sources suggest that the concept is defined on the basis of shared identities stemming from ethnic background, common religion, language, territory, and cultural and historical heritage, among others.[40] The problem is rather that it is impossible to prescribe the universal legal threshold for a group to qualify as a

---

[32] A Cassese, *Self-Determination of Peoples: A Legal Reappraisal* (Cambridge, Cambridge University Press, 1995) 11.

[33] ibid.

[34] ICCPR and ICESCR, Article 1.

[35] *R Miller, 'Self-Determination* in International Law and the Demise of Democracy?' (2003) 41 *Columbia Journal of Transnational Law* 601, 612.

[36] See B Roth, *Governmental Illegitimacy in International Law* (Oxford, Oxford University Press, 1999) 332.

[37] ICCPR and ICESCR, Article 1, paras 1 and 2.

[38] I Jennings, *The Approach to Self-Government* (Cambridge, Cambridge University Press, 1956) 55–56.

[39] See ch 4, 3. For more on this, see ch 5, 4.5.

[40] See ch 3, n 50.

people, what mixture of these identities the group needs to possess and how it is distinguished from the definition of a minority. The existence of a separate people is in the sphere of subjective collective identity rather than objective legal prescriptions.

Nevertheless, the identities relevant for the existence of a separate people are not based on political opinion and do not stem from party politics.[41] The right of self-determination in the UK, applies to several groups, such as the English, the Irish, the Scottish and the Welsh, but does not apply to the Tories, for example. On this basis, it cannot be said that where a government is not an outcome of multiparty elections, it prima facie violates the right of self-determination. Its non-democratic nature does not necessarily mean that the government discriminates against a certain people in the state's territory. The exclusion of the Kosovo Albanians from political life in the FRY under the Milošević regime resulted in a breach of their right of self-determination,[42] yet the non-democratic nature of the Milošević regime did not breach the right of self-determination of the Serbs and the Montenegrins within the FRY.[43] The qualification of a representative government for the purpose of the right of self-determination is narrower than its qualification for the purpose of democratic political theory.

Further constraints on self-determination in the UN Charter era stem from its codification as a human right and not as an absolute principle:

> [T]he right of self-determination is not an absolute right without any limitations. Its purpose is not directly to protect the personal or physical integrity of individuals or groups as is the purpose of the absolute rights and, unlike the absolute rights, the exercise of this right can involve major structural and institutional changes to a State and must affect, often significantly, most groups and individuals in that State and beyond that State. Therefore, the nature of the right does require some limitations to be implied on its exercise.[44]

The right of self-determination thus needs to be weighed against other human rights and against the principle of the territorial integrity of states.[45]

## 4.2  Secession, Human Rights and Democracy

As a consequence of limitations on the right of self-determination, secession is not an entitlement under international law and in the UN Charter era, the right of self-determination will normally be consummated in its

---

[41] See ch 3, 3.1.

[42] See ch 2, 6 and 3, 6.3.2.

[43] See ch 2, 3.7.

[44] R McCorquodale, 'Self-Determination: A Human Rights Approach' (1994) 43 *ICLQ* 857, 876.

[45] See the Declaration on Principles of International Law, UN Doc A/RES/2625 (24 October 1970), annex, principle 5, para 7.

internal mode.[46] The success of a unilateral secession will depend on international recognition and, when states consider granting recognition, even democratic legitimacy of secession may play some role.[47]

The only post-1990 example of unilateral secession that has attracted a significant number of international recognitions is Kosovo.[48] Its declaration of independence in 1991 was ignored by the international community.[49] In 1999, Kosovo did not declare independence; rather, the territory was put under an arrangement for international territorial administration.[50] In other words, Serbia's and the FRY's abuses of their sovereign powers did not directly lead to the creation of a new state. For this reason, Kosovo's secession in 2008 cannot be deemed to support the remedial secession doctrine, which stems from an inverted reading of the elaboration of the principle of the territorial integrity of states in the Declaration on Principles of International Law,[51] but acutely lacks state practice.

Unilateral secession is thus never a right or an entitlement under international law, not even where 'remedial arguments' could plausibly be advanced. This is due to the concept of the state and the nature of its emergence in contemporary international law. States do not emerge automatically on the basis of entitlement or meeting the statehood criteria. As a consequence of the principle of territorial integrity, the territorial status quo applies until the change in this status is accepted internationally. Historical entitlements existed for the independence of East Timor,[52] the Baltic States[53] and South Sudan,[54] and the peoples of these entities also suffered from severe oppression. Yet these circumstances did not have any direct legal implications for statehood and were not creative of states. The decisive factor was the political process which led to the consent of the parent state and thus acceptance of the change of the territorial status quo. To be sure, oppression and historical entitlement may well initiate the political process that ultimately leads to independence, but there still needs to be a political process; the territorial status quo is not moved automatically.

---

[46] See the *Québec* case (n 19), para 126.
[47] ibid, para 155.
[48] See ch 2, 6.
[49] See M Vickers, *Between Serb and Albanian: A History of Kosovo* (London, Hurst, 1998) 251. See also Crawford (n 5) 408.
[50] See UN Doc S/RES/1244.
[51] See the Declaration on Principles of International Law (1970), annex, principle 5, para 7. Arguments have been made that the elaboration of the principle of territorial integrity allows for an interpretation that a state, which has a government non-representative of all of its peoples, might not be entitled to limit the exercise of the right of self-determination of its oppressed peoples to the internal mode of this right.
[52] See ch 2, 5.
[53] See ch 2, 2.1.
[54] See ch 2, 2.4.

It is very difficult – and almost impossible in practice – to move the territorial status quo where the parent state does not give its consent. Secession (or an attempt at secession) is then unilateral. General international law does not prohibit unilateral secession.[55] As the Supreme Court of Canada held in the *Québec* case, '[t]he ultimate success of . . . [unilateral] secession would be dependent on recognition by the international community, which is likely to consider the legality and legitimacy of secession'.[56] Indeed, the principle of territorial integrity cannot be interpreted as if it were an absolute right of states which prohibits secession.[57] However, if the parent state does not consent to the emergence of a new state and does not waive its claim to territorial integrity, the legal status of the independence-seeking entity may remain ambiguous, even if recognition is widespread.[58]

Such ambiguity can sometimes only be clarified over time. It is in the nature of international law that it analyses practice over a longer period of time and, in so doing, reads history backwards. Five, 10 or perhaps 20 years from now, writers on statehood might argue that the legal status of Kosovo had been clarified or consolidated over a period of time. But writing in 2012, the objective legal status of Kosovo is ambiguous, as was the legal status of Bangladesh 40 years earlier.[59] This is a consequence of the concept of the state in international law: statehood is an international legal status, not an objective fact. As such, it can sometimes be ambiguous.

While, in principle, no ambiguity exists where the parent state consents to the emergence of a part of its territory as an independent state, it should be noted that such consent does not override those norms of international law which are capable of determining the illegality of a particular state creation. As the South African Homelands demonstrate, even in the absence of a claim to territorial integrity, a state cannot be created in violation of the right of self-determination and/or in pursuance of racist policies.[60] The episode with the Homelands proves that even where a state creation *is* consensual, it must not be illegal. Although human rights law does have an effect on the law of statehood, this cannot be extended to mean that there is a prescribed threshold of human rights protection or even a prescribed political system which influences the question of whether an effective entity would become a state. It might be possible to argue that the only human rights standards that determine the illegality of a state creation are those of a *jus cogens* character.[61] In the *Kosovo Advisory*

---

[55] See ch 1, 3.4 and 2, 6.
[56] The *Québec* case (n 19), para 155.
[57] Compare ch 1, 3.4 and 2, 6.6.
[58] *cf* ch 2, 6.6.
[59] See ch 3, 6.3.1.
[60] See ch 3, 3.5.
[61] See ch 1, 3.1, 1, 3.5 and 1, 3.6.

*Opinion*, even the ICJ cautiously associated the illegality of a state creation with the concept of *jus cogens*.[62]

## 4.3  The Will of the People and the Creation of New States

Before the legal status of a territory may be altered, the operation of the right of self-determination requires a consultation of the people inhabiting the territory in question. Such a requirement was expressed by the ICJ in the *Western Sahara Advisory Opinion*[63] and was later affirmed by the Badinter Commission in its Opinion on Bosnia-Herzegovina.[64] The question arises as to how the consent of the people is to be expressed and what the limits are of its application.

In the circumstances of an attempt to change the legal status of a territory, a referendum is the most common expression of the will of the people. While a referendum does not seem to be the only acceptable means of such an expression, it is not entirely clear under what circumstances a referendum may be considered unnecessary. Two observations can be made.

First, a referendum may not be required when the will of the people is obvious. This was implied even by the ICJ in the *Western Sahara Advisory Opinion*.[65] And in the absence of a referendum in Kosovo, there have been no doubts expressed internationally (or in Serbia) concerning the will of the Kosovo Albanians.[66] Second, general electoral results do not imply a decision regarding the legal status of a territory or that the right of self-determination can be exercised through general elections alone. In other words, an overwhelming vote for a political party advocating secession does not necessarily imply support for secession. The voting behaviour of people depends on a variety of issues, not only those concerning self-determination.[67]

When referenda on the change of the legal status of a territory are held, the democratically expressed will of a people in favour of independence does not necessarily create a new state. This is due to the fact that secession is not an entitlement under international law.[68] Nevertheless, the

---

[62] *Accordance with International Law of the Unilateral Declaration of Independence in Respect of Kosovo (Request for Advisory Opinion)*, ICJ Rep 2010, para 122.

[63] *Western Sahara Advisory Opinion*, ICJ Rep 1975, para 55.

[64] The Badinter Commission, Opinion 4 (11 January 1992), para 4, reprinted in S Trifunovska, *Yugoslavia through Documents: From its Creation to its Dissolution* (Dordrecht, Martinus Nijhoff, 1994) 486.

[65] *Western Sahara Advisory Opinion*, ICJ Rep 1975, para 59.

[66] See ch 2, 6.

[67] See R McCorquodale, 'Negotiating Sovereignty: The Practice of the United Kingdom in Regard to the Right of Self-Determination' (1996) 66 *British Yearbook of International Law 283*, 309–10.

[68] See the *Québec* case (n 19), paras 112 and 126.

democratically expressed will of a people in favour of secession cannot be ignored.[69] This means that such a will of the people would put an obligation on both the independence-seeking entity and on the parent state to negotiate a future constitutional arrangement of the entity in question.[70]

Such negotiations do not begin on the premise that the statehood-seeking entity would necessarily become an independent state.[71] The legal effects of independence referenda are thus another illustration of the nature of state creation in contemporary international law: states emerge in a political process which creates a new territorial situation under international law.

The episode with Québec's secessionist attempts generated a number of opinions by qualified writers as well as judicial and legislative responses to the situation. The analysis of these responses indicates the general procedural standard that both the referendum question and the deciding majority need to be clear.[72] It is difficult to prescribe a universally applicable standard of clarity. Some referenda questions in the practice of post-1990 state creations may have seemed unclear;[73] however, more specific wordings were probably prevented by complicated political situations (in some cases even by an emerging armed conflict). Even in such circumstances, no doubt existed among the people that they were consulted on independence.

With regard to the clear majority, in different societal situations, differently qualified majorities may be considered legitimate. In most post-1990 state creations, a majority of all valid votes cast was prescribed, while the majority of all those eligible to vote was commonly achieved.[74] At the same time, the case of Montenegro shows that in a complicated internal sociopolitical situation, a situation-specific majority may be prescribed in order to achieve the legitimacy of the decision-making.[75]

## 4.4 The Will of the People and the Delimitation of New States

The emergence of new states also leads to the problem of a new international delimitation. In the process of the international involvement in

[69] ibid, para 87.

[70] ibid.

[71] ibid, para 91. See also P Dumberry, 'Lessons Learned from the Quebec Secession Reference before the Supreme Court of Canada' in M Kohen (ed), *Secession: International Law Perspectives* (Cambridge, Cambridge University Press, 2006) 429.

[72] The *Québec* case (n 19), para 87. See also the Clarity Act (2000), Articles 1 and 2.

[73] See ch 3, 7.2 and 3, 7.7.

[74] The majority of all those eligible to vote was unequivocally demanded only in Slovenia (see ch 2, 3.4.2). At the same time, in all successful post-1991 state creations where independence referenda were held, a majority of all those eligible to vote was not achieved only in Montenegro (see ch 2, 4).

[75] See ch 2, 4.

the dissolution of the SFRY, the Badinter Commission interpreted the decision of the Chamber of the ICJ in the *Burkina Faso/Mali* case as an authority supporting the applicability of the *uti possidetis* principle outside of colonial situations.[76] Such an interpretation has been criticised on two grounds: first, it was argued that the *uti possidetis* principle is inherently associated with the process of decolonisation and, as such, is not applicable outside of this process;[77] and, second, the 'upgrading' of the former Yugoslav internal boundaries to international borders arguably disregarded people's ethnic identities, limited the will of the people and has been deemed to be a wrong approach in a situation of dissolution.[78]

In the Badinter Commission's view, the Chamber of the ICJ in the *Burkina Faso/Mali* case established that *uti possidetis* is a generally applicable principle of international law, that is, a principle not confined to decolonisation.[79] A full reading of the relevant paragraph of the *Burkina Faso/Mali* case reveals that the Chamber of the ICJ, in fact, stated that *uti possidetis* was a general principle of international law *where decolonisation is concerned*.[80] In the particular case, this meant a principle not limited to decolonisation in Latin America but also applicable to decolonisation in Africa.[81] The Badinter Commission thus supported the applicability of *uti possidetis* outside of colonialism by selective quoting the *Burkina Faso/Mali* case.

In relation to the criticism that the *uti possidetis* principle implies drawing international borders along lines which, at the same time, disregard people's existing identities and create new ones,[82] it is questionable whether the post-1990 practice really resorted to this kind of border-drawing. This is especially questionable with regard to international borders in Europe, ie, borders of strong historical pedigree. In the practice of all post-1990 state creations thus far, international borders were confined along the former internal boundaries.[83] The international borders of Eritrea, East Timor and South Sudan otherwise have colonial origins, but these state creations were not consequences of decolonisation. Thus, their delimitation was not a matter of *uti possidetis*.[84]

---

[76] The Badinter Commission, Opinion 3 (11 January 1992), reprinted in Trifunovska (n 64) 479.

[77] See P Radan, 'Post-Secession International Borders: A Critical Analysis of the Opinions of the Badinter Arbitration Commission' (2000) 24 *Melbourne University Law Review* 50, 60–62.

[78] See P Radan, *The Break-up of Yugoslavia and International Law* (London, Routledge, 2002) 234–43.

[79] The Badinter Commission, Opinion 3 (11 January 1992), reprinted in Trifunovska (n 64) 479.

[80] *Case Concerning the Frontier Dispute (Burkina Faso/Mali)*, ICJ Rep 1986, para 20.

[81] ibid.

[82] See ch 4, 2.

[83] See ch 4, 3.

[84] See ch 4, 3.2.2.

In other post-1990 state creations, former internal boundaries which became international borders commonly had a historical pedigree of more than arbitrarily drawn internal administrative boundaries. Indeed, the internal boundaries frequently adopted the lines of former international borders or internal borders within empires which delimited territories settled by distinct peoples.[85] In other words, a common pattern of the post-1990 new state creations is that international borders were confined along not just any former internal boundary but along those boundaries which delimited historically established self-determination units. The SFRY was not an exception to this pattern, but the situation was more complex there due to its non-consensual dissolution and ethnically mixed populations in Croatia and Bosnia-Herzegovina.[86]

International law does not prescribe an automatic 'upgrade' of an internal boundary to an international border. Indeed, the exact definition of borders may become part of the political process for the determination of the future legal status of a territory and an entity's possible path towards independence.[87] Where internal boundaries have a strong historical pedigree of delimiting self-determination units, practice has shown that these boundaries would form a strong base for the determination of the new international borders. And where internal boundaries were subject to relatively recent arbitrary changes, an argument in favour of the 'upgrading' of an internal boundary to an international border will be weaker, though not irrelevant.[88]

The different pedigree of internal boundaries and the fact that there is no presumption that international borders are automatically confined along the lines of internal boundaries in non-colonial situations thus show that it is incorrect to equate this process with the *uti possidetis* principle. However, the non-colonial determination of the new international border, just like *uti possidetis*, also limits the will of the people and cannot accommodate the wishes of all peoples and minority groups inhabiting the territory in question.

## 4.5  State Creation, International Delimitation and Limitations on the Will of the People

When new states are created, the rights of minorities and numerically inferior or otherwise non-dominant peoples within an entity wishing to become a state are an important consideration in the political process (potentially) leading to independence. This was expressly affirmed in the

---

[85] See ch 4, 3.2.4.
[86] See ch 4, 3.2.6.
[87] See ch 3, 2 and 4, 2.3.
[88] See ch 4, 3.1.

*Québec* case.[89] The standards of the protection of minorities and numerically inferior or otherwise non-dominant peoples were a concern of the international community with regard to both consensual and non-consensual post-1990 state creations.[90]

At the same time, the newly created minorities and numerically inferior peoples do not have a right to veto the secession or claim their own 'right to secession'.[91] This does not mean that the numerically inferior or otherwise non-dominant peoples are precluded from secession from the newly created state. Even in such circumstances, international law remains neutral on the question of secession and, ultimately, secession may or may not follow. The status of peoples within newly created states does not differ from the status of peoples in any other state.[92]

Where new states are created non-consensually, the position is more difficult, as the political process becomes entirely internationalised and not a matter of negotiation with the central government. The question is, then, not only who decides on a new state creation but also who decides on the new international delimitation. The *Québec* case implies that when states decide on granting recognition, the acceptance of a new international border along the lines of the internal boundary is part of the legality and legitimacy considerations taken into account prior to granting recognition.[93] The recognising states thus also recognise the internal boundary between Kosovo and Serbia, which otherwise has a strong historical pedigree, as the new international border.[94] When a non-consensual dissolution was at issue in the SFRY, the determination of international borders was also left to international involvement, and internal boundaries (which had a strong historical pedigree of delimiting self-determination units)[95] were upgraded to international borders (although the Badinter Commission incorrectly invoked the *uti possidetis* principle).[96]

Further, where internal boundaries are 'upgraded' to international borders, the constitutional order of the disintegrating states would seem to be determinative for both the state creation and the confinement of the borders of the new state. In the case of the SFRY, the EC only invited republics to opt for independence, although it could be argued that the right of self-determination was also applicable in some other subunits which were also delimited by internal boundaries of historical pedigree.[97] It is arguable

[89] The *Québec* case (n 19), especially paras 74 and 76.
[90] See ch 2, 2.4, 2, 3, 2, 5 and 2, 6.
[91] See ch 4, 3.1.
[92] See ch 3, 2, 3, 3.1 and 3, 7.1.2.
[93] The *Québec* case (n 19), para 155.
[94] For more on the historical origins of the borders of Kosovo, see the maps in N Malcolm, *Kosovo: A Short History* (London, Macmillan, 1998) xvii–xxv.
[95] See ch 4, 3.2.6.
[96] See ch 4, 2.2.
[97] See ch 2, 6 and 4, 3.2.6.

that Kosovo is a historically realised self-determination unit, although it only had the constitutional status of an autonomous province and not of a republic within the SFRY.[98] In the example of the consensual dissolution of the Soviet Union, it was also only republics that became states.[99]

Thus, in post-1990 dissolutions, the possibility of a new state creation has been overtly dependent on the constitutional order of the parent state. This puts peoples within federal states in a better position and discourages these states from establishing clearly delimited (federal) self-determination units as this could be (mis)used as a step towards independence.[100]

## 5 FINAL REMARKS: THE PLACE OF DEMOCRACY WITHIN THE PROCESS OF STATE CREATION

The post-Cold War practice shows a tendency towards the internationalised creation of a democratic political system in newly emerged states. This is not to say that the emergence of a new non-democratic state in international law is illegal. And the question here should not be whether democracy is a new statehood criterion. The emergence of a new state is a political process; it is not an objective fact arising from the fulfilment of a checklist of statehood criteria. Indeed, recent practice shows that meeting the statehood criteria may be neither sufficient nor necessary for an entity to become a state. A new state needs to overcome the hurdle of a competing claim to the territorial integrity of its parent state. Where this process is internationalised, the institutions of a democratic political system are internationally built into the foundational legal instruments of the new state.

Being a part of the internationalised political process leading towards statehood, democracy as a political system in contemporary international is as equally relevant or irrelevant as the Montevideo criteria. Both concepts shape the international practice of the emergence of new states. At the same time, neither not meeting the Montevideo criteria nor being non-democratic can prevent the emergence of a new state.

Democracy as a political system in the law of statehood should not be conflated with the operation of some democratic principles within the right of self-determination. This right requires a government representative of its peoples and the support of the will of the people before the legal status of a territory may be altered. Governmental representativeness in the context of the right of self-determination is not synonymous with

---

[98] In this context, it is argued that if Kosovo had acquired the status of a republic in the SFRY, it would have become an independent state in 1992: R Caplan, *Europe and Recognition of New States in Yugoslavia* (Cambridge, Cambridge University Press, 2005) 70.

[99] See ch 2, 2.1 and 4, 3.2.1.

[100] The Québec Report, ch 2.49.

governmental representativeness in democratic political theory and the right of self-determination is not a synonym for democracy. Moreover, the will of the people within the right of self-determination is subject to considerable limitations and popular support in favour of independence only very rarely results in a new state.

State creation in contemporary international law is not a factual occurrence on the basis of meeting the statehood criteria. It is a political process that changes the territorial status quo and alters the legal status of a territory. Statehood is a politically created international legal status. The process leading to it is governed by a legal framework. A state may not emerge in violation of some fundamental norms of international law, in particular those of a *jus cogens* character. And the right of self-determination requires for state creation to be a democratic process.

In the post-Cold War period, the practice has emerged not only of creating new states *democratically* but also of creating new *democratic* states. Democracy importantly shapes the political process of new state creations, but is not a legality requirement for statehood. Non-democratic states can emerge in contemporary international law, but so can states that do not meet the traditional statehood criteria.

# Bibliography

## MONOGRAPHS

Anderson, M, *Frontiers: Territory and State Formation in the Modern World* (Cambridge, Polity Press, 1997).

Aust, A, *Handbook of International Law* (Cambridge, Cambridge University Press, 2005).

Baerkin, H, *The Birth of Yugoslavia* (London, Leonard Parsons, 1922).

Baker, R and Dodd, W (eds), *The New Democracy: Presidential Messages, Addresses, and Other Papers* (New York, Harper, 1926).

—— and —— (eds), *War and Peace: Presidential Messages, Addresses, and Public Papers* (New York, Harper, 1927).

Barltrop, R, *Darfur and the International Community: The Challenges of Conflict Resolution in Sudan* (London, IB Tauris, 2011).

Bayefsky, A, *Self-Determination in International Law: Quebec and Lessons Learned* (The Hague, Kluwer Law International, 2000).

Beetham, D, *Democracy and Human Rights* (Cambridge, Polity Press, 1999).

Beigbeder, Y, *International Monitoring of Plebiscites, Referenda and National Elections: Self-Determination and Transition to Democracy* (Dordrecht, Martinus Nijhoff, 1994).

Berglund, S, *Challenges to Democracy: Eastern Europe Ten Years after the Collapse of Communism* (Chalthenham, Edward Elgar, 2001).

Bethlehem, D and Weller, M, *The 'Yugoslav' Crisis in International Law* (Cambridge, Cambridge University Press, 1997).

Bix, B, *Jurisprudence: Theory and Context* (London, Sweet & Maxwell, 2006).

Brierly, J, *The Law of Nations* (Oxford, Clarendon Press, 1963).

Buchanan, A, *Justice, Legitimacy, and Self-Determination* (Oxford, Oxford University Press, 2004).

Buchheit, L, *Secession: The Legitimacy of Self-Determination* (New Haven, Yale University Press, 1978).

Capatorti, F, *Study on the Rights of Persons Belonging to Ethnic, Religious and Ethnic Minorities*, UN Doc E/CN.4/Sub.2/384/Rev.1 (1979).

Caplan, R, *Europe and Recognition of New States in Yugoslavia* (Cambridge, Cambridge University Press, 2005).

Cassese, A, *Self-Determination of Peoples: A Legal Reappraisal* (Cambridge, Cambridge University Press, 1995).

Castellino, J, *International Law and Self-Determination* (The Hague, Martinus Nijhoff, 2008).

Charlesworth, H and Chinkin, C, *The Boundaries of International Law* (Manchester, Manchester University Press, 2005).

Cohen, L, *Broken Bonds: Yugoslavia's Disintegration and Balkan Politics in Transition* (Boulder, Westview, 1995).

Crawford, J, *The Creation of States in International Law* (Oxford, Oxford University Press, 2006).

Dahl, R, *Polyarchy: Participation and Opposition* (New Haven, Yale University Press, 1971).

D'Aspremont, J, *L'Etat non démocratique en droit international: Etude critique du droit international positif et de la pratique contemporaine* (Paris, Pedone, 2008).

Deeley, N, *The International Boundaries of East Timor* (University of Durham, International Boundaries Research Unit, 2001).

Diamond, L, *Developing Democracy: Toward Consolidation* (Baltimore, Johns Hopkins University Press, 1999).

Dixon, M, McCorquodale, R and Williams, S, *Cases and Materials in International Law* (Oxford, Oxford University Press, 2011).

Donnelly, J, *Universal Human Rights in Theory and Practice* (Ithaca, Cornell University Press, 2003).

Dugard, J, *Recognition and the United Nations* (Cambridge, Grotius Publications, 1987).

Ermacora, F, *The Protection of Minorities Before the United Nations*, 182 Recueil des Cours 247 (1983 IV).

Foley, C, *The Thin Blue Line: How Humanitarianism Went to War* (London, Verso, 2008).

Franck, T, *Fairness in International Law and Institutions* (Oxford, Oxford University Press, 1995).

Freund, G, *Unholy Alliance: Russian-German Relations from the Treaty of Brest-Litovsk to the Treaty of Berlin* (London, Chatto & Windus, 1957).

Fukuyama, F, *The End of History and the Last Man* (New York, Free Press, 1992).

Ghebrewebet, H, *Identifying Units of Statehood and Determining International Boundaries* (Frankfurt, Peter Lang, 2006).

Grant, T, *The Recognition of States: Law and Practice in Debate and Evolution* (Westport, Praeger, 1999).

Grawert, E (ed), *After the Comprehensive Peace Agreement in Sudan* (Oxford, James Currey, 2010).

Hainsworth, P and McCloskey, S (eds), *The East Timor Question: The Struggle for Independence from Indonesia* (London, IB Tauris, 2000).

Hannum, H (ed), *Documents on Autonomy and Minority Rights* (Dordrecht, Martinus Nijhoff, 1993).

——, *Autonomy, Sovereignty and Self-Determination: The Accommodation of Conflicting Rights* (Philadelphia, University of Pennsylvania Press, 1996).

Harris, D, *Cases and Materials on International Law* (London, Sweet & Maxwell, 2010).

Harvey, D, *A Brief History of Neoliberalism* (Oxford, Oxford University Press, 2005).

Held, D, *Democracy and the Global Order: From The Modern State to Cosmopolitan Governance* (Cambridge, Polity Press 1995).

Hill, C and Smith, K, *European Foreign Policy: Key Documents* (London, Routledge, 2000).

Hillgruber, C, *Die Aufnahme neuer Staaten in die Völkerrechtsgemeinschaft* (Peter Lang Verlag, Frankfurt, 1998).

Hunter Miller, D, *The Drafting of the Covenant* (New York, Putnam's Sons, 1928).

Huntington, S, *The Third Wave* (Norman, University of Oklahoma Press, 1990).

Ibrahimagić, O, *Državno-pravni razvitak Bosne i Hercegovine* (Sarajevo, Vijeće kongresa bošnjačkih intelektualaca, 1998).

Jellinek, G, *Allgemeine Staatslehre*, 2nd edn (Berlin, O Häring, 1905).

Jennings, I, *The Approach to Self-Government* (Cambridge, Cambridge University Press, 1956).

Johnson, D, *The Root Causes of Sudan's Civil Wars: Comprehensive Peace or Temporary Truce?* (Oxford, James Currey, 2011).

Kelsen, H, *General Theory of Law and State* (New York, Russell & Russell, 1961).

——, *Principles of International Law* (New York, Holt, Rinehart and Winston, 1966).

Koskenniemi, M, *The Gentle Civilizer of Nations: The Rise and Fall of International Law 1870–1960* (Cambridge, Cambridge University Press, 2002).

Kotkin, S, *Armageddon Averted: The Soviet Collapse* (Oxford, Oxford University Press, 2001).

Kreća, M, *The Badinter Arbitration Commission – A Critical Commentary* (Belgrade, Jugoslovenski pregled, 1993).

Krieger, H (ed), East *Timor and the International Community: Basic Documents* (Cambridge, Cambridge University Press, 1997).

—— and Rauschning, D, *East Timor and the International Community: Basic Documents* (Cambridge, Cambridge University Press, 1997).

Lalonde, S, *Determining Boundaries in the Conflicted World: The Role of Uti Possidetis* (Montreal, McGill-Queens University Press, 2002).

Lampe, J, *Yugoslavia as History: Twice There was a Country* (Cambridge, Cambridge University Press, 2000).

Lauterpacht, J, *Recognition in International Law* (Cambridge, Cambridge University Press, 1948).

Lenin, VI, *Questions of National Policy and Proletarian Internationalism* (Moscow, Foreign Languages Publishing House, year of publication unknown).

Lijphart, A, *Democracies: Patterns of Majoritarian and Consensus Government in Twenty-One Countries* (New Haven, Yale University Press,1984).

Linz, J and Stepan, A, *Problems of Democratic Transition and Democratic Consolidation* (Baltimore, Johns Hopkins University Press, 1996).

Lipset, S, *The Encyclopedia of Democracy* (Washington DC, Congressional Quarterly, 1994).

Lyons, T and Samatar, A, *Somalia: State Collapse, Multilateral Intervention, and Strategies for Political Reconstruction* (Washington DC, Brookings Institution, 1995).

Malcolm, N, *Kosovo: A Short History* (London, Macmillan, 1998).

Marek, K, *Identity and Continuity of States in Public International Law* (Geneva, Librairie Droz, 1968).

Marks, S, *The Riddle of All Constitutions* (Oxford, Oxford University Press, 2000).

—— and Clapham, A, *International Human Rights Lexicon* (Oxford, Oxford University Press, 2005).

Martin, I, *Self-Determination in East Timor: The United Nations, the Ballot, and International Intervention* (Boulder, Lynne Rienner, 2001).

McGoldrick, D, *The Human Rights Committee: Its Role in the Development of the International Covenant on Civil and Political Rights* (Oxford, Clarendon Press, 1991).

Mertus, J, *Kosovo: How Myths and Truths Started a War* (Berkeley, University of California Press, 1999).

Musgrave, T, *Self-Determination and National Minorities* (Oxford, Oxford University Press, 1997).

Nkala, J, *The United Nations, International Law, and the Rhodesian Independence Crisis* (Oxford, Clarendon Press, 1985).

O'Neill, W, *Kosovo: An Unfinished Peace* (Boulder, Lynne Rienner, 2002).

Oppenheim, L, *International Law* (London, Longmans, 1905).

——, *International Law: A Treatise* (H Lauterpacht (ed)) (London, Longmans, 1955).

——, *Oppenheim's International Law* (R Jennings and A Watts (eds)) (London, Longman, 1992).

Pavković, A and Radan, P. *Creating New States: Theory and Practice of Secession* (Aldershot, Ashgate, 2007).

Pavlowitch, S, *Yugoslavia* (London, Ernest Benn, 1971).

Peterson, MJ, *Recognition of Governments: Legal Doctrine and State Practice* (Basingstoke, Macmillan, 1997).

Radan, P, *The Break-up of Yugoslavia and International Law* (London, Routledge, 2002).

Raič, D, *Statehood and the Law of Self-Determination* (The Hague, Kluwer Law International, 2002).

Ramet, SP, *Whose Democracy?: Nationalism, Religion, and the Doctrine of Collective Rights in Post-1989 Eastern Europe* (Lanham, Rowman & Littlefield, 1997).

Reid, J, *The Concept of Representation in the Age of the American Revolution* (Chicago, University of Chicago Press, 1989).

Roth, B, *Governmental Illegitimacy in International Law* (Oxford, Oxford University Press, 1999).

Schumpeter, J, *Capitalism, Socialism, and Democracy* (New York, Harper, 1942).

Sen, A, *Identity and Violence* (New York, WW Norton, 2006).

Shaw, M, *International Law* (Cambridge, Cambridge University Press, 2008).

Singh, B, *East Timor, Indonesia and the World: Myths and Realities* (Singapore, Singapore Institute of International Affairs, 1995).

Slaughter, AM, *A New World Order* (Princeton, Princeton University Press, 2004).

Sorensen, G, *Democracy and Democratization: Processes and Prospects in a Changing World* (Boulder, Westview, 1993).

Stein, E, *Czechoslovakia: Ethnic Conflict, Constitutional Fissure, Negotiated Breakup* (Ann Arbor, University of Michigan Press, 1997).

Summers, J, *Peoples and International Law: How Nationalism and Self-Determination Shape a Contemporary Law of Nations* (Leiden, Martinus Nijhoff, 2007).

Taagepera, R, *Estonia: Return to Independence* (Boulder, Westview 1993).

Talmon, S, *Recognition of Governments in International Law: With Particular Reference to Governments in Exile* (Oxford, Clarendon Press, 1998).

——, *Kollektive Nichtanerkennung illegaler Staaten* (Tübingen, Mohr Siebeck, 2004).

Taylor, J, *East Timor: The Price of Freedom* (London, Zed Books, 1999).

Terrett, S, *The Dissolution of Yugoslavia and the Badinter Arbitration Commission: A Contextual Study of Peace-Making Efforts in the Post-Cold War World* (Aldershot, Ashgate, 2000).

Teson, F, *A Philosophy of International Law* (Boulder, Westview, 1998).

Tierney, S, *Constitutional Law and National Pluralism* (Oxford, Oxford University Press, 2006).

Trifunovska, S, *Yugoslavia through Documents: From its Creation to its Dissolution* (Dordrecht, Martinus Nijhoff, 1994).

Vickers, M, *Between Serb and Albanian: A History of Kosovo* (London, Hurst, 1998).

Vidmar, J, *Democratic Transition and Democratic Consolidation in Slovenia* (Frankfurt, Peter Lang Verlag, 2008).

Weller, M, *Contested Statehood: Kosovo's Struggle for Independence* (Oxford, Oxford University Press, 2009).

Wheatley, S, *Democracy, Minorities and International Law* (Cambridge, Cambridge University Press, 2005).

——, *The Democratic Legitimacy of International Law* (Oxford, Hart Publishing, 2010).

Wilde, R, *International Territorial Administration: How Trusteeship and the Civilizing Mission Never Went Away* (Oxford, Oxford University Press, 2008).

Wilson, W, *President Wilson's Foreign Policy: Messages, Addresses, Papers* (collected by J Brown Scott) (New York, Oxford University Press, 1918).

Ziemele, I, *State Continuity and Nationality: The Baltic States and Russia: Past Present and Future as Defined by International Law* (Leiden, Martinus Nijhoff, 2005).

[Unspecified author] *Collected Edition of the 'Travaux Préparatoires' of the European Convention on Human Rights*, The Council of Europe (The Hague, Martinus Nijhoff, 1975).

[Unspecified author] *Kosovo: Law and Politics, Kosovo in Normative Acts Before and After 1974* (Belgrade, Helsinki Committee for Human Rights in Serbia, 1998).

[Unspecified author] The 1981 Census in the SFRY, *Popis stanovništva, domaćinstava i stanova u 1981. godini* (Belgrade, Savezni zavod za statistiku, 1983).

## CHAPTERS IN EDITED COLLECTIONS

Abi-Saab, G, 'Le principe de l'*uti possidetis* son rôle et ses limites dans le contentieux territorial international' in M Kohen (ed), *Promoting Justice, Human Rights and Conflict Resolution through International Law* (Dordrecht, Martunus Nijhoff, 2007).

Angelet, N, 'Quelques observations sur le principe de l'uti possidetis à l'aune du cas hypothétique de la Belgique' in O Corten, B Delcourt, P Klein and N Levrat (eds), *Démembrements d'États et delimitations territoriales: L'uti possidetis en question(s)* (Brussels,Bruylant, 1999).

Beyme, K von, 'Institutional Engineering and Transitions to Democracy' in R Elgie and J Zielonka (eds), *Democratic Consolidation in Eastern Europe* (Oxford, Oxford University Press, 2001).

Bothe, M and Marauhn, T, 'UN Administration of Kosovo and East Timor: Concept, Legality and Limitations of Security Council-Mandated Trusteeship Administration' in C Tomuschat (ed), *Kosovo and the International Community: A Legal Assessment* (The Hague, Kluwer Law International, 2001).

Brady, H and Kaplan, C,'Eastern Europe and the Former Soviet Union' in D Butler and A Ranney (ed), *Referendums Around the World: The Growing Use of Direct Democracy* (Washington DC, AEI Press, 1994).

Clark, R, 'The Substance of the East Timor Case in the ICJ' in *International Law and the Question of East Timor* (Leiden, Catholic Institute for International Relations & International Platform of Jurists for East Timor, 1995).

Crawford, J, 'Democracy and the Body of International Law' in G Fox and B Roth (eds), *Democratic Governance and International Law* (Cambridge, Cambridge University Press, 2001).

D'Aspremont, J, 'The Rise and Fall of Democratic Governance in International Law' in J Crawford and S Nouwen (eds), *Select Proceedings of the European Society of International Law* (Oxford, Hart Publishing, 2012).

Daly, MW, 'Broken Bridge and Empty Basket: The political and Economic Background of the Sudanese Civil War', in M W Daly and A A Sikainga, *Civil War in the Sudan* (London, British Academic Press 1993).

Davison, G, 'Historical Reality and the Case of East Timor' in *International Law and the Question of East Timor* (Leiden, Catholic Institute for International Relations & International Platform of Jurists for East Timor, 1995).

Dinstein, Y, 'The Degree of Self-Rule of Minorities in Unitarian and Federal States' in C Brölmann, R Lefeber and M Zieck (eds), *Peoples and Minorities in International Law* (Dordrecht, Martinus Nijhoff, 1993).

Dugard, J and Raič, D, 'The Role of Recognition in the Law and Practice of Secession' in M Kohen (ed), *Secession: International Law Perspectives* (Cambridge, Cambridge University Press, 2006).

Dumberry, P, 'Lessons Learned from the Quebec Secession Reference before the Supreme Court of Canada' in M Kohen (ed), *Secession: International Law Perspectives* (Cambridge, Cambridge University Press, 2006).

Elgie, R and Zielonka, J, 'Constitutions and Constitution Building: a Comparative Perspective' in R Elgie and J Zielonka (eds), *Democratic Consolidation in Eastern Europe* (Oxford, Oxford University Press, 2001).

Franck, T, 'Democracy as a Human Right' in L Henkin and J Hargrove (eds), *Human Rights: An Agenda for the Next Century* (Washington DC, ASIL, 1994).

——, 'Legitimacy and the Democratic Entitlement' in G Fox and B Roth (eds), *Democratic Governance and International Law* (Cambridge, Cambridge University Press, 2001).

Hilling, C, 'Débats', in O Corten et al (eds), *Démembrements d'États et delimitations territoriales: L'uti possidetis en question(s)* (Brussels, Bruylant, 1999).

Himmer, S, 'The Achievement of Independence in the Baltic States and its Justification' in A Sprudzs (ed), *The Baltic Path to Independence* (Buffalo, WS Hein, 1994).

Kant, I, 'Perpetual Peace' (1795) in T Humphrey (ed), *Perpetual Peace and Other Essays on Politics, History, and Morals* (Indianapolis, Hackett, 1983).

Koskenniemi, M, 'Carl Schmitt, Hans Morgenthau and the Image of Law in International Relations' in M Byers (ed), *The Role of Law in International Politics* (Oxford, Oxford University Press, 2000).

Luker, M, 'On the Borders of Justice: An Examination and Possible Solution to the Doctrine of *Uti Possidetis*' in R Miller and R Bratspies (eds), *Progress in International Law* (Dordrecht, Martinus Nijhoff, 2008).

Mansfield, E and Snyder, J, 'Democratization and the Danger of War' in M Brown, S Lynn-Jones and S Miller (eds), *Debating the Democratic Peace* (Cambridge, MA, MIT Press, 1996).

McCorquodale, R, 'The Creation and Recognition of States' in S Blay, R Piotrowicz and BM Tsamenyi (eds), *Public International Law: An Australian Perspective* (Melbourne, Oxford University Press, 2005).

Miller, N, 'Serbia and Montenegro' in R Frucht (ed), *Eastern Europe: An Introduction to the People, Lands, and Culture* (Santa Barbara, ABC CLIO, 2005).

Peters, A, 'Statehood after 1989: "Effectivités" between Legality and Virtuality' in J Crawford and S Nouwen (eds), *Select Proceedings of the European Society of International Law* (Oxford, Hart Publishing, 2012).

Rosas, A, 'Internal Self-Determination' in C Tomuschat (ed), *Modern Law of Self-Determination* (Dordrecht, Martinus Nijhoff, 1993).

Salmon, J, 'Aspects of the Right to Self-Determination: Towards a Democratic Legitimacy Principle?' in C Tomuschat (ed), *Modern Law of Self-Determination* (Dordrecht, Martinus Nijhoff, 1993).

Scobbie, I, 'The Presence of an Absent Third: Procedural Aspects of the East Timor Case in *International Law and the Question of East Timor* (Leiden, Catholic Institute for International Relations & International Platform of Jurists for East Timor, 1995).

Simpson, G, 'The Politics of Self-Determination in the Case Concerning East Timor' in *International Law and the Question of East Timor* (Leiden, Catholic Institute for International Relations & International Platform of Jurists for East Timor, 1995).

Slaughter, AM, 'Wilsonianism in the Twenty-First Century' in GJ Ikenberry, TJ Knock, AM Slaughter and T Smith (eds), *The Crisis of American Foreign Policy* (Princeton, Princeton University Press, 2009).

Tancredi, A, 'A Normative "Due Process" in the Creation of States through Secession' in M Kohen (ed), *Secession: International Law Perspectives* (Cambridge, Cambridge University Press, 2006).

Taylor, J, 'Decolonisation, Independence and Invasion' in *International Law and the Question of East Timor* (Leiden, Catholic Institute for International Relations & International Platform of Jurists for East Timor, 1995).

Thornberry, P, 'The Democratic or Internal Aspect of Self-Determination with Some Remarks on Federalism' in C Tomuschat (ed), *Modern Law of Self-Determination* (Dordrecht, Martinus Nijhoff, 1993).

Warbrick, C, 'States and Recognition in International Law' in M Evans (ed), *International Law*, 2nd edn (Oxford, Oxford University Press, 2006).

[Several authors] 'The Territorial Integrity of Quebec in the Event of the Attainment of Sovereignty' (the Quebec Report) (T Franck, R Higgins, A Pellet, M Shaw, C Tomuschat), reprinted in A Bayefsky, *Self-Determination in International Law: Quebec and Lessons Learned* (The Hague, Kluwer Law International, 2000).

JOURNAL ARTICLES

Alvarez, J (2001), 'Do Liberal States Behave Better? A Critique of Slaughter's Liberal Theory' (2001) 12 *EJIL* 183.

Antonopoulos, C, 'The Principle of *Uti Possidetis* in Contemporary International Law' (1996) 49 *Revue hellenique de droit international* 29.

Bartoš, T, '*Uti Possidetis. Quo Vadis?*' (1997) 18 *Australian Yearbook of International Law* 37.

Blum, Y, 'Russia Takes Over the Soviet Union's Seat at the United Nations' (1992) 3 *EJIL* 354.

Burley, AM, 'Toward an Age of Liberal Nations' (1992) 33 *Harvard International Law Journal* 393.

Carothers, T, 'Empirical Perspectives on the Emerging Norm of Democracy in International Law' (1992) *ASIL Proceedings* 261.

Cassese, A, '*Ex iniuria ius oritur*: Are We Moving Towards International Legitimation of Forcible Humanitarian Countermeasures in the World Community?' (1999) 10 *EJIL* 23.

Cerna, C, 'Universal Democracy: An International Legal Right or the Pipe Dream of the West?' (1995) 27 *New York University Journal of International Law and Politics* 289.

Chinkin, C, 'Kosovo: A "Good" or "Bad" War?' (1999) 93 *American Journal of International Law* 841.

Craven, M, 'What's in a Name?: The Former Yugoslav Republic of Macedonia and Issues of Statehood' (1995) 16 *Australian Yearbook of International Law* 199.

——, 'The European Community Arbitration Commission on Yugoslavia' (1996) 66 *British Yearbook of International Law* 333.

Crawford, J, 'Democracy and International Law' (1993) 64 *British Yearbook of International Law* 113.

D'Aspremont, J, 'Legitimacy of Governments in the Age of Democracy' (2006) 38 *New York University Journal of International Law and Politics* 878.

——, 'Regulating Statehood' (2007) 20 *Leiden Journal of International Law* 649.

——, 'Post-Conflict Administrations as Democracy-Building Instruments' (2008) 9 *Chicago Journal of International Law* 1.

——, 'Responsibility for Coups in International Law' (2010) 18 *Tulane Journal of International & Comparative Law* 451.

Devine, DJ, 'The Requirements of Statehood Re-examined' (1971) 34 *MLR* 410.

Doyle, M, 'Kant, Liberal Legacies, and Foreign Affairs' (1983) 12 *Philosophy and Public Affairs* 205.

Elsuwege, P van, 'State Continuity and its Consequences: The Case of the Baltic States (2003) 16 *Leiden Journal of International Law* 377.

Falk, R, 'The Haiti Intervention: A Dangerous World Order Precedent for the United Nations' (1995) 36 *Harvard International Law Journal* 341.

Fawcett, JES, 'Security Council Resolution on Rhodesia' (1965–66) 41 *British Yearbook of International Law* 104.

Faye Witkin, M, 'Transkei: An Analysis of the Practice of Recognition – Political or Legal?' (1977) 18 *Harvard International Law Journal* 605.

Fox, G, 'The Right to Political Participation in International Law' (1992) 17 *Yale Journal of International Law* 539.

——, 'Self-Determination in the Post-Cold War Era: A New Internal Focus' (1994–95) 16 *Michigan Journal of International Law* 733.

Franck, T, 'The Emerging Right to Democratic Governance' (1992) 86 *American Journal of International Law* 46.

Ghabra, S, 'Democratization in a Middle Eastern State: Kuwait' (1994) 3 *Middle East Policy* 102.

Goy, R, 'L'indépendence de l'Érythrée' (1993) 39 *Annuaire français de droit international* 337.

Gray, C, 'The Eritrea/Ethiopia Claims Commission Oversteps its Boundaries: A Partial Award?' (2006) 17 *EJIL* 699.

Haile, M, 'Legality of Secessions: The Case of Eritrea' (1994) 8 *Emory International Law Review* 479.

Haile, S, 'The Origins and Demise of the Ethiopia-*Eritrea* Federation Issue' (1987) 15 *Journal of Opinion* 9.

Hasani, E, '*Uti Possidetis Juris:* From Rome to Kosovo' (2003) 27 *Fletcher Forum of World Affairs* 85.

Henderson, C, 'International Measures for the Protection of Civilians in Libya and Cote D'Ivoire' (2011) 60 *ICLQ* 767.

Herring, E, 'From Rambouillet to the Kosovo Accords: NATO's War Against Serbia and its Aftermath' (2000) 4 *International Journal of Human Rights* 225.

Hillgruber, C, 'The Admission of New States to the International Community' (1998) 9 *EJIL* 491.

Kritsiotis, D, 'The Kosovo Crisis and NATO's Application of Armed Force Against the Federal Republic of Yugoslavia' (2000) 49 *ICLQ* 330.

Lalonde, S, 'Québec's Boundaries in the Event of Secession' (2003) 7 *Macquarie Law Journal* 129.

McCorquodale, R, 'South Africa and the Right of Self-Determination' (1994) 10 *South African Journal of Human Rights* 4.

——, 'Self-Determination: A Human Rights Approach' (1994) 43 *ICLQ* 857.

——, 'Negotiating Sovereignty: The Practice of the United Kingdom in Regard to the Right of Self-Determination' (1996) 66 *British Yearbook of International Law* 283.

——, and Pangalangan, R, 'Pushing Back the Limitation of Territorial Boundaries' (2001) 12 *EJIL* 867.

*Miller, R, 'Self-Determination* in International Law and the Demise of Democracy?' (2003) 41 *Columbia Journal of Transnational Law* 601.

Orakhelashvili, A, 'Statehood, Recognition and the United Nations System: A Unilateral Declaration of Independence in Kosovo' (2009) 12 *Max Planck Yearbook of United Nations Law* 1.

Payandeh, M, 'The United Nations, Military Intervention, and Regime Change in Libya' (2012) 55 *Virginia Journal of International Law* 355.

Pellet, A, 'The Opinions of the Badinter Arbitration Committee: A Second Breath for the Self-Determination of Peoples' (1992) 3 *EJIL* 178.

Peters, A, 'Does Kosovo Lie in the Lotus-Land Freedom?' (2011) 24 *Leiden Journal of International Law* 95.

Pomerance, M, 'The United States and Self-Determination: Perspectives on the Wilsonian Conception' (1976) 70 *American Journal of International Law* 1.

——, 'The Badinter Commission: The Use and Misuse of the International Court of Justice's Jurisprudence' (1998–99) 20 *Michigan Journal of International Law* 31.

Radan, P, 'The Borders of a Future Independent Québec: Does the Principle of *Uti Possidetis Juris* Apply?' (1997) 4 *Australian International Law Journal* 200.

Radan, P, 'Post-Secession International Borders: A Critical Analysis of the Opinions of the Badinter Arbitration Commission' (2000) 24 *Melbourne University Law Review* 50.

Ratner, S, 'Drawing a Better Line: *Uti Possidetis* and the Borders of New States' (1996) 90 *American Journal of International Law* 590.

Rich, R, 'Recognition of States: The Collapse of Yugoslavia and the Soviet Union' (1993) 4 *EJIL* 36.

——, '*Bringing Democracy* into International Law' (2001) 12 *Journal of Democracy* 20.

Rosen, A, 'Economic and Cooperative Post-Colonial Borders: How Two Interpretations of Borders by the I.C.J. May Undermine the Relationship Between *Uti Possidetis* and Democracy' (2006) 25 *Penn State International Law Review* 207.

Ruffert, M, 'The Administration of Kosovo and East Timor by the International Community' (2001) 50 *ICLQ* 613.

Schiller, A, '*Eritrea*: Constitution and Federation with Ethiopia' (1953) 2 *American Journal of Comparative Law* 375.

Sereni, AP, 'The Legal Status of Albania' (1941) 35 *American Political Science Review* 311.

——, 'The Status of Croatia under International Law' (1941) 35 *American Political Science Review* 1144.

Shaw, M, 'The Heritage of States: The Principle of *Uti Possidetis* Today' (1996) 67 *British Yearbook of International Law* 75.

——, 'Peoples, Territorialism and Boundaries' (1997) 8 *EJIL* 478.

——, 'Title, Control, and Closure? The Experience of the Eritrea–Ethiopia Boundary Commission' (2007) 56 *ICLQ* 755.

Simma, B, 'NATO, the UN and the Use of Force: Legal Aspects' (1999) 10 *EJIL* 1.

Simpson, G, 'Imagined Consent: Democratic Liberalism in International Legal Theory' (1994) 15 *Australian Yearbook of International Law* 103.

——, 'Two Liberalisms' (2001) 12 *EJIL* 537.

Slaughter, AM, 'International Law in a World of Liberal States' (1995) 6 *EJIL* 503.

——, 'The Real New World Order' (1997) 76 *Foreign Affairs* 183.

Steiner, H, 'Political Participation as a Human Right' (1988) 1 *Harvard Human Rights Yearbook* 77.

Talmon, S, 'The Constitutive versus the Declaratory Doctrine of Recognition: *Tertium Non Datur*?' (2004) 75 *British Yearbook of International Law* 101.

——, 'De-Recognition of Colonel Qaddafi as Head of State of Libya?' (2011) 60 *ICLQ* 759.

Tepe, S, 'Religious Parties and Democracy: A Comparative Assessment of Israel and Turkey' (2005) 12 *Democratization* 283.

Teson, F, 'The Kantian Theory of International Law' (1992) 92 *Columbia Law Review* 53.

Thornberry, P, 'Self-Determination, Minorities, Human Rights: A Review of International Instruments' (1989) 38 *ICLQ* 341.

Türk, D, 'Recognition of States: A Comment' (1993) 4 *EJIL* 66.

Vidmar, J, 'The Kosovo Advisory Opinion Scrutinized' (2011) 24 *Leiden Journal of International Law* 355.

Warbrick, C, 'Recognition of States' (1992) 41 *ICLQ* 473.

——, 'Kosovo: The Declaration of Independence' (2008) 57 *ICLQ* 675.

Weller, M, 'Modesty Can Be a Virtue: Judicial Economy in the ICJ *Kosovo* Opinion' (2011) 24 *Leiden Journal of International Law* 127.

Wilde, R, 'From Danzig to East Timor and Beyond: The Role of International Territorial Administration' (2001) 95 *American Journal of International Law* 503.

# Index